ALI

The Life of Ali Bacher

D1607445

ALI

The Life of Ali Bacher

Rodney Hartman

with a Foreword by Nelson Mandela

VIKING

an imprint of

PENGUIN BOOKS

VIKING

Published by the Penguin Group
80 Strand, London WC2R 0RL, England
Penguin Putnam Inc, 375 Hudson Street, New York, New York 10014, USA
Penguin Books Australia Ltd, 250 Camberwell Road, Camberwell,
Victoria 3124, Australia
Penguin Books Canada Ltd, 10 Alcorn Avenue, Toronto, Ontario,
Canada M4V 3B2
Penguin Books (NZ) Ltd, Cnr Rosedale and Airborne Roads, Albany,
Auckland, New Zealand
Penguin Books India (Pvt) Ltd, 11 Community Centre, Panchsheel Park,
New Delhi – 110 017 India
Penguin Books (South Africa) (Pty) Ltd, 24 Sturdee Avenue, Rosebank,
Johannesburg 2196, South Africa

Penguin Books (South Africa) (Pty) Ltd, Registered Offices:
24 Sturdee Avenue, Rosebank, Johannesburg 2196, South Africa

First published by Penguin Books (South Africa) (Pty) Ltd 2004

ISBN 0 670 04796 1

Typeset by CJH Design in 10.5/14 point Charter
Cover design: Mouse Design
Cover photograph: Duif du Toit/Touchline Photo
Printed and bound by CTP Book Printers, Duminy Street, Parow 7500, Cape Town

Contents

Foreword by Nelson Mandela   vii
Message from the Chairman of Standard Bank   ix
Author's Notes & Acknowledgements   xi
'A Fortunate Man'   xiv
Preface   xvi

Prologue   1

Part I – Roots (1942-1970)
1   Farewell to Rokiskis   7
2   'The Boy Can Bat A Bit'   21
3   Medical School   35
4   Provincial Captain   51
5   Of Hat-tricks and Hoods   59
6   To England   66
7   Enter the Aussies   87
8   Bacher versus Barlow   100
9   The Greats Revisited   115

Part II – New Horizons (1971-1981)
10   Politics and Private Practice   125
11   Retirement   135
12   Enter the Young Turks   143
13   Business and Bypass   152

Part III – Epiphany (1981-1990)
14   The Defining Moment   161
15   'We're On Our Own'   174
16   Cloak and Dagger   184

17   'A Most Insular Man'   192

18   A Brutal Country   201

19   The Gatting Tour   209

20   A Call from Mells   229

21   Secret Rendezvous   251

Part IV – Unity (1991-2000)

22   Batting for South Africa   261

23   Making History in India   278

24   Dinner with 'The Don'   288

25   'Where's a Dakka Bakka?'   300

26   'Call Me Madiba'   308

27   The Second Unity   317

28   The Anonymous Benefactor   332

29   Fallout in the UCB   340

Part V – De Profundis (2000-2003)

30   Into the Darkness   355

31   Summoned by Lord Griffiths   386

32   The Final Tragedy   393

33   Inside the ICC   400

34   What they don't teach you in Medical School   424

Epilogue   436

Index   439

Foreword

THE WORLD STILL marvels at what is widely referred to as the miracle of our transition from the most structured form of racial rule and societal organisation to a non-racial democracy and open, inclusive society. It was generally expected that South Africa would descend into bloody racially based civil war, with the country, its people and infrastructure severely scarred in the process and set back for decades to come.

South Africa confounded the prophets of doom. Its leadership, first political and then over a broader front of social sectors, chose the path of negotiation, compromise and peaceful settlement. The people of South Africa gave their overwhelming support to this course of action, allowing reason and compassion to triumph over destructive emotions and animosities built up over centuries of colonialism and decades of apartheid rule.

We are now ten years into our democracy and despite many problems and great challenges we still face in transforming our society, South Africa counts amongst the most stable polities in the world, the fundamentals of our economy are universally hailed as being extremely sound and race relations have changed almost unrecognisably from our divided past.

Sport was an important social agent in this process, and leaders in different sporting codes will be remembered for their role in this period of epoch-making change in our country. And amongst those leaders Ali Bacher, for so long Mister Cricket in South Africa, will occupy pride of place.

We on the political front peacefully negotiated a fundamental change in the political order, wishing and assuming that leaders in the social, cultural and economic spheres would voluntarily and of their own volition follow suit to lay the foundations for a fully transformed society. It will always stand to the credit of the game of cricket that its leadership was amongst the first to take those steps. Even before the political negotiations were concluded they reached out to each other and formed a united South African body to lead and oversee the integration and transformation of the game.

Such achievements are never those of single individuals only; the collective efforts of a range of leaders and the masses of followers are required to reach such objectives and goals. The crucial role of individuals – their wisdom, insight and skills – can, however, never be ignored or underplayed in such processes. The figure of Ali Bacher looms large in that process of change in South African cricket and this book gives an invaluable insight into the man, his life and the role he played.

Ali Bacher is a great example of that kind of South African that made possible the form and nature of our negotiated transition. He stood back in the middle of a crisis, reflected upon the broader meaning and implications of the course he was following, learned to understand the views of those who differed most intensely with him, sought advice broadly and then gave a decisive lead in changing course for the greater good. It is that, amongst his many admirable traits, that I respect and admire most in this man.

His cricketing achievements are many, locally and internationally. Even in those years of seclusion on Robben Island we took note with pride, although we were naturally opposed to the racially exclusive nature of the team, how he led South Africa to victory against Australia. After readmission to the international fold, the cause of South African cricket was served and advanced due to his skills in international cricketing diplomacy and the respect he enjoyed wherever cricket was played. His work in developing cricket in the underprivileged areas of the country was pioneering and he is one person who can look with genuine pride on what has been achieved in this field. It was his briefing to me on what was being done for township development at the time that convinced me to throw my weight behind the unification efforts being overseen and driven by Steve Tshwete.

Since the attainment of democracy and our reacceptance into the international community South Africa has earned a proud reputation for the successful hosting of large international events. The Cricket World Cup of 2003 was one of the greatest and most splendid achievements in this regard; not surprisingly so, as Ali Bacher stood at the helm of the team organising and running the event. It was most fitting that his long career in cricket should conclude with such a grand finale.

Ali Bacher is a great South African who has brought pride to all of us and one has no doubt that he will continue to contribute to the growth and advancement of our society in other fields he may now choose.

Mandela

N R MANDELA
January 2004

Message from the Chairman

Ali Bacher has been intimately involved in cricket in South Africa for over fifty years. His progress through school, university, provincial and international cricket is well recorded, as is the fact that he captained his country with great distinction.

Off the cricket field he qualified as a medical doctor and became one of the ablest cricket administrators that this or perhaps any country has been privileged to produce. Both his cricket and professional careers brought him in contact with South Africans from every walk of our society. Through this he developed a deep conviction that cricket offered unique opportunities to bring South Africa's people closer together. This conviction became a reality particularly after the release of Nelson Mandela in 1990 and South Africa's return to democracy and the international playing fields.

The success of the ICC Cricket World Cup 2003 held in South Africa is surely the highlight of Ali Bacher's career. The foundations that have been laid by him and his committee will ensure that the World Cup will live in the fond memories of all for many years to come and that cricket has a vibrant future in our country.

It is appropriate that Standard Bank has the privilege of sponsoring the launch of Ali Bacher's biography. For over 125 years we, too, have been involved with life in South Africa at every level and have a keen understanding of the unifying effects that cricket has had on our society, particularly over the last decade. We are particularly proud of our direct involvement in the Cricket World Cup Legacy Projects which were designed to bring previously-disadvantaged people into mainstream cricket. These projects not only endorse the commitment that Standard Bank has made to the development of cricket in South Africa but underscore the bank's role as an integral part of the fabric of South African society.

It is an honour for Standard Bank to salute Ali Bacher's outstanding achievements which are a product of his integrity, professionalism and visionary leadership. His invaluable contribution has ensured that South African cricket can proudly take its place on the world stage and enjoy a promising and enduring future.

DEREK COOPER
Chairman Standard Bank

Author's Notes & Acknowledgements

Graham Greene, himself a Penguin author, makes the observation that a biographer may well set out cheerfully to the task, but will end up 'glowering with sullen determination and resentment at the huge mass of intractable material any life must represent'.

In researching and writing this biography, one had cause to be cheerfully determined most of the time, to have glowered sullenly on rare occasions, but never to have experienced resentment. Dr Ali Bacher's full life does indeed represent a huge mass of material but, in unearthing and assembling it, I am indebted to him for the hundreds of hours we spent together during the course of six months to ensure that the real story was told. This was helped in no small part by his willingness to open up his files and diaries and scrapbooks, so diligently assembled first by his late mother Rose, then by others like Trish Lewis, her daughters Judith and Francoise, and Rae Israel; and by his remarkable memory and his ability to open doors to important people with something of value to offer. Sincere thanks are therefore due to the following people who gave so willingly and generously of their time, knowledge or memories: Don Mackay-Coghill, Cecil Aron, Dr John Benjamin, Mark Henning, George Mendelsohn, Solly Krok, David Saks, Eli Goldstein, Rabbi Koppel Bacher, Hugh Reichlin, Dr Harry Phillips, Dr John Jamieson, 'Tiger' Lance, Les Evans, Gordon Draper, Dr Donald Beard, Joe Pamensky, Lee Irvine, Johnny Waite, Albie During, Dr Owen Dean, John Lobban, the office staff at King Edward VII School, John Jefferies, Barry Fowle, Robbie Muzzell, Don MacLeod, Percy Sonn, Arthur Turner, Ray Mali, Geoff Dakin, Gerald Ritchie, Brian Bath, Ian Fullerton, Ngconde Balfour, Graham Abrahams, Lulu Johnson, Mthobi Tyamzashe, Krish Naidoo, Professor Willie Esterhuyse, Amrit Mathur, Raymond White, Ray McCauley, Moss Mashishi, Pam Tshwete, Hintsa Siwisa, Kapi Nkwana, Mluleki George, Sam Ramsamy, Professor Michael Katz, Michael Watt, Roelf Meyer, Peter Pollock, Graeme Pollock, Mike

Procter, Jim Fitzmaurice, David Brink, Bob Cowper, Denis Lindsay, Helen Irvine, Kevin McKenzie, Mervyn King, Jeremy Gauntlett, Andre Pruis, Carié Maas, Dr Piet Koornhof, Phillip Glaser, Imtiaz Patel, Lord Paul Condon, Hoosain Ayob, David Graveney, Qamar Ahmed, Majid Khan, Urvasi Naidoo, Ashley Mallett, Aslam Khota, Tyronne Fernando and Aileen Ambler-Smith.

Special thanks are due to members of the Bacher, Weisz and Kirsh families for their input, encouragement and advice; to Bronwyn Wilkinson and Clifford Green for their important contributions, diligent reading and constructive suggestions; to Professor Jakes Gerwel for facilitating the foreword by Nelson Mandela; and to Niesha Green, and Lindy Leonhardt of Penguin Australia, for demonstrating to Dr Bacher the value of email communication.

Four great figures in world cricket, the Reverend Wesley Hall, Geoffrey Boycott, Steven Waugh and Sachin Tendulkar, willingly sent appraisals from a global perspective, excerpts of which are reproduced with sincere appreciation.

I also acknowledge with thanks: Shaun Johnson for permission to quote from his portfolio of columns on the 1992 South African cricket tour of the West Indies which appeared in *The Star, Saturday Star* and *Sunday Star*; Michael Shafto for his reports on the 1990 Gatting tour in *The Star* and its sister titles; Chris Gibbons for his graphic recollections of the 1991 South African tour of India; Zebra Press for bits borrowed from my book *Hansie and the Boys* (1997) on various issues; Johan Esterhuizen of *Rapport* for dredging up invaluable memories of his time spent with Ali Bacher during the Pietermaritzburg leg of the Gatting tour; Bruce Francis for selflessly sharing his memoirs of the Australian rebel tour; Frederik Van Zyl Slabbert and Allister Sparks for giving me free access to their written works and for verbal guidance; the various editors of the *SA Cricket Annual* for corroborating facts and statistics; Mihir Bose whose book *Sporting Colours* provided additional guidance through the political minefields; Mogamad Allie whose *History of the WP Cricket Board* was a source of inspiration; the late Hayward Kidson whose *History of Transvaal Cricket* helped jog the memory; *Wisden Cricketers Almanack* for always being on my desk; Christopher Martin-Jenkins whose *Who's Who of Test Cricketers* has become a dog-eared friend; any wordsmith who might unwittingly have influenced my writing; and a myriad of important people who, even if not mentioned by name, are part of the soul of this book.

In addition, thanks are due to *Veritas Transcription Services* for the King Commission excerpts in Chapter 30, and to cricket statistician Andrew

Samson for his numerical input in Chapter 9.

To my wife, Carine Hartman, I extend my love and gratitude for her professional advice and personal understanding, and especially for her technical expertise in preparing the majority of the photographs for publication. Most of these are from the Bacher private collection. Every effort has been made to trace other sources, and any infringement of copyright is inadvertent. If notified, the Publishers will be pleased to make appropriate acknowledgement in any future editions of this book. Dr Bacher joins me in expressing appreciation to Marc Blachowitz of Touchline Media and Pete Milne of Touchline Photo for supplying photographs from their archives of specific events.

To the good people at Penguin Group SA – Alison Lowry for pursuing the idea, Pam Thornley for her calming influence and wealth of experience, Claire Heckrath for her design expertise, and Janine O'Connor and Siobhan Walsh in the vital areas of sales and marketing – my sincere appreciation.

Finally, the generous sponsorship of Standard Bank South Africa ensured that the execution of this work could proceed 'simpler, better, faster'. We are most indebted to them.

Rodney Hartman
Johannesburg
March 2004

'A Fortunate Man'

A BOOK OF this nature affords one the opportunity to evaluate one's life. In opening up my memories, my files and my scrapbooks, and then reading the account of all this in sequential form, I am able to derive some context from it all.

The author of this biography describes my role in events of great and historic consequence for cricket and our country. These singular moments, when seen as a whole and in perspective, lead me to the unqualified conclusion that I have been a fortunate man.

I have been fortunate that my ambitions, dreams and desires from early childhood were able to be realised. I have always been mindful that the majority of South Africans were never given the same opportunities as I had to achieve these objectives. I trust that at all times throughout my playing and administrative career I did everything possible within my limitations to level the playing fields.

I am fortunate that my parents left eastern Europe ahead of the Holocaust because, had they not done so, there would be no book.

I am fortunate that I had a good upbringing, that I attended good schools, that I had excellent teachers and the best of sporting facilities.

I am fortunate that I was able to play cricket with so many exceptional cricketers who I still number among my friends.

I am fortunate that I was able to study to become a doctor and thereby understand the suffering and needs of others and learn the importance of good communication.

I am fortunate that I spent time in the business world where I learned invaluable lessons in commerce, marketing and public relations.

I am fortunate that I cheated death on two occasions through the intervention of doctors to whom I owe my life.

I am fortunate that I happened to be in the right place at the right time when my country underwent its miraculous political change to achieve true democracy.

I am fortunate that I was involved in the amazing unity process in South African cricket and in its subsequent reacceptance in the international family of nations.

I am fortunate to have worked alongside so many dedicated administrators and with staff I could trust and who gave one hundred per cent to the cause of cricket.

I am fortunate to have made friends with such great men as Nelson Mandela, Steve Tshwete and Archbishop Desmond Tutu.

In pursuit of my objectives, through great moments and tough times, I am fortunate to have had family and friends who I could always count on. Above all, I am a fortunate man to have a loving and supportive wife, Shira; wonderful and caring children, Ann, Lynn and David; and sons-in-law Darryl and Kevin and daughter-in-law Cindy; and five grandchildren who mean so much to me. I want all my family and friends to know that I am eternally grateful to them for their support, advice and encouragement at all times.

Dr Ali Bacher
Johannesburg
March 2004

Preface

LITTLE ARNOLD PERKINS, God bless him; he invented a nickname for his pal and unwittingly created an icon.

On his birth certificate he is Aron but no one, absolutely *no one*, has ever addressed him by that name since that childhood day on Dunbar Street when little Arnold dubbed him Ali.

People of every class and culture, of whatever political persuasion or religious affiliation; they have always called him Ali. To cricketers of whatever era, from whichever country or club or county, he was just Ali.

The late Arnold Perkins, all praise to him; he would be glad to know that the moment he decided that little Aron Bacher would become 'Ali' – when was it, more than 50 years ago? – it would create a resonance with cricket wherever the game was played.

To heads of state, cabinet ministers, ambassadors and sporting luminaries, it was always, 'Hello Ali' or 'Say hello to Ali, dear'.

And Nelson Mandela, he calls him Ali, too.

Even to those who do not particularly like him, he is Ali; and to those with little interest in cricket, they know what 'Ali' stands for.

In deference to his stature during the build-up to the ICC Cricket World Cup of 2003, one of the new staffers began calling him 'Doctor B', a name that was maddeningly adopted by many new acquaintances. This was a cause of mild irritation to those who had grown to know him because to them, of course, he could only be Ali.

That two of his small grandchildren are wont to call him 'Ati' is probably more a matter of elocution than any significant challenge to the legend. No doubt, in time, they will call him Ali, too.

For the purpose of telling his story, therefore, he will quite often be referred to as Ali.

Prologue

On 23 August 1939, the Fascists and the Communists cracked open a bottle of vodka in the Kremlin to signal the start of a terrible episode in the story of mankind.

On that day Adolf Hitler – via the hand of his foreign minister and errand boy Joachim von Ribbentrop – signed a non-aggression pact with Josef Stalin that was celebrated deep into the night in the inner sanctums of Moscow and Berlin. In simple terms, the treaty agreed that neither power would attack the other, either individually or in partnership with a 'third party'. It was a cynical agreement that underlined Hitler's cunning and Stalin's acquiescence. The truth was that Hitler was planning to invade Poland and he knew that Britain – clearly the 'third party' – had an agreement with the Poles to come to their aid in the event of an attack. By ensuring that Russia remained neutral at the outset, Hitler would buy enough time to gain an early advantage in his grand plan to overrun Europe. All of this, of course, made no allowance for the fury that would be unleashed on the people of eastern Europe and the terrible fate that lay ahead for the Jews of that region.

The non-aggression treaty was well publicised but the outside world was not aware of a secret deal contained in it: that Poland would soon be sliced up and taken over in equal parts by the two imperialist powers. Nor did it say that the Baltic states of Lithuania, Latvia and Estonia, which lay to the north of Poland, would become pawns in a dreadful theatre of war.

Nine days after Von Ribbentrop's trip to Moscow, Germany invaded Poland. Two days later, on 3 September 1939, England declared war on

Germany. A fortnight later, with western Poland overrun by German forces, the Soviet Union attacked eastern Poland to claim its spoils, lamely attempting to justify its action by claiming that Poland no longer existed and that it was simply taking back what belonged to it under former partitions.

By the end of the month the division of Poland was complete, the west under the Reich, the east under Russia, and soon thereafter the Baltic states were forced to accept Russian garrisons.

In May 1940, Hitler unleashed his massive offensive into western Europe, launching invasions into Luxembourg, Holland and Belgium, forcing the British Expeditionary Forces to retreat and evacuate at Dunkirk, bringing Mussolini's Italy into the war on his side and then forcing France to surrender. With the occupation of western Europe complete, all that was left was Britain itself; but this was proving a harder nut to crack. Hitler, however, was confident enough of the success of his western adventures to focus his attention again on the east.

Then, on 22 June 1941, he invaded the Soviet Union in flagrant breach of the non-aggression pact that Von Ribbentrop had signed over several glasses of vodka almost two years earlier. It was called Operation Barbarossa and Lithuania, now a Soviet-controlled Baltic republic abutting the German front, took the brunt of the early assault.

Three days later, the Nazis occupied Rokiskis[1] a provincial town in north-eastern Lithuania close to the Latvian border. About 40 per cent of its approximately 9 000 inhabitants were Jewish and the town's population had since 1939 become inflated by refugees from neighbouring areas who were attempting to use it as a springboard into Latvia en route to Moscow. In advance of the German occupation, however, the Nazis' Lithuanian collaborators – avowed anti-Communists who believed that Fascism would prove their salvation and were therefore at the Nazis' beck and call – began eliminating Jews at their masters' bidding in a killing frenzy of widespread and horrific proportions. These defenceless folk were driven from their homes, savagely beaten and burned alive; and many were herded into their synagogues and schools which were then doused with petrol and set alight. In Rokiskis, the Lithuanian fifth column intercepted Jews along the

---

[1] There are at least eleven different variations of the name, Rokiskis being the Lithuanian version. In Yiddish, the language of the Jews of eastern Europe, it is called Rokishok.

roads as they tried to escape by horse and wagon. In many cases they beat them to death with sticks.

A month later, on 25 July, the Germans captured the town of Slonim about 350 kilometres due south of Rokiskis. Slonim was situated on the high craggy banks of the River Schara in that part of the former Poland called White Russia[2] which had been occupied by the Russians as their share of the secret pact of 1939. Poland had changed hands and been partitioned so many times that its history and that of its neighbours was virtually one and the same. *Einsatzgruppen*, or Special Action Groups, followed the German brigades into Poland and the Baltic states. Their initial role was to round up Jews and herd them into ghettos ahead of what the inner sanctum of the Nazi party euphemistically called 'the final solution of the Jewish problem'. In time, the purpose of the *Einsatz* groups took on greater menace and they were transformed into extermination squads who massacred Jews and Communists indiscriminately. The usual method was to assemble these people under the pretence of 'repatriation', transport them into the forests, line them up and machine-gun them into mass graves. They were aided in their despicable purpose by local collaborators who played a prominent role in the massacre of Jews throughout the region.

On 14 August, in the first of these *aktions* in Slonim, 1 255 Jews were executed at a site called Petrolevits eight kilometres outside the town. Those murdered included intellectuals and members of the *Judenrat* or Jewish Council.

A ghetto[3] had been established in Slonim and thousands of Jews from surrounding towns were placed under concentration there. In the second *aktion* in the area, no fewer than 10 000 Jews were executed at a site called Chepilovo.

On 15 August, in an operation that left another 3 200 slaughtered, the remaining Jewish males of Rokiskis were separated from their wives and children and herded into the feudal lord's palace. A day later they were taken to the nearby forest where they were forced to dig their own graves before being gunned into them. Thereafter nearly all the women and children were killed.

---

[2] The country is known as Belarus which became an independent state in 1991.
[3] This ghetto became famous when it acquired arms from underground agents and established resistance groups or partisans in an adjacent forest. It was unheard of that Jews took up arms against the Germans but the Slonim partisans did this with some measure of success.

In one of many horrific incidents, two babies were snatched from the arms of their nanny and murdered. The woman, a non-Jew, was spared. She stood by helplessly, rigid with shock, as the clear, icy stream that bubbled merrily down from the forest to the town became a river of blood.[4]

[4] Sources include Masha Greenbaum: *The Jews of Lithuania*; Rabbi Ephraim Oshry: *The Annihilation of Lithuanian Jewry* 1995; Mr Solomon Krok: interview 24 July 2003; *The Encyclopaedia of the Holocaust*, Vol 4, Macmillan 1990; Eli Goldstein, Shtetl Connections.

PART I

ROOTS

Chapter 1

Farewell To Rokiskis

Koppel and Rose Bacher were looking forward to the birth of their fourth child. Koppel came from Rokiskis and Rose from Slonim, but they were thousands of miles away from the rivers of blood.[1]

They now lived in Johannesburg, South Africa, where on 24 May 1942 they became the proud parents of a third son. They named him Aron.

Nineteen years earlier, Koppel had left Lithuania as a boy of twelve, joining thousands of other Jews who had fled eastern Europe from the late nineteenth century onwards for reasons ranging from persecution by the Tsars, death at the hands of the Cossacks in bloody pogroms, abject poverty, mounting anti-Semitism and, in the 1930s, a fear of the looming Nazi menace.

Koppel came with his widowed mother Sarah, his sisters Freda, Edie and Dora, and his young brother Meishke or Morris. They were looking forward to being reunited with the eldest brother Saul who had gone to South Africa alone a year earlier. Their father Yitzchak Alter Bacher had passed away in Rokiskis after a failed trip to America, where he believed their future lay. He was a humble tailor who was described in the *Memorial Book of Rokiskis Jewry*[2] as 'a good-hearted Yid, whose pleasure was to do good deeds and to help others in time of distress'.

---

[1] The third *aktion* at Slonim began on 29 June 1942 during which a further 10 000 Jews were massacred at Petrolevits. When the Red Army recaptured Slonim in 1944, not a single Jew was left in the town.

[2] Translated and published in South Africa in 1952.

7

Rose Nochimovicz was fourteen when she left Slonim in 1928. Her father Louis was a carpenter who left his wife Mary and their four children in Poland in 1927 and came to South Africa to forge a new future for them. His elder brother Barnet was already in Johannesburg, a partner in a furniture firm called Steel-Barnet, and Louis got a job with them making furniture. He was a wood-turner of some distinction, having won gold medals for his work in Europe, and his speciality was magnificently carved wooden vases – which were often displayed at furniture fairs – and table and chair legs. He had such a 'good eye' that he never used measuring instruments for his work.

Louis assiduously saved his wages and nine months later he sent money home so that Mary and the children, Rose, 14, Gertie, 12, Jack, 10, and Aaron, 4, could join him.[3] They travelled by train from Slonim through Germany; and caught the boat at Hamburg, chief port of embarkation for thousands of German and Russian Jews.

IT WAS FROM Rokiskis that the Bachers came, a village that in Yiddish was called a *shtetl* and that was home to 2 013 Jews at the time of their departure in 1923. It had 29 streets with a total length of 10 kilometres, 551 houses, a power station, three flour mills, a woodcutting mill, a dairy, a factory for starch production, a metal working factory, a hospital with 65 beds, and two pharmacies. It was in truth an insignificant dot on the map of the world, yet inside Rokiskis beat a strange and amazing heart that would resonate in time with the public life of South Africa. For it was this *shtetl*, this insignificant place, that was the roots of such famous and successful South Africans as the philanthropists and entrepreneurs Solomon and Abraham Krok; the founder of the Investec banking empire, Stephen Koseff; the internationally renowned professional boxing promoter Rodney Berman, and the man who would become famous as his country's top cricket administrator, Aron 'Ali' Bacher. All of them had in common that their forebears came from Rokiskis in Lithuania at some point between the latter part of the nineteenth century and the first part of the twentieth.

Those who stayed any longer than that were destroyed in the unspeakable Holocaust that raged through their homeland in the awful months of 1941.

---

[3] Louis and Mary's fifth child, Yudel, was born in South Africa. He was known as Julius.

They said farewell to Rokiskis, and they never saw it again. The village disappeared slowly in the distance as the steam train headed away. They travelled the 250 kilometres on the railway, traversing the country from east to west. Through the cold they travelled towards the Baltic coast where the small cattle ship was lying in wait.

They waved goodbye to the mainland, the country of their birth and the land of their fears; and the cramped steamer ploughed on through the steel-grey Baltic Sea, leaving Lithuania behind.

Ahead of them lay a voyage of two months that would steadily improve once they had picked up the passenger ship in England to head due south into the other hemisphere. Behind them lay a country of clay and limestone, peat and dolomite that they were swapping for a place of diamonds and gold and other precious metals. They were about to embrace a land where opportunities abounded and where they would be free from the past and future tyrannies of eastern Europe. Their new home was a country blessed with the wealth of God's creation yet sadly cursed by the greed and arrogance and racism of its colonial settlers. The latter problem was of little consequence at the time but it would later rise up to shape the future of their adopted land.

For the Jews of eastern Europe, South Africa was a popular destination for various reasons, chief among which was the discovery of diamonds and gold between 1869 and 1886. Many Lithuanian Jews (they called themselves Litvaks) also heard tell of a certain Sammy Marks, one of their kind from Neustadt who had gone to South Africa to find fame and fortune. This he had succeeded in doing in abundance, becoming with his cousin Isaac Lewis a highly successful entrepreneur and industrialist and a personal adviser, fund-raiser and lifelong friend to President Paul Kruger. He was also on good terms with the British imperialist Cecil John Rhodes and during the Anglo-Boer War of 1899-1902 he was as friendly with Lord Roberts, commander in chief of the British forces, as he was with General Koos de la Rey, a hardline Boer commander. Marks' neutrality allowed him to straddle both sides and in this way he played a big role in brokering the talks that finally led to peace. Although Marks did not return to Lithuania, he sent money home on a regular basis to his mother. Word of his riches, aligned to Lithuania's ongoing repression by Tsarist Russia and crippling poverty, enticed fellow Litvaks to follow him to South Africa. This process became a trend and it was normal for the men (husbands or eldest sons) to travel to Cape Town or Johannesburg before making enough money to send home to the so-called 'ghetto banks' which were set up expressly to facilitate immigrants' travel arrangements. Some husbands, alas, created a new life for themselves in the sun and left their wives stranded forever on a cold continent. In the Litvak community, faithful fathers would tell their children: 'Shows you how much I loved your mother!' in demonstrating how they had honoured their promise to send for their womenfolk.

Koppel's mother, the matriarchal Sarah Bacher, was described as 'an unusually righteous woman'. She was born in an area of farms and forests on the outskirts of Rokiskis and despite the fact that during her early married life she lived in poor economic circumstances and an adverse climate, she went from house to house collecting donations for the poor families. When she became widowed, she spent much of her time collecting donations for the purpose of helping poor brides with the necessities for their wedding preparations.

When she immigrated to South Africa she continued this community work, collecting donations which she used to send parcels to her birthplace and surrounding places for needy families. The following is related by S Klass and translated by Sam Lichtenstein in the *Memorial Book of Rokiskis Jewry* of 1952:

I remember one early morning in Johannesburg a sudden knock on the door. Sarah Bacher brought two letters in hand. I directed her to a chair. She had just received two letters from Rokiskis, one from a young married woman wanting to join her husband in South Africa, the other from a young bride wanting to come to her future husband. Neither of them had money for travel expenses. I endeavored to persuade her that the weather was bad and that we should delay the trip for another day, but she was not prepared to accept it, demanding that we must obtain the money from some people.

We took a tramcar which took us to the end stop. There we went by another tramcar to Kensington and travelled to the last 'stop'. Suddenly a heavy rain came down. We then ran to a tree for shelter. The uphill climb left us breathless. When we reached the house of the Rokishker family, the lady of the house gave us a handsome donation for that purpose. From there we went to other homes, and none refused. On that day alone we collected 50 pounds. Within several days Chaya-Sarah-Ita Bacher collected 175 pounds, which she sent to Rokiskis to the interested persons, who quickly came to South Africa. She had done all her work in South Africa devotedly. Many women are thankful for her efforts, which has enabled them to escape the Nazi persecution and to come to South Africa. She has performed all her work alone, without any help from committees or societies, and with great dedication. No wonder her name is valued greatly by Rokishker Jews.

In the presence of her sons, daughters, sons-in-law, daughters-in-law and grandchildren she departed on the 28 September 1943.

One of those grandchildren was Aron Bacher who was 16 months old when his *Bobba,* his grandmother, died.

CECIL ARON LEFT Latvia for South Africa in 1924. He was 17 years old and he came alone. His tearful mother saw him off at the railway station at the start of a 12-hour rail journey to the coast. She was crying not because he was leaving her, but because she was afraid he would fall into the sea and drown.[4]

He sailed initially from the Baltic port of Libau in a 300-ton fishing boat. This took him to London where – like the Bachers before him – he was escorted to Whitechapel in the East End where he was accommodated at the Poor Jews Temporary Shelter that was established in the latter years of the nineteenth century with the express purpose of helping emigrating Jews in transit. From there he travelled by train to Southampton where he boarded the *Gascon,* a 6 000-ton vessel bound for Cape Town. Fellow Jewish immigrants met him there, gave him lunch and put him on the train to Johannesburg.

Doornfontein and Bertrams on the eastern fringes of the city of Johannesburg were home to the majority of Jews from the Baltic states. It was in Doornfontein that Cecil met the Bachers and where he would eventually marry little Aron's aunt, Freda Bacher.

It was also here that Koppel Bacher met Rose Nochimovicz, whose family would later change their name to Nickel.

The children could not speak a word of English when they arrived in South Africa, but Doornfontein was the site of the Jewish Government School, at the corner of End and Hancock Streets, where they gained their education. Established in 1896 by the Johannesburg Hebrew Congregation, its purpose was to assist children of eastern European immigrants integrate into the South African way of life.

At school, the young Rose learned to speak and write English and how

---

[4] Interview with Cecil Aron in Killarney, Johannesburg, 21 July 2003.

to play tennis and table tennis. She had a good eye and excelled at games. Her brothers, too, especially Aaron and Julius, were good at ball sports.

Rose left school at the age of 16 to go to work in order to help her father make ends meet in the midst of the Depression. Each week, uncomplainingly, she would hand over her wages. Out of this she would get a little pocket money.

Koppel Bacher and Rose Nickel were married in 1933. They opened a small trading store in Croesus, a tough industrial and working class area on the south-west side of the city. This consisted of a shop, which sold clothes and bicycles, and a cheap eating house catering for black workers from the nearby gold mines. They lived on the premises in a small zinc and wooden house, a far cry from the affluent suburbs on the northern side of town where the Randlords and the professional classes resided. They were a proud and stubborn young couple.

Like Koppel in Croesus, Cecil Aron owned a store and eating house in Primrose to the east of the city. Realising the huge potential of the black African retail market, the brothers-in-law decided to form a business partnership into which each sunk 1 500 pounds. Their new line of interest was as wholesalers of clothing and soft goods and they ran their operation from Magnet House in Market Street, the hub of the wholesale trade in the rapidly growing city of Johannesburg. As business improved, Koppel and Cecil branched out. They opened in Durban and even crossed the border to establish outlets in Bulawayo, Southern Rhodesia (now Zimbabwe), and Livingstone, Northern Rhodesia (now Zambia).

Koppel also bought a dairy farm near Roodepoort, a town on the West Rand, and the industrious Rose would be up at 5.30 each morning to drive the delivery truck on its rounds seven days a week. In time the farm would become a weekend retreat – Koppel built a swimming pool and a dance hall, and there were games and horse riding – and 'Bacher's Farm' grew to be a famous landmark in the Jewish community. It was also used by the Zionist Movement for the training of volunteers who went to Palestine in 1948 to fight in the war of independence out of which the State of Israel was born.

THE FIRST RECORDED Jews in South Africa were two Dutch soldiers, Samuel Jacobson, aged 20, and David Heijlbron, aged 22, who arrived in the Cape Province in the latter half of the seventeenth century in the service of the Dutch East India Company. According to records of the Dutch Reformed Church they were converted to Christianity by baptism on Christmas day in 1669 because only Protestant Christians were permitted to reside at the Cape under the control of the Dutch East India Company from 1652 to 1795; and this despite a significant number of Jewish shareholders in the company.[5]

The advent of the nineteenth century saw greater religious freedom. British Jews came with the 1820 Settlers and other European Jews began to stream in. In 1903, however, immigration laws were tightened. Jews were placed in the same category of immigrants as Asiatics upon whom there were renewed restrictions on entry. In order to bypass these, it was necessary to have Yiddish categorised as a European language and this was achieved in 1906. The 1930 Quota Act and the 1937 Aliens Act also impeded immigration. Without specifically mentioning Jews, they had the effect of limiting immigration according to 'assimilability'. Whatever this might have meant, it was a specious and unspecific criterion.

Of those Jews who became naturalised South Africans, the vast majority came from the Baltic and particularly Lithuania. South Africa was said to boast the biggest Litvak[6] community in the world, bigger than Lithuania itself. They came in search of a better life, and, as victims of terrible repression[7] themselves, they embraced a strong sense of social justice. They brought with them a robust cultural heritage, a hunger for hard work, and a burning ambition to rise above the average. This was their new world, their promised land, and they aimed to make the most of it.

UNLIKE JEWS FROM some other parts of Europe, the Litvaks were down-to-earth folk with no airs and graces. They were tolerant people who made friends easily and adapted well to new environments. They found South Africa to be an agreeable place with plenty of potential, and in return for this opportunity many of them made considerable contributions to their new country and some of them were outstanding people who became leaders in many different spheres. Among those of Baltic descent were the political leaders Joe Slovo, Helen Suzman and Tony Leon, the Nobel Prize winning novelist Nadine Gordimer and the hotel and casino magnate Sol Kerzner. In all walks of life – commerce and industry, the courts, sport,

---

[5] Source: South African Jewish Genealogy, Saul Issroff, London.
[6] Of the 80 000 Jews in South Africa in 2003, about 80 per cent had their origins in the Baltic.
[7] Historians estimate that 94 per cent of Lithuania's pre-war Jewish population of 220 000 perished in the Holocaust.

politics, the arts and the humanities – Jewish South Africans consistently played leading roles. Given that the Jewish population had never been higher than the 120 000 of 1980, their achievement ratio was quite extraordinary.

Of all the Jews who arrived in South Africa, two-thirds headed for Johannesburg where many set up home in the north-eastern suburbs of the city of gold with a strong sense of community and deep religious convictions.

THE VILLAGE OF Rokiskis was considered to be a fortress of the Lubavitch in Lithuania. Lubavitch, a sect of the Hassidic movement of orthodox Jews, is described as the biggest Jewish empowerment group in the world.[8] The Lubavitchers live by a spirituality that sets great store in the purpose of the individual and the promotion of fundamental human rights; and a characteristic trait of the Litvaks, whether or not they were members of the Lubavitch[9] sect, was a sense of justice for the downtrodden. It is not without significance that many of these Jews aligned themselves with the anti-apartheid movement and the liberation struggle in general in South Africa. In Yeoville, a middle-class residential area close to the city of Johannesburg, the Rokishker Jews, who were inspired in the project by little Aron Bacher's uncle Saul, were responsible for building the Hassidic synagogue on Yeo Street.

Yeoville was the home of Jewish merchants and shopkeepers, teachers and craftsmen. They lived in undistinguished houses, boxed tightly along narrow streets made more agreeable by rows of jacaranda trees that dropped a carpet of mauve petals in the spring. Among them lived professional people, doctors and dentists, lawyers and accountants who served the community of which they were an integral part.

After rising above the rather more humble circumstances of Doornfontein, the wood and iron shack in Croesus and a semi-detached house in Bertrams, it was to Yeoville that Koppel and Rose Bacher eventually moved.

In the late 1880s, property in the newly proclaimed Yeoville was offered to bidding at an auction. No bids were made because the area was thought

---

[8] Little Aron's cousin, Koppel Bacher, the son of Saul, went to America at the age of 14 to study for nine years. He became a rabbi and introduced the Lubavitch branch of Judaism to South Africa.
[9] Lubavitch is one and the same as the Chabad movement. It is named after the small Russian town of Lubavitch where it was founded.

'too far from town'. Thomas Yeo Sherwell, manager of City Deep Gold Mine, who was responsible for proclaiming the area, consequently sold his stands for one pound each.[10] In the 1940s, Yeoville was considered 'very close to town' and stands were now selling at about 2 000 pounds. The Bachers rented a house from an aunt who stayed next door.

Number 21 Dunbar Street was a simple abode of pine floors and cast-iron ceilings, and a small yard in which you could hardly swing an alley cat. There were three bedrooms. Aron, the youngest, shared with his sister Mushe, six years older than him; and his bigger brothers Isaac, who they called Issy, and Yudel were in the other. Their home was part of a small village in the heart of the growing metropolis. The suburb covered some 110 hectares that were imbued with a fine sense of community spirit. Here Jews and Gentiles lived side by side, but it was the Jews who formed the closer community, united by their faith and traditions that were the common thread in the Jewish Diaspora. Their 'portable culture'[11] was as much evident here as it was in the other prominent Jewish settlements of Brooklyn, New York, or Whitechapel, London, complete with all the Yiddish idiosyncrasies and the chicken soup.

There were no luxuries at No 21 Dunbar, but there was safety and security and few worries for a young boy. Aron was comfortable among his people, content with the lifestyle, and eager to make use of the opportunities that were coming his way.

AT YEOVILLE BOYS' School, in the heart of this bustling, high-density suburb, Aron Bacher developed into a little superstar who excelled in whichever sport he turned his hand to. He was particularly passionate about football, and filled the dual role of centre forward and captain. In four years, his team lost only one game, and that to a school from the tough Southern Suburbs who, it was suggested, were fielding boys aged 14 years in what was strictly an under-12 league. The Yeoville Boys' teams were so popular that the local shops would close for an hour on the Wednesday afternoons that they played. The whole community would be out in support.

When the 30 000-seater Rand Stadium was opened in 1951, Yeoville Boys had the distinction of being invited to play there in the Under-10 Final. Fighting back from 0-2 down, they equalised at 2-2 right on fulltime,

[10] Source: *North Eastern Tribune*, 1996.
[11] Description by David Saks, Jewish Board of Deputies, Johannesburg.

thanks to a Bacher penalty, and they won the match through an extra time goal.

It was a great little team. The flaxen-haired Graham 'Bones' Henning, whose family name was synonymous with golf and who would become a golf professional himself, was on the right wing; and Stanley Blogg was the goalkeeper who did not touch the ball once when Yeoville beat H A Jack School 16-0. One of the spectators at that match was a little H A Jack pupil named Shira Teeger. She was disappointed that her school's team was so badly beaten but she liked the look of the winning captain.[12] He was a strapping boy, dark and good looking.

There were names to conjure with at Yeoville Boys. Among them was a little fellow with a lisp named Ronnie Kasrils[13] who played in a team which included Aron's brother Yudel and was captained by another of the Henning brothers, Brian, who would one day become Tournament Director of the SA Professional Golfers' Association and take up a similar post on the United States Seniors golf tour. In 1949, their football team played and won 17 games, and scored 96 goals to 6. It was not hard to see why Yeoville Boys was so popular with the soccer-mad people in the suburb.

There was little Arnold Perkins whose family owned a carpet business. They lived on the corner of Dunbar and Bedford streets, a few houses away from the Bachers, and had a slightly bigger backyard – although, in truth, it was still the size of a postage stamp. It was here that the local boys would gather after school for regular games of soccer and cricket during which Aron would be the natural leader – he was after all captain of his school teams – and Mr Perkins would jokingly refer to the sports-mad gang as 'Ali Baba and his Forty Thieves'. This prompted little Arnold to invent a nickname for his pal; so Aron Bacher became 'Ali' to one and all and for the rest of his life, and even to those closest to him, he was never called Aron again. His sister Mushe says she cannot remember him ever being called Aron, and even the spelling of his given name creates confusion. Officially he is recorded as Aron, but Aaron is the more common name used by Jewish families and one of his uncles was Aaron. There are certificates from school that name him as 'Aaron' and in official cricket

---

[12] Ali Bacher married Shira Teeger on 4 April 1965.
[13] Ronnie Kasrils was a leading figure in the anti-apartheid struggle as a member of the ANC National Executive Committee and SA Communist Party. He was appointed deputy minister of defence in South Africa's first government of national unity in 1994.

records from his adult years he is often named Aron but also sometimes Aaron. His birth certificate, ID documents and passport all have him as Aron; but no one outside of the bureaucracy ever knew him again by that name.

There was a feeling among some of his kinfolk that 'Ali' was somehow more special than the other children; that he was the 'chosen one' who was born to lead. While his brothers and sisters had to get through life with their more formal Yiddish names, the name 'Ali' had a nice simple ring to it that somehow seemed more charismatic.

THESE WERE HEADY days at Yeoville Boys. Sport was everything to Ali; and he felt immense pride at representing the school.[14] On match days in the football season, the boys would go to school dressed in their soccer kit in preparation for the one o'clock kickoff that lay many hours away, and at which time the Yeoville shopkeepers would lock their doors and head for the field.

The influences around Ali were strong and positive. Each in their own way, the adults in his life were shaping his body and mind and spirit; and in return they gained the respect and devotion of a young boy who from an early age came to understand the values that a decent, hard-working life demanded. He soon recognised important allies in his growth in the form of his headmaster Mr Green, the sports master Mr Geldenhuys, and two devoted members of the PTA, Mr Srage and Mr Fisher, the latter being the local outfitter who kitted out the boys in the uniforms and playing strip that meant so much to them. Young and carefree he might have been, but Ali's intellect would grasp the importance of being surrounded by wise and influential people; and they would mould within him a fierce loyalty that would characterise his attitude and behaviour later in life.

In different ways, too, his parents were helping to shape Ali's outlook. From his father he learned about pride and ambition and a zealous work ethic, but it was his mother's passion to vigorously drive young aspirations and instil discipline that was perhaps more influential. It was not surprising that, from an early age, Ali would start developing strong leadership potential through the determination he learned from his parents; and that

---

[14] In December 1992, the Principal of Yeoville Boys' Primary School, N V Swain, acknowledged receipt of a cricket bat from Ali Bacher to be awarded each year to the top cricketer. Its first recipient was Anthony Cousins. At the same time, the fourth sports house at the school was named Bacher House.

he would embrace and respect the principles of rigid discipline and hard work.

He was captain of football in the winter and captain of cricket in the summer; and in between that he would captain his school at tennis, too. The school's high reputation for sporting excellence made him even more determined to do well and even as a six-year-old he was quite aware of the significance of a visit to the school by Alec Bedser, the great England cricketer; and he retains a clear memory of the famous man interrupting his tour of South Africa with George Mann's MCC team of 1948-49 to impart some wisdom to the young Yeovillites.

Julius Nickel was also very supportive. Ali recalls how his uncle returned penniless from a trip to England, where he had failed to establish himself in business. Ali and Rose met him at Park Station, the main railway terminus in central Johannesburg, and Julius immediately took him to Norman Gordon's sports shop and bought him a brand new cricket bat on tick. Julius was always a presence around the cricket fields where his nephew played.

Ali Bacher's first representative cricket match was at the age of seven. He was selected for the school's under-10 team in what was to become a significant pattern of achievement in that he was consistently considered good enough to compete equally alongside boys, and later men, of more advanced age. They took a bus to their match against a school situated at Milner Park which, although no more than a 15-minute journey to the west of Yeoville, would have felt like an away trip to an exciting foreign place.

Much closer to Yeoville Boys, in fact a mere stone's throw to the north across Louis Botha Avenue that separated Yeoville from the upper-class suburb of Houghton, lay two posh primary schools that did not deign to play against the 'lesser' mortals from across the road. The one was St John's Preparatory and the other King Edward Prep, universally known as KEPS, which were the direct feeder schools to St John's College and King Edward VII High School. In time to come, they would both get to know Ali Bacher.

In the mean time there were other adventures to tackle, other avenues to explore. There was Bacher's Farm on the West Rand which became the weekend haunt of the children, the place where their father could give expression to his love for the outdoors and where the children could pursue their sport and discover other exciting pastimes. There was horse riding, swimming, tennis, afternoon scones and tea from the small café, and dancing in the evenings. It was a fine diversion from the busy city life and Bacher's Farm would become a part of the history of Johannesburg's Jewish youth between the years 1945-50.

Ali would be allowed the privilege of inviting a friend or two to spend the weekend with him on the farm where, needless to say, they would use the dance hall for games of indoor cricket.

Probably as a result of the rural life in Lithuania, Koppel Bacher loved horses. Ali, on the other hand, had an aversion to them.

At the age of six, he was persuaded to mount one, whereupon the horse bolted, the boy was thrown from the saddle, his foot still caught in the stirrup and he was dragged upside down, as he recalls, 'like in the movies'. Shaken but not injured, he vowed never to ride a horse again. It would have been a great disappointment to his father that he resolutely kept his word. The other side of the coin was that Ali's love for cricket was not shared by his father who would take every opportunity to encourage his son but would never truly understand a game that was completely foreign to someone who grew up in eastern Europe.

Ali's mother was different. She immersed herself in the game for her sons' sake. Issy and Yudel, who were respectively eight and four years older than Ali, were fine allround sportsmen and his uncles Aaron and Julius were equally adept. Aaron Nickel, in fact, became only the second Jewish cricketer[15] to represent Transvaal at senior provincial level when he was capped in 1951.

ROSE'S MARRIAGE TO Koppel was troubled from the outset and the couple separated when Ali was very young. He could, in fact, not remember a time when his peripatetic father lived with them nor, for that matter, could he ever recall a family holiday.

He can remember travelling with his mother in her old blue Consul motor car for weekend breaks at a hotel in Warmbaths,[16] the hot springs resort town about 150 kilometres to the north of Johannesburg. During one such occasion, he learned for the first time of the Holocaust. Over after-dinner coffee in the evenings, fellow Jews in their company would tell horrific stories of the extermination of millions of their people – some of them members of their own families – and it had a devastating effect on

---

[15] Transvaal's first Jewish cricketer was the 1938 Springbok Norman Gordon.
[16] The town is now called by its Sotho name of Bela Bela (The Boiling Place).

the young boy. 'My mind could not grasp the horror, nor understand the mentality of its perpetrators', but it had a nightmarish impact as he sat with his mother, listening to these appalling accounts in a badly lit hotel lounge on those dark chilling nights.

His father was away in Durban, managing the business there, a restless man who was forever travelling in search of new outlets for the company. In time, his partnership with Cecil Aron would end in unhappiness when their business philosophy and strategy no longer corresponded. Cecil could not understand Koppel's obsession with expansionism, which at its extreme had him opening 29 shops around the country, and with it the resultant problems of inadequate stock control which created serious financial problems. By way of parting company, Cecil retained the Johannesburg operation and Koppel got the rest.

Through all of this, the remarkable Rose Bacher was ensuring that the children got a proper education and upbringing. She was a most attractive woman of an authoritarian nature. She totally committed her life to her children and single-handedly brought them up. Apart from Issy, Mushe, Yudel and Ali, there was a baby sister Sorrel, who was 10 years younger than Ali.

Ali was very fond of his mother, a tough, proud, resilient woman who brooked no trouble from her offspring. All of her children were achievers in their own separate ways, but in Ali she saw someone destined for greatness; and in later life he would say, 'my cricket became her life'. She bought him Bradman's *The Art of Cricket* – a book that would serve as his cricket bible throughout his playing career and beyond;[17] and at night while Ali slept she would read the book, carefully underlining key points and passages and, the next morning, she would give it to him so that he could study the parts she had highlighted. He learned a great deal from Bradman and adopted his closed left-hand Bradman batting grip.

---

[17] He eventually had two copies: one he lent to Hansie Cronje and the other to Graeme Smith who soon thereafter hit a SA record score of 277 against England at Edgbaston.

Chapter 2

'The Boy Can Bat a Bit'

In 1935, THE CITY fathers of Johannesburg donated a piece of farmland north of the city to the Jewish community for the purpose of building sports fields there. Leaders of the community named the venue Maccabi Park but a year later they decided to change the name – to avoid confusion with the Maccabi Games at which South Africa was now participating – and they called it Balfour Park in honour of Lord Balfour.[1] The concept of exclusive sports clubs for Jews was not a new one. They had made their first appearance in Europe towards the end of the nineteenth century as a counter to rampant anti-Semitism; and in Johannesburg, as in some other cities of the world, clubs existed that covertly discouraged Jewish member-ship. Furthermore, the Jews who lived in the poorer areas of Doornfontein, Bertrams and Bezuidenhout Valley could not join a club even if they wanted to because there was none in the vicinity to join. This was a community that did not have the wherewithal to enjoy the social pleasures of the wealthier townsfolk and, says George Mendelsohn,[2] who was a Doorn-fontein resident and Balfour Park stalwart, 'we had nothing but our sport'.

In the fine year-round weather that Johannesburg was blessed with, young men and women – particularly those who had come from inclement

---

[1] In 1917 the British Foreign Secretary, Lord Balfour, wrote to the British Zionist leader Lord Rothschild to assure him that the government supported the ideal of providing a homeland for the Jews. The 'Balfour Declaration' became the basis for international support for the founding of the modern state of Israel.
[2] George Mendelsohn interview, June 2003.

climes – derived great pleasure from participating in sport. And while the Jewish people put their faith in education, strong family and community ties and mutual support, it was equally true to say that they had a competitive nature that was well expressed through sport. As Mendelsohn pointed out, 'Balfour Park was our home. It was there that we all gathered and had fun. When we weren't working or at school, that's where you would find us. Life was sometimes tough; and this was like an escape for us.'

The Jewish sportsmen and women were proud of Balfour Park. They made it their responsibility to maintain and manage the facilities, which catered for sports that included football, cricket and tennis, and the players would arrive early on the day of the matches to mow and roll, erect the goalposts or wickets or nets, and mark out the creases or touchlines.

It is important to note that while Balfour Park was established by Jews on a site donated to Jews, those who ran the club did not discriminate against people of different creed or religion. Club membership was open to all, and many non-Jews joined its ranks and helped turn it into a popular, thriving club.

As for so many other young people, Balfour Park was a home from home for the Bachers. And it was there one Sunday morning that 12-year-old Ali was roped in to play his first cricket match for the club in a senior men's league fixture.

The boy was on the tennis court (his usual Sunday morning pursuit in those days) when his uncle Julius prepared himself on the nearby field to captain the club's 3rd team against Combined Banks. It was then that he realised that he was a man short. Ali answered the SOS for two reasons: he was very fond of this uncle who was particularly close to his mother, and he loved playing cricket. Julius Nickel, on the other hand, was happy to invite his nephew to play for one reason: he knew the kid could bat. In short pants and takkies[3] with full-size batting pads protruding uncomfortably near his waistline, the boy trudged in to bat in the lower middle order surrounded by men who did not know quite what to make of him. The Combined Banks bowler was Ralph Stork, a left-arm paceman. He shook his head in disbelief and informed the assembled company that he would have to bowl underarm for fear of hurting the boy. Three deliveries later he had conceded 4, 2, 4 . . . so he got angry and started bowling

---

[3] Takkies: Canvas sand shoes.

overarm. This did not help. The boy, cheered on by his teammates with each lusty blow, continued to plunder runs until he was finally out for 40-odd. It was the start of a glorious club career: by the time he was 15, Ali was playing for the Balfour Park 1st XI in the strong and star-studded Transvaal Premier League.

FOR THEIR SECONDARY school education the Bacher boys went to KES, an institution that was instantly recognisable by its acronymic name. In full, it was King Edward VII School, named as a memorial to that English monarch on his death in 1910, the year in which the Union of South Africa was established as a member of the British Commonwealth. The school, which was opened in 1911 on its current site at Houghton Estate, had undergone previous incarnations as the Johannesburg High School for Boys, opened in 1902 in a disused cigar factory in the centre of the burgeoning 'mining camp'; and then, two years later, as Johannesburg College in a location on the Berea Estate belonging to the diamond millionaire and landowner Barney Barnato.

It made sense that the Bacher boys should go to KES. It was a short walk from Dunbar Street and it enjoyed a fine reputation in both education and sport. Indeed, it was one of South Africa's finest schools – one of the so-called 'Milner Schools' that the British proconsul Lord Milner had endorsed after the Anglo-Boer war in 1902 to educate English-speaking boys – and it developed a strong network that 'recruited' pupils of promise. Thus it was that KES consistently delivered boys who would make their mark in society, be it as captains of industry, as noted academics, professional men, or top-class sportsmen.

The bigger Bacher boys, Issy and Yudel, were fine sportsmen. Issy was an excellent rugby, squash and hockey player, and Yudel played 1st team cricket and rugby, gaining fame in the latter game as a crash tackling centre threequarter. Although the bigger boys' exploits at KES probably helped to pave the way for their young brother to follow in their footsteps, word of his exploits at Yeoville Boys had already filtered across the road to the masters at KES. Even after Rose Bacher and her children – a family now enlarged by the arrival of little Sorrel – moved from Yeoville to Cyrildene, a few miles further east, KES was still well within their compass. Instead of walking to school, though, Ali and Yudel would catch the No 22 bus.

Their new home was at 18 Hettie Street, a red face-brick and tiled-roof house that Koppel Bacher had built in the manner of the smart dwellings that characterised the relatively new suburb of Cyrildene. A lot of its residents were Jewish folk who were doing well enough in their business ventures to begin upgrading their circumstances from Doornfontein, Bertrams, Bezuidenhout Valley and Yeoville. The Hettie Street house gave the bigger boys their own bedrooms, but more importantly it provided a lot more playing space than Dunbar Street, particularly the long driveway which was as wide as a cricket pitch. It was just bumpy enough, too, to encourage the batsman to be watchful. It was here that Yudel and Ali would bowl to each other hour after hour; and where Issy for the first time started taking notice of his youngest brother. Being eight years the senior, Issy had left home to become a veterinary surgeon – it seems that his father's love of farm life and horses might have influenced his choice of career – while Ali was still attending primary school. Issy was now boarding at the Onderstepoort Veterinary College near Pretoria, returning home at weekends. On one such occasion he bowled to Ali for a long spell in the driveway and was unable to get him out. 'I don't think I had taken much interest in him 'till then. Suddenly I realised that he could bat a bit.'

When his brothers were not available to bowl to him, he roped in his little sister Sorrel who proudly claimed she was his 'bowling machine'.

At KES, Ali surpassed his brothers at cricket by being named in the 1st XI at the age of 15 in Form III – when he shared the wicketkeeping duties – and that year, plus the two thereafter, he gained selection for Transvaal Schools. It is interesting that, although not captain of his school in Form IV, the provincial selectors named him as Transvaal Schools captain that year.

The next year, his last at KES, he was appointed captain of the School; and in achieving the pinnacle in any schoolboy cricketer's career, he played for SA Schools in 1959 and 1960.

His first Nuffield Week[4] was at East London in January 1958. It was there that, for the first time in many years, Transvaal beat Natal by three runs in a low-scoring match in which Ali failed to score. The Transvaal boys were overjoyed by their rare victory and it was clearly time to celebrate. But how to do so? The team included a few 'rough diamonds' who, among their sins, smoked cigarettes. So in the dressing room afterwards it was decided that everyone should smoke a celebratory cigarette. Now, the 15-

---

[4] The prestigious annual interprovincial schools tournament now known as the Coca-Cola Khaya Majola Week.

year-old Ali had never smoked a cigarette in his life and he was busy puffing away when the door opened to reveal the menacing figure of Mr Henry Beckwith, the tournament's organising secretary and chairman of the Transvaal High Schools Association. 'Most of the boys were clever enough to hide their cigarettes in such circumstances, but I just sat there with the evidence stuck between my lips' – and this from a boy who had not exactly made a huge contribution to the victory. Beckwith immediately gated him and he took no further part in the Week, the official excuse being that he had 'an ingrown toenail'. This catastrophe prompted Ali to confide to friends that he believed his cricket career was as good as over; but not only was it *not* over, it was proceeding so nicely that he was named as captain of Transvaal Schools the next season. Just before his 17th birthday in 1959, he led the provincial schools side against A P Walshe's Invitation XI, a senior team that included two very famous Springboks, the former South African captain Alan Melville, and the champion opening batsman Bruce Mitchell, who for a long time was South Africa's leading run-scorer in Test cricket. A third Springbok, the wicketkeeper-batsman Ronnie Grieveson, was also in the team for a Saturday match at the Wanderers. It was every schoolboy's dream to play there, and Ali lived it out by scoring 62 before retiring. He hit 10 fours and a six in an impressive knock, and Melville said afterwards: 'As a batsman he is years ahead of his age. If he keeps realising that there are lessons to learn every time you bat, I foresee a great future for him.'

The next day, the *Sunday Times* in Johannesburg carried a glowing report. Its author was R S 'Dick' Whitington who, before leaving his native Australia in 1958 to work as a sports editor and cricket writer in South Africa, played for South Australia for seven seasons from 1932 and for part of that time under the captaincy of Donald Bradman. He now wrote of the young Bacher:

> He has Bradman's stature, Bradman's lack of grace, Bradman's wariness, Bradman's drive against the point of the front toe and Bradman's time to play all his power-hit strokes – even Bradman's ability and time to correct a mistake and escape from it. Like Bradman, when he plays off the back foot he makes only one decisive movement into position. Like Bradman he is tremendously strong on the legside and off the back foot.

Not many South Africans had ever seen Bradman, so Whitington was fairly safe in making these comparisons; although it could be said that some of

25

his readers might not have known what to make of 'Bradman's drive against the point of the front toe'.

Arthur Goldman, in the press box that day for the *Sunday Express*, reported that Bacher's batting was 'a foe of dullness' and came to the conclusion that 'he will go a long way in cricket . . . and so will the bowling delivered to him.'

Goldman's article, however, was overshadowed by Whitington's which was reproduced a few days later in a daily newspaper under the headline: *IS THIS OUR BRADMAN?* It pointed out that Bacher was captain of the Transvaal Nuffield team even though he did not captain his school. In his characteristic personalised way, Whitington confided to his reader: 'I understand this was done because he is a far deeper student of cricket than any of his team colleagues.'

ALI'S REPUTATION PRECEDED him for his second Nuffield Week at Pietermaritzburg. At Durban Boys' High, a young pupil named Lee Irvine[5] had heard talk about this exceptional KES batsman who was being likened to Bradman. Lee and a pal decided to cycle from Durban to Pietermaritzburg to see for themselves. Unfortunately, Lee's bike broke down halfway there and they called off their escapade. In the mean time, Ali had met Dudley Nourse[6] for the first time. He was the convener of the SA Schools selectors and, as luck would have it, he was watching from the boundary when Ali scored a fine 92 in the first match against Western Province. In the second match against Natal, the Transvaal captain was disappointed not to repeat the victory of the previous year; and this time the defeat by four wickets included him being run out for one. It would not have meant anything to Ali at the time that the Natal team included the Hilton College batsman Raymond White[7] who was out for two. Ali's final innings of the tournament

---

[5] Lee Irvine was a gifted left-handed batsman who was a member of the Springbok team that Ali Bacher captained to a 4-0 Test series triumph over Australia. Irvine also played with Bacher for five years for Balfour Park and Transvaal, and is one of Ali's best friends.

[6] A D Nourse was a legendary figure in SA cricket, a former SA captain who played first-class cricket for Natal for 21 years during which he appeared in 34 Tests, toured England three times and once hit 231 against Australia in only four hours. He was the son of A W 'Dave' Nourse who is described as the 'grand old man of SA cricket'.

[7] Raymond White played Currie Cup cricket for Transvaal under Bacher's captaincy and was a prominent administrator who served as chairman of the Transvaal Cricket Council and president of the United Cricket Board of South Africa.

was a good 42 against Border, but he knew that it was the 92 at the start that earned his selection for the SA Schools side. This was a big moment in his life – to be named in the national team was the wish of every schoolboy cricketer – and sharing the honour with him for the first time was the fast bowler Peter Pollock[8] from Grey High School in Port Elizabeth. What a wonderful time this was because ahead of them lay the opportunity to play against the senior provincial team – which was the traditional end to Nuffield Weeks – and the Natal side included his Springbok heroes Jackie McGlew and Roy McLean. It was also a time to be reminded that cricket is a humbling game, a cruel game at times; going in to bat at No 5, Ali was out first ball to a catch in the covers. Nourse would still write in his tournament report:

> *A Bacher is a cricketer of promise. He was not as successful with the bat as was hoped after seeing his first knock of 92. This, it was felt, was due to his added responsibility in having to captain his team.*

DURING THE SAME season, Ali scored his maiden century for Balfour Park against Wanderers after which Whitington wrote in the *Sunday Times*, 'Bacher's batsmanship, particularly in its leg side strength and personal mannerism, is remarkably reminiscent of the young Bradman.'

It was in the midst of all these Bradmanesque achievements that Ali suffered a batting slump and returned home one evening after being dismissed for another nought. He was met at the front door by his mother: 'So, what do they call you now . . . Donald Duck?'

It has to be said that these comparisons with the great Australian batsman were a source of considerable embarrassment to Ali. Bradman was his hero and he knew there was none to compare with him – let alone himself. 'In my estimation, the only similarity between us was the closed left-hand grip.'

Ali was far and away the outstanding cricketer at KES during his years at the school. Initially he was seen as a useful spin bowler but in his second year at school he blossomed with the bat, averaging 97 for the under-14 A

---

[8] Peter Pollock played as a fast bowler alongside Ali Bacher in all 12 of his Test matches. His brother Graeme is regarded as South Africa's greatest batsman. Peter later became chairman of the national selectors and, while still in this role, his son Shaun was selected for South Africa, also as an opening bowler, and later became captain of the national team.

team, with two centuries and a top score of 125 not out against neighbouring St John's College.

The next year as a 'rookie' in the 1st XI he topped the batting with 392 runs at an average of 39.2 and hit 102 not out against St John's (the highest score by a KES boy that season). In his second year in the 1st XI, he topped the batting with 494 runs at 41.2 and 105 against St John's (the only century scored by the team that season). Apart from his excellent and consistent batting, it is noteworthy that Ali excelled when batting against St John's, whose sand and matting wicket allowed him to play to his strengths of cutting and pulling. One match in particular against that school remains vivid in his memory. It was played over two afternoons, starting on the Saturday and ending the following Wednesday, and on the opening day St John's were all out for 116 by the time tea was taken at 4 o'clock. In reply, KES reached 25 for one (Bacher adjudged leg before wicket for 23) and then suffered an awful collapse to be skittled for 31. There was, it should be noted, quite a lot of 'assistance' from the St John's umpire in the orchestration of KES's downfall. After this calamity, the St John's skipper suggested disdainfully that there was no point in playing again on the Wednesday because the match was already won. 'Not so,' said the shrewd Bacher, 'it's a two innings game. On Wednesday, we continue.'

It was a few days later in the school laboratory that Ali disclosed his strategy to his teammates, Sweet and Partridge. The lab at KES was a good place to do some extramural work. There was always a lot of activity there, with small groups of boys huddled around Bunsen burners and smelly test tubes, and science master 'Mango' Corbett not always knowing who was doing what. In a corner of the lab, Ali and his chums plotted.

On the Wednesday, Ali suggested to his rival captain that KES would follow on 85 runs in arrears. The plan was to score enough runs to set an inviting target. Bacher and Partridge set about the bowling, Bacher undefeated on 57 and Partridge 43, and Ali declared at tea on 161 for four. This left St John's 77 runs to win in 120 minutes. They managed 30. The spectacular triumph was due to the opening bowler, Anton Proctor, taking seven for 21 and their umpire, Bertie Buse, in Ali's words, 'not letting us down'.

Ali's final year at KES was by far his best. He scored 829 runs at an average of 43.6 (the next best aggregate was 462) with a top score of 136 against Natal's Hilton College, another acknowledged breeding ground of first-class players. No cricketer had made such a big impact at KES since Paul Winslow in the previous decade, and Ali's 829 runs surpassed the previous best 660 established by Winslow[9] 12 years earlier.

On the strength of all this, it was not surprising that Ali was characterised as a prodigy. He certainly was a rare talent, and there were a couple of good reasons for it. Firstly, he had assiduously studied the game virtually to the exclusion of any other pastime, devouring any cricket book he could lay his hands on, and especially those penned by or about Donald Bradman. Later, with *The Art of Cricket* at his side, and taking careful note of the passages his mother had underlined, he spent many lonely yet fulfilling hours refining his batting technique. Indoors, he would practise stroke after stroke in front of a full-length mirror and, outdoors, he would suspend a ball in a sock from a rope attached to a rafter in the garage at the Hettie Street house and bat it like clockwork with the strokes he chose to perfect. All of this was taught by Bradman, the greatest batsman in the world, through the pages of a book that was being devoured by a boy in Cyrildene, Johannesburg, 6 000 miles away from its author's home in Adelaide, South Australia.

Hour after hour, day after day, he refined his technique, becoming essentially a backfoot player because the matting wickets on which he played as a boy encouraged the cut and the pull shots. He was also blessed with a good eye that seemed to be a Nickel trait inherited from his wood-turning grandfather Louis Nochimovicz. Furthermore, he had quick feet, great powers of concentration and was able to pick his shots to pierce the field. In this, he undoubtedly modelled himself on Bradman who, by way of simple example, had written, '*A batsman should be able at any time to shut his eyes and visualise, just as though he were looking at a photograph, the exact position of every man on the field. Then and only then can he be mentally conditioned to the art of placing the ball.*'

Ali would constantly say that he was in awe of what he heard and read about Bradman. In the art of cricket, here indeed was a Michelangelo and a Rembrandt all in one.

Secondly, Ali gained a significant ascendancy over schoolboy rivals by being invited to play Premier League cricket for Balfour Park at the age of 15. This was unheard of among other Johannesburg clubs, but Balfour was different in that it was prepared to develop and encourage worthy youngsters from a tender age. At the centre of this noble strategy stood

---

[9] Paul Winslow played five Tests for South Africa. He went to his maiden first-class and Test century against England at Old Trafford in 1955 with a straight driven six into the car park. His first-class career included a stint for Sussex.

three men: the club president Tuxie Teeger, a Transvaal Cricket Union board member whose daughter Shira would one day marry Ali, its chairman Ruby Osrin and its treasurer Abe Levenstein.

At 15, Ali would play for the KES 1st XI on Wednesday afternoons and all day Saturdays, and then turn out for Balfour's senior league team on Sundays. The club cricket played in Johannesburg those days was of a very high standard, it being normal practice for provincial players and Springboks to turn out regularly in the league. Thus it was that the young Bacher gained invaluable experience each Sunday from facing the best bowlers in the province; and not only that, he now observed at first-hand the tactical and technical nuances of some great players and learned at their knee the great stories that were interwoven in the rich tapestry of the summer game he loved so much.

There might have been a third reason, too, for Ali's determination to succeed. There is no doubt that he was a very serious child who was possibly driven by a strong desire to do well for his mother's sake. He and his siblings were often exposed to their parents' acrimonious relationship, and Ali was very aware of the sacrifices his mother made on his behalf in what was essentially a one parent household. Perhaps the only way he could repay her was by making her proud of him. He was not in any way a 'Mommy's boy'; to the contrary, his mother was often hard on him. In such circumstances he might easily have rebelled against authority and taken an entirely different route into adult life; that he did not was the sign of a proud and strong-willed boy. He was, moreover, a non-conformist who stood up for his rights and spoke out against authority when aggrieved.

He was captain of his House and a respected school prefect who did not always follow convention. This is demonstrated in an incident involving a boy four years his junior named John Benjamin. He knew the Bacher boys by nodding acquaintance when they shared the No 22 bus. One day at school, John, a Form II pupil, was caught smoking behind the swimming pool. He was ordered to report to the prefects' room immediately after the final bell where the duty prefect would mete out the punishment. Offences like smoking were never referred to the schoolmasters, but dealt with by the prefects; and smoking was punishable with two or three cuts.

Benjamin reported as told. The duty prefect was Ali Bacher. John's confession was followed by a deafening silence as Ali pondered the case. He stared first at the ceiling, then at the floor, then at the wall. 'You better get out of here,' he told Benjamin.

The small boy was taken aback. 'But . . .'

'You heard me, get going.'

Benjamin[10] was puzzled. He decided later that Ali was not prepared to beat a boy smaller than him, in spite of what the rules required.

Many years later Ali Bacher would credit Dr John Benjamin with saving his life.

WHAT ALI MOST admired about KES was not so much the traditions and conventions but the quality of the teachers. Looking back, he would say 'the teachers made that school' through their total devotion to the institution over, in some cases, decades, and the excellence of their teaching. He always trusted their judgement. In Form I, when he showed no affinity whatsoever for the Arts, his teacher Tammy Mills chased him out of class. 'You're wasting my time and yours. Rather go and play cricket.' He did.

Another member of staff was Mark Henning whose first teaching post was at KEPS before he went up to the high school. His father D J Henning was head of geography, and when he took long leave his son stood in for him. It was during this time that Mark Henning taught Ali. Henning Junior also turned out for the Old Edwardians cricket team in the Premier League; and in two successive matches against Balfour Park, Ali's geography master was one of the bowlers who suffered through the schoolboy hitting two successive centuries.

Mark would later note, 'with no hard feelings', that it was Ali who displaced him in the Transvaal provincial team; and they would become firm allies in the administration of the game, Ali becoming vice-chairman of the Transvaal Cricket Council under Henning's chairmanship.

Ali also had a fondness for his cricket coach, the Somerset professional Bertie Buse who, according to notes in the school magazine, was 'the guide, philosopher and friend of every cricketer in the school.' Ali remembers him as the likeable rotund man who stood at the nets interminably bellowing 'FOR-WARD!' at the batsmen in his West Country accent, a command which clearly had little effect on young Bacher who persisted in playing mostly BACK-WARD!

During the course of his final year, Ali captained the 1st XI to a record that read *Played 21 Won 15 Drawn 6 Lost 0*, the first time the school was unbeaten over so many matches since before the Second World War. The school magazine was typically understated in its appraisal of an exceptional season but it did at least note that 'Bacher had to shoulder the lion's share

---

[10] Dr John Benjamin interview, July 2003.

of the batting and did this right well.'

It was during this year that the school's cricketers were treated to a visit by the Springbok captain Jackie McGlew and the Springbok wicketkeeper and Transvaal captain Johnny Waite. The two heroes were invited to address the boys and then take questions on any cricketing matter. It was not every school that could expect to host such honoured guests, but KES had been long regarded as a breeding ground for future international cricketers and enjoyed privileges of this nature. Among the cricketers who crammed into the main lecture hall that day was a scrawny new boy in Form I named Albert During who knew Ali by reputation and held him in the highest esteem. Boys wishing to ask a question of the Springbok captain would follow a set protocol: stand to attention, speak out clearly and politely, and prefix their question with the word 'sir'. Many questions were put in this way but it was Bacher who most impressed young Albie During. The Form V prefect lounged back in his chair, legs crossed at the ankles and one arm strung casually over the backrest; and when the time came for him to ask a question, he neither rose from his chair nor did he say 'sir'. He simply put his question. Not for a minute did During[11] think that this was disrespectful of the senior boy; it simply confirmed what he had heard – that Ali Bacher was a cut above the rest and could therefore deal with Springbok captains on level terms. Indeed, within 12 months of this meeting, Bacher would be batting for Transvaal against the champion Natal team led by Jackie McGlew; and, what is more, he would score freely against the ferocious fast bowling of McGlew's key strike bowler Neil Adcock.

A FURTHER MEASURE of Ali's non-conformity was in evidence during the rugby season in his final year. KES awarded different blazers for levels of proficiency and the much-prized colours blazer was traditionally only awarded to the most outstanding players. The 1st Rugby XV of 1959 was not an exceptional one yet, for some unknown reason, the school saw fit to award Colours to the entire team. To the proud young Bacher, this wholesale presentation of the quintessence of sporting proficiency somehow cheapened its worth. So, instead of parading in his bold red and white striped

---

[11] In the years ahead, Albie During would himself become a provincial cricketer, representing Transvaal schools in two successive years and then graduating to the senior provincial side where he would play under the captaincy of Ali Bacher. During served on the Transvaal Cricket Council board with Bacher for many years and would succeed him as chief executive.

colours blazer, Ali resorted to wearing his regular team blazer which was a plain green, braided garment. When the team travelled to Rustenburg in Western Transvaal to play a tough school from the *platteland* (rural areas), the hosts thought that Bacher's odd-one-out blazer was the mark of the real champion. He was 'nailed' throughout a hard game that KES narrowly won.

Ali Bacher loved rugby almost as much as cricket. He followed the fortunes of Springbok teams, at home and abroad, with a zealous passion. When the Springboks toured Australia and New Zealand in 1956, he would listen to the live radio commentary in the middle of the night and ache when they lost. As a flyhalf, he believed that his role was to create opportunities as the playmaker and that he was definitely not in the side to tackle.[12] He enjoyed it in later years when the great Northern Transvaal provincial coach, Brigadier Buurman van Zyl, made the point that his crack flyhalf, Naas Botha, was not selected in his team to tackle.

AT THE END of Ali's final year, the school received a surprise visit from Field Marshal Viscount Montgomery of Alamein who addressed the boys. He spoke to them of the importance of integrity and moral courage and then went on:

> I notice among chaps of your age, and a little older, when they are learning their professions, a great tendency to think all that matters in a profession is to achieve technical proficiency. Well, I maintain that's only half the game. The other half is knowing how to handle men, a knowledge of human nature. In the late war at one time I commanded more than two million men. I realised that bottled up inside those men were very great emotional forces. If I could win the hearts of those men and gain their confidence and their trust and use those emotional forces the right way, there was nothing that could not be done with them. That is a very important thing. Every one of you boys eventually will have to exercise responsibility and you will have to handle men. If you cannot handle men and win their hearts, your technical proficiency will be largely wasted.

It was a speech that would have made sense to Ali because, although he was probably unaware of it at the time, the seeds of strong leadership were sown in his years at KES.

After five years at the famous school Ali acquired a first-class University Exemption with a distinction in Mathematics. He was disappointed he did

---

[12] The School magazine of 1959 takes issue with this assertion. It says of Ali Bacher, 'Handled very safely and quickly. Did a lot of work on defence.'

not get a distinction in Latin, and his other favourite subject was Geography. He was never much good at his basic languages, his Afrikaans was very poor and for the rest of his life he lacked the confidence to attempt to converse in it. His English, too, suffered from a lack of reading. The only books he read were on cricket, foremost among them anything written by or about Donald Bradman.

HAVING NOW MATRICULATED, Ali bade farewell to his school days by playing n his third and final Nuffield Week in the first week of January in 1960 It was held in Johannesburg and after scoring runs consistently throughout the week, he was selected again for the SA Schools XI, this time as vice-captain to Nic Frangos, the opening batsman from Rhodesia. Their opponents in the showpiece game would be the Transvaal senior provincial side. Ali was down to bat at No 6, one place below the 15-year-old Graeme Pollock who was by far the best of the batsmen on view during the tournament. Ali had never seen him before but his teammate and friend from KES, Gavin Fairon, had. He told Ali, 'There's a young left-hander here from Port Elizabeth called Pollock, and he's got to be the best I've seen.' Graeme had hit two centuries during the week but, as luck would have it, he was out first ball. Ali had a much happier time of it, scoring a fine 34 in a losing cause before being caught behind by Johnny Waite off Eddie Barlow. The *SA Cricket Annual* recorded that 'Bacher's 34 was the innings of an accomplished batsman who displayed a wide range of strokes on both sides of the wicket.'

Dudley Nourse, still in charge of the selectors, wrote in his notes, 'A Bacher is an excellent on-side player who played his best innings in the final match against the provincial side.'

Exactly a week later, Ali was named in the Transvaal B team to make his first-class debut with his 18th birthday still more than four months away. The match at the Wanderers was an important one against Eastern Province who needed only to win on the first innings in order to be crowned the Currie Cup B Section champions. Ali batted at No 7 and in his only turn at bat scored 9 before being trapped in front by Peter Pollock. EP were beaten outright, and Transvaal B finished joint top of the log with them. The disappointed visiting captain was the opening batsman Geoff Dakin.[13]

---

[13] Geoff Dakin became one of South Africa's best known cricket administrators, serving as president of both the SA Cricket Union and later the United Cricket Board of South Africa. In both these capacities, he had Ali Bacher as his managing director.

Chapter 3

Medical School

IT IS SAID that the sons of English aristocracy are traditionally obliged to pursue a career in politics, the church or the army. In post-war South Africa, the male offspring of Jewish immigrants were expected to study for a profession. This was generally narrowed down to law, accountancy or medicine, three fields in which South African Jews have consistently excelled and in many cases become world authorities.

Koppel Bacher had impressed on his youngest son the need to follow one of these avenues. He reminded him that in times of economic depression, those without degrees were liable to suffer great deprivation. He told him of the Great Depression of the early 1930s when men had lost all they had. For Ali, this was too awful to contemplate but he had no clear idea of where his future lay. He sat down one night and listed three words on a piece of paper: *1) Lawyer 2) Accountant 3) Doctor*. He then began an elimination process and arrived at the following conclusions, in words to this effect: *1) Lawyer – not good at speaking in public or arguing. Don't read enough, apart from cricket books. English marks very average. 2) Accountant – little interest in financial issues and no accountancy at school. 3) Doctor – the only thing left.*

He had neither ambition nor calling to become a doctor but it was the only career on his list worth trying. In January 1960, he enrolled at Wits Medical School[1] at the University of the Witwatersrand in Johannesburg.

---

[1] Among its many notable achievements, the Wits Medical School started the first blood transfusion service in South Africa and undertook the first clinical survey of childbirth in African tribal conditions. (Ref: Wits University Archives.)

Wits University had a high reputation as a great seat of learning. It was also the most liberal university in South Africa and was viewed by the apartheid regime as a hotbed of communism. Wits was founded as an open university with a policy of non-discrimination on racial or any other grounds. This commitment faced its ultimate test when the government passed the Extension of the University Education Act in 1959, thereby enforcing university apartheid. The Wits community protested strongly and continued to maintain a firm, consistent and vigorous stand against apartheid, not only in education, but also in all its manifestations.

These protests were sustained as more and more civil liberties were withdrawn and peaceful opposition to apartheid was suppressed. The consequences for the University were severe. They included bannings, deportations and the detention of staff and students, as well as invasions of the campus by riot police to disrupt peaceful protest meetings.

Ali was not one of the student radicals, but he empathised with them. He soon realised that non-discrimination on the urban campus was a very noble policy but it was not going to do much good for black students who were financially disadvantaged or who fell foul of the apartheid laws.

Of the more than 200 students in his class, there were only eight blacks, one of whom, Benson Nghona from the Transkei, studied at night with a paraffin lamp in the blacks-only township in which he was forced to live. He would become a physician in Port Elizabeth. Of the others, Razak Moti became a cardiologist in Johannesburg, Farouk Dindar a neurologist who moved to Toronto, and Zarina Desai, a beautiful young woman of Indian extraction, became romantically involved with a white academic, Professor John Blacking of the Department of Social Anthropology,[2] and they were charged under the Immorality Act.[3] Both subsequently left the country, married and settled in Britain.

On a personal level, Ali was still not convinced that he was cut out to be a doctor, but some of the professors made a strong impact on him for the knowledge they imparted and for their strong character traits: the

---

[2] This department pioneered the study of what today is known as 'race relations'.
[3] Communism was banned by the National Party government. Apartheid legislation included the Prohibition of Mixed Marriages Act which forbade mixed marriages, the Population Registration Act which categorised the race groups, the Group Areas Act which defined areas for ethnic groups to live, the Reservation of Separate Amenities Act which, for example, prohibited mixed race public toilets, and the Immorality Act No 23 (Amended) of 1957 which prohibited sex across the colour line.

quiet and cerebral Phillip Tobias,[4] a diminutive man of monumental intellect who taught him Anatomy; the brash and humorous Harry Seftel,[5] a physician who taught Pharmacology and loved to prefix his statements with 'Harry says . . .' which meant 'this is the only way'; and the feared disciplinarian and inspirational Daniel 'Sonny' du Plessis who was Professor of Surgery and Chief Surgeon at Johannesburg General Hospital. Du Plessis' stature was such that the students dubbed him 'God' which inspired a one-liner that became part of Wits folklore. It is told that after the dictatorial surgeon was heard barking commands at an eminent physician, Dr Moses Suzman, one of the students was heard to remark, 'Thus spake God to Moses'.

Professor du Plessis[6] gave Ali a piece of advice that he would never forget and would always apply: 'Everyone is entitled to make a mistake once, but never make the same mistake twice.'

Ali found himself having to juggle his studies with his cricket commitments, which proved a difficult assignment. He was now a provincial player in the Transvaal B team and by the end of 1960 he would be in the senior provincial side. Cricket was his passion and he badly wanted to succeed in a game that was already offering opportunities for him to flourish.

FOR TRANSVAAL B'S match against Rhodesia in November 1960, Ali found himself on the train to Bulawayo. With him in the Transvaal B team was the 19-year-old Gavin Fairon, his pal from KES and teammate in the previous season's Transvaal Nuffield XI. It would be Ali's second game for Transvaal B and Gavin was making his debut. In those days the provincial teams travelled by train, and both youngsters were looking to have a rip-roaring time. They had heard talk that there were high jinks aplenty when

---

[4] Phillip V Tobias, Professor and Chair Emeritus of the Department of Anthropology, is one of the world's pre-eminent scholars of palaeoanthropology, recognised for his distinguished contributions in the fields of hominid palaeontology, human biological diversity and genetics, skeletal biology and comparative anatomy. He is the recipient of three Nobel Prize nominations and South Africa's Order for Meritorious Service.
[5] Professor Harry Seftel is Emeritus Professor of Medicine and a popular figure on radio and television shows for his down-to-earth advice on the maintenance of good health. At the time of Bacher's enrolment at Wits, Professor Seftel was in charge of the Non-European Hospital (NEH) in Johannesburg.
[6] Professor Daniel Jacob du Plessis became vice-chancellor and principal of Wits University in 1978 and did much to enhance its size and status in anticipation of the new South Africa. He died aged 81 in 1999.

teams travelled on trains. The team manager was Ken Viljoen,[7] a man much loved and respected for his great devotion to the game and something of a father figure to the younger players. He was a stickler for good behaviour, insisted on a proper dress code and did not smoke or drink. He saw the glint in the young men's eyes, so throughout the two-day journey he took them under his wing. For most of the time they talked cricket. Viljoen had a wealth of experience in the game and a fund of good cricketing yarns that he had acquired over decades of playing with and against some great cricketers. Ali was enthralled, particularly when Ken told of playing against Bradman on the 1931-32 tour of Australia and how, three balls in a row, the great batsman had hit boundaries through gaps in the field that were left vacant each time the Springbok captain Jock Cameron moved a fielder to another position in a vain attempt to contain him.[8] Perhaps Ali was inspired by this talk of his hero because at Bulawayo he picked the gaps to score 101, his maiden first-class hundred and the only century of the three-day match. The *SA Cricket Annual* reported that 'the youngster played the strong Rhodesian attack with confidence and displayed all the best strokes in the book.' Fairon did not rate a mention in the annual but he nevertheless came through his debut with distinction. He bowled tidy offspin to take five for 45 in the second innings as Transvaal B failed narrowly to take outright points.

Ali loved the train trips. 'We travelled second class, six to a compartment, and there was so much for us to learn from managers and senior players.' He was a great listener and absorbed the details of past exploits. He began to understand that a knowledge of cricket history was vital to his growth; and for the rest of his life in the game he would impress this on young players, some of whom were alarmingly ignorant of what had gone before them. As Ali put it, 'Cricket is a game that's all about the past ... it's the history of the game and the stories about the great players of yesteryear that spur us on.'

When he became a regular member of Transvaal's Currie Cup team, he

---

[7] Ken Viljoen was 16 years old when he made his provincial debut in 1926. His two Test centuries were 111 against Australia at Melbourne in 1931-32 and 124 against England at Old Trafford in 1935. In first-class cricket he scored 23 centuries, including three doubles. He served terms as president of both the SA Cricket Association and Transvaal Cricket Union and was manager of the famous 1952-53 Springbok team in Australia. He played 27 Tests for South Africa.
[8] In the 1931-32 series, Don Bradman hit four centuries, including 299 not out at Adelaide, 226 at Brisbane and 167 at Melbourne, and averaged 201.5.

counted himself privileged to listen to cricketing tales from team managers who included Jack Cheetham, Eric Rowan and Johnny Waite, and from senior players he admired, like Hugh Tayfield, Peter Heine and Russell Endean. He also spent long and enjoyable hours on train trips playing cards, and specifically a game called klabberjas; and one night each week, he was part of a klabberjas school with the other regulars, Rowan, Waite and the man they called 'The Butcher' – for that's what he was – the Transvaal legspinner Ronnie Carr. Teammate Tiger Lance was not a card player but he reckoned Bacher played klabberjas the way he outsmarted his opponents on the cricket field – with great bluff and daring. Playing cards, of course, did not stop the flow of cricket stories and the insights into the game that Ali was fast accumulating.

All these men had a big influence, one way or another, on Ali's cricket career. Cheetham and Rowan, so different in character and demeanour and background, were Springboks of legendary status during Ali's boyhood. Cheetham, the archetype gentleman, embodied the best virtues of sportsmanship and human endeavour and was always held up as the ideal kind of man to captain his country. Indeed, his legend was assured when he led a young and untried Springbok team to Australia in 1952-53 to achieve unexpected fame in sharing a Test series for the first time against the Aussies. Before they had even set sail from South Africa, Cheetham's Springboks were publicly denounced by Australian cricket bosses as not good enough to compete adequately against their team; and the only way the tour could proceed was for the SA Cricket Association to financially underwrite it. Even at home, the country's best known cricket journalist Louis Duffus, a former Transvaal cricketer himself, campaigned against the tour through *The Star* newspaper of which he was sports editor.

Against such odds, Cheetham[9] would certainly have won Ali's admiration for his remarkable leadership qualities (with the help of the trusty Ken Viljoen) in winning newfound respect for South African cricket and making many experts eat their words. For that tour Cheetham was best remembered for instilling a strong mental attitude among his players and, for the first time, giving high priority to fielding which was a department where the Australians were sorely lacking and which played a major role in his team's

---

[9] Jack Cheetham was captain in 15 of his 24 Tests against England, Australia and New Zealand. He was president of the SA Cricket Association at the same time as Bacher was Springbok captain, and is an honorary life president of Transvaal cricket. He died aged 60 in 1980.

unexpected success.

Cheetham's signature shot was the straight drive, which was totally in accordance with the way he played his cricket and lived his life. His friends called him 'Happy' and they rated him as South Africa's captain of captains who was so influential in his country's positive resurgence in international cricket following the Second World War.

If Cheetham was 'Happy' then Eric Rowan was 'Grumpy', and Ali admired him for different reasons. Whereas Cheetham was a role model of the highest order, Rowan was the *enfant terrible* of South African cricket who was dumped from the Springbok team after crossing swords once too often with officialdom. Once, when captaining Transvaal, he declared when Endean was 99 not out. Rowan said it was 'the right time' to declare, but Johnny Waite suggests he was not particularly fond of Endean.

Before and immediately after the Second World War, Rowan[10] was ranked alongside Dudley Nourse and Bruce Mitchell as South Africa's finest batsmen, but he was his own worst enemy and suffered through a reputation that was contemptuous of authority. It could be said that he was sometimes misrepresented and often misunderstood, but his cocky attitude and habit of calling a spade a bloody shovel clearly counted against him. He was manager of the Transvaal team on a trip to Cape Town when the Western Province batsmen came off the field for bad light. Eric was annoyed because he did not think the light was bad enough. He was expressing this view in the pavilion when the rotund manager of the Western Province Cricket Club, John Reid, who in Rowan's view was rather too posh for his liking, made a remark that was intended to further annoy the irascible Transvaal manager. Rowan shot back, 'Why don't you join Boswell's Circus, they're looking for fat men for clowns!'

Putting aside his faults, Rowan impressed Ali with his fine knowledge of the game, his keen sense of survival and, above all, his total dedication to the cause of Transvaal cricket. Eric *was* Transvaal cricket and he did everything there was worth doing for the province. Between 1929 and 1986 (save for one season when he played for Eastern Province) he devoted his life to Transvaal as a tough opening batsman, captain, selector and an

---

[10] Eric Rowan's first-class career spanned the years 1929-54 during which he scored 11 710 runs (average 48.58). In 26 Tests, he scored 1 965 runs (43.66) and his 3 Test centuries included 236 against England at Headingley in 1951 when he was SA's top batsman. After that tour he faced a disciplinary inquiry and did not play for South Africa again. He died aged 83 in 1993.

administrator whose acerbic wit and colourful language enlivened many a Transvaal board meeting. Eric was very fond of his fellow board member Tuxie Teeger who, as we know, was to become Ali's father-in-law. In respect of their personalities, Tuxie and Eric were like chalk and cheese, the one a quiet-spoken gentleman who was calm and reasoned in his approach, the other a man who could be perfectly charming the one minute and quite outrageous the next. Ali respected him for his commitment, and he in turn recognised the young man's potential from an early age and became an important ally.

As for Waite, Tayfield, Heine and Endean, here were players of great stature and popularity who were hero-worshipped in the post-war years. As a boy, Ali could not wait to go to Ellis Park or the Wanderers[11] Stadium to watch them play. At the Wanderers in 1956 and 1957, he sat on the open stands below the scoreboard on the eastern side of the ground often alone – for the full five days of the Tests against Peter May's England and Ian Craig's Australians. And at home in front of the big radiogram in the Hettie Street lounge, he would not miss a ball of the Springboks' adventures abroad. During the July school holidays of 1955 he would listen transfixed to the commentary of John Arlott, Rex Alston and Charles Fortune as they brought the cricket to him from Manchester and Leeds; and when 'Cheetham's Babes' were doing such fine things in Australia in 1952-53 he would be out of bed at 3 am, wrapped in a blanket, mesmerised by the short-wave crackle that carried the ball-by-ball commentary from Sydney and Melbourne and Adelaide.

Now, just a few years later, he was sharing a train compartment with some of these players – *one of them now* – and being taken into their confidence on so much interesting stuff. This was a rare privilege; and one that Ali would cherish long after his own fame had been achieved. He had learned as a boy to take nothing for granted and to thank God for the blessings that came his way. He was also taught never to allow privileged positions to go to his head; and when he eventually attained positions of great power and influence in cricket's administration he lived by the maxim that no man was bigger than the game. In later years his detractors would claim without conviction or proof that he was using the game to enhance his own status, but none could deny that his devotion to cricket's cause was anything but selfless.

---

[11] The Wanderers Stadium was opened in 1956 for the tour by Peter May's MCC team.

In the closing months of 1960, there were no such back-stabbers around as Ali set about scoring 78 against Border in his third and final game for Transvaal B. It was here that he would meet Robin Thorne, a Border allrounder 12 years his senior who he would grow to admire 25 years later when Robin spent countless hours coaching young cricketers in the black township of Alexandra.

Life at the Medical School was not easy. The zoology and biology lectures were becoming more and more burdensome, and Ali was experiencing a major conflict with himself. His cricket career was just starting and he was not sure that he really wanted to become a doctor. His growing cricket commitment to Transvaal was not the only thing cutting into his time; there was also Balfour Park. Ali loved Balfour and its people, he was their key batsman, and he would never have dreamt of switching his allegiance to the University cricket club or Old Edwardians, although he was qualified to play for either club, and they dearly would have liked him. He had been a Balfour boy since his school days – indeed, as a pupil at KES he was forbidden by school rules to turn out for the old boys' Old Edwardians Club because beer-drinking old boys were apparently not considered the correct company – and Old Eds understood this and, according to Mark Henning, an Old Edwardian of note, they never held this against him. Balfour Park's captain Jack Kerby had moved to Cape Town. The club needed a new skipper. There was much speculation because the two men in the running were an uncle and his nephew. Aaron Nickel had once captained Balfour Park but had been away for several years working in Natal. When he returned to Johannesburg, he found that Ali was his main rival. Many felt the club was faced with a delicate problem of having to choose between the two, but with a view to the future – and in keeping with Balfour's progressive policies – they opted for the younger man. Ali was now in charge of his club's Premier League team at the age of 20.

The appointment inspired him to give carefree expression to his talents and unconventional methods. When he took over the captaincy, he immediately decided that his strike bowlers were his three spinners – Morris Charnas, Joe Hansen and Godfrey Steyn. He had a limited number of seam bowlers in his uncle Aaron, Trevor Baillie and Terence Joffe, but he would often open the bowling with one of his spinners and ask them to deliver 75 per cent of the overs. Under his leadership, Balfour lost their first four matches and then won 14 in succession to win the Premier League.

The one aspect of captaincy that he did not relish was having to make speeches at the annual club dinners. He was neither articulate nor adept at writing and he would ask Tuxie Teeger and his wife 'Nana' – before and after they became his in-laws – to write them for him. He would then spend many hours memorising their excellent prose and recite it parrot-fashion on the night. It was always a nerve-racking experience.

Not unexpectedly, Ali's maiden century for Transvaal B in Bulawayo immediately pitched him into the Transvaal A team for the Currie Cup match against Natal ten days later. Natal were the champion team under Jackie McGlew but Ali was not at all nervous approaching the big game at the Wanderers. 'On the contrary, I counted down the days and could not wait for it to start.' The selectors obviously had great faith in him. Quite apart from the responsibility of being selected as a top-order specialist, he was also handed the wicketkeeping duties. Although Waite, the captain, was the country's best 'keeper, Ali was asked to don the gloves because Waite was suffering from a cracked finger. Bacher's wicketkeeping ability had come to the fore a couple of months earlier when Richie Benaud's International Cavaliers arrived at the Wanderers to play Transvaal. Waite was not available so the 18-year-old Bacher was asked to stand in for him against the star-studded visitors. In a dream outing, he took five catches, among them the England Test batsmen Ken Barrington and skipper Tom Graveney, and stumped the great Australian batsman Norman O'Neill for 66. The Cavaliers amassed 429, and Transvaal found themselves on 126 for five and floundering against the pace of the England new ball pairing of Fred Trueman and Brian Statham when Ali went in to bat. The precocious youngster was obviously unfazed by the reputations of his opponents. Early in his innings he had the temerity to sweep Trueman for a four – a shot that was unheard of against a pace bowler of this calibre – whereupon the fiery Yorkshireman glared at the young batsman: 'Aye lad, you think I'm a fookin' spin bowler, eh?' and proceeded to give him the full treatment on a pitch made greasy by on-off drizzle before finally bowling him for 16.

In naming him for his Currie Cup debut against Natal, the Transvaal selectors again made no attempt to keep Ali in cotton wool. He was named as the No 3 batsman to face an attack that was spearheaded by South Africa's version of Trueman – the fast and ferocious Neil Adcock – who earlier in the year had been the outstanding Springbok bowler[12] on the

---

[12] Adcock captured a record-equalling 26 wickets in the Tests (average 22.57) and 108 overall (average 14.02) on tour.

1960 tour of England under McGlew's captaincy.

Ali played Adcock superbly; indeed, he handled all the Natal bowlers well to hit top score of 75 that drew widespread praise. As always, Dick Whitington was keeping close tabs on the teenage batsman. He wrote:

> *It is no disparagement of the displays of McGlew and Goddard[13] to say that the finest batting came in an innings of rare quality, extraordinarily mature judgment and composure from the 18-year-old Ali Bacher. Judged on this display he is more advanced in his stroke production and generally considerably sounder in technique than were Norman O'Neill[14] and Ian Craig[15] at the same age.*

As for Ali's dismissal, Whitington informed his readers that:

> *He fell to an amazingly acrobatic catch by Goddard at gully from a ball of Adcock's which seamed back from the legside and rose sharply from a goodish length. Doubts were expressed in the covered stand by those blessed with binoculars (German as well as Japanese) whether Goddard had snaked his prehensile left-hand under the slow-falling ball.*

Whitington not only entertained his readers with his quaint turn of phrase but he also, as always, gave them the confidential line, in this case, 'Those close to the catch, including Bacher, are, I understand, satisfied that it was cleanly made.'

Bacher again distinguished himself as wicketkeeper, making four dismissals, including McGlew, Goddard and McLean, in Natal's only innings.

Up in the press box, Peter Walker, the Glamorgan and England allrounder who was Ali's professional at Balfour Park, remarked on his club teammate's powers of concentration. 'Sometimes when one bats with him, he hardly appears to know what you are saying when you approach him for a chat in between overs or between balls – always a sign that the batsman is really knuckling down to the job.'

---

[13] Trevor Goddard scored 145 and Jack McGlew 79 in Natal's victory by an innings.
[14] Norman O'Neill was acclaimed as 'the new Don Bradman' when he averaged over 43 as an 18-year-old in his first season with New South Wales in 1955. He would play 42 Tests for Australia.
[15] Also compared to Bradman, Ian Craig was just 17 years old when he scored 213 not out for New South Wales against the 1952-53 Springboks which propelled him into the Australian team as his country's youngest player in Test cricket. He was 22 when he captained Australia in South Africa in 1957-58.

Those who worked closely with Ali decades later would recognise this observation of Walker's as a reason for the blank looks they sometimes got when attempting to talk to him at the wrong time.

In summing up his first Currie Cup match, Whitington referred to Ali as 'that new morning star' and urged skipper Waite to allow him to concentrate on his batting and not force him to keep wicket as well.

WHITINGTON TRAVELLED TO Durban early in 1961 where he watched Ali score his first A Section century off the impressive Natal attack – with Adcock at his most hostile. Ali was learning how to deal with the Springbok fast bowler. He would greet him with a 'Morning, Mr Adcock' and then, during the course of play, the odd 'well bowled, Mr Adcock!' or even the occasional 'good ball, sir' would ensure, as he put it, that he didn't get too many deliveries aimed at the heart. In the days before chest protectors, helmets and forearm guards, batsmen did well to employ every method not to get hit. Adcock was more than 11 years older than Ali so he appreciated the kind of respect the young batsman accorded him; but the fact that Ali took 100 off him in the most difficult conditions during an innings in which Adcock's figures read 26-12-51-6 bore testimony more to his batsmanship than his flattery of the great bowler. By this stage Whitington himself was searching for adjectives to describe the young man's performance. He dubbed him the 'Boy Methuselah' which was a puzzling comparison seeing that Methuselah was a biblical character who had lived for 969 years; suffice to say that no one had any doubt that the sportswriter saw him right up there with people who had survived in very trying circumstances. His 102 was a fine knock and, when it finally ended, Ali was not dismissed by Adcock but by Clive Halse who trapped him leg before wicket.

It was an extremely hot and humid January in Durban, prompting a cartoonist in the morning newspaper to suggest that 'a thermometer may be Natal's best hope of beating Ali Bacher's 102 at Kingsmead'. It really *was* hot. Ali packed three shirts and flannels in his bag, and wore all three sets on the first day. His proud mother was there to watch him; and she performed minor miracles to get the shirts and trousers washed and dried in time for the start of the second day. Ali needed them because he was undefeated on 40 overnight and reached his hundred, dripping wet again, just before lunch on the second day.

Ray Woodley, popular sports editor of the *Sunday Express*, had also become a big Bacher fan. He wrote, 'I would like to punch on the nose the wise boys who are trying desperately to get Ali Bacher to change his batting style.'

The 'wise boys' had always reckoned that Ali would be 'found out' because of his unorthodox batting grip and leg-side technique, but with each new innings their wisdom seemed more and more misplaced and the mild-mannered Woodley was now ready to punch them in the nose. Ali himself was not too fussed. His technique was working for him and he rated his Kingsmead innings very highly. Shira Teeger was also watching, and she liked what she saw. She and her family were holidaying down the south coast at Margate but they travelled up to Durban to watch Ali play. Ali's brother Issy was also there; but he became so nervous when his little brother batted that he chose to walk round the ground rather than sit and watch.

The Afrikaans press – not particularly big into cricket in the early sixties – now also took note of the young run-getter. The *Landstem*, a big circulation Sunday newspaper, called him the cricketer with the 'funny name' and suggested he was the kind of batsman that South Africa needed against the visiting New Zealanders[16] in the season ahead. The paper also made mention that Ali had played rugby for KES which was important information for Afrikaans readers because rugby was their game of choice. It was a pity that the *Landstem* did not know that Ali had recently played at centre for the Wits Medical School XV which beat their counterparts from Pretoria 16-3 in their annual intervarsity match. Pretoria was the heartland of *Landstem*'s circulation, and Pretoria University was at its epicentre. Be that as it may, Bacher would become an enduringly popular figure among Afrikaner sports lovers who admired nothing more than a sportsman with courage – a quality that had recently been remarked upon by Dudley Nourse who watched Ali's century at Kingsmead: 'The lad is brimful of promise and has one very valuable characteristic – guts. A young cricketer can go a long way with this asset.'

The one occasion when Ali decided to dispense with this asset came not in cricket but in rugby. One of his good pals at medical school was Alan Menter who had attended Parktown Boys' High and was a teammate in the Transvaal Nuffield XI of 1959. Menter's real game, however, was rugby. He was the university's flyhalf, and he would go on to play provincial rugby and tour France with the Springboks in 1968.

---

[16] This did not materialise. His medical exams coincided with Transvaal's three-day game against the 1961-62 New Zealanders and he was forced to miss this important match.

It was Menter who got Ali involved in rugby at Wits when he persuaded him to play for the medics in an interfaculty rugby day. Having done quite well, and a few beers later, Ali agreed to attend the next club practice. Before he knew it, he was selected as flyhalf for the university's 2nd team. A couple of times a week the 'firsts' would practise against the 'seconds' and coach Sid Newman was a hard taskmaster who drove his men to their physical limits. Ali didn't fancy this one bit, especially when the time came to run up and down a steep embankment at the end of the field. After practice one evening, he told Menter he'd had enough; but his pal would have nothing of it and, after some cajoling, the two devised a plan. Before the next practice, Menter approached Newman. 'Coach, I think you should go a little easier on Bacher . . .'

'Why? He's a bloody loafer!'

'But don't you know he's got this problem if he overexerts himself?'

'Oh yes, and what's his problem?'

'He's only got one lung.'

'Crikey, I didn't know!'

Rugby now became a pleasant pastime for Ali. While the other players were slogging it up the embankment and around the field, he was allowed to sit on the sidelines and do light exercises. Only when the actual rugby began did Newman call him into action. In this way he enjoyed himself as a second team regular who was not without natural talent.

The president of Wits Rugby Club was Dr Norman Helfand who happened to be Shira Teeger's uncle. One day while chatting with him, Sid Newman remarked: 'You know, Doc, I'm really impressed with this Bacher chap. What with his medical problems and all that, he's a real trier.'

Helfand was curious. 'What medical problems are you talking about, Sid?'

'Oh, don't you know; he's only got *one lung*.'

'One lung, my foot!' laughed Helfand. 'There's nothing at all wrong with him.'

Rugby practices with Sid Newman[17] would take on a new meaning . . . particularly after he had chased his victim around the field while whipping

---

[17] S C (Sid) Newman played for Northern Transvaal in 1939 and Transvaal in 1940. After the Second World War he studied at Oxford University when he was selected for England at fullback and played three internationals for that country in 1947-48. He returned to South Africa and played for Free State in 1952.

him with the leather thong attached to his whistle.

Ali finally gave up rugby when the very peak of his career was in sight. It happened when he was told that his big moment had arrived: Menter was injured and the selectors had decided that he would replace him in the 1st team. The next match was against Vereeniging, a club of steel-workers who were led by a man-mountain named Piet Bosman, a provincial forward. 'Thanks for thinking of me, chaps,' Ali told the selectors, 'but I really think this is an opportunity for a younger player to gain some experience.'

And with that he bade farewell to rugby, although he always remained a fan.[18]

AMID ALL THE fun came the shock. The young Bacher's life was thrown into turmoil when he received his examination results; he had failed first year. He had had a wonderful year of cricket but his studies had suffered as a result. This was not surprising. On many occasions he had skipped important lectures, and he felt bad because he had let down his parents. He had also hidden the fact from them that he was unhappy at medical school. His real joy was on the cricket field. He knew, though, that he was not going to earn a living from playing cricket. South African players were amateurs, getting what amounted to pocket money for each game they played; and professionalism was not a prospect. He was also worried that Wits might not want to give him a second chance. As he later described it, he was in a state of conflict. Perhaps the best way was to drop out of university. In desperation, he went to see Wilf Isaacs who was a benefactor and mentor to so many young cricketers in the Transvaal. Each season the Wilf Isaacs XI – consisting of past and present star players – would play against the schools, and Wilf was also a Transvaal Schools selector. He knew Ali well, liked him and rated him highly. Ali told Wilf of his plight, and suggested he might find a job for him in the pharmaceutical industry.

Isaacs advised him not to quit, but Ali was still worried that Wits might not allow him to repeat the year. In that case, he would have to try to enrol at the University of Cape Town, which would mean having to leave Johannesburg . . . and Transvaal and Balfour Park. The thought was too awful to contemplate but fortunately Wits did not turn him away – although

---

[18] He attended the semifinals and final of the 2003 Rugby World Cup in Australia as a special guest of the International Rugby Board.

it was made perfectly clear that there would be no more chances. If he failed again, he was automatically out. Whether he liked it or not, the grim reality was that he would have to put his studies ahead of his cricket. It was an exhausting time. He would attend lectures during the day, practise his cricket until the sun went down, take a couple of buses home or, if he was lucky, cadge a lift in a teammate's car, have supper and be asleep at eight. Each night he would set his alarm clock for two or three o'clock, then get up and study until it was time to catch the bus to lectures again. As a schoolboy he had adhered to the regimen of going to bed early and then getting up to study before the sun came up, and it now became a way of life. Later, when he found himself in the forefront of South Africa's cricket administration, he would normally wake up at three o'clock each morning. Regularly at those times bright new ideas and clear-cut decisions would inspire him to leave his bed and make fresh entries in his diary, ready to put them into action once his colleagues and associates had begun their working day. Ali would never cease to marvel at the intricate workings of the brain and, even allowing for his medical background, he was constantly intrigued by the way it seemed to be programmed during his sleeping hours to sort through the clutter and offer him precise direction the next day.

IT WOULD TAKE Ali eight years to complete his six years of study to qualify as a doctor. The two years that he failed, in 1960 and in 1963, were very good ones for his cricket; in fact, he found that his performance in the examination room was usually inversely proportional to his performance on the cricket field. This is most certainly borne out in his first year in both university and first-class cricket when academic misery coincided with his being named as one of the five Cricketers of the Year by the editor of the *SA Cricket Annual*, a huge honour that has been perpetuated down the years by each succeeding editor in the same way that *Wisden Cricketers Almanack*, the acknowledged Bible of the game, acclaims cricketers worldwide on an annual basis.

In pointing out that Bacher had made four scores of 75 or more and two centuries in his first eight provincial matches, the Annual said in its citation that 'the youngster bore a striking resemblance to "The Don" at the same age'.

The comparisons with Bradman would just not go away and although he continued to feel embarrassed by them, it was clear that his close study of his Australian hero had paid its dividend and that unconsciously he

49

might even have adopted some of Bradman's characteristics. It is significant that when he sought out advice of a real technical nature it was to Bradman he turned. His first ever contact with him came towards the end of Ali's playing career when he posted a simple handwritten letter to an address in Adelaide in which he asked Sir Donald for his views on such esoteric subjects as the pros and cons of the front foot no-ball law and the six and eight-ball overs. He was astonished to get by return of post a detailed 12-page typewritten[19] letter in which the celebrated cricket knight spelled out his theories in elaborate detail.

---

[19] Sir Donald Bradman ('The Don') received hundreds of letters a week throughout his life. It is said he made a point of answering each and every one of them. He typed them himself.

Chapter 4

Provincial Captain

He came across as an honest-to-goodness boy next door, a young man with no airs or graces; and his little mannerisms and characteristics endeared him to the fans ... the distinctive, splayed-feet waddle, the stooped shoulders, and the cap jammed jauntily on his head at a rakish angle. He was every bit a man with no vanity; what you saw was what you got.

He was also very untidy. Those who 'roomed' with him on away trips tell how he read the morning newspaper in the bath, and would deposit it, page by page as he finished reading them, in the bath water. Roommates were amazed to discover that he squeezed the toothpaste out of the tube without ever taking it out of the box – he did not much care for the minutiae of life – and would leave a trail of clothing around the hotel room. Over a few beers with a group of teammates one night, Johnny Waite announced that Ali slept with his socks on. Everyone laughed and said, 'C'mon Johnny, pull the other one', but Waite dug in, the bets were struck, and the players crept into his bedroom, where he was sound asleep, and lifted the blanket to find out. 'Is it unusual to sleep with your socks on?' asked Ali sheepishly when he heard the story.

As a batsman, blessed with strong hands and forearms, he would work the ball around the field, particularly powerful, as we know, on the on side but eminently capable of scoring runs on both sides of the wicket. 'If you didn't dismiss him early, you knew you were in for a long afternoon,' remembers Mark Henning.

He was ostensibly a backfoot player whose main weapons were the cut and the pull, the hook and the leg glance. He was not in truth a very stylish batsman but he was a busy and consistent accumulator of runs. 'It was like nothing was happening out there,' says Tiger Lance, 'but you'd look up at the scoreboard and suddenly he had 30 or 40. When you were batting with him you knew you were in for a lot of running – he was always fit but, apart from playing some squash, he didn't seem to train – and he would be prodding and pushing into the gaps, looking for singles all of the time.'

When dismissed, he would return to the pavilion, sit down, drop his gloves and bat on the floor and immediately light a cigarette. If the match situation was really tense, he would sometimes be seen with two burning cigarettes. He would remove one pad and drop it on the floor, then become distracted and pace across to the other end of the dressing room, at the same time yelling advice to the batsmen. Then he would remove the other pad and drop it on the floor, the cap might come off and be left on a bench, and his box would be discarded in another part of the change room or perhaps on the balcony. Sometimes he would be seen at lunch still wearing a thigh guard, maybe even one pad. At the end of the day's play a major search would be conducted to find his belongings.[1]

In those days, the lifestyle of the cricketers was, shall we say, quite indolent. Most of the players smoked, and after the day's play the beer flowed freely. Ali's prematch preparations were two games of squash a week and a couple of net practices. He laughs when comparisons are drawn between the fitness regimen of the current cricketers and those of earlier eras. 'I remember seeing a photograph of Donald Bradman tossing the coin just before the start of a Test match. I mean, he was dressed in a three-piece suit, a tie and a trilby hat!'

His introduction to captaincy at provincial level provides a telling insight into his lateral thinking. During the course of a Currie Cup match against Western Province at the Wanderers in February 1963, the skipper, Waite, left the field for an hour on the second afternoon to attend to a finger injury. As he departed, he called to young Bacher, then 20, to take over the captaincy. This raised eyebrows among the senior players because he was the 'baby' of a side that included several Springboks. Waite's departure coincided with a critical period: Transvaal had totalled 431 for seven declared, of which Ali scored 3, and Western Province at 180-odd for seven

---

[1] In later life, he became a very fastidious person.

suddenly and maddeningly decided to stop scoring to delay the arrival of the second new ball which in those days was available once 200 runs were scored. They seemed particularly fearful of facing the fast bowlers Kenny Walter and the left-arm Mike Macaulay in the lengthening shadows of the late afternoon. Gentle half-volleys, even long hops, from the Transvaal bowlers were simply ignored, and Gerald Ritchie's ten overs cost him nine runs.

Ali's eldest brother Issy was watching from the grandstand with the former Springbok batsman Scotch Taylor. They played hockey together and Taylor was a Transvaal cricket selector. Issy watched in disbelief as his young brother took the ball and marked out his run-up. His teammates liked to say that Ali could not bowl 'a hoop down a hill', and here he was, having been invited to take over temporarily as captain of Transvaal, about to make a total idiot of himself.

Worse was to follow, however, as Bacher proceeded to deliver some of the worst leg breaks that had ever been bowled at the Wanderers. Issy was filled with embarrassment and Taylor was growing angrier with each delivery. They did not know that the young stand-in skipper was in the process of setting up his opponents for the kill.

Before bringing himself on to bowl Ali had carefully briefed Waite's understudy wicketkeeper, Syd O'Linn. What followed was a deliberate load of leg spin rubbish that instantly yielded a stream of wides and byes. Ali had reasoned that if the Western Province batsmen did not want to help themselves to runs, he would help them, so he literally set out to bowl the ball to the boundary. The runs mounted quicker than the batting side would have liked, the new ball was soon taken, Walter and Macaulay rattled through the tail, Western Province were asked to follow on, and the next day Transvaal won by an innings and 66 runs.

In the Transvaal dressing room, Ritchie joked, 'I hope when you become captain, you won't ever bowl again!' and Ian Fullerton, one of the more senior players who had scored a century on the opening day, congratulated him on his cunning. 'We didn't have an official vice-captain to Johnny,' recalls Fullerton, 'so when he handed the reins over to Ali, there were mutters of "who's this little upstart?" Some of the blokes reckoned he was only in the team because Tuxie Teeger was a selector, but I told them, "listen, we're going to back this little bugger!" Little did we know how far he would go.'

IN THE AUTUMN of 1963, Ali Bacher was officially appointed as Transvaal captain. He was 21. The appointment was not entirely unexpected because Waite had already told Eric Rowan that a younger captain needed to be groomed, and that Bacher was his choice. In the coming season, of course, Waite would be absent in Australia with the 1963-64 Springbok team. Ali had the greatest respect for Waite and still rates him the finest wicketkeeper-batsman to represent South Africa. Anyone who had the good fortune to watch him will know exactly the qualities that Ali saw in him: ramrod tall, composed and elegant, and as smooth as velvet when standing up to the spinners and seamers alike. He was not regarded as the most adventurous of captains but Ali loved to listen to his wealth of stories and learn from his wide knowledge of cricket.

In 1963-64, it was only Jackie McGlew's Natal that by a whisker denied Bacher the honour of walking off with the Currie Cup trophy in his first season as captain. In his six matches in charge during that campaign, he was unbeaten at home and scored away wins over Western Province (a rare achievement by six wickets) and Eastern Province. The last match of the season in Durban would decide the champions.

Throughout the campaign, Ali led from the front, topping the Transvaal first-class batting averages on 62.80 runs per innings. Even accepting that Trevor Goddard's Springboks did not play in the tournament because of their concurrent tour of Australia, Bacher's consistent batting form and winning ways could not be underestimated. His 628 runs in six matches was the highest aggregate in South Africa in 1963-64, surpassing Roy McLean's 577 and McGlew's 538, although both veteran Natal Springboks[2] had better averages. McGlew had secured five outright wins to Transvaal's four, and Natal's only defeat came in the annual 'Boxing Day match' at the Wanderers with a jubilant Bacher undefeated on 54 when the winning runs were scored. It was the first time in five years that Transvaal had comprehensively beaten the Cup holders.

That half-century was one of five that Ali scored in his first six innings as captain. In the seventh, he made a century. His scores in his first season as captain bear recording: 76 and 53 against Eastern Province; 23 and 54 not out against Natal; 97 and 53 against Western Province; 128 in 145 minutes against Eastern Province; 36 and 38 against Western Province in a victory that shot Transvaal to the top of the log with a three-point lead

---

[2] McGlew and McLean were among Ali's boyhood heroes. When the Springboks toured England in 1955, he followed their fortunes with great interest, hardly missing a ball on the short wave BBC radio coverage of the Test matches.

heading into the deciding match against Natal at Kingsmead; and finally 4 and 67 in that match in question.

Natal at Kingsmead was the ultimate test and it turned out to be a fascinating encounter in more ways than one. McGlew's plan was to go for Transvaal's jugular with a four-man pace attack, backed up by his off-spinner Norman Crookes. So, putting his faith in his speedsters, Trimborn, Dumbrill, Schultz and Cole, he ordered a grassy green top.

The Kingsmead groundsman was Frank Lange and, for reasons best known to him, he was not very supportive of Natal. After Transvaal's practice on the eve of the match, he told Ali that McGlew's order was for a green track. Ali grimaced. 'Would you like me to take the grass off?' asked Lange. Ali was dumbfounded to be asked such a question by the home groundsman, but he nodded in approval.

When the covers came off on the morning of the match, McGlew could not believe his eyes. Frank's mower had been at work.

The last thing the Natal captain wanted was to undermine the credibility of his pace battery so, having won the toss, he still sent Transvaal in. Although his fast bowlers did a magnificent job in reducing them to 41 for five, the visitors' total of 341 was impressive, thanks to Gerald Innes's 140. Natal then also recovered from an early collapse but their 308 total meant that they had lost on the first innings. The equation was simple: Natal had to win outright to take the championship, and Transvaal needed only to draw to regain the Currie Cup for the first time in five years.

It was then that the groundsman's ploy backfired badly. Bereft of grass and suffering from wear and tear, the pitch began to take spin at an alarming rate. Crookes spun a web to take five cheap wickets and McGlew saw a chance to show off his leg spin and promptly took a hat-trick. Ali's gutsy 67 represented almost 50 per cent of his team's disappointing second innings total of 150, and Natal were left 275 minutes to score the required 184. This was by no means an easy task on the turning wicket, and Ali used his opening bowlers for just three overs before tossing the ball to his spin bowlers Atholl McKinnon and Tony Tillim. 'In order to get the shine off the ball as quickly as possible,' recalls Ali, 'the slips were instructed to roll it back to me at mid-off.' The left-arm McKinnon, in particular, turned the ball square and bowled with great accuracy over and around the wicket to concede 42 runs in 27 overs without taking a wicket. Each run had to be earned as Natal ground their way to victory. Later, Ali conceded that in trying to contain the batsmen, he had been far too defensive in his field settings.

If that result signalled the death knell of Transvaal's Currie Cup challenge, it might reasonably be argued that they had let things slip earlier in the season when Bacher officially took over as captain in the match against Eastern Province. At the Wanderers, Transvaal were put in to bat and amassed a formidable 402, yet they could take only first innings points. On the final day, Rose Bacher decided it was time to give her son some advice. She never missed a match that Ali played at the Wanderers and was in her usual seat in the grandstand to witness her son's captaincy debut. With Transvaal batting on and on in their second innings, she marched off to the dressing room. 'People are saying you should have declared already,' she scolded Ali, 'and I agree. You better declare now!'

Bacher returned to his teammates. 'Listen chaps, my mother reckons we should declare,' and he duly did so. His opponents' target was 313 runs in 280 minutes, but they had no intention of chasing the runs. They were also determined not to give Transvaal an outright win. Ali used no fewer than nine bowlers – including himself – to try to budge them but when time was called his opponents were 192 for four. On reflection, the new Transvaal captain conceded that he had not given his bowlers enough time to take 10 wickets.

His mother was right.

WHAT THE SEASON proved beyond doubt was that captaincy sat well with Ali Bacher. He was the youngest[3] player in the Transvaal team when he first led them on to the field on 30 November 1963 and he never allowed the added burden to affect his ability to score runs. In fact, as captain his batting blossomed.

Just as he did when captaining Balfour Park, he showed great faith in his spin bowlers McKinnon and Tillim. It was not unusual to see both of them operating to an attacking field early in the first session of play.

Out on the field, he cut a distinctive figure. When he was plotting the next move, he would caress his chin and stare at the ground, deep in thought; when he had figured out what to do he would stroll nonchalantly, arms behind his back, to impart his wisdom to the bowler; and when he was at his most confident, you would see him, hands on hips, staring down the batsman. One of the qualities that endeared him to his teammates

---

[3] In that team were four Springboks – including senior players Syd O'Linn, Gerald Innes and Atholl McKinnon who were respectively 15, 11 and 10 years older than Bacher.

was his courage. He was a fearless catcher in close positions in front of the wicket.

There is no doubt that his captaincy came as a breath of fresh air to Transvaal, but the question is how his older teammates related to so young a leader. The answer lay in the small gold mining town of Stilfontein in the Western Transvaal.[4] It was there, a couple of weeks after the opening match against Eastern Province, that Bacher captained Transvaal for the second time. The three-day match was against the SA Universities XI[5] during which he encountered some trouble from a few of the senior players. The men who came to his aid were Innes and McKinnon, an ebullient character with a strong personality. Echoing what Fullerton had said earlier, they commanded their teammates to support their new skipper. From that moment on, he was firmly in charge.

There were many strings to his captaincy bow and his teammates and opponents agreed early on that he had a wise old head on his young shoulders. Above all, he knew how to bring out the best in his team. He did this by establishing special relationships with all the players.

'He had this knack to make each player feel that he had a very special role to play in the team,' says Brian Bath,[6] his trusty opening partner at Transvaal. 'He would consult with his players and ask their advice. Sometimes he would take it – even if he knew it wouldn't work – just to make them feel special.'

Barry Richards once wrote a newspaper article comparing Bacher's captaincy with a computer. 'It was anything but,' refutes Bath. 'It was all about exploring and developing player relationships.'

He was, however, by no means a pushover; and three of Transvaal's Springboks found this out to their cost. He once ordered McKinnon off the field because of his attitude, he locked Peter Carlstein in his hotel room to stop him from going out on the night before an important innings, and he bowled paceman Kenny Walter into the strong wind at Newlands to discipline him for some wayward behaviour.

On the field, he was always innovative and unorthodox, making decisions on the spur of the moment; but he also could be ruthless. 'He

---

[4] This region is now known as the North West province where Potchefstroom is the cricket headquarters.
[5] SA Universities was captained by Transvaal's Don Mackay-Coghill who led his team to victory over his provincial teammates in a low-scoring match.
[6] Brian Bath would succeed Mackay-Coghill as chairman of the Transvaal Cricket Council in 1986 before emigrating to Australia shortly thereafter.

had this way,' says Lance, 'of lulling the batsmen into a false sense of security by allowing them to score runs off our weaker bowlers. Then, just at the right moment, he would bring back his strike bowlers and he was like a wild dog going for the throat. He made things happen.'

Chapter 5

Of Hat-tricks and Hoods

CLUB CRICKET IN Johannesburg during the sixties and early seventies was a fine mix of good competition, fierce rivalries, boyish pranks, tough talk and eccentric behaviour. These were qualities that appealed to Ali Bacher's instincts; and it made a nice change from his school days when he was altogether too serious.

Among his chief rivals was an irreverent character named Don Mackay-Coghill who captained Wits University where he was studying economics. Initially, they were 'mortal enemies' who were constantly at each other's throats, and the start of their relationship bears this out. While leading Wits at Balfour Park, Coghill rudely asked, more by way of command than enquiry, 'Where are the bloody drinks?'

Bacher, batting at the time, shot back, 'If you talk like that here, you'll get no bloody drinks!' As the home captain he then gave instructions that drinks would not be required until much later and the Wits bowlers and fielders continued to toil away under the hot sun.

In time they warmed to each other and a fine mutual respect developed, although the teasing and jousting never stopped. Ali liked 'Cogs' for his blunt sense of humour and rosy-cheeked choirboy looks that disguised a fine disregard for the conventional. As a non-conformist at heart, Bacher could easily identify with this sort of outlook and, in the tall and good-looking extrovert, he found the perfect foil to his more serious, introverted nature. Coghill clearly brought out the best in him, allowing him to explore a mischievous streak of his own that would have been inhibited by a strict and regimented childhood. Ali's inhibitions seemed to melt away in the company of 'Cogs', and it was not surprising that they developed a strong bond that would last for the rest of their lives.

In the Transvaal team they formed a rare alliance that would allow Coghill to flourish under Bacher's captaincy. The left-arm fast bowler's consistent match-winning performances had a lot to do with his captain's encouragement and Coghill became known as the 'best bowler[1] never to play for South Africa'. Ali, typically, preferred honing in on his friend's batsmanship in order to get a rise out of him: 'You made cricket history,' he would regularly remind him, 'as the only batsman to start your first-class career at number four and finish it as a number eleven!'[2]

After attending school at Kimberley Boys' High, where he was selected for three Nuffield Weeks exclusively as a batsman, Coghill went to Rhodes University where he enjoyed two 'social years' before dropping out. Ali claims he has information from no less a person than Dr Conrad Strauss, a former chairman of Standard Bank who was then in charge of the hostel at Rhodes, that his pal was 'the naughtiest student of all time', a claim which Coghill does not dispute convincingly.

A fellow student at Rhodes was Colin Bland who would later be acclaimed as the world's greatest fielder. In an interesting aside, Coghill points out that Bland's fielding ability in the covers was not as instinctive as his fans thought. 'At Rhodes, I would spend hours and hours with him – sometimes four hours a day – helping him with his fielding drills. We would put up one stump, I'd act as catcher and thrower, and he would throw at the stump from all angles and distances, hour after hour.'

In time, the tall, graceful Bland would distinguish himself in the Test arena by swooping on the ball – he became known as the 'Golden Eagle' – and running out countless victims by scoring direct hits. His seamless pick-up and flat throw would regularly take out the one stump he could see from square on to the wicket. The sportswriters ascribed it to his 'uncanny ability' but Coghill says it was the result of 'sheer hard work'.

From Rhodes, Coghill went to Johannesburg to work for the Chamber

---

[1] Mackay-Coghill became Transvaal's leading wicket taker with 245 first-class wickets, a record that stood for six years after his retirement in 1974.
[2] Mackay-Coghill was selected as a No 4 batsman on his provincial debut for Transvaal B against Griqualand West in February 1963 and scored 47. During the late sixties he was also a regular No 4 in the Currie Cup team. For his final match in February 1974 he was the No 11 – but was not required to bat – in Transvaal's 82-run win over Western Province. At the Wanderers in 1965/66, he and Tiger Lance established a SA record 174 for the 10th wicket against Natal.

of Mines, not because he had any designs on a career in the gold mining industry but simply because he liked the office hours. Knocking off each day at four o'clock gave him the time to practise his cricket. It is ironic that his cricket would eventually play second fiddle to the gold mining industry in which he distinguished himself internationally after putting the famous Krugerrand on the global map.[3]

ON THE CLUB cricket scene, there was no shortage of nourishment for Ali's dry sense of humour. Tears came to his eyes when he told of a former Balfour Park captain named Zunky Kaplan who could not bear the sight of his little batsman Joe Hirshowitz being felled, not once but three times, by short deliveries from the fearsome Neil Adcock,[4] one of the famous Jeppe Old Boys club's galaxy of Springboks. So Zunky Kaplan stomped out to the middle, hurled a towel on to the pitch and announced to the fielding captain, 'My boy's had enough!', and guided little Joe back to the safety of the dressing room. It is not clear whether the entry in the scorebook read 'retired hurt' or 'retired had enough'.

Bacher himself was a central figure in many peculiar situations and on one occasion created what was surely cricketing history. This particular story is part of cricket folklore in Johannesburg and, as is the nature of good yarns, there are several variations to it. We shall look at just two of them. Balfour Park was caught on a wet wicket by their arch rivals Old Johannians, a club for which Coghill was now playing, and were skittled out for 64 or 79, depending on which version you choose. Bacher insists it was 64 and they were in all sorts of trouble when the Old Johnnies openers reached 20 without loss. So he tossed the ball to Les Evans, an enthusiastic medium pace bowler who was a contemporary of his but had attended the less fashionable Athlone Boys' High School where, in Ali's words, 'he was a sporting icon with colours scrolls on his blazer down to his knee'.

Things were looking bleak for Balfour when Evans made the break-through, having Des Sacco caught. The next ball he clean bowled Brian

---

[3] In 1978, Mackay-Coghill received the South African Marketing Award of the Year for his outstanding international marketing of the Krugerrand, which created the first global market for bullion coins. In 1986 he left South Africa, but kept his citizenship, to take up the dual position of Chief Executive Officer of GoldCorp Australia and Managing Director of the Western Australian Mint. He retired in June 2003 and was formerly a director of the World Gold Council.
[4] Neil Adcock played for Transvaal for much of the 1950s before relocating to Natal.

Clark. Two wickets in two balls and out to the middle strode Coghill. Everyone held their breath, in came Les, out went Coghill, dismissed first ball.

According to Bacher, he then complimented Evans on his hat-trick but, 'because he sometimes got a bit carried away with his own importance I immediately took him off. I told him "it's always good to get out while you're still on top".'

Evans, a larger than life character who does hilarious impersonations of famous people (including Ali, naturally), tells the story somewhat differently. 'We were all out for 79 and Old Johnnies were 21 for three. I had taken nought for 21 and Richard Dumbrill[5] had taken three for 0. So Ali strolled over to me in the middle of the over and said, "Look Les, it's a bit wet and your foot's slipping. I think we take a little break after this over and I'll bring Joe on." I couldn't argue with him because I was bowling a shower. But I had three balls left. With those balls, I had Sacco caught at backward square, uprooted Clark's middle stump with a cutter, and dived full stretch to take a one-handed catch from Mackay-Coghill. Now Johnnies were 21 for six! An over later, Ali said "well bowled, Les" and tossed the ball to Joe (Hansen). I said, "Hey, I've just taken a hat-trick!" and he repeated, "Well bowled, Les", and started setting the field for Joe. So I yelled, "Hey, can't you count, I've just taken three wickets?" but he ignored me.'

As Ali pointed out, 'Les had done a job and I didn't want him to push his luck. We bowled them out for 45 and Dumbrill took six for 12.'

In retrospect, Evans accepted that Bacher was right. 'When he made up his mind about something, there was no point in arguing with him. I mean, he played a league match like it was a Test match. He knew what he was doing. He had a certain magic, a charisma, about him.'

In another match against Old Johnnies, Coghill came to the crease and Bacher tossed the ball to Evans. 'Now look, Les, this is what you do: the first two balls you bowl inswing, then the third ball you bowl the away swinger.'

Evans did precisely that and the third ball, the away swinger, found the edge and an irate Coghill was caught by Bacher at slip. Evans was extremely proud of himself. He had done the captain's bidding and executed the

---

[5] Richard Dumbrill was a Springbok allrounder who played his provincial cricket for Natal before relocating to Johannesburg where he joined Balfour Park.

plan to perfection.

'Hey, doc, that wasn't a bad piece of bowling, eh?'

'Excuse me, Les, it was *my* wicket, not yours . . .'

As Evans would put it many years later, 'He was always the boss and he kissed no ass'; or as Coghill points out, 'If he decided on a course of action, you could stand on your head but he wouldn't change it.'

There is nothing Ali loved more than to recall the funny stories from the past. Long after their playing days were done, he and two of his closest friends, Coghill and Lee Irvine, would dine out on those stories. They were real raconteurs and he would sit back and listen to them, laughing till the tears rolled down his cheeks. 'They would tell the same stories every time, and each time they would be funnier and we would laugh even louder.'

There is no question that in the years when Bacher became embroiled in the serious problems of cricket's administration and was heavily weighed down by them, the only way to bring him out of his shell was for 'Cogs' or Lee to invite him out for dinner. Coghill's annual visits to South Africa from Australia would become one of the highlights of Ali's year; and the reunions would grow more nostalgic and hilarious.

They would remind Ali of the day the 'hoods' arrived at the cricket match in which they were all playing. 'It was during the tea interval at Old Johnnies one Sunday afternoon,' says Irvine, 'when suddenly these two big limos pull into the ground. Out of them step these blokes in black suits and fedoras and they walk straight towards us. "Crikey, here come the hoods," says someone, and the big guy in front steps up and says, "Where's Ali?" in a rather menacing way. We all disappear into a corner of the hut but Ali steps up and says to the big guy in a friendly sort of way, "Hi, Cecil, how you doing?" and we all look at each other and say, "Crikey, Ali's one of 'em!"

'Turns out the leader is Cecil Sweidan, a big stockbroker who is throwing money around like you can't believe. He says to Ali, "Your bowlers are crap, who do you want?" which is not nice because all the bowlers are listening. So Ali says, "John Snow[6] would be good" and we all know that John Snow doesn't come cheap . . .'

Coghill picks up the tale, 'I'm having tea with my Old Johnnies'

---

[6] John Snow was a Sussex and England fast bowler who was playing in Johannesburg for the Southern Suburbs club.

teammates when this bunch of hoods approaches us with Ali in tow. I wondered what the hell was going on when Ali introduced me very warmly to Cecil Sweidan who was a real high roller and a director of the Highlands Park Football Club.[7] Ali says, "Hey, Cogs, Cecil wants to give some money to the Transvaal team", and I say, "How much?" and he replies, "Seven and a half thousand rand", which I know is a lot of money in those days. So a day later, we have a meeting. There's Ali, Lee, Bubbles[8] and me. What to do with this money? Ali's already got the cheque. I say, what the hell, we're the top players in the team, let's just share it among ourselves and we get into a heated debate. I remember our wives were there, too, and one of them piped up, "You can't leave out Viv Greve!"[9] and one of us said, "Why, he's not much of a player!" and she replied, "Oh, but he's *so* good looking!"

'So our meeting ended without resolution and a couple of days later Ali phones me and whispers, "Cogs, have you seen the front page of the *Rand Daily Mail*?" and there splashed all over it is this shocking news that Cecil Sweidan has committed suicide after a huge fraud had been uncovered in his firm.' The uncashed cheque was still burning a hole in Bacher's pocket but he knew what to do with it: he went straight to the firm and handed it in.

YEAR, AFTER YEAR, after year Marists Old Boys, or Old Maristonians, would try to beat Balfour Park. Each time they would be thwarted. Never, in fact, had they beaten their hoodoo team, and victory over them became their obsession. Finally, their day seemed to have come. Bacher's men were battling. They were caught on a wet wicket chasing 140 for victory and staring down the barrel at 120 for nine. It looked like 'game, set and match', which was the way Ali, a tennis player at heart, liked to put it. But Les Evans, the No 11 batsman, would hear nothing of it. He unleashed some blazing shots to take the total to 139 for nine. With just two runs to win now, Harry Avnit put down a simple catch at mid-on after Evans had mistimed a big hit off Ronnie Carr's leg spin and skied the ball. The Marists

---

[7] Ali Bacher was by now a qualified medical doctor who acted as team doctor for the crack Highlands Park team in the National Football League. It was there that he met Sweidan.

[8] Brian 'Bubbles' Bath and the other three were at this stage playing together for Transvaal and were considered the nucleus of the side.

[9] Viv Greve was a blond, tousle-haired spin bowler for Old Edwardians and Transvaal.

players went berserk. Avnit lay on the pitch beating the turf with his hands in anguish and shame while his teammates screamed at him for fluffing a chance to pull off a famous victory. All the while, no one thought to retrieve the ball and have a shy at the stumps, so the Balfour batsmen helped themselves to the two runs required . . . and Marists Old Boys still had never beaten Balfour.

Bacher's teammates came from all over town. Kenny Siebert was a tough character from the southern suburbs, an amateur boxing champion who found his way to Balfour Park. During one match Ali spotted him in the dressing room holding his bat under the shower. 'What you up to, Kenny?' he asked casually.

'I'm giving my bat a shower.'

'I can see that, Kenny, but why?'

'I want to soften the wood.'

'Why's that, Kenny?'

'So that the umpire won't hear the snicks.'

Chapter 6

To England

SHIRA TEEGER FOUND Ali Bacher 'a bit odd' when she first invited him to tea at the family home in Waverley, Johannesburg. He spent the entire visit 'breaking in' a new cricket bat by clobbering it with a ball contained in a sock; and he did not have much to say by way of conversation amid the constant dull thud of the hard ball striking the new willow.

He arrived at her house on his clapped-out motorcycle, a gift from his father, which was his mode of transport in his last two years at school. He was also missing a front tooth that he had lost on the rugby field and which his mother was reluctant to replace because the same tooth had been repaired[1] the previous year when he got a cricket ball in the mouth while keeping wicket and standing up to a medium pace bowler.

Shira, an attractive brunette, had first met Ali when a cousin of his had taken her to a party at the Bacher home. Ali was secretly impressed by her because she had a good all round knowledge of cricket and came from a family steeped in the game. She found him a mature boy, 'quiet and deep', but when she asked him what he was going to do when he left school, he replied tersely, 'Become a traffic cop'.

They would see a lot of each other during their teenage years because they were both closely associated with Balfour Park, she as the club president's daughter, he as the star batsman; and the swimming pool at the club was where all the young people socialised. They began dating

---

[1] The dentist was Dr Nomis, father of the Springbok rugby player Syd Nomis.

when Ali left school and were engaged five years later, on Shira's 21st birthday, 11 November 1964. The date for the wedding was set for the following April.

In March 1965, the last thing on Ali's mind was cricket as he made his way to the Teeger residence in Knox Street, Waverley, to visit his fiancée. In a month's time he would marry his sweetheart in the Great Synagogue. At this time only two things occupied his thoughts – his studies and the wedding. This weekday in March he had been downtown looking at clothes. He would wear a formal morning suit for the wedding and he needed to find the right outfit. Ali hated leaving things to the last minute, although it is hard to imagine that he ever went shopping.

As he approached 45 Knox Street he noticed an unusually large number of cars parked in the street outside the house. He was puzzled and a little concerned. Was something wrong? Had there been a death in the family? Heaven forbid.

It never crossed his mind that the visitors were there for him. Earlier in the day his Aunt Gertie from Durban (who apparently did not have a big interest in cricket) had telephoned the family in Johannesburg to offer her congratulations. She had heard his name read out over the radio. He had been named in the Springbok team to tour England. This was news to the family. They could not believe it. In their view, Ali had fallen out of the selection frame after a poor domestic season with Transvaal. No one even knew that the team was being announced that day.

The news spread like a veld fire and friends and family had gathered to slap him on the back. Ali could not believe what he was hearing. He had not even been considered good enough for a 'shadow' Springbok team that was named earlier in the season, and in his heart of hearts he did not regard himself as a contender. This was borne out by the decision to get married on the fourth of April – only ten weeks before the departure of the team for England – which would not have been a rational idea had there been even an outside chance of a long trip abroad. It was not as if he had given up hope of playing for South Africa but, after the disappointments of the previous season, he did not think his time was about to come.

Now suddenly he *was* a Springbok; his boyhood dream had come true at last. 'Mazeltov, Ali!' They hugged him and kissed him and slapped him on the back. 'Congratulations!'

He was absolutely staggered. He had passed third year medicine at the end of 1964 because of his decision to concentrate more on his studies

67

that year at the expense of his cricket. He had already proved to himself that success at his studies could not be accomplished without an adverse effect on his cricket. It was either one or the other. In 1964, he had resolved to allow his third year studies to take precedence. This may well have been a result of his disappointment at having been overlooked for the 1963-64 Springbok tour of Australia after he had had a particularly good domestic cricket season but had failed his 1963 university exams. On that occasion, he had put his cricket first, but to no avail.

The 1964-65 season was dominated by a long and dull MCC tour of South Africa. It ran for 19 matches between October and mid-February, and in between there were a few friendly interprovincials. By the time Mike Smith's MCC played Transvaal in November, Ali had had few matches to prepare. What was more, he was in the middle of his exams, one of which clashed with the start of the four-day match at 11 am. Through a special arrangement with the dean of his faculty, the Transvaal captain wrote his exam between 7-10 am. He sat alone in a room with an invigilator who, once the exam was over, escorted Ali straight to the Wanderers. There had to be no contact with other students who were yet to write the paper. It was an agreeable arrangement for the invigilator who received a complimentary ticket and spent the rest of the day watching the cricket.

Ali won the toss and, as always, he elected to bat. Before long he realised it was the wrong decision because the pitch was still a little damp. Batting at No 3, he top edged an attempted hook and was caught at third man for 2. Transvaal were all out for 125, eventually losing by an innings to the strong English outfit.

Ali's fondest memory of that match was the bowling of Peter Heine. The Springbok paceman had been persuaded to come out of retirement at the age of 36 because Don Mackay-Coghill had gone down with the mumps. On his day he was one of the world's most feared fast bowlers; now he was no more than medium pace. Yet some excellent England batting practitioners – among them Ken Barrington who eventually scored 169, and skipper Smith who also hit a century – treated him with the circum-spection and respect that he commanded when, for example, he took five for 60 on debut on the first day of the Lord's Test in 1955. Heine was all heart, one of Ali's favourite players, and he responded magnificently when the Transvaal captain, 14 years Heine's junior, asked him to bowl no fewer than 41 overs during which he took five for 110 in MCC's 464 for nine declared. Heine was one of two players who inspired the young Bacher with their determination and tenacity. The other was Hugh Tayfield, South

Africa's greatest post-war spin bowler who had occasionally captained Transvaal and impressed Ali with his shrewd leadership qualities.

Transvaal's improved second innings effort of 257 included 32 from Bacher, and ten days later at Berea Park in Pretoria, during a final North vs South trial match, he again caught the eye with 77 in the first innings. This was overshadowed, however, by the South's No 3 batsman, Derek Varnals of Natal, who scored a century and a 50 in the match. In truth Ali was never in the running for the forthcoming Test series because the experienced form batsman Tony Pithey was already in place to fill the important No 3 slot. Varnals, however, had done enough to warrant selection but he made his debut in the first Test batting at No 8 and failed in both innings.

The Test series was by no means memorable. England secured a big win in the first Test and then sat on the splice for the rest of the five-match series. Trevor Goddard's Springboks had performed admirably to share the spoils in Australia the previous season but there were mutterings now on the selection panel about Goddard's captaincy, notwithstanding the fact that the pitches for the last four drawn Tests were lifeless strips.

Through all of this, Ali was confined to the sidelines, more intent on becoming a doctor than a Test cricketer and with little prospect, it seemed, of achieving his childhood ambition to play for South Africa. Thus, the announcement that he was in the team to tour England in the winter of 1965 came as astonishing news to him. He learned later that it was Eric Rowan who had championed his cause. Rowan had been watching him since his schoolboy days and was convinced that he had the right stuff. The old Springbok spoke to Arthur Coy, the convener of the national selectors,[2] explaining that all the boy needed was to be given a chance away from his exhausting medical studies. He told Coy that he was certain that Bacher would not let them down. For all his failings, Rowan carried some considerable weight in cricketing circles at all levels of the game, and this would surely have had a positive influence on the chairman of selectors.

THERE IS AN interesting sub-plot to Coy's decision to back Bacher. Outside of the Jewish community, it was not commonly known that Arthur Coy had

---

[2] The national selection panel that caused a surprise by selecting Ali Bacher in 1965 was Arthur Coy (chair), Alan Melville, Lindsay Tuckett and Dennis Dyer.

been born Arthur Cohen, a Jew who later converted to Christianity and changed his name. Some sections of the Jewish community were of the opinion that Coy, through his conversion, was practising anti-Semitism, and that it was unlikely that he would select a Jewish cricketer to represent South Africa. In selecting Bacher, he effectively destroyed this insinuation and, what is more, five years later it was the selfsame Coy who oversaw the process of appointing him as South Africa's captain. Ali was obviously aware of the evil of anti-Semitism. It was by no means rife in South Africa, but there were isolated incidents of Jews being victimised. 'There was always a wariness within the Jewish community that this could escalate. Throughout the history of the Jews there were different periods when it was rampant and I guess there was always an uneasiness that it could resurface.'

Throughout his cricket career, Ali encountered it only once. It was in the change room after a club game against Old Johannians that he heard a blatant anti-Semitic remark from a member of the opposition team who was in the shower cubicle alongside his. 'The player who made the remark obviously did not know I was there, but I said nothing. I simply went to my players afterwards and told them that, although we had won, we would not be staying for the usual after-match drinks with the home team.'

The next day Don Mackay-Coghill, a member of the Old Johannians team, phoned to ask why he and his teammates had not stayed for a drink. Ali gave him the reasons and he was horrified.

In 1965, Ali reasoned that his selection for England might have been helped by his performance in a match the previous October that he believed should never have taken place. In what he viewed as a ludicrous decision by certain South African administrators, a four-day game was played at the Wanderers between Goddard's Springboks and a Rest of South Africa XI. Goddard's men had proved their mettle in Australia earlier in the year, so why challenge this? Did certain officials think that the team was not the best one at South Africa's disposal? The Springboks were not impressed at having to play this match, and they took out their anger with a vengeance. Winning the toss and batting first, they amassed 618 for four declared with superb centuries from Tony Pithey, Graeme Pollock, Colin Bland and Denis Lindsay – and all in a single day's play. The *pièce de résistance* came from Bland and Lindsay who flayed the attack for 267 runs in the final 99 minutes of the innings. It said much for the Springboks' superiority that the second best XI in South Africa could then muster a total of 483 runs in two innings, leaving them defeated by an innings and 135 runs.

Ali was out for 14 to a bat-pad catch to Lindsay at short leg; but in the second innings he hit a fluent top score of 61 before being dismissed by Goddard. This inspired the *South African Cricket Annual* to note that 'Bacher impressed as an enterprising and promising batsman who handled Peter Pollock and (the Natal speedster) Clive Halse with confidence'. Indeed, Ali would go away thinking that he had encountered Pollock, in particular, at his most aggressive and had played him well. He was also aware that all the national selectors were there, but did not think that this was of much significance.

As it turned out, Goddard announced he was unavailable to tour England after his fallout with the selectors, and Pithey could not take the time off. These top-order vacancies left a spot for Bacher, and the team would have a new captain in Peter van der Merwe.

THE WEDDING CEREMONY took place on schedule in the Great Synagogue. The handsome groom was not yet twenty-three and the blushing bride was six months shy of her twenty-second birthday. They set up home in a small flat in Berea, the 'flatland' adjacent to Yeoville.

Two weeks after their marriage, however, they were forced to part company because of Ali having to spend six weeks at the Queen Victoria Maternity Home in Johannesburg while studying obstetrics. Shira went back to living with her parents while working as a receptionist in a surgeon's rooms. Ali took his Gray-Nicolls cricket bat to the 'Queen Vic' where he would practise his shots in front of a long mirror whenever he had a free moment. This was the way the new Springbok had to prepare for his first major tour.

The young couple were reunited for only a few days before it was time for him to board the Boeing 707 for England, and his first trip outside southern Africa.

Everything had happened so quickly: his selection for South Africa, his marriage to Shira, the pre-tour preparations, sorting out his life at university; it was all like a blur, and a happy blur at that. Even if Ali had wanted to take Shira with him, it would have been out of the question. All the players (and their wives) were obliged to sign an agreement that forbade spouses on tour. Wives had accompanied their husbands on the Springbok tour of England in 1947, and this was now decreed an undesirable practice in that it apparently created divisions in team ranks between the singles and the couples. Ironically, girlfriends would be exempt, because, unlike wives, they could not be made to sign any agreement. There is no suggestion, however, that any player exploited this loophole.

In an age before direct dialling and cellular telephones, communication between the players and home was by airmail. Ali wrote regularly to Shira and to other members of the family, and all the time he encouraged Shira to keep her letters coming 'because they are the only thing that keeps me going here'.

That might have been so during the low moments on tour, but spending two and a half months playing cricket in England for one's country was any young man's dream. For Ali, it had been a long time coming, there had been the disappointments of non-selection during the past couple of years and now what lay ahead seemed too good to be true.

The start of the adventure, however, was not short of incident for the young debutant. In years to come, Ali's absent-mindedness would become part of the Bacher legend and now, at the age of 23, it would receive a public airing for the first time. As the players settled into their seats in the big jet prior to take-off, the cabin intercom crackled into life: 'A message for Mr Ali Bacher: would you kindly return your father's motor car keys . . . he can't get home.' A red-faced Ali unbuckled his seat belt, located the keys in his pocket and handed them over to the air hostess who tossed them to a messenger standing on the tarmac below.

The experience of flying to London was a new one for the young cricketer, a fact borne out by an observation he made in a postcard to his teenage sister-in-law Debbie Teeger: 'The plane flies so high in the sky that it is above the clouds . . .'

On 16 June 1965 the Springboks checked into the Waldorf Hotel in London where Ali learned a signal lesson that he would apply assiduously throughout his life. Ahead of the opening match against Derbyshire, team practices were scheduled at Lord's Cricket Ground at 9 o'clock. One morning he awoke to the awful realisation that he had overslept. Arriving embarrassingly late at Lord's, he was taken aside and given a dressing down by the team manager Jack Plimsoll, and the captain Van der Merwe. For the rest of his life, he would religiously book a wake-up call every night he spent in a hotel.

Plimsoll and Van der Merwe constituted the team management. They seemed to get on very well and the players had confidence in them. As a player, Plimsoll toured England with the 1947 team as a left-arm fast-medium bowler, taking 68 wickets in all but playing in only one Test. The tall, bespectacled Van der Merwe was the captain of Western Province, had toured Australia with Goddard, and played in the disappointing series against Smith's England. On both tours he learned a lot about Test captaincy from Goddard, South Africa's outstanding left-handed allrounder who captained his country 13 times.

Throughout the 18-match tour of England in 1965, Plimsoll and Van der Merwe came across to all concerned, and particularly to the players under them, as a happy and formidable duo. 'It surprised me,' says Ali, 'when Plimsoll confided to me some years later that he and the captain had not got on particularly well. If that was the case, they concealed their disagreements very well, for none of the players had any hint throughout the two and a half month tour of anything untoward between them.'

The team was a happy one, and Van der Merwe – 'Murphy' to his teammates – infused a fine sense of spirit in the ranks. In his post-tour report, Plimsoll praised him for his inspiration and leadership.

At the start of the tour the Springboks attended the traditional MCC dinner at Lord's. Ali found himself sitting alongside Russell Endean, the former Springbok batsman who now lived in England and with whom he had played in his early days with Transvaal and greatly admired for his integrity and cricketing skills. They spoke at length about the challenges and opportunities of playing cricket in England, and they recalled how Eric Rowan would tell any youngster willing to listen that no one could consider himself a real cricketer until he had toured England. As the tour progressed Ali would come to understand exactly what Rowan meant by this. After each day's play, he would make a point of spending time with the older English professionals in order to learn from their experience, gain fresh insights into the game, acquire new tricks of the trade and hear never-ending stories of teams and players, of amazing deeds and hilarious moments. This was a cricket fraternity that Ali admired, a cricketing atmosphere that he loved; and the old English pros were not in the least averse to welcoming new disciples and sharing their wisdom and expertise. On a couple of Sundays Ali also played in charity matches.[3] He learned quickly and picked up so many new tips and ideas that, according to Tiger Lance, some of the senior Springboks began to 'pick his brain' on different

---

[3] One of these matches was umpired by Sir Learie Constantine, the legendary former West Indies allrounder and Trinidad government minister. He was not friendly towards Ali, who put this down to the West Indian's abhorrence of apartheid.

tactical issues as the tour progressed. Van der Merwe was the captain, Eddie Barlow the vice-captain, but Lance and others saw in Bacher a shrewd and valuable tactician and a Test captain in the making.

As for his own batting technique, Ali arrived in England as essentially a backfoot player and returned home as a batsman who had mastered front foot play. He learned that by getting the front foot well forward he could narrow the angle of the ball and reduce the risk of getting himself trapped in English conditions that were conducive to swing bowling and on pitches that turned. The mastery of this technique became evident in the second innings of the final Test at The Oval after five of the top six South African batsmen (including Ali for 28) were given out leg before wicket in the first innings. In the second innings, however, he scored a worthy 70 and, as Louis Duffus wrote in *The Star*, 'After the five lbw decisions given against them in the first innings, the South Africans adopted a policy of going out to the ball; and none applied it more successfully than Bacher.' Denis Compton, the former great England batsman writing in the *Sunday Express* in London noted:

> Ali Bacher has played some sterling innings for South Africa when most wanted. Once more now he showed his fighting qualities. He is a rather strange looking player with a number of unorthodox strokes in his repertoire. Yet since arriving in this country he has learned fast the most effective way to play on our wickets. He is exclusively a back foot player in South Africa, but now he plays forward extremely well and often.

It becomes more and more obvious that Bacher put in a lot of extra work during the tour to improve his game and gain a mastery of the English conditions. He endured some sleepless nights at the outset when a few batting failures led him to question his ability, perhaps somewhat too harshly, but he scored runs at critical times to emerge as a first-choice player. He also relished the chance of facing so many top-class bowlers in different batting conditions in every match he played – John Price of Middlesex, John Snow of Sussex, Jeff Jones and Don Shepherd from Glamorgan, Brian Statham and Ken Higgs from Lancashire, David Brown of Warwickshire, Pat Pocock of Surrey, David Larter of Northants and Fred Rumsey of Somerset. Some of these bowlers were regulars in the England team but those who were not were top players on any other day of the week.

THE 1965 TOUR of England is generally remembered for the batting of Graeme Pollock, the bowling of Peter Pollock and the fielding of Colin Bland, but it is sometimes forgotten that this was a tour that established Ali Bacher as one of South Africa's key players. He was, after all, the only player with Graeme Pollock to pass 1 000 runs on tour and he finished second to Pollock in the batting averages. As we have seen, Compton rated him a batsman capable of playing an important innings when most needed, and Louis Duffus observed:

> The team went abroad endowed with the heavy onus of finding a new opening batsman (for Goddard) and a new number three (for Pithey). With admirable adjustment to the conditions Bacher has shown ideal qualifications for the position of first wicket down (No 3). To me, defiant little Ali Bacher is the find of the tour.

Other journalists who accompanied the team were as effusive, and none more so than Harold Butler of the *Cape Times* who covered the tour for South Africa's morning newspaper group and the *Sunday Times*.

The view he shared with his readers was that:

> No player in the Springbok touring party has made more progress than Ali Bacher, the most consistent Springbok batsman and a player mature beyond his years. There has been no other batsman in the team better qualified to play the type of cricket Bacher has played on this tour when the team has been in a spot. Cool, composed and thoughtful, he oozed confidence and his ability to concentrate was a pronounced aspect of his cricket.

Butler added that he had played with a spirit and character that suggested 'he is destined to play an important part in the future of South African cricket'. Indeed, in the speculation that followed the tour, Bacher's name was mentioned frequently as a likely successor to Van der Merwe. The highly respected sportswriter, and future editor of the *SA Cricket Annual*, Eric Litchfield, wrote in the *Sunday Times* that although Eddie Barlow was a dynamic personality and cricketer and vice-captain in England, 'among men of cricketing experience it is being said that Ali Bacher would be the better man for the (captaincy) job'. It should be said that this was not a vote of no confidence in Van der Merwe, who had done a good job, but rather conjecture as to what the future might hold. It was the start of one of the hottest debates in South African cricket – the burning question of Barlow or Bacher for captain – and it would rage on for several years and cause great division among cricket supporters and huge rivalry between the players in question, both of them provincial captains, and the teams they led in the Currie Cup.

In the mean time, Bacher was drawing higher praise than Barlow for his deeds in England, and Barlow's batting average of 38.84 would come in third behind Pollock's 57.35 and Bacher's 40.32.

English critics and former players were full of praise for the Springboks and admired the gritty determination of Bacher. A back-handed compliment came from one of cricket's most celebrated knights, Sir Leonard Hutton: 'Bacher is the type of batsman who infuriates the bowlers. He plays the majority of shots with a cross bat, but he gets away with it.'

The team was well liked by the media and Ali got on well with the travelling pressmen. Charles Fortune, the eloquent schoolmaster turned radio commentator who eventually became secretary of the SA Cricket Association, became a firm friend. In his commentaries he would always pronounce Bacher as 'Backer', something that infuriated the Jewish community who were Ali's biggest fans; he later confided in Ali that he did it on purpose to get a rise out of the listeners.

THE 1965 TOUR was plagued by rain, which badly hampered the Springboks' preparations, and it also did not start well for them or for Ali. They lost the opening match against Derbyshire in two days. Ali remembers the match on two counts – his failure in both innings while batting at No 3 and England's top umpire Sid Buller no-balling the former England fast bowler Harold Rhodes for throwing.[4]

Ali was distraught at being out for single figure scores in both innings of his first match in South African colours. 'It was the most depressed I had ever felt playing cricket. My big moment had arrived, and I had messed it up. In the second innings, I took about 50 minutes to score 5 runs. On the bus that night driving south, Colin Bland could obviously see that I was feeling down. He came and sat next to me and told me to keep my chin up. "Don't worry, Ali, the runs will come." '

Although Bland would continue to encourage him during the nerve-racking settling-in period on tour, Bacher's despairing mood did not improve when he was named as 12th man for the second match against Yorkshire

---

[4] Playing for Derbyshire against the 1960 Springboks, Rhodes was called six times for throwing by umpire Paul Gibb.

at Bramall Lane. He now began thinking that he would become one of the 'also rans' in England and his burning ambition of course was to produce good early batting form to secure a place in the Test team. The first Test at Lord's was still three weeks away when he was selected for the third match against Essex at Colchester, but this time he was down to bat at No 6 with Denis Lindsay at No 3. Given his support off the field, it seemed eminently appropriate that it was Bland with 94 who took the lead in a glorious 148-run partnership in 115 minutes with Bacher. Ali went on to score 59 but not before he 'broke his bat' on a delivery by the leg-spinner Robin Hobbs who went up for the catch by the reserve England wicketkeeper Bob Taylor. Ali stood his ground and umpire Buller kept his hand in his jacket pocket: not out.[5]

Ali generally walked when he knew he was out, but, as we know, he was desperate to get runs under his belt and took the view that if England's top umpire was not prepared to uphold the appeal, he was happy to abide by his decision. In the second innings, Hobbs dismissed him for 28, the match was drawn and Lindsay's scores of 48 and 52 ensured that he kept the No 3 spot for the next match against Surrey at The Oval. There were now four fixtures left before the Test. Against Surrey, Peter Pollock's five for 50 in the first innings and Barlow's 110 – the first century for the South Africans – were the highlights of a drawn match in which Bacher batted briefly only once for 6 not out before the declaration. The next match against Gloucestershire did not help much either, as two of the three days were rained out at Bristol, and Ali was among a majority of Springboks who did not get a chance to bat. What that match did signal was the depth of South African cricket because two Natal teenagers – Barry Richards and Mike Procter – were included in the county side on trial, and together they flayed the Springbok attack in a partnership of 116 in just 93 minutes. 'We wanted to show them up, but they actually showed us up,' recalls Ali of his first contact with two players who would become such important allies in the years ahead.

Two matches to go now before the Lord's Test and suddenly it all turned

---

[5] Robin Hobbs was a member of the Derrick Robins team that toured South Africa in 1973. At a cocktail party at the Wanderers club on the eve of their match against Transvaal, Hobbs spotted Bacher on the other side of the room. He immediately walked across and without any fanfare asked pointedly, 'Do you sleep well at night?' He was deadly serious. Bacher hit top score of 147 for Transvaal against the Robins XI.

rosy for Bacher and set him on course for the rest of the tour. Against Minor Counties at Newcastle-on-Tyne he was back at No 3 (Lindsay was tried as an opener) to score 121 and 34, and he followed this up against Leicestershire with 119 batting at No 6 again (for once, Lindsay failed at No 3). His confidence was running high again, particularly after Leicester where he and the Pretoria fast bowler Jackie Botten – with whom he forged a strong friendship on tour – had a glorious time in putting on 181 runs for the ninth wicket in just over two hours. Botten scored 90 batting at No 10 and their partnership broke a 30-year-old record. The next match was the first of the three Tests and, following his back-to-back hundreds, Ali's place in the team was assured.

LORD'S CRICKET GROUND is a singular place made extra special in July 1965 by its hosting of the 100th Test between England and South Africa.

'I was now at the holy of holies,' recalls Ali, 'and my nerves were shot as I sat in the dressing room and put on my boots and flannels. Peter van der Merwe won the toss and decided we should bat. I was down to go in at No 6 but I was so nervous I couldn't watch any play. I just sat in the dressing room listening to the applause and then the roar, which I knew meant that someone was out.'

So acute was his anxiety at having to walk out on to the hallowed ground that he grappled with ways to calm his jangling nerves. Deciding that reverse psychology would provide the remedy, he succeeded in persuading himself to accept the hypothesis that this was 'just another game at just another ground'. 'It worked too well. When I went in to bat after tea (at 155 for four), I was almost flippant. My mental state had altered by 180 degrees.'

In this carefree frame of mind he was almost out first ball on his Test debut when a delivery from David Brown passed just over the middle stump. Then, having scored 4, he tried to sweep Fred Titmus coming round the wicket and was struck on his back leg to be given out lbw.

He did not enjoy batting at Lord's – later in the tour he failed in both innings there against Middlesex – because the famous slope of the ground made him feel like he was about to lose his balance and topple over.

England took control of the Test from the outset and was the dominant force for four days. On the fourth afternoon, Bacher came to the crease to join Bland with the team struggling. 'We were in trouble and I knew it was vital for me to bat through to the close. Colin and I added 50 runs before he was out for 70. Without him, I knew that if I go, we lose. I knew that the longer I occupied the crease, the faster England would have to score on the final day. It really was a grim struggle. I don't think my batting was very nice to watch, but I was fighting for survival, for myself, my team and my country.'

At stumps he was unbeaten on 25 and, as he sat in the dressing room afterwards, Denis Compton walked through the door and sat down with him. 'Eddie (Barlow) then joined us and both were very complimentary. They didn't praise me for a fantastic innings – because that it was not – but they knew what I was trying to do out there, hanging in for my country, and they were very supportive.'

The next morning, he added 12 more runs before the wily Titmus bowled him with his faster ball, and when the South African innings closed on 248, England were left to score 191 runs for victory in 236 minutes. 'We were back-pedalling for four and half days,' recalls Ali, 'and then suddenly we almost snatched victory. I can remember Peter Pollock felling John Edrich with a ball to the head (England's No 3 was taken to hospital and took no further part in the series) and suddenly they were five down for 121.'

The bowling hero was Richard Dumbrill with four wickets on his Test debut, but the England tail managed to hold out for the draw with three wickets in hand at the close.

'We travelled by bus to Canterbury that night for our next three-day game against Kent. We were drinking beer and our spirits were high. It was great being part of such a young, confident and jubilant side. After our experience at Lord's we knew we had the beating of England.'

THE SPRINGBOKS THRASHED Colin Cowdrey's Kent in two days with Graeme Pollock showing his batting mastery with an undefeated 203, and brother Peter taking five for 28 as Kent were skittled for 74. Ali and Graeme shared a third-wicket partnership of 137 before Bacher's illustrious partner ran him out by the length of the pitch for 57. Peter Pollock also did the Springboks a favour by giving Cowdrey a mauling. England's experienced No 5 was his victim in each innings for an aggregate of only 3 runs. The other notable deed of the game was Mike Macaulay's second innings hat-trick to remove the last three Kent batsmen.

The Kent team included a player just turned 20 who bowled what can only be described as left-arm slow-to-medium spin-scam. He made so little impression at the time (conceding 87 runs in 21 overs) that Ali did not even notice his name. In years to come, Derek Underwood would become such a unique force in international cricket that his teammates nicknamed him 'Deadly'. In 1968, after Underwood had taken seven for 50 for England against Australia at The Oval, Ali was asked by his Balfour Park teammate Joe Hansen what it was like facing him. He replied, 'I never played against him.' It was only when Hansen showed him the scorecard of the 1965 match against Kent that he realised who the strange 'unknown' bowler[6] was that he had faced that day at Canterbury.

At Swansea, Ali met up with an old friend in the former England allrounder Peter Walker[7] who played in the Transvaal in the English winters and was a teammate at Balfour Park. It was Peter who had persuaded him a few years earlier to change his grip to present a more open-faced bat that enabled him to score more freely on both sides of the wicket. Walker was now a member of the Glamorgan team that almost inflicted a humiliating defeat on the Springboks on the eve of the second Test. The respective batting and bowling heroes of the county were their No 3 batsman and former Cambridge University captain Tony Lewis who scored an undefeated 146 (earlier that season he had hit a century against the touring New Zealanders) and the spin bowler Jim Pressdee who finished with a match analysis of seven for 80 on a turning wicket. Pressdee forged strong links with South Africa as a provincial player and coach for North Eastern Transvaal[8] over several decades and Lewis – who went on to play nine Tests for England and was elected president of the MCC – became a friend of the Bachers and would entertain Ali and Shira on many of their trips to the UK.

In reply to Glamorgan's 301, the South Africans could total a miserly 144 – with Ali scoring exactly half of those runs. Before he reached double figures, though, he was given a big let-off when Walker – reputed to be the safest catcher in Glamorgan's history – put down a dolly catch off Jeff Jones. Bacher's 72 and Bland's 32 were the only scores of note, and things did not improve much in the follow-on innings. Ali was out for 7, caught Walker, bowled Pressdee, and only a fighting half-century by Dumbrill down the order helped the South Africans hold out for a draw.

---

[6] The previous year (1964) Underwood took nine for 28 for Kent against Sussex, and among his subsequent match-winning performances was his eight for 51 for England against Pakistan at Lord's in 1974. In the twilight of his career, he toured South Africa with the first rebel English team in 1982.
[7] Peter Walker represented England in three of the five Tests against Jackie McGlew's Springboks in 1960.
[8] Later Northern Transvaal, now the Northerns Titans.

THE SPRINGBOKS PUT the narrow squeak at Swansea behind them as they travelled to Nottingham the next day for the Test match at Trent Bridge. Their mood was helped by a marked improvement in the weather after heavy rains during the past few weeks but, after Van der Merwe won the toss and decided to bat, they were in early trouble at 80 for five, including Bacher, the No 6 batsman, bowled by John Snow for 12. At that point England would have been forgiven for believing that they were well set for victory but they did not reckon with Graeme Pollock. His 125 out of 140 runs scored in 160 minutes was acclaimed as one of the finest innings ever seen at Trent Bridge, or anywhere else for that matter, and such was his dominance that he contributed 91 in a 98-run partnership with Van der Merwe. In what was remembered as the 'Pollocks' Match', Graeme scored 59 in the second innings and Peter returned a match analysis of ten for 87 for South Africa to score their first win in England in ten years and inflict on England their first defeat in 15 Tests.

Ali had been promoted to No 3 in the second innings and survived an early chance off Snow – when a catch flew between slip and gully – to play an innings of great character and value for his first half-century in Test cricket. He and Barlow shared a 99-run stand before he was trapped in front for 67 by the tall fast bowler Larter. The *Sunday Tribune* reported:

> For just over three hours Bacher played an innings of inestimable value for his side . . . in which he revealed his temperament for a tight corner, a cool head, the technique to play correctly, the footwork to get to the pitch of the ball and the strokes to score on either side of the wicket.

South Africa's second innings of 289 – the work largely of Barlow (76), Bacher (67) and Pollock (59) – left England the task of scoring 319 runs for victory in two full days plus 35 minutes. There was still a full day remaining when they were bowled out for 224, with Peter Pollock's bowling analysis of 24-15-34-5 worthy of gold-plated inscription. Pollock later wrote, 'I believe Trent Bridge was one of the greatest and most significant Tests of the era . . . a moment of destiny.'[9]

The celebrations afterwards were legendary. In the misty dusk, after all the spectators had left, several players stripped to their underpants, raced on to the pitch and planted two beer bottles neck downwards in the turf.

---

[9] *God's Fast Bowler* by Peter Pollock (Christian Art Publishers 2001).

Two of the players wore police helmets, the owners of which were giving mock chase. One of the policemen then solemnly measured out his run-up and bowled a beer bottle down the pitch towards five crouching Springbok fielders, four of them wearing baggy white Y-fronts. They roared an appeal, sent the policeman headlong, and wrestled with a police dog that lay on its back and wagged its tail. Photographic evidence suggests that those in their undies were Denis Lindsay, Graeme Pollock, Colin Bland and Eddie Barlow, while Atholl McKinnon was still wearing his full cricket kit, and Ali Bacher was dressed in his whites but without shoes or socks. An incongruous sight was Peter Pollock, smartly dressed in white formal shirt and tie, his hair neatly combed.

He tells that during the tense final stages of the Test he had offered a silent prayer for the Lord to help him take the three remaining wickets. In return he would not touch a drink that night. When his prayer was answered, Peter had to stick to the deal and so, while his teammates were downing beers and champagne in the dressing room, he went away quietly to shower and dress.

Bacher says that McKinnon and Bland led the celebrations, but it is certain that everyone played their part. If anything, this tomfoolery shows just how much cricket has changed. Had it happened 30 years later – and that probably would have been impossible – the media would have turned it into a sensational story that would no doubt have cost a couple of policemen their promotions and placed several Springboks in front of a disciplinary committee. In 1965, however, it was the kind of laddish fun that cricketers should be allowed to engage in when the day is done.

The policemen, of course, were not there by chance. Throughout the tour, officers were assigned to keep an eye on the South African dressing room because of threats of anti-apartheid demonstrations. This did not materialise and only twice during the whole tour did the players see minor protests at Colchester and outside The Oval.

After the Trent Bridge triumph, Bacher scored half-centuries against Hampshire and Warwickshire and was then given a well-deserved rest, along with Peter Pollock, when the Springboks played Sussex at Hove. It was there that the two of them spent a day together on the Brighton beach and, away from cricket for once, cemented a close relationship that would endure for a long time. 'Both of us were headstrong men who had the odd blow-up as administrators in the years ahead, but not once did we surrender our mutual respect,' says Ali.

WITH MORE HALF-centuries[10] than anyone else on tour, Ali always felt that the elusive Test century would eventually come; and at The Oval on 28 August it looked to be imminent. In the Saturday afternoon gloom of the second innings, he batted with great application and resourcefulness to reach an undefeated 70, his highest Test score to date, with the fourth day on Monday still to come. The English cricket writers liked what they saw: 'Bacher's innings was all arms, legs and stickability' . . . 'an innings not glittering with strokes but an intelligent one of rigid application', and Compton wrote, 'He has played some fine innings when most wanted, but this could well be the most vital innings he has played.'

South Africa's overall lead was 169 with seven wickets in hand; and Ali's dogged batting in variable light gave rise to optimism in the South African camp that victory could be theirs – despite the fact that his 62-run partnership with Graeme Pollock was tragically ended in the first over after tea when the left-hander was run out. Pollock called for a quick single after steering the ball directly to a fielder, Bacher sent him back, and Pollock turned and dived full length . . . but was beaten by Eric Russell's pinpoint underarm throw from cover point.

In Bacher's defence, *The Times* cricket correspondent noted that 'Pollock sees a run more quickly than he calls it' and this time he made off for a single 'without extending a clear invitation to Bacher to join him'.

HE STRODE OUT on the Monday morning full of confidence, buoyed by the telegrams from home that willed him on. He was out first ball, to a bat-pad catch by Mike Smith off Brian Statham; and to this day his disappointment is discernible.

The Test ended in an anticlimax when rain put an end to some unexpectedly audacious run chasing by the England batsmen and some unpopular delaying tactics by the South Africans. The question left unanswered was 'Who did the rain really save?'

Set to score a nigh impossible 399 to win,[11] England ended 91 runs short of the target with 70 minutes and six wickets remaining. They had been roundly criticised for their slow batting in the first innings, but now their scoring rate, particularly after Barrington and Cowdrey had added

---

[10] Bacher scored eight half-centuries in all in England with Eddie Barlow the next best with six.

[11] By that stage, only Australia in 1948 had scored more than 300 runs in a fourth innings to win a Test match.

135 runs in 142 minutes, suggested that they could have pulled it off. That they did not do so meant that South Africa had won its first Test series in England since 1935.

The Times assessed Ali's performance at The Oval as follows:

Not for the first time in the series Bacher played a significant part. The basis of his batting is an eye that enables him to tuck the ball away to leg with unusual facility. He also uses his feet well – to the quicker bowlers as well as the spinners. In fact, on their recent form, England's batsmen can learn from Bacher as to how best to use the ability they have.

IN THE FINAL match of the tour, Ali unwittingly transgressed a line of cricketing etiquette. It happened against T N Pearce's XI at Scarborough in a so-called festival match that caused some confusion and controversy. The home side was loaded with no fewer than ten England Test players who all took it rather seriously, while the Springboks played it as a light-hearted, farewell romp for which they were criticised. The first ball that Ali received was a benign full toss from Fred Rumsey that he viciously pulled for four. Rumsey was enraged, and immediately quickened his pace. It was only later that Ali found out that the unwritten law at Scarborough was that the bowler always gave the new batsman a 'dolly' ball to allow him to get off the mark with a single.

Ali hit eight more boundaries in his quickfire 60, and was by far the best of the Springboks who generally engaged in high jinks. At one stage Lindsay switched to batting left handed and hit Rumsey for a four; Graeme Pollock hit a catch back to the bowler, charged down the pitch, made a mock attempt to hit him with his bat, and was run out in the process; McKinnon amused spectators with some byplay on the boundary, putting up a huge umbrella and limping when an attractive nurse passed by; Bacher and Bland bowled for the first time on tour, and Ali also spent time keeping wicket when the two regulars, Lindsay and Gamsy, fielded. Thus it was that they were beaten with a full day to spare, with Duffus telling his readers that the Springboks had paid dearly for their frivolous approach. Ali recalls that in the dressing room afterwards, Eddie Barlow, who was not playing, gave his teammates a tongue-lashing for their behaviour in South African colours. An argument ensued but, in the end, Ali accepted that Eddie was right.

His other abiding memory of that match was of the man who dismissed him for 60. Trevor Bailey was then forty-one years old, a craggy former

England allrounder and arch-professional. 'I first saw him when he played against us for Essex near the start of the tour. He was their captain and he looked an excellent cricketer. He scored 70-odd in the first innings, and batted superbly on a fast pitch with Peter Pollock bowling flat out. At Scarborough, he bowled me three successive balls that were truly amazing: the first, a perfect outswinger; the second, a perfect inswinger; and the third, an off-cutter that knocked out my middle stump.'

As THE LONG tour neared its completion, Ali wrote to Shira that he was growing more homesick by the day. 'I've realised that there's more to life than just cricket.'

Little did they know the extent to which the game would consume their lives in the years still lying ahead.

THE RENEWED DEDICATION that Ali had been putting into his studies was paying dividends. In spite of undertaking a long tour of England, he was delighted to pass his fourth year medicine at the end of 1965 and was by now relishing the prospect of becoming a doctor. Fourth year had been his most enjoyable by far because of the practical nature of the work in the wards – a nice change from the claustrophobic theory of the preceding years. The second year had been the toughest when he spent every day of his July holidays studying for a solid month in the main library to get on top of his work, but now it was all turning around for the better. 'In fourth year I realised that my decision to hang in was the right one – and I was forever grateful to Wilf Isaacs for persuading me not to give up after I had failed my first year.'

It was therefore with some degree of enthusiasm that Ali returned to his studies. On his first day back at Johannesburg's old General Hospital following the tour of England, he was part of a group of students who had their blood taken as part of a study being undertaken by Dr Menof, the physician in charge of the ward. This was designed to establish the association between the thyroid gland and cholesterol metabolism.

'On my third day back in the ward I was suddenly surrounded by physicians and registrars. "What's up?" I asked. They replied, "Does your family have a history of heart disease?" I said "Why?" and they said, "Your cholesterol level is sky high." '

Ali now learned that his condition was a hereditary one that afflicted Jewish, Indian and Afrikaner families in particular and in each generation it could be transmitted to every second child. He, of course, was the fourth of five siblings.

At the time, he was not particularly concerned about this trait but he began taking daily medication to keep his cholesterol level under control.

It was also during this time at medical school that he examined his mother and discovered that she had a heart murmur, which necessitated periodic visits to a cardiologist.

These discoveries would later have dire consequences for both of them.

Chapter 7

Enter the Aussies

ALTHOUGH ALI BACHER'S international experience was limited to playing against only England and Australia, those countries did after all represent two-thirds of South Africa's opponents during his playing days. The third of the traditional rivals was New Zealand, which completed the four-nation 'white bloc' of world cricket, and against whom he would have played, at least for his province in 1961-62, were it not for his studies.

The one sadness is that he never got the chance to tour Australia and play on such famous grounds as Melbourne, Sydney and Adelaide. Given the nature of those pitches, it is likely that he would have done very well batting in that country, although we shall never know for sure.

In South Africa, however, he relished his tussles with the Australians; and his first encounter with them in 1966 was the stuff of storybooks. It became known as 'Bacher's Match' and, given the lack of counter-attractions of those times, it was inscribed in banner headlines on the front pages around the country.

It happened over four days of great cricket and mounting tension in November 1966, the third match of the tour by Bobby Simpson's team against Transvaal at the Wanderers. Apart from scoring 235 in what was then the highest score by a South African against Australia, Bacher took what was described as 'the catch of the decade' to dismiss Bob Cowper; and he simply shone as the captain to orchestrate a famous nail-biting victory with eight minutes of the match remaining. 'Both teams played exhilarating cricket,' says Ali, 'and the match set the tempo for an exciting summer.'

Ahead of the arrival of the Australians, he had made a concerted effort to get into shape. In what he called an exhaustive training regimen, Ali would use his lunch hour on campus to jog eight laps of the rugby field three times a week and indulge in a weekly game of squash. His friend Don Mackay-Coghill would have accused him of overdoing things because Coghill's fitness training was a vigorous burst in the dressing room shortly before going into the field to open the bowling. This energetic display consisted of touching the top of his shins, as opposed to his toes, several times. In his defence, it should be said that Coghill was constantly plagued by back and knee problems and often had to take painkillers to help him get through a match; but while he was touching his shins, the chain-smoking Bacher would have been puffing away on a final pre-match cigarette.[1]

Ali's desire to be as fit and ready as possible for the Aussies was aimed, of course, at retaining his place in the Springbok team for the five-Test series. There was growing competition for several places in the side, including his own top-order slot where the young Natal batsman Barry Richards was making ever stronger claims. Ali's form in the Transvaal match suggested to him that he had 'peaked' too soon but his performance at least provided the clincher for national honours and his side's remarkable victory, albeit against opponents who refused to go on the defensive and battle out a draw, provided the spur for South Africa to approach the Test series with added confidence.

Louis Duffus, a cricket writer not given to hyperbole, saw an even greater significance in Bacher's performance: 'The Aussies are no longer bogeymen. It was Bacher with his resourceful captaincy, brilliant catching and his great gallivanting innings who ripped off their masks.'

His double-century in the second innings (he scored 45 in the first) was only the fourth[2] by a South African against an Australian team. He batted just over five and a half hours. Twenty-four of his 37 boundaries were struck through the on side. And Duffus wrote, 'Because it was achieved against Grimmett and O'Reilly in a Test match, Dudley Nourse's 231 at the old Wanderers was a feat in a higher class, but Bacher's barnstorming 235

---

[1] Statistics are not available, but it is likely that the majority of cricketers smoked. Cigarette adverts regularly used sportsmen as their role models and a brand called *Springbok* was known as *The Sportsman's Cigarette*.
[2] The others were all scored in Test matches: Dudley Nourse 231 (at Johannesburg 1935-36), Aubrey Faulkner 204 (at Melbourne 1910-11) and Eddie Barlow 201 (at Adelaide 1963-64).

remains a monument to a non-stop impulse to attack, to faultless timing and sustained skill.'

What Duffus did not add was that there was also a little motivational challenge contained in a note that was handed to Ali by the 12th man during a drinks break when he had scored 130-odd. *'If you don't get 200, you're not a batsman!'* read the note, and it was signed by Eddie Barlow.

'It was one of those innings,' recalls Ali, 'when everything just falls into place. From the first ball I faced late on the Saturday afternoon, I just felt good: my feet were moving well, I saw the ball early and my reflexes were sharp. The next day was the rest day and I was undefeated with about nine runs; but on the Monday when we resumed, everything worked again for me. The longer I batted, the better I felt.'

Apart from Bacher's 235, Tiger Lance scored a delightful 107 in the second innings – his third century in four innings – to help his captain take the total from 172 for three to 409 for four before the declaration came at 422 for six. This was a crucial match-winning partnership, one of many that the two shared over the years during which a fine mutual respect developed. Lance was a man who worked hard and played hard and even though he was a professional footballer in the National Soccer League he was envious of Ali's level of fitness.

Ali liked Herbert 'Tiger' Lance. He was street-smart and tough and his highly original sense of humour was a feature of South African cricket and an important ingredient in a happy dressing room. Bacher rated him among the best allrounders of his day and a stroke-playing batsman who stood back to no one.

Up in the press box, the former Australian captain Richie Benaud, who was a professional journalist even before he became a famous cricketer and then television commentator, punched the following out on his portable typewriter:

> *It was like slaughter on tenth avenue as Bacher and Lance tore the heart out of the Australians. I am more and more impressed with Bacher every time I see him, for whilst it is true that he is predominantly an on-side player, he is also possessed of a sound defence and the ability to time the ball perfectly from a limited back lift. In addition, he has that priceless gift of good temperament and though not stylish to watch, he is devilishly hard to dismiss.*

The occasion also summarily dispelled the pre-match gossip that Lance was not likely to crack the Test team. Quite apart from his splendid batting, he underlined his value as an allrounder by clean bowling four Aussies with his seamers in the first innings as he and Atholl McKinnon reduced them from 228 for four to 254 all out on an excellent pitch and an outfield that was very fast.

McKinnon also clinched his place in the Test team by answering his captain's call in sending down a 27-over marathon spell to take five wickets, three of them to catches by Bacher in close positions in front of the wicket. The catch that dismissed the left-handed Cowper was described as 'miraculous'. It came from a full-blooded pull that Ali caught left-handed while fielding at silly mid-on, the force of the shot knocking him off his feet and on to his back while he clutched the ball above him. Coghill watched in disbelief. 'He was standing no further than five metres from the bat when Cowper hit it right in the meat. It was all reflex action from Ali and the ball came at him so hard and fast that it knocked him on to his bum. I walked up to him as he lay there. "You can open your eyes now," I said.'

The taciturn Cowper remembers it none too fondly. 'It shouldn't have happened; it was brilliant for him, but not for me. I whacked a short-pitched ball and, as far as I was concerned, it was going straight to the boundary. It was an impossible catch; if not a fluke, then miraculous. Ali and I have been firm friends ever since.'[3]

Many years later, after the advent of Jonty Rhodes and the dawning of the age of the super fielders, Ali would play down the Cowper catch as 'nothing more than the norm today'. That may or may not be so (for a start, silly mid-on is a position that has all but disappeared in the modern game) but it was a classic reflex catch that was as spectacular in November 1966 as it would have been in November 1996.

McKinnon, of course, was so pleased that he gave his captain a big hug. He was a rotund man of over 200 pounds – 'I am what you might call a bonny baby,' he would say – who did not indulge in any serious training programme yet was in good enough shape to bowl 27 economical overs of left-arm spin to international batsmen of the calibre of Simpson, Lawry, Cowper and Chappell. 'Reckon I must be fit,' he said at the time. 'Why, I can still get into last season's togs!' He was a garrulous man whom the fans adored, and he once told how his Test captain, Peter van der Merwe,

---

[3] Bob Cowper interview, November 2003. Note: Cowper scored 307 against England at Melbourne in the season prior to coming to South Africa.

had removed him from the attack when he smelled the alcohol on his bowler's breath from his imbibing with spectators while fielding on the long leg boundary.[4]

Australia were set a victory target of 490 runs in 400 minutes, and it was to their credit that they went for the runs. At 370 for six, with an hour remaining, a draw seemed the likely result, but Eddie Barlow took two quick wickets that were immediately followed by a run-out and suddenly the Australians were 400 for nine with 33 minutes left. Tail-enders Jim Hubble and Neil Hawke defended dourly and just when it looked like they might carry it through, Bacher's decision to put his faith in the wrist spinner Tony Tillim paid off. With fielders crowded all round the bat, Hawke failed to pick a perfect googly and it cannoned back into his off stump with eight minutes remaining.

A crowd of 37 000 had watched all four days and there were ecstatic scenes afterwards – with Ali carried shoulder high from the field – in celebration of Transvaal becoming the first team ever to beat an Australian side in South Africa. 'The Aussies arrived with this tag of invincibility, but we proved that they could be beaten. The Transvaal team was not a great team by any yardstick, but it had all the confidence in the world. We also refused to be overawed by the Aussies and I had a quiet confidence in our determination.

'What was also very significant for me was that, for the first time, thousands of Afrikaners came to watch the cricket and show their support. This continued throughout the Test series when Afrikaans folk became very committed cricket fans. I believe they were attracted by our success.'

The newspapers bought into the euphoria in a big way, trumpeting the 24-year-old Bacher as the new 'general' who was now ready to take over as Springbok captain. Van der Merwe was the man in possession but several cricket writers started questioning whether his batting was good enough to justify his selection. In the speculation, the two candidates as captain-elect were Bacher and Barlow but, as it turned out, 'Murphy' scored a timeous 60 while captaining Eastern Province against the Aussies a fortnight later and kept the job. Barry Richards made another claim for his first Test cap by scoring a century while batting No 3 for a SA XI against the touring

---

[4] Atholl McKinnon died in his sleep aged 51 in December 1983. At the time he was assistant manager of the rebel West Indies team touring South Africa. Peter van der Merwe described him as 'the finest team man I knew'.

team in East London, but the selectors looked no further than Bacher for the Test team. Years later, Ali would say to Richards,[5] 'My greatest batting achievement was keeping you out of a Test series!'

ALI FOUND THE Aussies to be very tough in their on-field conduct, much more so than the England players he had encountered in 1965. The English, he recalled, were generally quite polite, often acknowledging a good shot or a good delivery with a nod or a 'well done' or a 'nice shot'. Not so the Aussies. There was no 'sledging' of the kind of in-your-face bad-mouthing that is prevalent in modern-day cricket, but things were said in conversation among the fielders that was just loud enough for the batting 'victim' to hear. Ali went out to bat in the Test series and instinctively felt the lack of warmth and the increased pressure. He remembered that Graham McKenzie, their ace fast bowler, was quite genial during the Transvaal match, but when the Test series started he suddenly became frosty. In the first innings of the first Test at the Wanderers he gave nothing away to rip out the heart of the Springbok innings and finish with five for 46 in a total of 199. He was far and away Australia's best bowler, ending the series with 24 wickets, more than double the number of the next best Aussie; and of the eight times that Ali was out in the series, McKenzie claimed five. At the end of his playing days Bacher would say without any hesitation that the man they called 'Garth'[6] was by far the best bowler he ever faced from another country. He had a deceptive change of pace, was as quick as any other bowler and hit the deck hard enough for the ball to carry sometimes over the head of the 'keeper. His stock ball was a very late away swinger from his classic sideways-on action that often found the outside edge.

In that first Test at the Wanderers, McKenzie dismissed Barlow (13), Bacher (5) and Bland (0) in a devastating eight-ball burst, and inside the opening hour the Springboks were down and out on 41 for five. The uncertainty of Test cricket, however, is such that South Africa came back to win the match by 233 runs. This was due to a remarkable second innings total of 620 which was a record for South Africa in a Test match. Amazingly that huge total included only one individual hundred, Denis Lindsay's maiden Test century of 182. There were, of course, good contributions

---

[5] Barry Richards was so highly rated as a batsman that he was the only South African included in Sir Donald Bradman's mythical team of all-time greats.
[6] Graham McKenzie was fair and good looking with an athletic physique that reminded his teammates of a comic book hero called *Garth*.

from all the batsmen and, when Ali had moved past the 60-mark and was batting soundly, he again felt confident that he could convert it into his first Test century. On 63, however, he was adjudged run out; and umpire Les Baxter was roundly booed by the spectators sitting square to the wicket who were convinced the batsman had made his ground. There was no television, of course, to test the veracity of this; and it was only many years later, when Bacher introduced the innovation of the third umpire to international cricket that the problem of line calls was solved.

Lindsay's century was the start of a golden summer. In all he hit three lusty Test scores of 182, 137 and 131 and his aggregate of 606 came at an average of 86.57. He was also responsible for 24 dismissals behind the stumps. The one thing about Lindsay's performance that always stuck with Ali was his relationship with the Australian fast bowler Dave Renneberg. The tall, angular Aussie would persist in bowling short on the leg stump, which was meat and drink to the belligerent batsman. In the first Test, for example, Lindsay swatted these deliveries away and turned five of them into sixes. Then, after close of play each day, Lindsay and Renneberg would get together for a few beers in the change room and then go out for the evening . . . and the next day Renneberg would be back to feed him the short stuff again. It was a ritual that endured throughout the series and Ali could never quite figure it out. Maybe it made some sense to Renneberg in the second Test at Newlands when Lindsay miscued a big hook on to his forehead and the ball rebounded back down the pitch for Renneberg to dive full stretch to take the return catch and dismiss his friendly foe for 5.

The most of the action that Ali saw at Newlands (he was dismissed for 0 and 4 by McKenzie) was acting as Graeme Pollock's runner after the left-hander pulled a leg muscle while fielding on the second day. This did not stop him from hobbling out later and scoring 209 in what, alas, turned out to be a losing cause.

The damage had already been done much earlier when Simpson won the toss and Australia scored 542 with centuries from their captain and Keith Stackpole. The latter's dismissal for 134 is indelibly etched in Ali's memory. 'I was fielding in the slips and the wind was howling. Eddie bowled the last ball of the over, a bouncer to Keith. He attempted to hook it, missed the ball and walked for tea.'

In the heat of the moment, someone appealed, the umpire saw Stackpole walking (only for tea, mind), and instinctively stuck his finger in the air. Out! Stackpole stopped in his tracks and glared at the umpire in utter disbelief.

Victory for Australia by six wickets came quite easily after they were left to score 179 in the final four hours. Ali made a mental note of an article by Richie Benaud in which he expressed surprise that the Springboks did not encourage McKinnon to bowl his left-arm spin from *over* the wicket. In this way he might have exploited the rough outside the leg stump and made the batsmen's life far more difficult on the final afternoon.

Ali rated his twin batting failures at Newlands as the most depressing time of his entire Test career. 'I remember on my first trip to Newlands as a youngster for Transvaal, the older players were negative about playing there and warned that you had to be careful driving the spin bowlers when they floated the ball into the south-easterly wind. They also said that the ball never deviated off the pitch. In the Test match, McKenzie bowled me what I can only describe as a fast off break to bowl me in the first innings.

'Batting can be so tough. In tennis, you can be two sets down and come back to win; and in golf you can trail over three rounds and still win it in the fourth. In batting, you've got one chance; when you're out, that's you, and you're out of the game.

'I felt really rotten during that Test match; my heart was breaking, and I could have cried. I was determined, though, not to show my feelings. I remembered what Eric Rowan always told us about putting on a brave face when we lost – "Smile, smile, I feel like crying".'

Bacher's failure at Newlands again gave rise to questions as to when Richards would get his first cap.[7] In the five innings he played against the Aussies for Natal and SA Invitation XIs, the 21-year-old former SA Schools captain scored 385 runs at an average of 77. Bacher knew as well as the next man that this was, in his words, 'a genius in the making'. Ali spent an anxious couple of weeks awaiting the announcement of the team for the third Test at Durban and recalls 'coming out of bioscope one Saturday night with Tiger and his wife and seeing my name (and Lance's) in the team printed in the late edition of *The Star*'. He read it with a deep sense of relief.

A new name also appeared, one Michael John Procter who was Richards' chum from Natal, and he would relish the chance of making his Test debut

---

[7] As far back as 1963, when Barry Richards was still 17, Denis Compton wrote an article in the *Sunday Times* headlined 'Send Richards to Australia'. The great England cricketer had watched him in action and bowled to him for an hour in the nets and was convinced that the Durban High School prodigy should be included in the Springbok team for the 1963-64 tour of Australia.

in an all-pace and seam attack on his home ground of Kingsmead. This he most certainly did, proceeding to take seven wickets in the match to emerge by far the most successful bowler, and in time he would stamp his authority on a game in which he would become one of the world's foremost allrounders.

Ali, in the mean time, had realised that the Kingsmead Test was 'do or die' for him. 'Before play began, Arthur Coy (chairman of selectors) came into the dressing room and wished me well. He knew and I knew that this was my last chance.'

Simpson won the toss and put South Africa in on a green-top. Start of play was scheduled for 10.30 but, for whatever reason, the umpire called 'Play!' at 10.26. Ali recalls what happened next: 'McKenzie bowled the first ball from the Umgeni End and it was almost as though he hadn't warmed up properly, the way he ambled in and sent down a real loosener, almost a practice ball, a gentle full toss. Eddie hit it straight back to him and was caught and bowled. My heart sank, Eddie's out first ball, and I'm in. The clock says 10.30 and I'm now virtually opening the innings against McKenzie, who can only get better.

'In retrospect, it was best for me that I got in early. If I'd had a long wait in the dressing room, my nerves would probably have got the better of me. I had no time to be nervous; I was out there now, facing McKenzie with the new ball.'

Bacher batted through until lunch and was out thereafter for 47, and in the second innings he scored an undefeated 60 in the Springboks' eight-wicket victory. He had entrenched his position in the side, and Richards would have to wait a while longer for his first Test cap.

The Kingsmead Test would also give Ali another insight into top-class captaincy. He was amazed when Simpson, having asked South Africa to bat on a well-grassed wicket, introduced Cowper, no more than a part-time spinner, into the attack during the second hour of the opening day. Simpson judged the prevailing weather conditions to be perfect for Cowper to bowl floaters into a strong breeze blowing in from leg to off. This inspired move met with immediate success as he sent back Goddard,[8] Pollock and Lance cheaply for South Africa to be reeling on 94 for six – before the

---

[8] At Durban, Trevor Goddard became the third South African to capture 100 Test wickets and by the end of the series he had passed 10 000 first-class runs. He captured 26 wickets at 16.23 in the series – the best aggregate and average by any bowler – and his batting average was 32.66.

golden boy Lindsay again performed his heroics with 137 in a total of 300. Throughout all of this, Ali was highly impressed with the way Simpson kept Cowper plugging away with his drifting deliveries in an unbroken spell of 37 overs covering four and a half hours; and his figures of 37-14-57-3 bear repeating.

With South Africa now 2-1 up in the series, it was only heavy rains in the fourth Test at the Wanderers that saved Australia from a huge defeat. The batting hero was again Lindsay who reached his third century of the series with a six off Cowper.

The day after this rain-ruined match, 9 February 1967, Shira Bacher gave birth to Ann, the first of the couple's three children. Two weeks later, the proud new father travelled to Port Elizabeth where the Springboks wrapped up the series 3-1. Graeme Pollock scored a century on his home ground of St George's Park, and Ali hit 40 in the second innings of a comfortable seven-wicket win.[9]

The victory signalled a first series triumph over Australia and with it the continuation of a golden age for South African cricket.

THE GREAT SADNESS of that triumphant series was the cruel injury that put a premature end to Colin Bland's career. In the first Test at the Wanderers, the long-limbed Rhodesian, racing to cut off a ball on the square boundary in front of the dressing rooms, failed to pull up in time, and crashed into the railings, severely damaging an already suspect knee. He would never play Test cricket again.

'He was really a dear friend,' says Ali, 'and an inspiration to me when he encouraged me while I was feeling down in the early part of the 1965 tour of England. Apart from his exceptional fielding ability, he was a very stylish and elegant No 5 who had a very good Test average.[10] I felt very sad that his career had ended that way.'

Many years later, Jonty Rhodes emerged as a fielder who was often compared to Colin Bland, if not for their similarities, then for their effectiveness. They could not be compared, says Ali; they were simply the two best outfielders he had seen throughout his 40-plus years of involvement in cricket as a player and administrator.

---

[9] In his nine innings in the Test series Ali Bacher totalled 244 runs at an average of 30.50. Heading the batting averages was Denis Lindsay's 86.57 above Graeme Pollock's 76.71.
[10] In his 21 Tests, Colin Bland scored 1 669 runs at an average of 49.08.

'On the field, Colin was always immaculately dressed in his creams that were never discoloured; Jonty's clothes always showed green patches from where he had dived. Colin fielded in the covers; Jonty preferred backward point. Colin was very graceful, sheer poetry in motion; Jonty hustled and bustled and was always very busy. Colin was the better thrower; Jonty saved more runs from his diving and extra pace around the field. Colin was quiet and unassuming on the field; Jonty was always exhorting his teammates to raise their game . . .'

AT THE END of 1967, Ali finally became 'Dr Bacher', and baby Ann was with Shira to witness his graduation in Wits University's Great Hall. Ali would spend the next two years serving his internship at Baragwanath[11] – the only public hospital in Soweto serving more than three million people – and at Natalspruit Hospital near the black township of Thokoza east of Johannesburg. He was at 'Bara' for 18 months, which was equally divided between practising the disciplines of medicine, surgery and paediatrics; and at Natalspruit he had six months of gynaecology and obstetrics.

Baragwanath was a legendary institution and one of the great teaching hospitals.[12] Some of the teachers were renowned in their fields, men like Leo Shamroth in cardiology and Asher Dubb in medicine. It was under their wing that Dr Bacher earned his stripes. Every fourth night he worked a 24-hour shift in order to manage the intake of new patients from casualties, and he soon found that he had to be ready to cope with every kind of medical emergency. 'To learn in this environment was a rare privilege,' he says; and it was not surprising that many South African doctors enjoyed such a high standing internationally.

This kind of work, of course, was not conducive to playing a team sport. There were practices to attend, matches over weekends. At Baragwanath the intense activity stopped for no one. Ali, however, found willing allies among his fellow interns. During the cricket season they would double up for him, particularly over weekends, and in the winter months, he would repay them in kind.

---

[11] Chris Hani Baragwanath Hospital, with its 3 000 beds, is the largest acute hospital in the world. It is situated to the south west of Johannesburg, on the southern border of Soweto. The hospital grounds cover an area of 173 acres, and there are 429 buildings with a total floor area of 240 000m².
[12] The greater part of the teaching and clinical research for the Faculty of Health Sciences of the University of the Witwatersrand takes place at this hospital.

In spite of this busy life, it did not escape his attention that storm clouds were gathering on the sports political front. The MCC[13] was due to tour South Africa in 1968-69 and the problem centred around a player named Basil D'Oliveira. He was a South African of the 'Cape Coloured' community and in non-white cricket in South Africa he had no peer as a batsman of the highest class. Because of his race classification under the apartheid laws, he was prevented from representing the country of his birth in international cricket so, after years of failed attempts to play in England, he had been finally accepted in 1960 by the Middleton Club in the Central Lancashire League. From there, he joined Worcestershire in the county championship and in 1966, having become a naturalised British citizen, he was selected by England for the home series against the West Indies; and produced consecutive Test scores of 76, 54 and 88 against the world's most feared fast bowling duo of Wes Hall and Charlie Griffith.

The alarm bells immediately began ringing in the corridors of the apartheid regime, and in January 1967, while the Australians were happily playing in South Africa, the minister of the interior Pieter le Roux warned that D'Oliveira might be banned from touring with the MCC the following summer. He reminded English cricket authorities that sport between players of different race groups was forbidden in South Africa.

In the South African winter of 1968, however, D'Oliveira was dropped from the England team after the first Test against Australia – but the South African-born cricketer refused to give in. Recalled for the final Test at The Oval, he scored 158 and helped England share the series. A day later, the MCC announced the names of the 16 players to tour South Africa. D'Oliveira was not among them. The secretary of the MCC, Billy Griffiths, insisted that 'nothing else was discussed at the selectors meeting other than cricketing considerations' but John Arlott, the renowned broadcaster and writer who had helped D'Oliveira play in England, called his omission 'the ultimate betrayal'.

Then, a fortnight later, the fast bowler Tom Cartwright withdrew with injury from the touring team, and D'Oliveira was named as his replacement. The next day in Bloemfontein, the South African prime minister, B J Vorster, addressed a National Party congress. People cheered him when he announced that his government would not accept the new MCC team

---

[13] At that time, England teams toured abroad as the MCC (Marylebone Cricket Club).

'that is being thrust upon South Africa by the Anti-Apartheid Movement'.

On the night the tour was cancelled, Dr Bacher was doing his rounds during a 24-hour shift at Baragwanath. 'When I heard the news, I was disappointed for about 12 hours, but then life went on. I always knew there would be a conflict because the National Party had always maintained that blacks and coloureds were inferior to whites and it would undermine their racist philosophy to have a coloured South African playing cricket at the highest level against an all-white Springbok team.'

In time, Bacher would publicly criticise the government for its policies; and in 1969 he and the two Pollock brothers appealed for black and white cricketers to be allowed to play together. The next day Ali was driving to Natalspruit Hospital and on his car radio he listened to a vitriolic attack on the three players. It was broadcast by the SABC in a daily government propaganda bulletin called *Current Affairs,* which gave the party line each morning on issues in the news.

There was no MCC tour in 1968-69; indeed, there would be no MCC tour to South Africa ever again;[14] but for Ali it was still the most memorable of seasons. Now at the peak of his form, he led Transvaal to their first Currie Cup title in ten seasons to finally break Natal's hold on the coveted trophy. His aggregate of 904 first-class runs in nine matches was a new record[15] for the province and he became the first Transvaal batsman in almost 50 years to score three successive Currie Cup hundreds – 189 against Rhodesia, and 152 and 144 in home-and-away matches against Eastern Province. In addition, he made several scores in excess of 80 to end with an outstanding average of 75.33.

'It was my best season ever and it put us in a winning frame of mind. We went on to win the Currie Cup five years in a row – sharing it once with Western Province – because winning becomes contagious. Once you've done it, you tend to know how to do it; and although it looked as if we were lucky at times, we would always find a way to sneak in because of the winning habit.'

---

[14] England next toured South Africa in 1995-96, by which stage they were no longer called the MCC.
[15] Bacher's record stood for ten seasons before it was bettered by Graeme Pollock when he moved to Transvaal from Eastern Province.

Chapter 8

Bacher versus Barlow

BILL LAWRY WAS a dour opening batsman from the State of Victoria who was called 'Phantom' by his teammates. In 1966-67, he was vice-captain to Bobby Simpson; four seasons later, he returned to South Africa at the age of 32 as captain of Australia. And he came with a not unimpressive record.

In his four series to date he had led his country to a 4-0 crushing of India in Australia, a share of the Ashes series in England, a 3-1 defeat of West Indies in Australia and, immediately prior to his arrival in South Africa in January 1970, a 3-1 triumph in India.

The man named to oppose him as the new Springbok captain was the 27-year-old Ali Bacher. He learned of his appointment from Jack Cheetham, president of the SA Cricket Association. 'He walked up to me during a club game at the Wanderers early in January and told me the news. I was thrilled, but some of the other selections surprised me. Where were Denis Lindsay and Tiger Lance?'

That apart, there was great celebration in the Bacher household which had grown five months earlier with the birth of their second daughter, Lynn. Little did they know that the four-Test series would make cricket history for Ali and his team, assuring some of them a place in cricket's hall of fame, before the curtain of international isolation came down with frightening finality on the South African stage. In the build-up to the tour, however, South African cricket supporters were not so much concerned about the political forces looming ominously on the horizon as about who would get the nod as the new skipper.

Tension had been mounting for some time as the debate raged over the credentials of two players – Ali Bacher and Eddie Barlow – and the intense rivalry that existed between them. Who would it be?

Throughout the ages, cricket had enjoyed fierce rivalry between players who had raced flat out to be the first among equals; and this one was a classic case. Both were born leaders, both were excellent cricketers, both were very ambitious, very influential and very determined to be the chosen one. Both had attended Wits University where, according to one observer,[1] they were poles apart in terms of their personalities: 'Quiet Ali you never heard, but bouncing Barlow was everywhere.'

Eddie was the showman – in fact at times he was a positive show-off – and the fans loved him while some players thought him a bit full of himself.

They played in the same teams at provincial and national level and Barlow, being the senior by about two years and with considerably more matches to his credit, would have felt that he had the inside track. The fuel in the fire of their relationship was a race to ascend the national cricket throne which was complicated by their respective appointments along the way: for example, although Ali captained him at Transvaal, Eddie was appointed vice-captain of Springbok teams in 1965 and 1966 of which Ali was a member; and Eddie already had 18 Tests to his name by the time Ali was selected for his country for the first time.

But perhaps more than anything else was the reputation that Barlow gained in Australia in 1963-64 when he was acclaimed as the player who pointed South Africa down the road to a bright new dawn; he was inspired, he said, to spearhead a positive and aggressive approach because 'for years we were the gentlemen of cricket, so nice in fact that we let other teams win to avoid any problems'. Louis Duffus, widely held to be the top cricket writer in South Africa, wrote of Barlow: 'I am inclined to contend that he had more influence over South African cricket than any single player I know . . . he did more than anyone else to break down the timid defensive tactics which for so many years kept South Africa a second-rate cricket country.'

Don Mackay-Coghill recalls: 'He went to Australia and performed phenomenally well. He also apparently got right up the Aussies' noses. He probably saw Ali as a new upstart coming through and, there's no question, he didn't like it. He saw himself as the heir apparent and Ali as the usurper.'

---

[1] Unidentified author in *Convocation Commentary*, official organ of the Convocation of the University of the Witwatersrand, March 1970.

It was therefore hardly surprising that Barlow wanted to be a Currie Cup captain with his sights set firmly on captaining South Africa and he left Transvaal in order to achieve this, first captaining Eastern Province and then Western Province. On the provincial front, however, Bacher was regarded as the pre-eminent captain and his celebrated style of leadership could not have been more different from his rival's.

Barlow loved to lead from the front in a boisterous almost boastful manner. Those who knew him as a schoolboy at Pretoria Boys' High say he had such confidence in himself that he believed he could do anything and, indeed, wanted to do everything: open the batting, open the bowling, captain the team, keep wicket, hit the winning runs, take the important wickets. He had to be in the forefront and he thrived when others followed. In trench warfare, he would have been the first one over the top.

He rolled up his sleeves high above his elbows, flexed his muscles and bounced on to the field like a prize fighter emerging from his corner; he was a burly, broad-shouldered man who looked every bit like a boxer – in spite of the spectacles – and he loved to take the fight to his opponent, whether it be as a top-order batsman or medium fast bowler.

They called him 'Bunter' after the fictitious schoolboy anti-hero Billy Bunter, although in character he was quite the antithesis of the fat and lazy schoolboy. The only similarities were the spectacles and the impression of a physical roundness of body and ruddy cheeks.

Bacher, on the other hand, was the consummate puppet master who unobtrusively pulled the strings to get each player to perform to his maximum ability. The proof of this lay in Transvaal's success, and in the way he had gained the respect of so many senior cricketers and Springboks who had played under him while he was still barely into his twenties. On the basis that eleven men could not all be playing brilliantly at the same time, he would concentrate his efforts on those individuals who were not performing well in order to lift their confidence and performance, and he would ensure that his star players were handled in just the right way. Graeme Pollock, for example, needed to be told how well he was batting and how much he meant to the side. It would have been all too easy to take such a great and consistent player for granted but Ali realised that Graeme, despite his stature in the game, needed constant reassuring. As a captain, he also played up the 'threat' of Barry Richards to push Graeme into maintaining his position as the leading batsman, and he used the rise of Mike Procter to inspire his senior fast bowler Peter Pollock to bowl even faster. Away from the action, it was also important for Ali to put the right players together. For the first Test at Cape Town, he and Richards were roommates and the other new cap in the team, Lee Irvine, was required to share with Barlow, the vice-captain. Another skipper might have thought nothing of putting the two new boys together in the same room.

Bacher also made it his business to find out what made his teammates tick. He had learned at Transvaal that Coghill performed best when aggressive, so he would find ways of provoking his opening bowler. In the case of Barlow, he always timed to perfection the moment to unleash him on a couple of batsmen who were badly in need of dislodging. In simple terms, Bacher was a shrewd captain who practised psychology through meticulous analysis of his teammates and opponents. And he was, if the truth be known, more popular among the other players than the impulsive Barlow.

Their undisguised rivalry became one of the great talking points in sporting circles. Neither man would stand back for the other and when they captained rival provincial teams those involved would describe the matches as 'wars'.

Prior to touring England with the 1965 Springboks, Barlow had packed his bags at Transvaal and relocated to Port Elizabeth where he played briefly under the captaincy of Graeme Pollock before taking over as skipper of the province. When his team journeyed to Johannesburg for their Currie Cup match in the summer of '65-66, he adopted his own form of psychology. Only a few months earlier he had shared the Springbok dressing room with three Transvaal players – Bacher, Lance and McKinnon – now he was not even talking to them. McKinnon went over to him. 'What's up, Bunter?'

Barlow snapped back: 'We've come here to win points, not friends!' and turned away.

Transvaal sent Eastern Province packing in two days and McKinnon bade Barlow farewell: 'Sorry Bunter, no points *and* no friends!'

Barlow's bellicosity intensified when he moved to Cape Town a couple of seasons later to take over the captaincy of struggling Western Province. It was then that the Bacher-Barlow rivalry escalated along with the North-South hostility that already existed in the South African sports culture, and it was exacerbated at this time in the late sixties because the tour by the Australians was drawing closer and the race was on for the Springbok captaincy. 'When we played him at Cape Town, it was like the Vietnam war,' recalls Ali.

The flames were fanned in the media, and particularly by Cape newspapers that supported Barlow and Transvaal newspapers that supported

Bacher. It was the kind of plot that might have been invented by a boxing promoter hyping up a big fight showdown. Yet had it all taken place, say, 30 years later, it would have dominated the media far more than it did at the time. There was no television in South Africa in those days and no talk radio; so public figures were not exposed to media grilling or live interviews conducted by confrontational journalists or talk show hosts. A live head-to-head TV interview with Bacher and Barlow would have made for compulsory viewing.

On the question of the captaincy, the public was divided but, it seems, the players were not. The respected Cape sportswriter A C Parker had the ear of almost every sports official and player in the country (the *Cape Argus* regularly devoted an entire page to his weekly column of behind the scenes developments and interviews) and this is what he later said: 'I knew from soundings that I had taken among South Africa's Test players that most of them leaned towards Bacher who was also the choice of the retiring captain Peter van der Merwe and his predecessor Trevor Goddard. I also felt that three of the four national selectors would support Bacher on the grounds that he was a better catalyst; that is to say he would get on more harmoniously with the players. To put it another way – with Bacher as captain there was little likelihood of differences arising within the team than with Barlow in charge.'

Procter – who as a youngster played all seven of his Tests in the company of Ali and Eddie – makes the point that some players might have felt pressurised by Barlow, and that he was likely to be less forgiving than Bacher if they did not come up to his expectations.

As for A C Parker, he confessed that Barlow was his personal preference, and so too did the other cricket-writing heavyweight Louis Duffus and the old captain-turned-columnist Jackie McGlew. In McGlew's view, Ali was a good captain but he felt that the pressure of being a medical doctor might be a burden.

It would have been difficult not to support Barlow because of his incredible confidence and fighting spirit, but Bacher was a subtler leader, a cooler customer who had an amazing calming influence when things were going wrong, and was far less excitable. Barlow, on the other hand, could become quite caustic when his plan did not come together. He had an excellent mind and a razor-sharp wit – but beware those who were the target of his sarcasm – and he had extremely strong and sometimes unique views on just about everything. He was a paradox: the original team man, yet the original one-man show.

Somewhere in there was the reason why Ali Bacher got the Springbok captaincy and Eddie Barlow did not.

As it turned out, Ali was hugely successful in the four Tests in which he was in charge, slicing up the Australians with clinical efficiency – he was, after all, the first medical doctor to captain a country since W G Grace for England in the nineteenth century – to inflict a four-nil thrashing that Australians still prefer not to talk about.

Lawry's team came to South Africa after a very tough and at times dangerous tour of India – 'without doubt the toughest I've been on,' said the captain in something of an understatement – on what Australians will say was a foolhardy venture. The South African leg was hastily arranged after Australia's planned tour of Pakistan, which was to follow India, fell through. The Aussies might have won handsomely in India but they were physically and emotionally drained when they arrived in South Africa to play what would emerge as arguably the best team in the world. Their matches in India were disrupted by riots over disputed umpiring decisions, and there were stampedes and pitched battles among ticket-seeking fans in Calcutta that left six people dead. They also needed 24-hour police and army protection after Communist Party propaganda against cricketer-soldier Doug Walters (who was accused of fighting in Vietnam when in fact he had not set foot in the place), and accusations against Lawry that he had assaulted a photographer. Missiles were thrown at the players during games and on one occasion Johnny Gleeson was hit by a bottle and Lawry by a wicker chair.

Lawry was not a popular figure in South Africa; but nor was he in India where one reporter,[2] in summing up the tour, wrote that 'Lawry captained the side most efficiently. His bowling changes and field placing deserve the highest praise, if at times not his sportsmanship.'

In South Africa, he did not always speak publicly when it was normal for a captain to do so after matches, he did not impress reporters when he refused to make himself available for interviews, and some of his gestures and utterances did not endear him to local fans. Of course, the India campaign (which actually started in Ceylon[3] in mid-October 1969) had been a long and taxing one and ongoing defeats in South Africa placed the

[2] Rusi Modi, writing in the *Playfair Cricket Monthly* magazine, February 1970.
[3] Now Sri Lanka.

105

Australian captain under what was said to be extreme pressure. Not that South Africans cared. Ali got calls from old Springboks who had been thrashed by Australia back in the 1930s: 'Ali, don't let up, give it back to them!'

Bacher could sense that Lawry's Aussies were not happy campers. Cracks continued to show and one of their players, Keith Stackpole, suggested later that for the first time in his experience there was not total unity in an Australian team; furthermore, a few players apparently did not go along with Lawry's autocratic style of captaincy and his vice-captain Ian Chappell[4] did not live up to his captain's expectations.

When they arrived in South Africa, Lawry described Chappell as 'the greatest batsman in the world in all conditions'. In the nine Tests he played in South Africa between 1966-1970 his best score was 49;[5] he had a big heart, but it did not help him. The bottom line was that the Aussie batsmen simply could not cope with South Africa's fast bowlers. Of the 80 wickets they lost in the series, 52 were captured by Procter, Pollock and Barlow; and Procter's dominance was such that he accounted for half of these.

On the flipside, Australia's pace bowler of the decade, Graham McKenzie,[6] could take only one wicket in the entire series – one for 333 to be precise – and that just about tells the story of the Springbok batting. More to the point, four Springbok batsmen averaged over 50 (Pollock, Richards, Barlow and Irvine) and the first two had averages better than 70. For the Aussies, one batsman, Ian Redpath, averaged in the 40s. Ali won the toss in all four Tests, and batted first each time.

At the first team meeting before the first Test at Newlands, Trevor Goddard, the most senior player in the team, stood up and addressed his teammates. He told them that Bacher could expect his full support and that he hoped they would all follow his example. This was a great endorsement from the former Springbok captain and made the new skipper feel a lot more comfortable. Barlow as vice-captain also promised his total support and his performances underlined this: in the second Test at Kingsmead in Durban he joined the attack to take three wickets in nine

---

[4] Ian Chappell topped Australia's batting averages in India with 46.28.

[5] Chappell's highest score in eight innings in the 1970 series was 34 and his average 11.50. On the 1966-67 tour his top score in ten innings was 49 and his average 21.77.

[6] During the 1960s, Graham McKenzie became the youngest bowler to take 100, 150 and 200 Test wickets. In the five Tests alone in India in 1969-70, McKenzie bowled 222 overs and took 21 wickets.

balls; he re-entered the fray in the second innings to take three wickets in eleven balls; and in the next Test at the Wanderers he dismissed Australia's captain and vice-captain with successive deliveries. Tiger Lance, who at Ali's instigation was recalled to the team for the second Test, provided the final word on the Bacher-Barlow rivalry: 'I stood next to Eddie in the slips for a long time during that series and not once did he ever utter a single word of criticism against the captain. Whatever the Doc asked him to do, he did it without complaint. I think that says a lot about both those guys.'[7]

JOHNNY GLEESON WAS a country boy who came to first-class cricket at the Sydney Cricket Ground at the relatively advanced age of 28. The newspapers called him a mystery spin bowler because he bowled off breaks or leg breaks with equal facility without apparently changing his action. How he did this was to grip the ball between his thumb and folded middle finger and flick it out of his hand, this way, then that, in the manner of the original Australian mystery spinner Jack Iverson who baffled batsmen in the years immediately following the Second World War. Gleeson's right hand was so valuable to him that he insured it for $10 000.

He was highly effective under Lawry's captaincy in the series against West Indies and England but to a lesser extent in India where he was upstaged by his spin partner, the off-break bowler Ashley Mallett.[8] Nonetheless, the Aussie skipper resolved to project Gleeson as his trump card in South Africa. The tactic was simple: when Gleeson played against provincial teams, Lawry would immediately take him out of the attack when a recognised Test batsman came to the crease. Apart from denying them a sniff of his medicine, this had the effect of creating some apprehension in the South African camp.

In the first hour of the first Test, Lawry tossed the ball to Gleeson. Bacher was on strike, virtually opening the innings after the early dismissal of Goddard, and it was his dubious pleasure to become the first South African Test batsman to meet the 'Mystery Man'.

At this level of the game, batsmen find ways to 'read' bowlers to identify the type of delivery that is heading their way. A batsman like Barry Richards

---

[7] Tiger Lance interview, July 2003.
[8] Ashley Mallett was not a factor in the Test series in South Africa, taking six wickets to Gleeson's 19. Also, in the Australians' match against Western Province, Mike Procter hit Mallett for five sixes off successive balls. Mallett was the quietest man in the Australian team. His nickname was 'Rowdy'.

could spot the difference by the way the bowler gripped the ball, while others could tell from how it left the bowler's hand and/or spun through the air. There were also those who 'read' the ball off the pitch, which was a rather riskier business, particularly against a canny fellow like Gleeson. In his experience against spin bowlers, Ali would get an idea from the way the ball was spinning in the air after it had left the bowler's hand, but this time he did not have a clue what was coming.

'The most embarrassing time in my entire cricket career was when I faced the first two overs from Gleeson,' he says. 'I played the first ball as an off break, and it went the other way, right past me into wicketkeeper Brian Taber's gloves. The second ball I played for the leg break and it went the other way, into Taber's gloves. I then got a ball at my ankle, got the faintest of nicks, but Taber dropped the catch. It was such a faint nick that I don't think many people on the field even knew it was a chance.

'This went on for two overs. I felt like an absolute clown facing him. If someone could have shown me an underground tunnel to exit the ground, I would have disappeared down it.

'At the end of two overs, I told myself that if I carried on like this, playing and missing, I would become a laughing stock. In order to avoid further embarrassment, I decided to go on the attack. I thrust my front foot well down the pitch and started hoicking him over midwicket. Somehow it just kept working for me, and I ended up scoring 57.'

In the Springbok dressing room the amateur sleuths were all trying to solve the mystery of the Australian spin bowler. Ali was impressed that only one batsman – and the most junior one at that – seemed to have worked it all out in less than a day. Richards told his teammates that it was simple: if you could see one finger and the thumb, it was the off break; if you could see more than one finger over the top of the ball, it was the leg break. For what it is worth, Gleeson did not dismiss Richards once in the seven[9] innings he bowled to him; and the Springbok opener occupied the crease for long periods in compiling scores of 29, 32, 140, 65, 35, 81 and 126. 'Barry was so confident that he could read Gleeson,' says Ali, 'that he would go down the track to drive him . . . while the rest of us continued to play him from the crease.'

---

[9] As it turned out, these seven innings were all that Barry Richards played in Test cricket: a total of 508 runs at an average of 72.57.

BEFORE THE START of the Test, Peter Pollock quit smoking with the help of a hypnotist. He had not been bowling well, his rhythm seemed to have deserted him, and some of the critics were beginning to mutter. He resolved to get fit, practise like a Trojan and ensure that no critic could have justification in calling for his scalp. This was all well and good but Ali noticed that all he could talk about was that he had stopped smoking, and that this, he felt, was taking his mind off his cricket. He suggested to him that he would be better off smoking again: 'You do know what happened to Arnold Palmer when he gave up smoking? He lost his putting stroke.'

So Pollock started puffing again, the rhythm suddenly returned and he proceeded to take four wickets, including Lawry, Chappell and Walters. 'See what I told you,' said Ali afterwards. As a smoker himself during his playing days, Ali always had his game plan at his fingertips; that is to say, he used the back of his cigarette boxes to jot down his batting orders, fielding settings and other assorted information.

Pollock's four wickets in the first innings was a feat emulated by Procter in the second. There was a lot of debate around Bacher's decision not to enforce the follow-on but it turned out to be the right one, and South Africa completed its first victory at Newlands in 60 years and Australia its first defeat on the ground in seven visits. Victory came by a massive 170 runs and boosted the Springboks' confidence to such an extent that the margin of victory grew bigger and bigger as the series progressed.

THE SECOND TEST at Kingsmead – victory by an innings and 129 runs – was set up by a record total of 622 for nine declared which was remarkable for several things, including the fact that Ali had to be persuaded by some of his teammates to declare. He was quite intent on batting on, thoroughly enjoying the sight of the last wicket pair of Peter Pollock and John Traicos advancing the total by 42 runs before reluctantly calling a halt.

Traicos was another of the players who had been selected at Bacher's instigation. Like Lance, he had not played in the first Test, during which Ali had discussions with Arthur Coy, the convener of selectors, and asked for these changes. It said a lot for their relationship that Coy acceded to this request. Traicos was an off-spinner who was born in Egypt of Greek parents and raised in Rhodesia. As it turned out, his bowling was not really needed in the series, largely because of the dominance of the fast bowlers.

The conditions at Kingsmead were excellent, with a fast outfield and a good pitch. When he won the toss, Bacher had no hesitation in batting –

to which decision some thought there was more than met the eye. He had invited Lawry to toss earlier than usual, explaining that he wanted to get news of the match out on the radio in order to attract more people into the ground; he was already showing the media and marketing skills that characterised his management style in later years. Lawry saw no problem with this and the toss was conducted about an hour before the scheduled 10.30 start of play. In doing so, however, neither captain bothered to inform the umpires, Gordon Draper and Carl Coetzee, of their decision.

In recalling the incident, the Australian writer Mike Coward suggested that Lawry had been 'duped at the toss'. He wrote:

> No doubt relieved by his highest score in six Tests on the exhausting tour – a second innings 83 at Cape Town – Lawry was more relaxed in Durban and saw no reason to object when Bacher asked if they could toss earlier than was customary. As Lawry returned to the change rooms to inform his jaded and crestfallen bowlers that he had lost the toss and they needed to fix their bayonets and go over the top once more, Doug Walters suddenly exclaimed that the ground staff were mowing the pitch again. Lawry quickly returned to the middle in search of an official explanation.[10] To his chagrin, he learned that he had been duped by Bacher who had superior knowledge of the small print within the laws of the game and knew that the pitch could be mowed until 30 minutes before the start of play.[11]

At no stage did Lawry ever raise the matter with Ali but seven months later a report was published in the *Daily News* in Durban headlined *Kingsmead Incident Recalled: Bacher bears no blame, says Test match umpire.*

It was in response to fresh allegations made by Lawry that there had been 'sharp practice' on Bacher's part in the matter of the toss before the Test. Umpire Draper, who lived in Durban, felt that Lawry's claim demanded a response so he went public by issuing a statement which was the basis of the *Daily News* article. While he conceded that the Australian captain had every right to make critical comments, he felt that he as the umpire had to respond because there were now unfounded accusations of sharp practice and ulterior motive on the part of the South African captain. Draper pointed

---

[10] Taking grass off the pitch could be seen as giving an unfair advantage to the batting team.

[11] From *The Chappell Years, Cricket in the 70s* (ABC Books 2002).

out that the Playing Conditions for the 1970 tour were identical to those that governed the tour by Simpson's Australians three seasons earlier; and that 30 minutes prior to the commencement of play it was the umpires' duty to oversee the cutting and rolling of the pitch.

He added, 'Neither captain advised us that the toss had been done earlier and we were quite unaware of this when we supervised the mowing. What (grass) came off would not have filled a match box and would have had no bearing on the match.'[12]

What did have a major bearing on the match was the batsmanship of Graeme Pollock – who bludgeoned 274[13] to record the then highest individual score by a South African batsman in a Test match – and Richards whose 140 was described in one report as being 'as technically perfect as human artistry could make it'.

At lunch, Richards had scored 94 out of a total of 126 for two, coming maddeningly close to becoming the first batsman to score a century before lunch in a Test match in South Africa. Ali was bowled around his legs for nine in the over before lunch while trying to nudge a single to give Richards the strike. There was so much that was remarkable that day but the one aspect of it that was common to all accounts was the hour after lunch. It was then that Pollock and Richards were at their imperious best in adding 103 runs – Richards having moved to his century in 116 balls – in a manner that inspired their captain to say it was batting of a quality he would never see again.

All else paled against their performance; Barlow was out for a single, saying there was 'no price' batting after Pollock and Richards, but 'Bunter', of course, would find other ways to make his contribution, and he did so in spectacular fashion after Bacher had enforced the follow-on with a 465-run advantage. It was during the course of the afternoon on the fourth day, with the Australian batsmen grinding out what was shaping as a biggish total, that Ali was handed a telegram. It was from Barlow and it read, *PLEASE DOC, GIVE ME A BOWL!* It was an offer that was just too unique to

---

[12] Gordon Draper interview, July 2003.
[13] Graeme Pollock reached his second double-century in Test cricket in 284 balls with 32 fours and a five. His 274 included 177 runs in boundaries and bettered Jack McGlew's previous SA record 255 against New Zealand in 1952-53 and Dudley Nourse's 231 against Australia in 1935-36. In March 1999 Daryll Cullinan scored 275 not out against New Zealand at Auckland; in December 1999 Gary Kirsten scored 275 against England at Durban; and in July 2003 Graeme Smith scored 277 against England at Birmingham.

resist, so with the total 264 for five and the second new ball just ten overs old, Ali tossed the ball to the telegram sender. Eleven balls later, Australia were 268 for eight.

FOR THE THIRD Test at the Wanderers, Ali got what he reckoned was his strongest team after the recall of Denis Lindsay to replace Dennis Gamsy. For the second innings he changed the batting order, with Barlow promoted to open with Richards – and 'Bunter' responding with an innings of 110 – and Procter and Goddard at Nos 8 and 9 completing a dream batting line-up. Ali's scores were 30 and 15, but the depth of a happy team meant that there was always someone ready to take responsibility for scoring the runs. As for the bowlers, Pollock and Procter were devastating and dangerous, particularly with their over-zealous use of the bouncer on the bouncy Wanderers wicket, a tactic that drew some criticism. Pollock was clearly inspired by the super-fast and destructive Procter, bagging five wickets in the first innings from which the Aussies never recovered; victory for South Africa this time came by 307 runs.

Ali was impressed with his teammates, not just because they were performing so well – 'It was like everyone hit his peak at exactly the same time' – but because of their attitude. He was surrounded by some great players, and the absence of arrogance and self-importance was reassuring. It helped, of course, that they were captained by a down-to-earth skipper with no airs or graces who had the knack of bringing the best out in his men and making them want to 'be there' for the next man. For the rest of his days, he would modestly say that a monkey could easily have captained the 1970 South Africans – by this he meant they were so good they did not need a captain – but the truth is that a team of stars often achieves little without the right leader, and many of his illustrious teammates would confirm that point.

THE ONE SADNESS of the series was the omission of Goddard for the fourth and final Test. The 38-year-old had announced he would not be available to tour England in the coming South African winter, that his race was run; but many felt that with the Springboks already 3-0 up in the series the selectors could have given him a big send-off. By his own high standards, he had not had a very successful series – particularly with the bat – but his pinpoint left-arm seam bowling in the second innings of the Wanderers Test proved yet again his inestimable value; he took three wickets while conceding 27 runs in 26 overs. One of his victims was Ian Chappell whose square drive was taken by Lance at a close backward point position. Chappell thought the ball might have bounced so he asked, 'Did you catch it?' and Lance said 'Yes', so Chappell departed. Later someone told Chappell that the ball had indeed bounced. He confronted Tiger in the dressing room who explained, 'You asked me if I *caught it* – not if it *bounced!*' Later, Lance was to confide: 'He didn't have a good tour; I just put him out of his misery', which might have been true because Chappell had been labouring at the crease for three hours for his 34 runs.[14]

As it turned out, Goddard's last ball in Test cricket claimed a wicket when he dismissed Connolly – this time to a perfectly legitimate catch by Richards – to end the match. Taking all of this into account, his omission upset him and his teammates. They had been together through an extraordinary period and Goddard – South Africa's outstanding allrounder till the emergence of Barlow – was the senior player and a steadying influence. Ali had the utmost respect for him, a man who never smoked or drank and later became a church minister; and the captain had a tear in his eye when he called a team meeting to calm the emotions. He told the players his information was that Goddard had not been dropped in the strict sense of the word but that the selectors thought this a good opportunity to give his Natal teammate, Pat Trimborn, an outing ahead of the England tour. It was a rather sad end to a great career.[15]

THE FOURTH TEST in Port Elizabeth was a triumph for the triumvirate of Richards, Procter and Irvine, all of whom had their roots in Natal cricket. Procter blasted out nine Aussies, including six in the second innings, Richards scored 81 and 126 and the left-handed Irvine hit his maiden century. Trimborn also grabbed his chance by taking four wickets in the match, including the last one when Ali held the catch to remove Connolly. Little did the captain know it would be the last catch he would take in Test cricket, that Trimborn would never get to bowl in England, and that little Lee Irvine, celebrating his 26th birthday, would never have another chance in the Test arena – an exquisite young batsman who averaged over 50 in his only series.

---

[14] Tiger Lance interview, July 2003.
[15] Trevor Goddard was the only South African to score 2 000 runs and take 100 wickets in Test cricket – until the advent of Shaun Pollock and Jacques Kallis who would play considerably more Tests than his 41 and against a greater variety of countries. On two occasions he got more than 200 runs and 20 wickets in a series – in England in 1955 and against Simpson's Australians in 1966-67.

At the end of the Test, Bacher spoke to the crowd, but Lawry refused to leave the dressing room. It was left to the likeable Australian team manager Fred Bennett to do the honours, and he graciously acknowledged South Africa's superiority, which the critics agreed would have translated into 5-0 had there been a fifth Test.

'Was it the best South African team ever? I would have to think so,' says Ali. 'Jack Cheetham's team in 1952-53 were phenomenal when, against all expectations, they drew the series in Australia; but if I look at the calibre of the players in 1970 I think man for man it had to be the better team. I reckon that if you added Hugh Tayfield to that side it would have been the most complete South African team of all time.'

THE 1970 SPRINGBOKS would never play together again. At least, if nothing else, their legend was assured; and some people were lucky enough to see them play.

Chapter 9

The Greats Revisited

MUCH HAS BEEN said and written about those players who were part of a golden age of South African cricket, and almost without fail the discussions or essays on that period elevate two players – Graeme Pollock and Barry Richards – and the rest follow thereafter.

Now, as he reviewed[1] the cricketers who played under his captaincy, Ali Bacher made a new and significant assertion: 'We always talk about Graeme and Barry as the two real stars but I would like to revise that to say that there were *three* players in the same category – Graeme, Barry and Mike Procter – and to my mind they were the greatest cricketers produced by South Africa. People use the word "great" far too easily but these guys were great and that's no exaggeration.

'We need only remind ourselves of what Sir Donald Bradman said of two of them: he told me that Pollock was the greatest left-handed batsman of all time, marginally better than Sir Garfield Sobers, although he did of course acknowledge that Sobers was easily the best allrounder. Of Richards, he told me that he was the equal of Sir Leonard Hutton and Sir Jack Hobbs. If you go to England, the experts will tell you that Hobbs was the best batsman produced by that country.

'One of the key attributes of great batsmen is that they are perfectly still at the moment of delivery. This applied to both Graeme and Barry. They were absolutely still, and particularly Barry. We'd sometimes test

---

[1] Ali Bacher interview, January 2004.

him in the nets. The bowler would bring his arm over but wouldn't release the ball. Barry would not move an inch.

'Early on in his Test career, Graeme had an apparent weakness on the leg side. During the 1964-65 tour of South Africa by the MCC the English off-spinners David Allen and Fred Titmus contained him in the early Tests by directing their deliveries at his middle and leg stumps. In order to counter this, he developed a ferocious pull shot and a very good on drive.

'One thing that was absolutely certain about Graeme was that if you bowled a bad ball to him, it went for four. He was the first to use a heavy bat and his placement was terrific. Of all his magnificent strokes, he will always be remembered for his great cover drive; and he was able to execute it even if the ball was pitched halfway down the wicket.'

Ali was one of a select panel of 'selectors' who were invited by Wisden Cricketers Almanack to choose their five best players of the twentieth century for inclusion in the year 2000 edition. From all of those polled, the select five emerged as Donald Bradman, Garfield Sobers, Jack Hobbs, Vivian Richards and Shane Warne.

Ali had selected four of them but instead of Viv Richards he opted for Graeme Pollock. There cannot be higher praise than that, but how then does Barry Richards rate with Pollock?

'We shouldn't try to compare the two of them. Both were great players but very different in approach and style. From the first ball, Graeme was always positive, always looking for early runs, and able to score very quickly. Barry, on the other hand, was the most complete batsman I encountered. He could play off the back foot, he could play off the front foot; he could play to the off side and the on side, he could play spin and he could play pace. He could do it all and we knew that when he was motivated he would get a hundred.'

On Boxing Day in the late sixties, Transvaal were playing Natal in their traditional festive season match at the Wanderers, and Richards was taking the home side to the cleaners. Don Mackay-Coghill was halfway through an over to the Natal maestro when the Transvaal captain intervened. 'I stopped the game,' says Ali, 'and changed the field. I put five men on the leg side, including a leg gully, which is unheard of nowadays, and instructed Cogs to bowl a full inswinger at his leg stump. I can still see Barry sniggering at me at mid-off as Cogs approached the wicket. The delivery was spot on, Barry flicked the ball and it flew straight into the hands of Willie Kerr at leg gully – and that was the end of Barry Richards.

'We then travelled round the country telling everyone that we had sorted him out; that Richards was no longer a factor. We now arrive in Durban for the return match. Barry batting, Cogs bowling, I set the five-man leg side field. What does Barry do? He takes guard a foot outside the leg stump. Cogs has no option. He's got the new ball in his hand and he has to aim at the exposed stumps. It was easy for Barry; he just kept hitting him through the covers.'

Coghill would also recall Richards cutting him between the leg stump and the wicketkeeper.

'Barry was way ahead of us,' recalls Ali. 'It took him just one innings to figure out Johnny Gleeson: if he saw lots of fingers over the ball he played for the leg break; if he just saw the thumb and the forefinger, he played for the off break. He just went down the track to him and drove him through the covers.'

So much for Graeme and Barry; what of Mike Procter? Mention of the name conjures up vivid memories in Ali's mind. 'He was probably the most naturally talented of them all, an extraordinary cricketer. When he was 17 he was described by Jackie McGlew as not only good enough to play for Natal, but good enough for South Africa. Outside of Natal no one had heard of him and we thought Jackie was getting carried away. But, no, he was right. He was another Garry Sobers, not in the same class, but probably second to him.

'He bowled very, very fast with a whirlwind action. Some people thought he delivered off the wrong foot but in fact it was just his quick arm action that made it look like that. In spite of his express pace, he had the ability to swing the ball prodigiously. He bowled both kinds of inswing: the big "banana-like" delivery from the arm and the one that swung very late into the batsman. By way of variation, he would come around the wicket and get the ball to deviate away from the batsman. He was hostile and he had an enormous heart; even on slow wickets he would pound in, ball after ball. He was captaining Rhodesia at Salisbury (now Harare) in the mid-sixties, came around the wicket to me and hit me on the head.[2] I staggered towards gully and he came across to ask me if I was all right. I told him that my daughter Ann was faster than him. "Really?" he replied.

'He then lengthened his run-up and, again from round the wicket, he

---

[2] Bacher played all his cricket before the advent of the batsman's helmet. He was hit twice on the head during his career, the other occasion by Peter Pollock at the Wanderers when the ball ricocheted to the boundary and the umpire signalled four runs.

bowled me a second vicious bouncer. "Now how does that one compare with Ann's pace?" he asked.

'He could also bowl off spin. Against Rhodesia at Bulawayo, Proccie left us (Transvaal) to score 311 for victory. He dismissed Norman Feather-stone in his opening over but then Bubbles Bath and I took the total past the 100-mark without further loss. At this point Proccie brought himself back and switched to off breaks. He then had a 30-over spell in which he took eight[3] more wickets and bowled us out for 197 with his off spin.

'Batting-wise, he was a beautiful timer of the ball. In the 1965-66 season, Natal were in big trouble on 18 for four in reply to Transvaal's 290. I even suggested to Johnny Waite that we might enforce the follow-on. Procter, still 19 years old, came in and we never got another wicket that day. He and Berry Versfeld put on 289 for the fifth wicket and Proccie was unbeaten on 129, his maiden first-class century.'

As good a bowler as he was, Procter much preferred batting, and he scored runs in spectacular fashion, often at his best when the chips were down. He once scored six centuries in successive innings[4] to equal the world record of Don Bradman and C B Fry of Sussex and England.

Unlike many other fast bowlers who patrol the boundary, he was also an excellent slip fielder and close-to-the-wicket catcher.

'He was such a magnificent allround cricketer. I believe that given greater international exposure (he played only seven Tests, yet took 41 wickets at 15.02) in the seventies and early eighties, he would have eclipsed the Ian Bothams, the Imran Khans, the Richard Hadlees and the Kapil Devs as the second best allrounder of all time to Sobers.'

In making sure that this assessment was not unfair or unfounded, Ali studied the comparative career statistics of those four top allrounders of Procter's era: Botham, Imran, Hadlee and Kapil Dev. He discounted Test career records (where Procter's bowling average of 15.02 is far and away the best) on the basis that, for example, Procter played seven Tests against Kapil Dev's 131 and this was therefore not a true reflection. He also discounted first-class career records because these include Test appear-

---

[3] Procter's figures of nine for 71 in October 1972 were the best of a first-class career of 401 matches. The only batsman he did not dismiss was Ali Bacher who was out to the left-arm spin of Richie Kaschula for top score of 62.

[4] In successive innings for Rhodesia in 1970-71, Procter scored 119 vs Natal B, 129 vs Transvaal B, 107 vs Orange Free State, 174 vs North-Eastern Transvaal, 106 vs Griqualand West and 254 vs Western Province.

ances; although here, as a matter of interest, Procter's 48 centuries and 109 fifties are far superior to anyone on the list (Botham's 38 centuries and 97 fifties, Imran's 30 and 93, Kapil Dev's 18 and 56, and Hadlee's 14 and 59) and his bowling average of 19.53 is bettered only by Hadlee's 18.11.

On the basis of their careers in English county cricket, where they all played with distinction on what could be termed a level playing field, Kapil Dev has the best batting average (42.81) compared to Hadlee (39.09), Imran (38.44), Procter (36.17) and Botham (33.80), although Kapil Dev, for example, batted 64 times compared to Procter's 411; and in the bowling list Hadlee is tops with 14.50 and Procter second on 19.58. If the best way to judge allrounders is to compare the differential between their batting and bowling averages then Hadlee in county cricket lies first; but a straight comparison between Hadlee and Procter on the basis of their Test, first-class and county career averages combined gives Procter a better differential of 14.39 to Hadlee's 14.35 in the top two positions.

Could it be argued therefore that a fraction as tiny as 0.04 puts Procter second to Sobers? Statistically, the answer has to be yes; but emotionally there will be several schools of thought that will argue in a number of different ways. What is important is that Bacher's assessment is not far fetched, and in his heart of hearts he knows just how outstanding Procter was.

Talk of Sobers[5] opens up a new South African angle. When the great West Indian stopped playing county cricket, Nottinghamshire contracted Clive Rice in his place. Rice appeared in more first-class matches (482) than any other South African and was in the top echelon of world-class allrounders. Indeed, Ali singled him out as one of the outstanding allround cricketers he played with – along with Trevor Goddard, Eddie Barlow and Tiger Lance – and suggested that Rice was probably the most competitive of them all.

DURING THE 1970s, Bacher was persuaded by *The Star* in Johannesburg to produce a weekly column. This was ghost written by one of South Africa's favourite sportswriters, Michael Shafto, and they called it *Ali Bacher Opens Up*. In the manner of such things, Shafto suggested that Ali select his best

---

[5] Batting in Test matches, he averaged 57.78 and in first-class cricket 54.87; and his respective bowling averages were 34.03 and 27.74.

SA XI from the cricketers he had played with and against. He surprised some people when he omitted Roy McLean and Peter Pollock. In the middle order, he preferred Lee Irvine to McLean, and his opening bowlers were Neil Adcock and Peter Heine, who he called 'The Terrible Twins', whose strike rate was almost identical. In both choices he claimed justification and said some kind things about those he omitted: 'It may seem almost sacrilege to leave out a player like Peter Pollock, with more than 100 Test wickets to his credit . . .' and '. . . McLean, the darling of Kingsmead, was a magnificent cricketer. Anyone who could turn the tide of a game and make 100s in such quick time against the likes of Brian Statham, could not be anything else . . .'

Yet Ali had seen the 'unrealised potential' of Irvine once the little left-hander moved from Durban to Johannesburg before the 1969-70 campaign, the same season that Irvine was selected for South Africa. In his first season for Transvaal under Bacher's captaincy, he amassed 872 runs in nine matches and smashed three centuries – his best season. In his column in 1976, Ali made the point that he had seen every innings that Irvine had played in the five seasons they had played together and he selected him ahead of McLean because 'he is a batsman in the Pollock grade'.

To back up that assessment almost 30 years later, Ali asked the cricket statistician Andrew Samson to dig up the figures: of the leading run-scorers in first-class cricket in South Africa for those five seasons between 1969-70 and 1973-74 only Richards and Procter scored more runs than Irvine, and only Richards had a better average. Ali was heartened to learn this because, as he had pointed out, Irvine emerged during that period as a world-class batsman. 'His problem was that he played in an era dominated by two of the greatest batsmen the world had ever seen. In any other era, he would have been recognised as a top-class international batsman.'

For the record, Richards's average over those five summers was 75.76 and Irvine's was 52.88. Procter averaged 47.93, Barlow 45.70 and Pollock 45.37. Richards scored 5 000 runs (including 20 hundreds), Procter 3 739 (12 hundreds), Irvine 3 702 (13 hundreds), Barlow 3 108 (10 hundreds) and Pollock 2 904 (7 hundreds).

Irvine, of course, was more than just a dashing, nimble-footed batsman. He was a good wicketkeeper – nicknamed 'Bert' by his teammates after the dapper Aussie 'keeper of old, Bert Oldfield – and he was more than a useful seam bowler who was described by Ali as a man who could bowl cutters, swingers, yorkers and bumpers . . . a complete cricketer to be sure, whose only failings came when he was appointed Transvaal's captain in succession to Bacher and the province, having been dominant for several seasons, went into a slump.

Omitting Peter Pollock from his team in *The Star* in 1976 would not have been easy for Ali. Looking back, he points out that Pollock carried the South African attack for a major part of the sixties and was 'fast, aggressive, hostile and very successful . . .'

There again, he had huge respect for Adcock and Heine and felt he had to play them in tandem.

His team as published in 1976 was: Jackie McGlew (capt), Trevor Goddard, Barry Richards, Graeme Pollock, Lee Irvine, Eddie Barlow, Mike Procter, Johnny Waite, Hugh Tayfield, Peter Heine and Neil Adcock. 12th man – Colin Bland.

The one man he would love to have included was his trusty provincial lieutenant Don Mackay-Coghill – 'during the time that I played, the best cricketer not to play for South Africa' – but he already had a truly wonderful attack in Adcock, Heine, Procter, Goddard, Tayfield and Barlow that would have taken on any team in the world. It was the unfortunate lot of the left-arm Coghill that he played at a time of such bowling riches in South Africa. As we know, he was originally a top-order batsman who moved gradually down the order as his bowling took over. Initially he opened the bowling with his left-arm inswing to a field that included a leg slip and leg gully. Later in his career he developed the away swinger and also the leg-cutter with the older ball to a predominantly off side field.

Ali enjoyed Coghill for his 'BMT', or big match temperament. 'If there was nothing in the match, he was no good; but give him a needle match, a tight finish, and he would rise magnificently to the occasion. No one I knew was capable of such dramatic response to a challenge.'

Ali particularly remembered the time when Barlow, in his column in a Cape Town newspaper, criticised him and claimed it was 'boring' to play against Transvaal. It was a remark that upset him and, although he said nothing about it at the time, Coghill sensed that his skipper was hurt. When Barlow's Western Province arrived for their next match at the Wanderers, Coghill was so belligerent that he walked through the opposition dressing room, telling them exactly what he was going to do to them. Then he went out and took seven wickets, including Barlow's with a beauty that pitched on leg and hit the top of the off stump.

Coghill enjoyed landing the big fish, never more motivated than when bowling to the top batsmen. He reckoned Richards was his 'bunny' and match after match against Natal, as the ace opener walked in to bat, he would update him on the number of times he had dismissed him: 'Hello Barry, just to remind you that it's now up to number seven' . . . and with each succeeding game the count would increase . . . 'We're now up to number 10, Barry, in case you've forgotten . . .'

By the time his career ended in 1974, he had scalped Richards no fewer than 14 times which, in Transvaal folklore at least, is reckoned to be a record for any bowler anywhere.

Ali says of his great pal and vice-captain: 'We won the Currie Cup for five consecutive years and, although I am loath to acknowledge it to him, it is doubtful that we could have achieved it without him.'

PART II

NEW HORIZONS

Chapter 10

Politics and Private Practice

THE SEVENTIES BROUGHT revolution to the world of cricket. It was a decade when the players flexed their muscle to challenge the system for the first time, when the Gentleman's Game was taken over by an unruly generation of players of rebellious inclination, and when the frown of disapproval grew ever deeper on the forehead of the game's creaking Establishment. Yet it was a vibrant time when players emerged on the world stage who were so good that sportswriters coined a new word and called them 'Superstars'. This was not to say that they were necessarily better than the heroes of previous generations, but they were now being built up as marketable commodities in a game that was straining on the leash as commercialism beckoned.

They were exciting and exacting times that were characterised by a growing anticipation and apprehension that international cricket was about to undergo radical change; and South Africa, with the exception of the few individuals who were able to play their cricket abroad, was left out in the cold. For most of the cricketers of this beleaguered country it was not so much a dramatic decade as a deep trough of depression. International competition had dried up, the domestic game took precedence, and the warring factions in South African cricket administration became polarised under the heavy heel of apartheid.

In relation to the other three decades of his life in cricket, the seventies were the least memorable for Ali Bacher.

Given the fallout from the D'Oliveira affair, it should not have come as a surprise when the scheduled Springbok tour of England in the winter of

1970 was cancelled by English cricket authorities at the request of their government. The previous year, the MCC Council had voted unanimously in favour of it proceeding, and Ali had been holding out hope that it might take place. At that point, his team was arguably the best in the world but, because of apartheid, they would never play together again. That would be a great sadness for him but, in truth, he did not have a thorough understanding of the political problems bedevilling his country. He was not alone; the majority of white South Africans were living in a cocoon of ignorance or disinterest. Naively, they wondered why politics was being dragged into sport.

Ali did not question the advisability of touring England in 1970, just two years after the D'Oliveira affair, and he felt cheated when it was called off. He was, after all, a simple cricketer intent on doing his best for his country. There is no question that he was appalled by the iniquities of apartheid and was in the forefront, often the initiator, of public pronouncements against a system that barred black cricketers from provincial and national teams. But in hindsight he will admit that he and his fellow sympathisers were simply making the 'right noises' to articulate their opposition. The bland truth was that whites were conditioned to believe that the system was entrenched – backed by an inflexible political, bureaucratic and military machine – and that it was beyond their means to depose it. Ali admitted that as much as he was determined that apartheid should be abolished, he did not believe it would happen in his lifetime. Paradoxically, blacks in the liberation struggle were certain that it was only a matter of time before they would install democracy in their country. At the time, white South Africans had little or no contact with the black activists, otherwise they might have revised their conditioned thinking.

When it was still thought possible that his Springboks would tour England in 1970, Ali was surprised when Wilf Isaacs called to say that the prime minister wanted to see them. Isaacs had taken his private team to England earlier in the year, and their tour had been disrupted by anti-apartheid demonstrators under the leadership of Peter Hain. Earlier, too, Hain and the demonstrators had hounded the Springbok rugby team throughout its problematic tour of the British Isles.

Isaacs and Bacher travelled to Pretoria where they were ushered into the prime minister's office and, after a lengthy monologue by Isaacs about his own contributions to the cause of young cricketers, B J Vorster raised a bushy eyebrow and asked, 'Right, gentlemen, what can I do for you?'

Bacher was taken aback. It was his understanding from Isaacs that

Vorster had sent for them – not *them* seeking an audience – and when the prime minister sensed the hesitation he grabbed the initiative. He indicated that the Springbok captain should use the opportunity of touring England to voice support for the policies of the National Party government. Ali was angry at the way things had turned out. 'I'm sorry sir, but I cannot do that. I do not believe in the policies of the National Party.'

The meeting ended immediately, and there would be no more with the prime minister.

In 1970, Dr Ali Bacher decided to go into private practice as a general practitioner. He had discussed the possibility of a partnership but reckoned that option was too fraught with problems ranging from raising the upfront money to petty jealousies among partners. He decided to do it on his own, so with Shira as his receptionist he acquired rooms at Admiral's Court in Rosebank, Johannesburg. He would provide services at the following rates: R3 per consultation, R4.50 per house call, and R5.50 for a weekend visit.

The profession's code of conduct forbade doctors from advertising their services so new GPs had to be prepared to exercise a lot of patience. Dr Bacher opened his doors on a Saturday morning in March and waited . . . and waited . . . and waited. One patient came in that day, a young woman who had fainted in a downstairs shop that sold bridal wear. In time to come, the proprietor of the shop, Mavis Crote, would refer many more fainting brides to the grateful doctor; but in the mean time ways would have to be found to attract patients. Lee Irvine and his wife Helen, a close friend of Shira, would go to the rooms with a group of friends to pretend to be patients. 'We were trying to make the rooms look busier than they really were,' says Helen, 'and I remember that Ali's mother would arrive each day with sandwiches for her son and old magazines for the waiting room.'

Slowly, the patients started drifting in. The first of the cricketers was Sibley McAdam, who played for the Wanderers club; and he was followed by Hans Knuttel, a chef at the nearby Oxford Hotel, who later started his own catering business and became the chief caterer at the Wanderers stadium and for the big cricket functions in and around Johannesburg.

The Irvines, of course, became patients, and so too did Kevin McKenzie, another of his Transvaal teammates. Ali's opening batting partner Brian Bath had a BCom degree, so he did the doctor's books.

McKenzie recalls how his wife would take their little boys, Gavin and

Neil,[1] to the doctor. 'Ali was always so pleased when patients pitched up who were involved in cricket that he would almost forget the purpose of their visit and talk cricket all the time. Eventually, she would have to go and find his stethoscope and say, "Hey, Ali, would you *please* examine the kids!" There was also the time I came home from hockey with a splitting headache. It got so bad I called Ali and asked him to come and see me urgently. He pitched up and all he talked about was cricket – what I thought I should be doing next season, what he thought we should be planning on doing – and it's the middle of winter, the cricket season is six months away and I'm lying there feeling like I'm about to die. In between all of this, he keeps reaching for my cigarettes on the bedside table (Ali had a reputation for always smoking other people's cigarettes) and lighting up. After about six smokes and more cricket talk, he finally examined me and diagnosed that I was suffering from encephalitis.'

In order to make a living in his early years in practice, Ali performed locums and assisted specialists in surgery. One of these was Dr Clive Noble, an orthopaedic surgeon who became well known as a sports specialist. The medical practice at Admiral's Court began to thrive and eventually he was seeing up to 50 patients a day. In the mornings he would make his house calls, carefully drawing up a rough little map to arrive at the most practical sequence of appointments. One Sunday morning he was called out to 51 Sussex Road in a suburb of Johannesburg where the streets were named after English counties. At No 51, he found the front door open so, in the manner of GPs, he walked straight in and located the bedroom. It was the first time he was seeing this patient and, after introducing himself to the man lying in the bed, he began examining him. He then checked the medicine on the bedside table, wrote out a new prescription and handed it over. The patient gratefully accepted it and then asked, 'Who was it who asked you to come and see me?'

Dr Bacher answered, the man looked puzzled. A further exchange of questions and answers ensued.

'This is 51 Sussex Road, isn't it?'

'Oh no, this is 51 *Worcester Road.*'

Notwithstanding the funnier moments of his life as a general practitioner, Ali was by all accounts a very good and compassionate doctor. He was popular in the sporting fraternity and, apart from many cricketers and

---

[1] Neil McKenzie is a current South African Test cricketer.

their families, Highlands Park footballers were constantly under his professional care. His surgery became a place where they could discuss their personal problems and their football careers in the comfort of confidentiality. As the official team doctor, however, he felt obliged to pay special attention to anything that might affect the club. He was alarmed to hear of the amount of backstabbing that was going on among players and certain officials. How, he asked himself, could the team ever hope to succeed if people were sticking the knife into each other? Eddie Lewis, a former Manchester United player, was the team's new manager, and Bacher told him in confidence what the players were saying behind closed doors. Lewis was not a happy man. He, too, had become a victim of the backstabbing in a club that was troubled by power struggles. Lewis asked him to give his boys a pep talk. 'I had the greatest of respect for him and he was a comfort to me during a very unhappy time,' says Lewis. Drawing on all the skills he had acquired as a successful cricket captain, Bacher told the soccer players that they could never make headway as long the team was fractured by internecine battles. That year, Highlands finished second in the league and reached the final of the national knockout competition. 'Because of Ali's involvement at the club, I saw him more as a soccer official than a doctor,' says Lewis. 'One day he wanted to give me an injection but I was so afraid of needles that he ended up chasing me round his rooms!'

Bacher's own cricket teams were happy and united outfits that benefited from the individual attention he gave each of his players. 'He shouldn't have been a doctor,' says McKenzie. 'He should have been a psychiatrist.'

In September 1970, Bacher was invited to join a group of players to take part in a double-wicket tournament that traditionally heralded the start of the new cricket season in Rhodesia. Among the other South African players lined up for the two-day festival in Salisbury were Eddie Barlow, Barry Richards, Mike Procter, Lee Irvine and Don Mackay-Coghill – but the big catch was the world's greatest allrounder, Garry Sobers. He had played with Barlow in the England vs Rest of the World XI series that had been hastily arranged to replace the Springbok tour of England, and at Barlow's invitation the West Indies captain agreed to pay his first visit to southern Africa at an appearance fee of six hundred pounds. His partner would be Ali Bacher who he had never met before. At the pre-tournament reception, Coghill told Sobers: 'The organisers are very clever; they've totally nullified your ability by giving you Bacher as a partner!'

The point of a double-wicket tournament is that each player has to bat and bowl; and everyone knew that Ali couldn't bowl a hoop down a hill.

Most of the players thought it a good idea to pool the prize money and share it out equally, but Barlow, who was partnered by the Rhodesian and Springbok spin bowler Jackie du Preez, would hear nothing of it. 'Winner takes all!' he announced, and he aimed at winning.

Sobers was looking forward to the challenge, blissfully unaware of the hornet's nest that he had unwittingly stirred up. In fact, the 48 hours that he spent in Salisbury unleashed a hurricane. It started when a Barbados trade union criticised him for going to 'an area that is an offence to the dignity and character of West Indians'. It got worse when he had lunch with the Rhodesian prime minister, Ian Smith,[2] and described him as a great man to talk to. 'It was a personal opinion and had nothing to do with me playing cricket in Rhodesia, nor was it an opinion on his politics or his role as a leader,' wrote Sobers later.[3]

In his autobiography, Sobers says that before accepting the invitation, he checked that apartheid did not exist in that country and was assured this was the case; moreover, their national football team were all black and there was no discrimination in the selection of their sports teams. He was living in England at the time and was not aware of attitudes to Rhodesia in the Caribbean. The secretary of the West Indies Cricket Board issued a statement saying it was Sobers's decision and had nothing to do with the Board. The problem was that one of the West Indian prime ministers was at that very moment visiting Gambia in West Africa and telling his counterpart that they were blood brothers. The Gambian leader wondered how this could be when Sobers, a revered figure in world cricket, was lunching simultaneously with Smith, regarded in Gambia as a white supremacist.

The Caribbean erupted in rage and indignation. Forbes Burnham, prime minister of Guyana, said Sobers would not be welcome in his country until he apologised, and the Guyana Cricket Board demanded an apology from the cricketer. The Jamaican government demanded that he resign as captain of West Indies and other politicians jumped on to the bandwagon. India's prime minister Indira Gandhi said she would not allow the Indian team to visit West Indies until the matter had been sorted out.

---

[2] The international community regarded the Rhodesian government as illegal and racist, and the UN imposed economic sanctions on the country after Ian Smith unilaterally declared independence from Great Britain in 1965.
[3] Garry Sobers, *My Autobiography* (Headline 2002).

In his native Barbados at least, Sobers received support. His prime minister Errol Barrow, cut short a trip to the United States to return home to meet with Sobers after he had returned from Rhodesia. He was totally sympathetic, and wrote a letter to the West Indies Cricket Board that Sobers signed and which conveyed his sincere regrets for any embarrassment which his actions might have caused. Sobers was adamant, however, that he was not apologising. Later, various politicians who had stacked up against him admitted that they used the affair to score political points.

As for the tournament in Salisbury, Ali recalls: 'I'm told that when I bowled my first ball, Garry, standing behind me at mid-on, just shook his head.' Be that as it may, Bacher and Sobers were drawn to play Barlow and Du Preez in the last game of the round robin tournament. The situation was simple: Ali and Garry were out of the running for the first prize but, if they beat their opponents, they would deny them the winner-takes-all cheque.

'There's a bit of tension,' says Ali by way of understatement, 'and we bat first and total 32. Their plan is to block Garry and then score the runs off me. I bowl Eddie a lollipop, he tries to hit it into the Zambezi, but it goes straight up and he's caught. Jackie then goes on a big drive, hits the ball straight back to me, and he's out caught and bowled! Eddie is not impressed, I'm the hero of the day, and the other teams are so delighted that they form a guard of honour for Garry and me as we leave the field.'

Bacher found Sobers to be 'a great guy with no airs or graces' and years later the great West Indian would embrace him for his statesmanship in world cricket . . . but in September 1970 Sobers left Rhodesia vowing never to return.

When the new year dawned in 1971 Transvaal were in Cape Town for their traditional Currie Cup match against Western Province over the festive season. In Bacher's early years in provincial cricket Transvaal teams had a mental block about playing at the lovely Newlands Cricket Ground in the shadow of that part of Table Mountain called Devil's Peak. Ali recalls how on the train to Cape Town there would be a lot of negative talk which normally translated into defeat, or at best a draw, against opposition who were generally weaker than Transvaal and who were regularly thrashed when they played in Johannesburg. The Cape's notorious south-easterly wind would faze the opposition and the dry pitch would turn alarmingly. Ali would chuckle at the memory of Transvaal players looking for excuses not to play in Cape Town, and how a great fast bowler like Neil Adcock would 'suddenly pull a muscle before the game' because, if the truth be known, bowling on the flat and slow-paced Newlands wicket was not a prospect he savoured.

Over the new year of 1971, Transvaal readied themselves for a tough battle against the team that had shared the Currie Cup title with them the previous season. This game was very important – if Barlow's team won, they would probably go on to win the title, whereas Bacher was happy to settle for a draw because he knew his team would beat Western Province in the return match at the Wanderers, as they always did. On New Year's Day, Ali lost the toss for the first time in 17 matches. Barlow elected to bat and hit top score of 76 in a total of 326. On the Saturday, with the house full signs up, Ali and 'Bubbles' Bath opened the Transvaal innings. The fast bowler John Cawood was bowling with the new ball into the wind from the Kelvin Grove End. Ali hit the ball hard and it flew like a bullet to gully where Richard Morris took the catch; out for a duck in a disappointing total of 197. The next day was the traditional 'rest day', and it saw the mischievous Coghill 'taking bets around the country' that his captain would bag a pair for the first time in his career.

Monday dawned and, again facing Cawood but this time from the Wynberg End, Ali edged a delivery to Hylton Ackerman at second slip before he had opened his score. 'The ball went to him low, he claimed the catch and they all appealed. There was a cloud of dust gusting around so I wasn't certain myself that he had taken a clean catch. I wasn't going to walk unless I was sure. So I stuck around and the umpire said, "Not out". There was a lot of chat directed at me, and Bubbles walked down to my end. "You okay?" he asked.'

Bath recalls: 'There was a bit of a standoff between him and Barlow – you could say they were vigorously competitive – and I went to give him some moral support and he said to me, "Okay, I'll be all right now!"'

The next ball, however, was edged again and this time Bacher was caught fair and square by André Bruyns.

'Ali looked down the pitch at me,' says Bath, 'and winked with both eyes. That was Ali, he always winked with both eyes at the same time.'

Bacher continues: 'As I walked off the field with the crowd going mad, I spotted a beaming Cogs at the top of the dressing room stairs applauding me loudly every step of the way. "Well done," he laughed, "I'm proud of you!"'

After the match, Ackerman told Ali that the catch he had taken was a fair one; the ball had hit his boot and popped into his hands. Bacher confronted Coghill, 'You can say what you like, I'm the first player to bag a pair and be dismissed *three* times for nought in a first-class match!'

It might have been an embarrassing time for the skipper, but it was altogether a happy new year for Transvaal. Barlow's sporting declaration had set them a victory target of 295 in 270 minutes and they slumped to 185 for eight before the tail-enders mounted a stout rearguard action amid nail-biting tension in the closing overs to hold out for a draw. WP would have felt that they were robbed, but Ali's men had done enough to keep them in contention for the title.

THE SPIRIT AND competition in the Currie Cup remained of a high standard, but the cricketers of South Africa were losing patience with the politics. Before the cancellation of the England tour, the president of the SA Cricket Association, Jack Cheetham, had announced that future Springbok teams should be multiracial and selected on merit. Prime Minister Vorster told Cheetham to jump in a lake. Now the scheduled 1971-72 Springbok tour of Australia was approaching and SACA officially requested permission from the government to include two non-white players in the touring party. When Vorster rejected the request, the players decided to stage their own demonstration. In April 1971, as part of the Republic Festival, a Rest of South Africa XI played the Currie Cup champions, Transvaal, in a three-day match at Newlands, after which the Springbok team for Australia would be announced. Ali was unable to play. His medical practice was keeping him busy and he did not want to leave it for what was only a festival match. He was, however, in contact with the other players and expressed his solidarity with them. Mackay-Coghill would captain Transvaal.

The players' initial plan was to boycott the match in protest at their government's stand but after a group of them had consulted with Charles Fortune, a friend and father figure to all cricketers, it was decided to stage a walk-off instead. Coghill says Fortune was still in bed early on the morning of the opening day when he and the two Pollock brothers went to see him. 'He agreed with our sentiment but he was against a boycott because he felt the public should not be made to pay for the government's position.'

Mike Procter bowled the first ball to Barry Richards,[4] who was 'guesting' for Transvaal, he in turn pushed it away for a single; and the players then

---

[4] Richards had just concluded the first personal sponsorship in South African cricket and would earn R2 a run. The original plan was for him to pat the first ball back to Procter, but he deviated from it and took a single. Procter chided him, but he responded, 'That's two bucks in the bank!'

walked off the field. The ground was packed to capacity and four cabinet ministers were present. Confusion reigned. Coghill, as the batting captain, was under instructions to read out a statement in the press box and he duly did so:

> We cricketers feel that the time has come for an expression of our views. We fully support the South African Cricket Association's application to include non-whites on the tour of Australia if good enough and, furthermore, subscribe to merit being the only criterion on the cricket field.

That done, the players walked back and the match resumed. Afterwards the Springbok touring team was named: Ali Bacher (captain), Eddie Barlow,[5] Barry Richards, Anthony Biggs, Hylton Ackerman, Graeme Pollock, Lee Irvine, Denis Lindsay, Mike Procter, Peter Pollock, Pat Trimborn, Clive Rice, Graham Chevalier, Peter de Vaal and Vintcent van der Bijl.

Coghill was not surprised that his name was not among them. Eric Rowan, one of the selectors, saw him as one of the ringleaders of the walk-off and, after Coghill had read the statement to the media, Rowan snarled at him, 'That's it, you've just done your dash!'

Coghill says he was prepared to accept the consequences of his actions. 'Conscience-wise, I never sacrificed my principles.'[6]

If that was the reason for his non-selection, it was a spiteful one. Procter says he remembers telling an administrator, 'I hope you don't think this walk-off is just so that we can go on tour.' In other words, he was saying that the demonstration was a genuine protest against government policy, and he adds, 'My only regret is that we never did more to try to change things (because) the decision to cancel both tours (to England and Australia) was the right one. People said they were sorry for me because I didn't play more than my seven Test matches, but that was not the point. What was more important, one cricketer or 30 million people?'[7]

Did Ali think the Newlands walk-off would make any impact on apartheid sport? 'I never held out any hope of going to Australia. I always felt that we might get to England, but when that tour was cancelled, I realised it was the end of the road for us.'

---

[5] Eddie Barlow later withdrew and was replaced by Arthur Short.
[6] Don Mackay-Coghill interview, October 2003.
[7] Mike Procter interview, September 2003.

Chapter 11

Retirement

THE SEVENTIES MIGHT have been the least memorable decade for Ali Bacher, but it still changed the direction of his life. The medical practice was expanding, his daughters were growing up, Shira was pregnant with their third child David, and his priorities were shifting. After a dozen years of simply playing and enjoying the game, his perspectives began to alter, in some cases unconsciously, in significant ways.

In October 1973, he took the decision to retire from first-class cricket at the end of that season. The tour to Australia had been torpedoed, there was no prospect of international competition to maintain his interest, he was becoming distracted by the political situation, and he felt strangely ill at ease with his game. At the start of his provincial career, he could not wait for matches to begin and was never prone to nervousness in domestic cricket; now, in spite of all his experience out in the middle, he was growing more and more edgy. It reminded him of his Test debut at Lord's where it was understandable that a young cricketer would feel overwhelmed by the occasion. 'We were playing at Newlands over the new year of 1972-73. They got a 70-odd run lead on the first innings, and we basically had to bat out the whole of the third day to save the match. My nerves just got the better of me. I sat in the toilet for about 45 minutes before play started. I had never felt this way before and, although I scored 65 and we drew the match and went on to win the Currie Cup, I knew it was time to get out.'

His final taste of 'international' cricket in the South African context came during that season when Derrick Robins, a British cricket benefactor, brought his private team of mainly English professionals and a few Test players on a short tour. Leading Transvaal against the Robins XI, Ali scored 147, his first century in 15 months.

When, later that year, he announced his intention to retire at the end of the 1973-74 season, the news was received with sadness and some considerable opposition. A hard-hitting article in the *Sunday Express* said bluntly, 'Ali Bacher is unquestionably the most successful cricket captain produced in South Africa. He is retiring too soon.' The newspaper reminded him that the Robins XI was returning for a second tour in 1974-75 and that they were scheduled to play three matches against a SA Invitation XI (the Test team by another name). The *Express* insisted he should be there as captain.

In Ali's view, however, there was no turning back. Once he had made up his mind about something, he never changed it. He was already a member of the Transvaal Cricket Union board, was one of the provincial selectors, and was becoming so embroiled in problems off the field that he was losing his zest for the game on it. He had become a benefactor of cricket in the black townships and, having spotted the talents of an outstanding black schoolboy prospect, Edward Habane from the Eastern Cape, he personally arranged for him to move to Johannesburg for specialised coaching. He was also becoming more outspoken on the racial problems besetting the game; and voiced public criticism of the apathy of many whites on the question of merit selection.

In mid-1973, he was guest speaker at a Maccabi dinner where he asked: 'How many (white) players and administrators have made a concerted effort to watch blacks play, or have had frank discussions with them? No wonder the whites have failed to convince the blacks of their sincerity. Our cricketing future lies in their hands and theirs in ours . . .'

He had never been a political animal but his innate belief in basic human rights and the welfare of others was leading him unconsciously into the realm of his country's politics. By propagating genuine black advancement, as opposed to the cosmetic 'expansion' that the National Party would later embark upon, he was positioning himself in direct conflict with the policies of the apartheid regime.

When Ali announced his pending retirement, the *Rand Daily Mail* wrote in its top leader:

Ali Bacher has spoken with great poignancy about his retirement from first-class cricket. There is his admission that the intrusion of politics had blunted his enthusiasm for the game; instead of deriving joy from training and then competing keenly, he found his thoughts directed to all the problems off the field. This is the antithesis of what sport is all about, and Bacher's reaction is, sadly, only too understandable.

His final two matches, both against Natal under their new captain Barry Richards, are remembered for different reasons in an emotional climax to his career. Both teams were in line for the provincial 'double' of the Currie Cup and the Gillette Cup[1] and they would contest decisive matches over successive weekends in Johannesburg and Durban. In the first, his farewell game at the Wanderers, Ali led Transvaal to a nerve-racking 10-run win in the Gillette Cup Final. It had been an interesting day in which his tactical nous was again to the fore. 'When Natal batted second, the rain clouds began building up and it became very dark. Barry Richards and Henry Fotheringham were batting. If the match was left unfinished because of rain, they could win on a technicality as long as they didn't lose any more wickets, so Barry's tactic was to tell Henry that they should just block it out and wait for the rain. Our priority was to get through our overs as quickly as possible, so I brought on 'Bubbles' Bath to bowl his off breaks and we were rattling through the overs at about 22 an hour. It was a real chess game out there. Suddenly, the clouds started lifting and the threat of rain disappeared. Then Natal were under pressure and they started hitting out. With one over to go, they needed 18 runs with the last pair in.'

The final wicket fell with three balls to spare and fittingly it read: *Trimborn c Bacher b Coghill 4.* It was Mackay-Coghill's last match for Transvaal and, of course, Ali had entrusted the final over to his chief lieutenant, and then took the vital skied catch off him at mid-on. The Transvaal players celebrated their Gillette Cup triumph with a mixture of beers and tears as they bade farewell to 'Cogs'. The next weekend they would go to Durban for the match that would decide the Currie Cup, but they would do so without him because his work demanded that he attend an important meeting abroad.

It was on their home ground of Kingsmead that Natal took their revenge, thrashing their rivals by an innings and 48 runs to wrest back the trophy. Ali concedes that, on this occasion, his tactics backfired. 'We had to win outright to take the trophy and I elected to bat first on a perfect batting

---

[1] The popular 60 overs a side tournament was introduced four seasons earlier when South Africans got their first taste of limited overs cricket.

wicket which I believed would take turn later. We simply did not score enough runs in the first innings, and that was that.'

In his final first-class innings, Ali was out for 20, caught and bowled by the spinner Pelham Henwood; and he was given a standing ovation all the way back to the pavilion. It was a poignant moment for him, but he did not regret his decision to call it a day. Natal's giant fast bowler Vince van der Bijl recalls the presentation ceremony: 'Ali took the microphone (something he was not comfortable with because he was not a natural public speaker) and he told us, "You outbatted us, you outbowled us, you outfielded us, and to you Barry, I must say you outcaptained me." It really was quite touching, the humble way he delivered that little speech to end his career.'[2]

The cold statistics show that Ali Bacher was a very fine cricketer. In a first-class career spanning 1960-74, he played 120 matches, scored 7 894 runs at an average of 39.07 and hit 18 centuries and 45 fifties. In his 12 Tests he averaged 32.33 with six half-centuries; and was unlucky on at least two occasions not to score a Test century. In all, he took 110 catches and made one stumping.

- In 1972 he became the first batsman to score 5 000 runs in the Currie Cup, breaking Dudley Nourse's record of 4 478 runs. His career aggregate of 5 640 runs was a South African all-time record that stood until Barry Richards finally moved past it in 1975;
- His 6 183 first-class runs for Transvaal was a provincial record that was broken by Jimmy Cook 13 years after he retired;
- His 904 runs in 1968-69 was a Transvaal record that stood for ten years before Graeme Pollock broke it;
- His 72 captaincies for Transvaal was a record that stood for 16 seasons before it was bettered by Clive Rice;
- His 88 catches for Transvaal was a record that stood for ten seasons before Kevin McKenzie bettered it.

'If I had one regret, it was that I did not score a Test century. In a very tough provincial environment I got a century or two against bowlers – Adcock, Procter, Pollock – who, apart from Graham McKenzie, were better than any of the other fast bowlers I faced in Test cricket. In my humble

---

[2] Vince van der Bijl interview, October 2003.

opinion, I always believed that I had it in me to score a Test hundred, but it was not to be.'

Those who played with him and against him will testify to his humbleness and friendship, his courage as a batsman, and his exceptional and somewhat unorthodox style of captaincy. 'He would make things happen,' recalls Tiger Lance. 'Sometimes he would do funny things by way of bowling changes and so on, but when the other blokes said "what the hell's he doing now?" I'd tell them not to worry because he knew what he was doing – and he did.'

'Sometimes it seemed like luck, but almost always he would make the right moves,' says Mike Procter. 'He was a fierce competitor but there was never any animosity directed at the opposition if he lost. I played under three men who captained South Africa – Jackie McGlew, Peter van der Merwe and Ali Bacher – but if I was forced to make a choice, Ali would be my captain.'

'I would like to have played more under him,' says Denis Lindsay. 'What I always liked about him was that he respected the game of cricket and not once did he ever get into trouble or cause any incidents. He also had the total respect of his players. He knew them all like the back of his hand, and he expected you to give one hundred per cent. He was a private man, though, who would never allow you to get into his life. He kept you at arm's length. As a batsman, he was very underrated; just look at his record.'

Graeme Pollock agrees. 'People sometimes saw him only as a very successful captain and they tended to underestimate his own contributions as a specialist No 3 batsman who scored runs at vital stages. What I liked about him as a captain was that he played to win from ball one. He was a great motivator which was shown in the 1970 Springbok team where there were eleven very classy cricketers all wanting to do well for the team. There was a great team spirit.'

Peter Pollock recalls how he and Ali had spent some quality time together on the pebble beach of Brighton when they had a couple of days off on the 1965 tour of England. 'He had been going through a bit of a bad patch so we talked a lot, and I'd like to think I helped him. Then in 1970, people were suggesting that my days in cricket were over but he supported me wonderfully as my captain. He did for me in 1970 what I might have done for him in 1965. I had the greatest respect for Ali – and that's never changed.'

Lee Irvine, who succeeded Bacher as Transvaal's captain, believes the respect that Ali received from his teammates in the 1970 Springbok team stemmed from his unselfishness. 'He realised that he was batting with some guys who were on another planet – Pollock and Richards for example – and when he batted with them he spent most of the time ensuring that they got as much of the strike as possible. In feeding them the strike, he effectively limited his own chances. Also, the amazing thing about him was that he never trained. He played a couple of games of squash a week and when he was batting he got a lot of exercise because he ran so quickly and so often between the wickets. But he wouldn't for example do much running when we were training. I don't know, maybe it had something to do with the heart condition, the cholesterol problem, he knew he had.'

When Irvine first played for Natal against Transvaal, his first impression of Ali was that 'he was not a very friendly bloke' and that he behaved older than his age. For years, Irvine was convinced that he was much older than he really was. He was also intrigued by Bacher's leg-side technique. 'He hit most of his shots through mid-on. Once I remember him sweeping Pat Trimborn for four. It really was a most unusual shot.'

Irvine had one criticism of Ali's batting: that he tried to modify his closed left-hand grip to play more shots on the off side because he believed that the bowlers he was facing season after season were starting to work him out. Irvine did not think this was at all necessary because at Natal he had played with two fine batsmen, the Springboks Kim Elgie and Roy McLean, whose techniques were similar to Ali's and who remained highly effective throughout their careers without resorting to any alterations.

Don Mackay-Coghill probably knew him best. 'There were only three things in his life – cricket, medicine and his family. That was all he knew, all he wanted to know. Because of this narrow focus, he spent so much time thinking about the game. He was a very strong captain and his overwhelming ability was to motivate and to mould. He had an ability to get people behind him – he even had a way with Eddie Barlow – and he had an innate sense, something that he never cogitated, of getting people focused on the task at hand. If the Springboks had gone to England and Australia, there is no doubt that he would have been revered among the great Test captains.'

'Cricket was everything to him,' says Kevin McKenzie, 'and he gave everything for his players. He ruled with an iron fist but he was always fair. I was only a junior in his Transvaal team, but he gave me so much of his time. On the Sunday rest day during a match, he would call me to the nets. Only he would be there, and he would spend a couple of hours throwing down at me when he could have been doing something else.

People would later compliment me on my hook shot; but he taught me how to hook. One Sunday he threw down bouncer after bouncer at me until I got it right. I was due to face Procter the next day and he knew I would have to deal with the short stuff. The next day I scored quite a few runs. He was the best captain I ever had.'

'Bubbles' Bath played under Ali at Transvaal for seven seasons, and shared many big opening stands with him. 'People would ask me what we talked about during our mid-pitch conferences that took place after every over. Well, nine times out of ten we simply discussed where we would pinch the next single . . . nothing more profound than that. Earlier in his career Ali was a much more prolific scorer. In the end we both became more limited and spent our time just looking for singles.'

Bath gained many insights into Ali's personality. 'He was never the supremo; he never spoke down to anyone. He was always just part of the side but he earned enormous respect. You knew where to draw the line with him. If he asked a player to see him, he always gave very careful counselling. He might have given the impression that he was stern but this is not how he was.'

He also fondly recalls the fun he had playing in those Transvaal teams. 'There has never been another period in my life when I laughed so much. There was great humour in that side. I honestly cannot believe that any other team could have enjoyed such incredible camaraderie; you had to see it to believe it. We would joke about things that weren't worth a row of beans, and Ali would laugh his head off at the smallest thing.'

Bacher's own idiosyncrasies, his malapropisms and absent-mindedness, were a constant source of mirth to his teammates. He had absolutely no knowledge of, nor interest in, anything technological. He was known for his punctuality, but he once arrived late for the toss and McKenzie says he announced to the dressing room that 'the geyser blew up'.

'Gee,' someone asked, 'did it make a mess of the house?'

'Wotcha mean, the house? The geyser in my *car* blew up.'

He was referring, of course, to the radiator.

'In those days,' says McKenzie, 'we would wear suits when we travelled away. Ali pitched up one day in a very fashionable three-piece aubergine coloured suit, with matching shirt and tie and new shoes. We commented on his new outfit, and he said, "I've got four more in my suitcase". He then sat down and crossed his legs. He had forgotten to put on socks.'

'There was this amazing contrast in Ali as a man,' says Bath. 'He said he couldn't budget, he couldn't change a tyre on his motor car, he had difficulty keeping the blade of his bat open long enough to play a cover drive, and he laughed at his own limitations. In fact, he imposed these limitations on himself – his inability to do a lot of very simple things – and yet he had an unbelievable insight into how others operated and how to get the best out of them.'

Bath makes a telling point on Ali's awareness of the bigger problems around the game: 'On the political level at the age of 23 he had a basic understanding of these issues and at the heart of it was an appreciation of the dignity of the individual. While the average 23-year-old is certainly not busy looking at the dignity of other individuals, it was deeply embedded in him.

'He was 23 . . . and he was also 33.'

Chapter 12

Enter the Young Turks

Dr Ali Bacher was convinced that the only solution to South Africa's predicament was the abolition of apartheid. Moves were already under way to introduce so-called multiracial sport but these generally crashed headlong into the brick wall of apartheid legislation. It was obvious that the apartheid regime was disingenuous about real change.

He immersed himself in his new role as a cricket administrator, both as a board member and a selector. He largely stayed out of the political side where Joe Pamensky was involved in the initiatives at both national and provincial level to find common purpose with the government and the rival national cricket body, the SA Cricket Board of Control (Sacboc).

Don Mackay-Coghill followed Bacher on to the Transvaal Cricket Union (TCU) board where Coghill would become the ringleader of a failed coup by what Ali called the 'Young Turks'. These were players of recent vintage who believed new blood was needed on the board. The object of their interest, in particular, was Eric Rowan who they reckoned had become a disruptive and obstructive influence.

'In those days,' says Ali, 'we would use the Wits University club to get former players of our choice on to the board. Because of the nature of their set-up, Wits often found it difficult to send a delegate to annual meetings. We would then get them to agree to put up people who we suggested. Raymond White, for example, played for the Wanderers club but Johnny Waite was already their delegate; so we put Raymond up as the Wits delegate.'

The Young Turks held many meetings during the winter months to

143

plan their strategy; and even when Ali took Shira on holiday to Durban he would keep in constant touch with Coghill to find out how things were progressing. 'There were no cellphones, of course, so I would have to leave Shira on the beach and go back to the flat to use the phone. I had to tell her a white lie about my visits to the flat because Tuxie Teeger (her father) was on Eric's side on the board.'

Rowan, of course, was a wily and well-connected man and, at the eleventh hour, he got wind of the palace revolution. Just two days ahead of the annual meeting he and his allies plotted a counter-coup and the Young Turks, with the exception of Ali, were soundly defeated. Several years later, however, the new blood represented by Coghill, White, Brian Bath, Lee Irvine and Albie During would hold sway on the board.

In the mean time, however, there were more pressing issues. The buzzword of the seventies was 'normalisation', the process by which cricket officials attempted to get multiracial sport off the ground. The exercise, however, was anything but normal and it inspired the rallying cry in sport's anti-apartheid ranks of 'No normal sport in an abnormal society'.[1]

It was during this process that cricket would go head-to-head with the sports minister Dr Piet Koornhof, who took over the portfolio in March 1974 from a former Springbok rugby player, Frank Waring, and was a man of bizarre contradictions. In his doctoral thesis at Oxford – where he went as a Rhodes Scholar to study social anthropology – he postulated that the only solution to South Africa's problems lay in racial integration. 'It was crystal clear to me, I was outspoken on it and in the end I was right,' he says.[2]

From Oxford he returned to South Africa where, for his field studies, he spent 12 months living in a Zulu kraal, which he rated as one of the happiest periods of his life. All this happened only a few years after the National Party came to power in 1948 and began the process to institutionalise racial segregation; and it was this selfsame regime that Koornhof would later join as a cabinet minister who held a variety of portfolios. He explains this conundrum away by saying that the trick was to 'kill it (apartheid) from the inside' which, some might argue, did happen in the end, although this was hardly apparent amid the confusion of the 1970s.

---

[1] This famous rallying cry is variously attributed to the ANC's Dullah Omar, Sacboc president Hassan Howa and a sports journalist, Jimmy Atkins.
[2] Piet Koornhof interview, October 2003.

Koornhof became known for the promises he made about a bright new dawn for South African sport, and how those promises were systematically rendered hollow because of the apartheid regime of which he was a part. A cheerful optimist, he even went to Washington where he told the National Press Club: 'Apartheid is dead!'

His outspoken views resulted in some of his cabinet colleagues calling him a 'traitor and a communist' but on the question of his sports policy the MPs in the National Assembly were far more facetious. 'When I explained my sports policy in parliament, they thought I was joking; and when I was joking, they thought I was explaining the sports policy.'

He became caricatured as 'Piet Promises' and his sports policy would, indeed, have been a joke were the situation not so serious.

Bacher liked Koornhof as a person, but certainly not for the system he represented. He believed, like most, that the man's heart was in the right place and that he was far more enlightened than many of his cabinet colleagues. In trying to further his multiracial sports policy, he seemed to operate on an ad hoc basis, which gave rise to the view that no sports policy existed at all, and at times he secretly gave permission for mixed competition in the hope that the white electorate would not come to hear about it. He was ever conscious of his prime minister's warning that, whatever they did, they could not afford to lose votes.

Koornhof says his major problem was how to 'educate (right wing) voters who were reluctant to be educated' and, he adds, 'this was not something you could achieve before breakfast'.[3]

Shortly before he took over as sports minister, Koornhof held secret talks with Hassan Howa, president of Sacboc, an organisation committed to non-racial cricket and diametrically opposed to the whites-only SA Cricket Association (SACA). At this meeting, he told Howa of his three-year plan for mixed cricket which would include a 'multinational' team playing Australia in the first year, a 'merit selected' South African team playing New Zealand in the second, and fully integrated cricket from club to provincial level in the third. This all sounded very grand, but there was one glaring omission – his plans catered for whites, coloureds and Indians, but not black Africans.

The Transvaal Cricket Union (TCU), of which Bacher was a board member, pressed on with its own plans. Koornhof got wind of this and

[3] Piet Koornhof interview, October 2003.

summoned various TCU board members, including Ali, Mark Henning and Joe Pamensky, to Pretoria where he berated them. Henning recalls Koornhof sounding off for 90 minutes without interruption, at which point he tried to interject and was abruptly told by the minister, *'Hou jou bek!'* (Shut up!).

Henning says he came away from the meeting with the impression that Koornhof was adopting a heavy-handed approach in reaffirming the party line for the sake of it, but that privately he supported their initiative. 'He gave us a big wink' when he had finished his diatribe. Ali recalls vividly how Koornhof walked with them to his car afterwards and said, 'Chaps, well done, keep it up!' Bacher's view was that Koornhof felt compelled to castigate them in the meeting, only because another government official was present. Koornhof does not recall that particular meeting, but admits it would not have been out of character for him to privately give his blessing to multiracial moves. 'It was the only way,' he insists, and suggests that he personally was hamstrung by apartheid.

The TCU proceeded to arrange talks with the Sacboc-aligned Transvaal Cricket Federation with a view to integrating club cricket in the province. These plans initially floundered but later the Transvaal African Cricket Association was drawn in with the Federation and it was agreed that three Sacboc teams – Crescents, Kohinoor and Rangers – would play in the Premier League in the 1976-77 season. Several leading white cricketers joined these clubs in a show of solidarity, and Ali was one of them. He had a season as player-coach with Rangers.

A united front in South African cricket was still a very long way away, but amid all the confusion, the semblance of a seed had at least been planted. Other provinces followed Transvaal's example, but there were soon more problems. Sacboc was sharply divided on the issue, particularly in Howa's militant constituency in the Western Cape; and in other areas government bureaucrats simply cancelled matches involving different race groups. Mixed cricket seemed to imply that players of different races could play together in the same team – which happened in the Transvaal – but elsewhere the policy seemed to be that teams representing different race groups could play *against* each other but not as integrated teams. In Kimberley, police moved in to stop a multiracial trial match. The situation was further inflamed when the president of SACA, Billy Woodin, said: 'We and the minister agreed to club cricket matches between clubs of different race. We never agreed to multiracial clubs.' This statement did not help men like Pamensky who was at the forefront of negotiations with Sacboc

146

with a view to normalising cricket at all levels.

If there was a new official sports policy, it was being interpreted in an ad hoc fashion, and no one could be certain from one day to the next what was permissible and what was not. In some provinces, attempts to organise mixed race club cricket simply failed, were restarted, and failed again.

Like many people, Ali found the whole situation very bewildering and just another example of apartheid obfuscation; but he was happy to play for Rangers where he encountered some fine players and made new friends. He established a good relationship with Abdul Bhamjee, captain of the Sacboc-affiliated Transvaal team, and arranged for these players to practise in the Wanderers nets – a far cry from the rundown facilities they were used to – and also be his guests for dinner at the Bacher home. Ali was still playing club cricket for Balfour Park, now under the captaincy of Lee Irvine, and some officials of the club were none too impressed when he announced that he was moving across to Rangers. He explained that he was not *leaving* the club as such, but simply going to Rangers to help them through a transitional phase. He captained his new club and kept wicket at times; and, for only the second time in his career, he bagged a pair against West Rand when a provincial fast bowler, Marinus van Wyk, dismissed him for nought in each innings.

It was not the first time that Bacher was playing with cricketers from other race groups. As far back as 1 April 1961, in what some people in apartheid South Africa might have interpreted as an April Fool's joke, two teams – one white, one black – decided to play a match with little regard for the country's laws. It took place on the Natalspruit sports ground between John Waite's XI and Mr S A Haque's XI, and it featured players from the upper echelons of the game. Waite's team, for example, included nine players who were either Springboks or would become Springboks: Waite, Russell Endean, Ali Bacher, Syd O'Linn, Peter Carlstein, Mike Macaulay, Jackie Botten, Derek Varnals and Kenny Walter. The two other members were John Corbett and Graham Kemp.

Mr Haque's team might have included a couple of Springboks, had South Africa been a normal nation.

Sayed Abdul Haque was his community's best-loved sports organiser and benefactor. He would often pop into Waite's sports shop in central Johannesburg and on one such occasion, while he was purchasing badges, Waite learned that he had his own cricket team. Why not have a match? Both thought it a good idea. Waite asked Haque how good his team was in order to judge what sort of side he should select. 'Pick the best team you've got,' he replied ominously.[4]

So Waite did just that, and Haque selected the following side: Abdullah Rubidge, Samson Ntshekisa, Amien Variawa, Saaidin Kimmie, Osman Latha, Solly Chotia, Abdul Latief 'Tiffie' Barnes, Sallie 'Lobo' Abed, Judas Ndlovu, Ebrahim Akhalwaya and Abdul Bhamjee.

They played on a matting wicket on a dusty ground, and Waite's team lost by 20 runs. 'The result was not important,' he says. 'It was just a wonderful weekend's cricket and it showed how stupid the apartheid system was. They had some very good cricketers, and they beat us with some excellent fielding and bowling.'

The authorities turned a blind eye to the match, but Waite knew that an attempt to have regular games between the teams would probably be stopped. The return match never took place.

FIFTEEN YEARS LATER, moves were afoot to 'normalise' cricket throughout South Africa, but the mood in the country was hardly conducive to improved race relations. In the black townships, resentment of the injustices of apartheid was reaching boiling point and when, on 16 June 1976, thousands of Soweto school pupils marched in protest at the compulsory teaching of the Afrikaans language in their classes, the powder keg exploded and left 13 pupils dead from police bullets. The fury swept the country and by August 1976 a further 23 people had been killed in unrest in townships in the Western Cape.

Against this backdrop, cricket was making a semblance of progress. Meetings were taking place between the various cricket bodies which would culminate in the formation of the multiracial SA Cricket Union (SACU) in September 1977. Its first president was Johannesburg businessman Rashid Varachia who had succeeded Howa as president of Sacboc and had become his sworn enemy. When Varachia and other Sacboc people broke away to throw in their lot with SACA, they were labelled 'sellouts'; and Sacboc hardliners immediately established the SA Cricket Board (SACB) with Krish Mackerdhuj, an analytical chemist at the petroleum refineries in Durban, as its first president.

SACU[5] now claimed to represent the interests of all cricketers in South Africa and, under the heading *One Body at Last!* the *SA Cricket Annual*

---

[4] John Waite interview, July 2003.
[5] In the vernacular, SACU was pronounced 'Sarkoo' and SACB as 'Sackbee'.

148

naively declared that 'with cricket administration in South Africa now sorted out, those who rule the game overseas must surely start thinking seriously about South Africa's re-entry into Test cricket . . .'

In the view of Mackerdhuj and his SACB, cricket was hardly 'sorted out' and they immediately went on the offensive to convince the world that this was not so. SACU's counter-offensive was to send Varachia and his former SACA colleagues Joe Pamensky and Boon Wallace on a series of goodwill visits to speak to representatives of the Test-playing nations. These included meetings with officials from Pakistan, India and the West Indies which were all very cordial but not terribly productive. The trio did at least persuade the ICC – a body of which South Africa had ceased membership when prime minister Hendrik Verwoerd withdrew from the Commonwealth in 1961 – to send a fact-finding delegation to South Africa. This they did in 1978 but the three-man delegation were all representatives of the white bloc so their mission proved futile.

In keeping with developments at national level, the white provincial unions engaged their black counterparts and set up new bodies that were a mirror image of SACU. The Transvaal Cricket Council (TCC) was established with Mark Henning elected as its first chairman and Ali Bacher its vice-chairman. Its board included Varachia, Pamensky, and Ali's former teammates Waite, Mackay-Coghill, White and During.

There were further interesting developments that scratched the granite wall of apartheid; among them, the selection of several black players for a Transvaal Invitation XI and two of them, Morris Garda and Solly Chotia, being named for the Transvaal B team. In their communities, however, they were seen by many as 'sellouts'.

International cricket was also in upheaval. The Australian TV mogul Kerry Packer had formed a breakaway body called World Series Cricket (WSC) and dozens of the world's top players had defected from their national teams to join him. Packer was offering the players the kind of money they had only dreamed of to play in a series of televised 'Super Tests' featuring all the top cricketing nations. He had been inspired to unleash this crisis on the Establishment when his Channel Nine network failed to get the television rights to broadcast Tests under the auspices of the Australian Cricket Board (ACB).

Among his innovations was international cricket under floodlights and the players turning out in garish coloured clothing. South Africans were not exempt – Graeme Pollock, Eddie Barlow, Barry Richards, Mike Procter, Clive Rice, Garth le Roux and Denys Hobson all signed up as non-aligned players, but Pollock and Hobson were paid out without getting a chance to play because, unlike the other South Africans, they did not play county cricket in England. This curious logic was based on the governments of the West Indies, India and Pakistan informing Packer that their WSC players would not be allowed to play against cricketers who were 'based' in South Africa.

After an acrimonious series of court battles and bans being slapped on players, the Establishment had no option but to ensure that their Test cricketers would receive improved remuneration; and this would also become an issue in South Africa when WSC players returned home. Clive Rice, in particular, began demanding appearance fees and salaries for his fellow Transvaal players; and as captain of Nottinghamshire, a professional cricketer and one of the world's top allrounders his views could not be ignored in the wave of 'Player Power' that Packer had unleashed. Rice's outspokenness would have major repercussions at Transvaal, where he was accused of being a 'mercenary', and it represented the start of a process that would ultimately lead to a new professional dispensation in which Bacher would play a central role.

Ali's role now in the Transvaal set-up was as the new chairman of selectors; and his unorthodox methods were soon to the fore. On one occasion, he dropped three players – 'Jumbo' Klette, Miles Conte and Morris Garda – who had just scored 154, 101 and 54 respectively for the provincial B team against Griqualand West. 'They had been selected as stand-ins for three highly promising young players – Lee Barnard, Wynand van der Linden and Noel Day – who were writing university exams. We simply brought the youngsters back for the next game.'

THE *SA CRICKET ANNUAL*'s assumption that the formation of SACU had solved the country's cricketing problems was a view not shared in the international community. At a meeting of Commonwealth prime ministers at Gleneagles in Scotland in 1977, it was agreed to discourage any further sporting links with South Africa. Its signatories included all the Test-playing nations, including those from the 'white bloc' who were traditionally more sympathetic with their old 'World War ally'. The Gleneagles Agreement would thus be used as another important weapon in the fight against apartheid and would provide further ammunition in SACB's mounting fight with SACU.

The view was growing in white South African cricket circles that the only way out was to go the Packer route and effectively buy teams of international players. Having played and watched international cricket, white South Africans believed it was their fundamental right to continue to have such competition; so, amid the frustration, South African cricket became abuzz with rumour that waxed and waned, from where no one could always be sure, that plans for some form of Packer-style rebel circus were being hatched. Some cricket reporters seemed to exist solely on a diet of unsourced stories from unnamed (or unknown) informants that became embellished with revelations of secret meetings with players' agents and entrepreneurs. Contracts worth astronomical sums of money were reportedly being bandied about; and occasionally the name of some prominent foreign cricketer would emerge and soon thereafter he would issue an emphatic denial or even threats of litigation. It was a surreal world in South Africa in more ways than one; and everyone seemed trapped in the Koornhof conundrum.[6]

---

[6] After taking up several other portfolios in the cabinet, Dr Piet Koornhof later left to become South Africa's ambassador in Washington.

Chapter 13

Business and Bypass

ALI BACHER LOVED his work as a doctor. He was thankful that he had listened to Wilf Isaacs's advice all those years ago and not dropped out of medical school. To him, there was nothing more rewarding than to help people suffering from illness, and to deal with each patient on a personal basis in order to understand their individual needs and attempt to allay their fears.

Through this he came to understand the value of sound communication and the vital need for confidentiality. To keep a secret is a vexing problem, and often the temptation to break a confidence without considering the consequences can prove irresistible and damaging. Ali worked extremely hard on keeping his patients' secrets, and he also developed the skill of listening. They were to become two important characteristics of the way he approached all his working relationships for the rest of his life.

'I also learned about deprivation and desperation. I saw many patients afflicted with both; among them were many black folk who came to my rooms in a state of poor physical, mental and financial health.' They were treated with care and respect in return for a nominal fee, and sometimes for no charge at all.

He was liked and respected by his patients for his care and compassion, but, as much as he enjoyed what he was doing, the work was beginning to take its toll on his own health. By 1978, his practice was a big one by any yardstick. He was seeing up to 50 patients a day, each consultation and visit was unique, and the heavy workload was beginning to open up some telltale cracks. This was literally the case because the skin on his elbows, knees, scalp and the soles of his feet began to break out in angry eruptions.

The stress of the job, and of his getting too emotionally involved with his patients' problems, had brought on a condition called psoriasis.

Ali would roll up his sleeves to reveal itchy, scaly sores on his elbows, some of them at times oozing blood through ugly cracks. There was no known cure for it but he reasoned that changing his career path, perhaps working in a less stressful environment, might just alleviate the problem.

On a Sunday morning in 1979, Ali was playing tennis at the home of his eldest sister Mushe.[1] She was married to Issie Kirsh, a top businessman who had run a milling company with his brother Natie in Potchefstroom before moving to Johannesburg to diversify into new business ventures and the media industry. He and Natie, a tycoon who had moved to Swaziland to set up the headquarters of an impressive business empire, were joint majority shareholders in Metro Cash & Carry, a nationwide chain of wholesalers that serviced mainly small black-owned retailers. Natie told Ali that he was currently doing a deal with a large pharmaceutical company and was looking for someone to run this operation.

'How about you, Ali, wouldn't you like the job?'

Bacher did not take the offer seriously and replied, 'Why don't you make me an offer I can't refuse . . .'

Two days later, Natie Kirsh made his offer. Six weeks later, Dr Ali Bacher quit medicine and sold his practice at Admiral's Court. Taking everything into consideration, and particularly his stress-related condition, he resolved that it was probably a good idea to move on and change his lifestyle. He had no difficulty selling his practice in what he described as a break-even deal; and he now became managing director of Delta Distributors. 'I was ready to take on the world!'

Delta was a new company that was equally owned by SA Druggists and Metro Cash & Carry, and it manufactured patent medicines and distributed them through Metro and other wholesale outlets.

Dressed in a smart new suit and feeling rather important in his new life as a businessman, Ali duly moved into his office at SA Druggists, not far from his old medical practice in the smart suburb of Rosebank. On his desk, awaiting his expert opinion, was a thick document on market research that the company had commissioned. He picked it up and began reading.

---

[1] Mushe Kirsh has performed outstanding community work over decades in both South Africa and Israel.

Five minutes later he put it down again. 'I didn't have a clue what it was about,' he says. 'It was full of marketing jargon I had never seen before. It was all gibberish to me, totally confusing. I was floundering before I had even begun.'

He continued to struggle in this strange new world for several more months. Then three things emerged: Delta Distributors was not attaining its business projections; the market was not as big as originally forecast; and a company called Commercial Commodities went into liquidation. It was this company that turned out to be Delta and Ali's salvation. It had a factory at Heriotdale, an austere industrial area east of Johannesburg, and it produced and bottled in volume such products as methylated spirits, vinegar, bleach and benzine. It was, in Ali's estimation, a good business waiting for a good man; so Delta immediately bought it. He now diversified the business into the manufacture and distribution of household commodities. The takeover would necessitate a move, so he packed up in Rosebank and relocated to an office block in Heriotdale.

The working conditions at the factory and bottling plant were appalling. He had a staff of some 60 people in a rundown facility which he knew would have been closed down by the trade unions had they not been restricted by the apartheid government. He resolved that the only way to make life more bearable for his workers, who were mostly black, was to treat them as best he could. He became a popular boss and, what is more, he was now getting the hang of the commercial world.

His growing business acumen also received an invaluable boost from a surprising quarter. One floor up from his office he met up with an old boyhood pal, Manfred Frysh, who was the South African agent for a men's deodorant called Brüt, a major brand in the marketplace. Frysh, a paraplegic confined to a wheelchair after a horrific motor car accident, was an astute and creative businessman. He and Ali got on well and Manfred was happy to share his expertise with his old friend. Through his influence, Ali learned about graphic design, copyrights and the secrets of good marketing. He rolled up his sleeves and threw himself wholeheartedly into the work.

Through Metro Cash & Carry and other wholesalers, retailers were snapping up large volumes of Commercial Commodities' products; so, with the company growing at a remarkable rate, Ali resolved to diversify even further. He developed two more household products – a fabric softener called *Softpal* and a dish washing liquid he named *Ali's Magic Dishwasher*. He was now becoming a super salesman, personally making presentations to large retail outlets and opening doors for his company. At the Pick 'n

154

Pay Hypermarket at Boksburg on the East Rand he found himself in the office of its main buyer Peter Dove, a rising star in a nationwide chain that turned over millions of rands per day. Ali sat across the desk from Dove and took out his notes on which he had listed the cost prices, the mark-ups and the suggested selling prices of his goods. These were, of course, for his eyes only, but he had not reckoned on Dove's ability to read upside down. 'Your mark-up's too high,' the chief buyer bluntly told his startled visitor; and that was that. It was the start of an excellent business relationship, and by the end of the meeting Dove had ordered 5 000 bottles of *Softpal*. Ali was particularly proud of the new product in its flashy pink container and, excited at Dove's support, he sallied forth to set out a marketing promotion of the kind that Manfred had taught him. The strategy was simple: he persuaded Shira to take a few of her friends to the Hypermarket at month's end to 'hype up' the fabric softener with the customers. They patrolled the aisles of the huge shopping facility and extolled the virtues of *Softpal* to every housewife they encountered. They performed this function so well that Shira rushed home with the news that every bottle of *Softpal* had been sold on its first day in the market. Dove immediately doubled up on his order and decreed that *Softpal* would be given prime shelf position. 'I could not believe my good fortune,' says Ali. 'Products from the giant Lever Bros group, which traditionally dominated the market in household cleaners, were now being downgraded on to the lower shelf space.'

Lever Bros might well have been concerned after ACNielsen, the world's leading marketing information company, listed Commercial Commodities as having captured five per cent of the retail market. The ACNielsen ratings of retail measurement and consumer purchases were universally held to be above reproach, and the Durban-based Lever Bros was so concerned that they flew one of their top people to Johannesburg to find out what was going on.

A month later, Shira and her band of friends returned to the Hypermarket on yet another promotional mission. To their shock they found row after row of flashy pink bottles gathering dust on the prime position shelves. *Softpal* was not moving. What was up? Instead of a marketing promotion, they now patrolled the aisles on an exercise in market research. Why, they asked the consumers, were they not buying *Softpal*? The responses were unanimous: 'It's no good, it doesn't work!'

To his growing list of maxims, Ali wrote: 'You can't fool the public. If your product is no good, you'll be found out.' In the years ahead, he would apply this rule assiduously.

As for *Ali's Magic Dishwasher*, it was a reasonable product that was received in the marketplace as a better buy than *Softpal*. There was just one problem: a company called Royal Baking Powder advised Ali that they owned the registered trademark 'Magic' and that only their household cleaner *Gillette's Magic* had the right to use it; an interdict was issued on the basis that, in calling his dish washing liquid 'Magic', Commercial Commodities was infringing their trademark.

'I wasn't wedded to the name,' Ali says, 'but I had produced a lot of labelled stock and I needed to move it. I spoke to a trademark attorney, Owen Dean.'

Dean went back to Royal Baking Power and effectively told them to jump in a lake. He argued that Ali's use of the word 'Magic' was not confusingly similar. They refused to budge, so Dean advised Ali to alter the name of his product to read *Magio* instead of *Magic*; it would simply mean a little work with a felt-tipped pen to change the letter 'c' to 'o'.

Royal Baking Powder still would not accept it, claiming that changing 'Magic' to 'Magio' was not going far enough. Dean consulted with one of South Africa's foremost advocates, Sydney Kentridge QC, and their case was successfully argued in court. *Ali's Magio Dishwasher* could remain in the marketplace . . .[2]

It had been one of the more intriguing episodes in the hard grind of business, but with three years' experience of the ups and downs of the commercial world, Ali was still not sure that it was the place for him. It had been tough going learning the business and he had more or less been left alone by his principals to find his own way. It did not make him particularly happy. He had always had a good sense of timing and he felt the time to move on was fast approaching; among other things, the Heriotdale factory was dilapidated and he knew it would not be long before a new one would have to be found or built. He had no inkling where he might go, or what do; but he finally made his decision after a development involving one of his best clients, Chipkins, who regularly bought vinegar from him to supply to hotel chains and restaurants. When they informed him that a competitor had outpriced him, and that they could save a few

---

[2] In 2002, Dr Owen Dean and Clifford Green, the ICC Cricket World Cup 2003 lawyer of the law firm Edward Nathan & Friedland, worked closely with the Department of Trade and Industry on legislation to prevent ambush marketing during the event.

cents on his price of 89c per 5 litres, he knew he had had enough. To lose a customer for a trifling amount in a business that operated on the basis of high volume/low margin was the final straw. He contacted Natie Kirsh and suggested they sell the business.

He was happy with the thought of moving on, although he still had no idea where he would go. The three years with Delta Distributors and Commercial Commodities had been a new and demanding exercise, and he had learned a great deal. He felt that he had acquired important insights into marketing and promotion and had developed a good 'feel' for these fields. Perhaps he could find a job where he might utilise these disciplines . . .

It was June 1981. Ali was driving to work one morning and pondering his options. Suddenly he felt a very heavy, pressing pain in his chest. For five minutes the crushing ache persisted. He knew what was happening, and he was afraid. Seven years earlier, his father, Koppel Bacher, had dropped dead from a heart attack in the forecourt of a petrol station halfway between Durban and Johannesburg. Ali drove on to Heriotdale, walked stiffly into his office and picked up the phone. 'Harry, you've got to get a physician to see me.'

Dr Harry Phillips had been in the same class as Ali at medical school and was one of his best friends. He advised him to go immediately to the Rand Clinic and in the mean time would arrange for a physician to be on hand.

Ali spent the next two days in ICU. Blood tests and electrocardiograms revealed nothing. The diagnosis was pericarditis, an inflammation of the pericardium sac enclosing the heart; it was a condition that was not considered overly serious. The physician detected 'pericardial rub', which meant he could literally hear the inflammation through his stethoscope.

Dr Phillips was not happy with the diagnosis. He immediately called in a cardiologist, Dr John Benjamin. At King Edward VII School, John had escaped punishment for smoking when the prefect Ali Bacher could not find it within himself to cane the smaller boy. After their schooldays, John had again been a junior to Ali when they were at medical school.

Dr Benjamin went immediately to the clinic and checked out the details of the case. He was also not convinced that the diagnosis of pericarditis was correct. Worried, he contacted John Barlow, the esteemed Professor of Cardiology at Wits Medical School, outlined the case, and expressed his views and concerns. Professor Barlow was worried, too. He examined Ali and ordered further tests. All remained negative.

157

A month later, Professor Barlow ordered another stress cardiogram. For the first time, the graph changed. The diagnosis was now angina, a condition caused by momentary lack of blood supply to the heart muscle that is characterised by a sudden acute pain in the chest. There was clearly a blockage of sorts. He sent Ali for an angiogram to assess the arterial blockage status. It revealed an 80 per cent blockage. The coronary artery lumen was irreparably narrowed due to an accumulation of fatty deposits over the years.

Four days later, in the J G Strijdom Hospital,[3] Professor Robin Kinsley performed cardiac double-bypass surgery on Ali Bacher, aged 39. He had never had an operation before, and he was terrified. Heart surgery to the coronary arteries was also relatively rare at the time; and as this was one of the first double-bypass procedures performed in South Africa, it was uncommon enough to make front page news.

At 7 am they wheeled him into the operating theatre. As the anaesthetist readied himself, Ali wondered whether he would live to see another day.

'At about 11 pm I woke up and saw blurred lights. I stared hard at them in an attempt to work out where I was. After a while I could distinctly make out the twinkling lights of the western suburbs of Johannesburg. I was lying on my side staring out the window of my post-operative ward. I remember saying to myself "I'm alive, I've made it!" It had to be the most precious moment of my life.'[4]

It was a very emotional and trying time and his teenage daughter Ann felt overwhelmed by it all. 'This kind of operation was almost unheard of, and I knew how serious it was. The newspapers were full if it, and his ward reminded me of a florist's shop. It was a really tough time for my dad – he would have to spend six weeks on his back recuperating.'

---

[3] Now the Helen Joseph Hospital.
[4] Ali Bacher still visits Dr John Benjamin at Morningside Clinic for six-monthly check-ups.

PART III

EPIPHANY

In Yeoville, circa 1946, Rose Bacher has little Ali on her knee, with Issy and Mushe behind her and Yudel on the ground

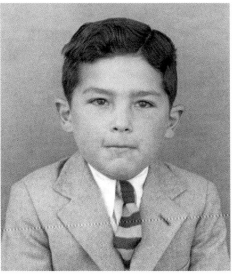

Ali in his first year at Yeoville Boys School

Aged 9, Ali, centre middle row with ball, captains his football team at Yeoville Boys School. Seated in the same row, far left, is Arnold Perkins and, far right, Graham Henning. The adults are messrs Green (headmaster), Srage (PTA), Geldenhuys (sports master) and Fisher (PTA)

Ali, third from left front row, is vice-captain of the SA Schools team in 1960. Next to him in the centre is the captain Nic Frangos and, far left front row, Graeme Pollock

The Bacher children, from left, Yudel, Mushe, Sorrel, Ali and Issy

Dr Ali Bacher on graduation day at the University of the Witwatersrand in 1967

On the day of his Springbok selection in 1965, Ali embraces his mother Rose and fiancée Shira as his future in-laws Tuxie and Nana Teeger look on during the unexpected celebrations at the Knox Street house

The 1965 Springbok team in England. Standing: Dennis Gamsy, Norman Crookes, Richard Dumbrill, Mike Macaulay, Herbert 'Tiger' Lance, Harry Bromfield, Atholl McKinnon, Jackie Botten, Ali Bacher, Mitch McLennan (scorer). Sitting: Denis Lindsay, Graeme Pollock, Peter van der Merwe (captain), Jack Plimsoll (manager), Eddie Barlow (vice-captain), Colin Bland, Peter Pollock

The Springbok team that beat Australia in the third Test at Kingsmead in January 1967. Standing: Jackie du Preez (12th man), Pat Trimborn, David Pithey, 'Tiger' Lance, Mike Procter, Ali Bacher. Sitting: Denis Lindsay, Trevor Goddard, Peter van der Merwe (captain), Bob Williams (manager), Eddie Barlow (vice-captain), Peter Pollock, Graeme Pollock

Photo: Charles Bird Studio, Durban

The Balfour Park club team that won the Transvaal Premier League in 1965-66. The player top right is Ali's brother Yudel, fourth from left middle row is Les Evans, seated are chairman Ruby Osrin, the Springboks Richard Dumbrill and Ali Bacher, vice-captain Lou Harris, Joe Hansen and president Tuxie Teeger. Behind Teeger is co-president Abe Levenstein.

Photo: Sid Cohen, Johannesburg

During 'Bacher's match' against the Australians at the Wanderers in November 1966, clockwise from top, Ali Bacher goes on the sweep during his record innings of 235; takes the 'catch of the decade' to dismiss Bob Cowper; and is chaired off the field by fans after Transvaal's famous victory   **Photos:** *Bacher private collection*

Arch-rivals and good teammates, Ali Bacher and Eddie Barlow, pictured at the Wanderers stadium with the old grandstand in the background **Photo:** *Courtesy Convocation Commentary, Wits University*

The all-conquering 1970 Springbok team pictured outside the Wanderers dressing room before another big victory over Australia. Standing: Brian Bath (12th man), John Traicos, Barry Richards, Mike Procter, 'Tiger' Lance, Denis Lindsay, Lee Irvine. Sitting: Graeme Pollock, Trevor Goddard, Ali Bacher (captain), Wilf Isaacs (manager), Eddie Barlow (vice-captain), Peter Pollock

Onto the Transvaal Cricket Union board for the first time in 1972, Ali Bacher is pictured third from left in the back row with Johnny Waite next to him, fourth left. Seated are Tuxie Teeger, Eric Rowan, Mark Henning (vice-chairman), Joe Pamensky (chairman), Jack Cheetham (president), Peter van der Merwe (treasurer) and Charlie Jones (manager)

The Transvaal team that clinched a fifth successive Currie Cup title in 1972-73. Standing: Doug Neilson, Viv Greve, Danny Becker, Jimmy Cook, Albie During, Clive Rice. Sitting: Robbie Muzzell, Don Mackay-Coghill, Ali Bacher (captain), Johnny Waite (manager), Lee Irvine, Ray White, Brian Bath **Photo:** *Commercial and Industrial Photographers, Durban*

Chapter 14

The Defining Moment

THE DEFINING MOMENT in Ali Bacher's life came while he lay in his hospital bed. It had nothing to do with his heart condition, nor was it about the operation or the great sense of relief when he realised that he was alive. No, it came in the library of St Stithians College where Don Mackay-Coghill had called a meeting. Four people, men who constituted the core sub-committee of the TCC board, attended it.

Coghill was by now vice-chairman of the TCC and he had organised the meeting because his chairman was lying desperately ill in the J G Strijdom hospital on the other side of town. The object of the meeting, however, was not to talk about the chairman. It was to discuss the health and future of Transvaal cricket.

The choice of venue was self-evident; Mark Henning was the rector at St Stithians, a sprawling Methodist Church school situated in acres of parkland at Randburg, north of Johannesburg. He was the chairman who Ali had succeeded the previous year and although he was no longer on the board, he was a man whose wise counsel was highly sought after.

Coghill was a visionary man. He had seen the fallout from the Packer revolution, and he had seen the future. Transvaal cricket needed to make an important decision, and there were two options that he placed on the table in the St Stithians College library. It really was quite simple: was Transvaal cricket going to remain in its semi-amateur, old fashioned mode, in which it was governed by men on a part-time basis for small honorariums; or was it going to grasp the nettle and set course on the modern road to professionalism?

As the biggest province in South Africa, and one that had all the potential to become the champion team again, Transvaal could point the way. He put it to his colleagues, Henning, Joe Pamensky and Jack Warner, the veteran Transvaal secretary and a former Test match umpire.

'I certainly knew which way we had to go,' says Coghill. 'If we remained amateur, we would start to lag behind the world and our cricket would stagnate. I made the point that professionalism didn't mean just paying the players. Crucially, in order to be really successful, we needed to establish a highly professional administration; and we needed to find the right guy to head it up on a full-time basis.'

The board members were doing a good job, Warner was in charge of the office in a full-time capacity, and the chairman had always been the focal point in all the decision making. What Coghill wanted was a man who could front up the cricket operation and take Transvaal to the top. In a game that was rapidly changing and becoming more demanding, it was a task that a part-time chairman and his board could not accomplish.

In his view there was only one man capable of doing the job: Bacher.

Pamensky had been involved in Transvaal cricket for 25 years. He was a former chairman and was now joint president of the TCC with Rashid Varachia. He agreed with Coghill, but wondered whether Ali would be available.

The previous day he had undergone major heart surgery, there was no clarity on the state of his health, and there was no certainty that he would be in a position to take on the job.

Coghill telephoned Shira to get her opinion. He was not going to trouble Ali before he had spoken to her. A day later, he and Shira visited the patient in the hospital's intensive care unit. He had staples running down his chest, pipes coming out of his body and when he saw them he cried. 'He was just so happy to be alive and I became very emotional too,' recalls Coghill. 'I thought it a good idea to get him to start focusing on the future and not to dwell on what he had just gone through. I knew that he wasn't happy doing what he was doing in business and that he was getting bogged down in the minutiae, the small things. He hated it because he is a big-picture person. I knew how much he loved cricket so, there and then, I put it to him about running Transvaal. He looked at me and said, "Jeez, Cogs, look at me. I'm lying in ICU, being held together with staples, there are pipes coming out of me all over the place and you come in with this proposal!" '

Clearly, he would have loved nothing better than to accept this extraordinary offer, but his recuperation was foremost in his mind.

Pamensky also visited Ali in ICU. They had been very close for many years and Ali put a high price on Joe's friendship and integrity. 'He was emotionally drained,' says Pamensky, 'and he was in tears when he told me that he was so grateful to be given a second life. He said there was nothing that he wanted more in life now than to be involved in cricket on a full-time basis. I assured him that we would work out the details of how best to sell the idea to the board.'

Pamensky saw himself as mentor to Bacher. A dozen years separated them in age and Pamensky had known and admired him since Ali's teenage playing days at Balfour Park. Pamensky had played his club cricket as a wicketkeeper-batsman for Wits University and Pirates, but he seemed more interested in administration and was first elected to the Transvaal board at the age of 25. He was a top accountant who established his reputation as managing director of the Schlesinger Group before starting his own business to provide personal financial services to the rich and famous.

Joe was one of Ali's 'Three Wise Men' – the others were Professor Michael Katz and Mervyn King – to whom he would turn whenever he needed guidance and advice on a variety of issues; and Ali had the highest regard for him as a cricket administrator.[1] 'He was a man for all seasons who, as an allround administrator, would have to be the best I encountered. He taught me a lot, particularly how to draw up contracts, which I was eventually able to do by myself. He was a very thorough man, brilliantly able to interpret the small print, and his eye for detail was unfailing. He went through the minutes of meetings with a fine toothcomb and refused to be rushed. As a chairman, he might have been a managing director's nightmare!'

Pamensky was essentially an admin man, an expert with figures, but he developed a strong network in the game, was elected a life member of the MCC, and could hold his own on cricketing issues. He was always proud to say that he numbered Sir Donald Bradman as a close, personal friend.

He and Coghill set about 'selling' their idea to the board. 'Essentially, we had to find a way to afford to employ Ali, so we came up with a formula

---

[1] In March 2003, Ali Bacher was instrumental in organising a gala banquet for Joe Pamensky and his family to honour him for his 50 years of service to Transvaal and South African cricket.

in which he would effectively pay for himself.'

What this meant was that Bacher would be given free rein to raise sponsorships for Transvaal cricket and, with new money coming in, the board would be able to pay him the equivalent of a managing director's salary. What this boiled down to, in effect, was that his financial security would be in direct relation to the amount of success he could bring to the province. He would assume duty as Director of Cricket at the beginning of the 1981-82 season at a starting salary of R3 000 per month. In addition, the board gave him permission to do private marketing and promotional work in order to augment his income.

Ali's recuperation was his first priority. In order to give the new job the attention it deserved, he would have to be physically and mentally strong. He would be eternally grateful to Drs Phillips and Benjamin and Professor Barlow for saving his life. 'If I had been discharged from hospital before Dr Phillips and Dr Benjamin saw me, would I be alive to tell this story? I doubt it.'

The crisis had given him an acute sense of his own mortality and affected him in a variety of different ways. When he returned to his desk at Delta Distributors four weeks after surgery, he found that his confidence had taken a knock and that he had also become quite aggressive. Uncharacteristically, he would become involved in confrontational flare-ups in business and cricket meetings. He was feeling insecure.

On the positive side, the life-threatening experience helped him break a debilitating habit. He had begun smoking whilst at medical school and had been a slave to the nicotine habit for more than 20 years. At Delta Distributors, he was smoking up to 60 cigarettes a day, and could not make an important telephone call or go into a business meeting before he had had a smoke. The onset of his heart condition forced him to give up smoking instantly and totally because, as he explained it, 'there aren't any ashtrays in ICU'.

On the question of his lack of confidence and aggressive tendencies, Ali resolved to practise some reverse psychology. As a boy, athletics was the one sport he particularly disliked and running around a field held no appeal for him. So, within six weeks of undergoing major surgery, he took up jogging because he hated the thought of it. The key, he reasoned, was to do it each day without fail, and to stick to the practice through rain or shine. In time, his jogging became an obsession. As regular as clockwork, each morning he would be on the road performing what affectionately became known as the 'Ali Shuffle'.

The practice would endure throughout his life and in the years ahead his sessions on the road would become something of a daily catharsis during which some of his most important ideas and decisions would be made. He would carry his ubiquitous cellphone in his pocket and think nothing of making instant phone calls on the road when he needed to discuss an issue or idea, or simply give an instruction. Those who were to work closely with him in cricket administration would become accustomed to hearing their slightly breathless boss on the other end of the line.

ONCE COMMERCIAL COMMODITIES had been sold, Bacher said farewell to business to take up his position at the Transvaal Cricket Council in October 1981. The first thing he did was to inform the new chairman, Don Mackay-Coghill, that he intended moving premises. For years the Transvaal cricket offices had been located in two rooms at Hatton Gardens in downtown Johannesburg but he could not understand 'how you can run cricket from the middle of town'. Hatton Gardens was miles away from the action of the Wanderers stadium and its rooms were becoming far too cramped. So the staff packed up and relocated to the Wanderers to take up premises where Johnny Waite and Syd O'Linn's old sports shop, L F Palmer, now stands. There was Jack Warner, now in the position of Director of Administration, Cathy Bray, a secretary who took the minutes at meetings, Edward Cebekulu, the general assistant, and Ruby Osrin, a retired Balfour Park stalwart who operated the switchboard. 'The only problem with Ruby,' laughs Ali, 'was that his vision was impaired and so he would constantly hit the wrong buttons.'

Bacher's first secretary was Aimée Swersky. She was a feisty young woman who, Ali says, 'bulldozed her way in and said she aimed to become MD of Transvaal cricket'. Over the years in Transvaal and later South African cricket, he had various other secretaries or personal assistants – Gilda Sasse, Daphne Bradbury, Diane Sime, Jenny Curnow, Sheena Knox, Annette Campbell and Bridget Sprague. Daphne worked for him for two spells, three years at Transvaal and two at the national body, but none of them stayed for more than three years at a time. 'They were all excellent contributors,' says Ali, 'but the pace and demands were very onerous, there were the early morning calls from me and often work to be done on Saturdays and Sundays. Any secretary who joined me never lasted more than three years maximum.' The notable exception was Niesha Green who joined him in March 1998 and remained his PA, even after he had left cricket.

PRIOR TO ASSUMING duties as the first full-time cricket administrator in South Africa, Ali formed a company that he called Century Promotions. Its function was to manage the private work that the board had granted him permission to do. He became the South African agent for a British manufactured bowling machine, which he sold to schools and clubs. 'I realised very quickly that there was a conflict of interests here. How could I be working full-time for Transvaal cricket and then approach teams in my private capacity to do cricket business with them from which I would benefit? Nine months later I personally took the decision that Century Promotions would cease to trade, and that the company would continue to exist in name only.'

This, however, did not prevent occasional negative connotations being attached to Bacher's now dormant company; and some years later, during the rebel cricket tours of South Africa, it became the object of interest of South Africa's most celebrated investigative journalist, Kitt Katzin. 'There were suggestions,' says Ali, 'that I was getting commissions on every player I signed and also taking kickbacks from vendors and food outlets at the stadium. This was absolute rubbish, but Katzin phoned me and asked me if we could meet. It was a drizzly, misty morning, I remember, and he was wearing a light brown trench coat. I thought to myself that he looked just like Columbo.'[2]

Katzin was an exceptional reporter for the *Sunday Express* who made his name during the so-called Info Scandal that had rocked South Africa in 1979, and which uncovered widespread corruption within the Department of Information of the apartheid regime and led to the resignation of Prime Minister Vorster.

He was a journalist who left no stone unturned and developed an exceptional network of contacts. Like the best of private eyes, he regularly 'got his man', but when he came after Bacher, he drew a blank. Ali never asked him who his source was (he would never have disclosed that, anyway) but he had strong suspicions about the person's identity which, he says, was later all but confirmed. Be that as it may, Katzin could find nothing untoward in Ali's dealings. 'I was pleased when the *Sunday Express* came out and refuted the allegations against me. During the rebel tours I was the chief negotiator and signed up on my own the Australians, the West Indies and the members of Mike Gatting's English team. I can say

---

[2] The name of an American private eye in a popular television series running at the time.

166

categorically that I have never asked for or received a single cent for any player I signed up or any business transactions – sponsorships and TV deals – related to cricket that I concluded. Even when I was offered a fee to deliver speeches, I insisted that the money be paid into cricket's development fund. I instructed my staff members that they must do the same.'

Mackay-Coghill, who took over as chairman upon Ali's full-time appointment and served in this capacity for the next five years, confirms Bacher's integrity. 'He was always a scrupulously honest man.'

EARLY IN HIS term at Transvaal cricket, Ali began forming strong relationships with the media. He befriended the cricket writers on the Johannesburg newspapers and made good contacts in radio and television. He also hosted weekly media briefings in his office and personally telephoned reporters to update them on developments. 'It was set out in my employment contract that one of my responsibilities was to promote and market the game. If I had an important story or item of cricket news, I wouldn't wait for the media to phone – I would be on to them immediately.' In this way he ensured that cricket got a better press than ever before. In doing this, he admits he took a leaf out of Abdul Bhamjee's book. Bhamjee was a good cricketer, but he was a better soccer official. He worked for the National Soccer League as its flamboyant public affairs manager and he had developed media relations into something of an art form. He was a showman par excellence and each Tuesday he would host a media conference at his offices in Johannesburg in which he played the starring role like some Las Vegas showman. Professional football attracted big sponsorships and it was Bhamjee's mission in life to sing his sponsors' praises at every opportunity. They adored him for the extraordinary amount of 'mileage' he gave them; the media, in turn, fell for his sheer effrontery and the number of stories – normally sponsor-related – that he handed them on a silver platter.

Ali's media briefings were not characterised by the same sort of hoopla, but his more subtle approach was no less effective. At one point, in fact, Bhamjee complained to a Johannesburg sports editor that his paper was giving too much coverage to cricket at the expense of soccer.

Coghill was delighted with the new course that Transvaal was steering with Bacher firmly at the helm. 'I had conceived the idea of turning Transvaal into a totally professional outfit – putting together a strong team of players, securing sponsorships, selling corporate suites at the stadium and having the best administration – but all the kudos must go to Ali. He put it all together.'

The working relationship, too, was excellent. 'I had zero problems with him on the board. He always kept me informed of what he was doing, and I let him get on with it.'

It did not take long before Ali was promoted from Director of Cricket to Managing Director of the TCC, again the first appointment of its kind in South Africa. Innovations under his direction came thick and fast. The first professional player contracts in South Africa were drawn up by a lawyer named Delano Chessler, a partner of Tuxie Teeger's; and these were used as the core contracts for Test players when South Africa re-entered international cricket ten years later, as well as the basis for contracts that some other Test-playing nations offered their players in the years ahead.

Sunday cricket was also introduced to South Africa at the Wanderers. Under the government's Sunday Observance Act, the playing of organised sport on the Sabbath was forbidden. By 'organised', the Act stated that gate money for entertainment events could not be taken on Sunday. 'Cogs came up with the idea,' says Ali, 'that we should find a way around this because there was great desire from the cricket public to watch their team on Sundays. 'We went to see Michael Katz[3] and he suggested we should form a Transvaal Supporters Club for members and their guests. The spectators would arrive at the stadium as usual, sign in and pay their membership; and that's how we started getting our biggest crowds on Sundays and the experiment became the norm. In a short time, people just bought their tickets like any other day.'

Another 'first' for South African cricket was the introduction of season tickets in various categories, which, in some cases, included lunch in a big marquee on the rugby field adjacent the stadium.

When, in December 1981, Rashid Varachia died of a heart attack after attending a sponsor's champagne breakfast in Johannesburg, Pamensky took over as president of SACU. His new deputy was Geoff Dakin, his old schoolmate from Port Elizabeth and president of the Eastern Province Cricket Union. And it was Dakin who began articulating the mutterings of cricket officials around the country who were becoming increasingly disenchanted with Transvaal's pre-eminence.

Just as rival American baseball clubs would come to hate the New York Yankees for their power, wealth and arrogance, so too did the other

---

[3] One of South Africa's foremost commercial lawyers.

provincial unions develop a distinct dislike for Transvaal for much the same reasons. And because of his position and growing influence, Ali had become synonymous with Transvaal's unpopularity. So, too, for that matter had the new skipper Clive Rice who had also developed an impressive media network and was constantly in the limelight. The cricket writers liked Rice because he was 'always good for a quote' and, if he wasn't sounding off at opposition teams, then he was sounding off at the Establishment. Rice called a spade a spade, as did Geoff Dakin. He blamed Ali for emasculating the other provinces by 'buying up' their star players; Ali, in turn, was adamant that he was doing nothing of the sort. Players, he said, were coming to Johannesburg of their own volition to explore better business opportunities in South Africa's biggest and richest city.

Dakin ignored Bacher's explanations and trotted out the names of those he believed had been 'bought' – Graeme Pollock and Rupert Hanley from Eastern Province, Henry Fotheringham from Natal; and he was furious when one of his star players, the fast bowler Etienne Schmidt, phoned him to say that Dr Bacher wanted him to play for Transvaal for more money than he could earn at Eastern Province. Dakin says he gave Ali 'a blast' and Schmidt remained in Port Elizabeth.

Dakin blamed Bacher for assembling a player base in the Transvaal that was the genesis of the all-conquering 'Mean Machine' of the 1980s; and in this way secured the best sponsorship deals at the expense of the national body and the other provinces. He cited a case of Ali negotiating a R250 000 sponsorship from the nationwide Checkers supermarket chain – and then even agreeing to brand his team 'Checkers Transvaal'. Dakin angrily pointed out that Checkers was a national brand and it had no business adopting one provincial team.

Transvaal's rivals complained that growth in the game was being concentrated in one area only, and this did have a ring of truth to it. Bacher had assembled at Transvaal the most powerful provincial team in South Africa and by the nature of things this had become the epicentre of national affairs. Also, given that Pamensky and Bacher were from Transvaal, that the team under Rice had mercilessly closed out the challenge of every other provincial team and, what's more, that they were backed by the most influential newspapers in the country, it was hardly surprising that the other provinces saw the Wanderers and everything it stood for as being rather too big for its boots.

It was at a function at the Wanderers Club that Dakin – who years later succeeded in shifting the power base of South African cricket from

Johannesburg to Port Elizabeth – rounded on the local cricket writers and, in typical strident and vocal fashion, accused them of being 'the Transvaal Mafia' who presumably answered to the 'Godfather' Ali. In truth, these ink-stained *'Mafiosi'* were very fond of Geoff Dakin, a big ramrod of a man who always looked like a million dollars. He could be overbearing at times, but they respected him for his loyalty to cricket, his knowledge of the game, and his willingness to give anyone, and particularly the players, the time of day. Behind his brash and bluff exterior lay a sensitive and soft-hearted man; but he would see red when he reckoned he was being upstaged. Dakin's view that the majority of the Johannesburg cricket writers were biased was only in keeping with the times: in the absence of a national team to unite the country, rank provincialism had fractured sport into warring factions based on the geography of its provinces. Indeed, Test match cricket of the twenty-first century would be highly envious of the size of the crowds that pitched up to watch provincial cricket in South Africa in the eighties.

It was easy to target Bacher as the man who made things happen, but was he to blame for turning Transvaal into the main cog of cricket's wheel? He had been empowered by the TCC to make the province the richest and the strongest; and he performed this role with single-minded commitment, and with the skills he had acquired during his sojourn in the world of commerce. He had learned a signal lesson from the *Softpal* experience – success could only be acquired by putting a product into the market that worked; and his new 'product' was Transvaal cricket.

The truth of the matter was that he virtually had the field to himself. There were no other full-time administrators operating elsewhere and, with professionalism still in its infancy, he had no real opposition. The closest to this was Eddie Barlow[4] who, while still captaining Western Province, had been appointed as that union's cricket promoter and organiser of contracts. Barlow, however, did not need to look elsewhere for talent. His best players were traditionally home-grown and loyal, the likes of Peter Kirsten, Allan Lamb, Garth le Roux and Steve Jefferies, and they had no intention of leaving Newlands or Cape Town – although Lamb did in time take the gap through the apartheid wall to become a Test player for England.

---

[4] Eddie Barlow retired from first-class cricket in 1983, ending his playing days at Boland, and then went on to become chairman of the short-lived SA Cricket Players Association, South Africa's 'roving sports ambassador' based in London, and unsuccessfully stood for parliament in opposition to the ruling National Party.

THE MAKINGS OF the 'Mean Machine' came with the arrival in Johannesburg of Pollock and Fotheringham. 'Graeme came up for business reasons and was talking about giving up the game,' recalls Ali. 'I went to see him after he had arrived and talked him out of it. He was still an excellent player and had a lot to offer. I suggested to him that this would be another challenge for him (to play for Transvaal) and that he would help us to draw the crowds. He was the key.'

Pollock confirms that cricket had nothing to do with his move to Johannesburg. He extended his cricket career for nine years with Transvaal, which he rates the most enjoyable of his 27 years in first-class cricket. 'It was the most professionally run outfit, and Ali Bacher was at the heart of it.'

Fotheringham was an opening batsman from Natal with an excellent pedigree when he was transferred on business to Johannesburg. 'He was a class batsman but he struggled at the start,' says Ali. 'I could see a mile off that he had no confidence, so to allay his fear of being dropped I guaranteed him three successive matches, without the other selectors knowing.' Fotheringham blossomed and would forge a long and memorable opening partnership with Jimmy Cook.

New developments in Transvaal came thick and fast. Bacher's appointment coincided with David Dyer being axed as the captain and opening batsman after he had led Transvaal to a hat-trick of triumphs in the previous three Datsun Shield limited overs finals. 'He was a good captain,' says Ali, 'but his batting had slumped. He took the opportunity to regain his form in the B team, but it didn't work for him.'

The captaincy now switched to the controversial Rice whose relationship with Bacher was as stormy as it was successful. They were both strong-willed characters who clashed on any number of issues. Rice's experiences as captain and top allrounder at Nottinghamshire, and then with Packer's WSC, had given him insights into cricket which did not necessarily coincide with the priorities at the Wanderers; but Bacher knew what he was getting when Rice was appointed captain. 'I wanted him because he was such a fierce competitor and led by example. He was a truly outstanding allrounder who in my opinion was in the Procter/Barlow/Goddard class and he was one of the most, if not *the* most, competitive cricketer that I had seen.'

As he had done as a captain, Bacher took a personal interest in all the players. Alan Kourie,[5] for example, was overweight; so to encourage him

---

[5] In the 1982-83 season, Alan Kourie took 63 first-class wickets in 13 matches.

to slim down Ali procured a personal sponsorship from a diet supplement company that would pay the big left-arm spinner rands per wicket – on condition that he lost weight and maintained it below a certain limit throughout the season. 'He would come into the office each week so we could weigh him,' says Ali, 'and he kept it up and did a great job.'

As the 'Mean Machine'[6] continued to take shape, it was decided that, for the first time in their history, Transvaal would hire an overseas professional. It had previously been a firm policy not to use foreign players on a regular basis, but the time had arrived to contract a world-class fast bowler. 'We also agreed that this player should be black,' says Ali, 'because that would heighten an awareness in what we were trying to achieve and also be an inspiration for the young black kids.'

Several names came up, but the man Transvaal wanted most was Imran Khan of Pakistan. Not only was he a world-class fast bowler, he was also among international cricket's leading allrounders. Imran and Bacher spoke on the phone, but the Pakistani declined the offer.

Ali phoned Rice, who was leading Nottinghamshire to their first County Championship title in 52 years; and he advised that there was a player available, but that he was a specialist left-handed batsman, and not a fast bowler. Rice had just played against Alvin Kallicharran in a Sunday League match when the little West Indies and Warwickshire batsman had scored a swashbuckling run-a-ball century. Ali telephoned David Brown, the former England fast bowler who had almost dismissed him first ball on Ali's Test debut at Lord's in 1965. They had become good friends and Brown was now manager of the Warwickshire team. Negotiations continued and, with Brown's support, the deal was done and Kallicharran left Birmingham under a veil of secrecy to prevent the anti-apartheid lobby from talking him out of it. Although apartheid was still entrenched, it had by now become permissible for black cricketers to play in South African provincial teams, but this was the first time that a foreign player would be one of them.

Kallicharran arrived in Johannesburg the day before Ali moved into his new office and Transvaal viewed it as a major coup. The Guyana-born batsman had played 66 Test matches, making his debut with a century against New Zealand in 1971, and captained West Indies during the exodus

---

[6] Under Clive Rice's captaincy, Transvaal won the Currie Cup five times in seven seasons, the Datsun Shield four years in a row, and the Benson & Hedges Night Series three times in its first four years.

of players to Packer's WSC when he was the only top West Indian to reject a contract offer.

Bacher took the diminutive cricketer under his wing. 'I arranged for him and his family to live in an apartment close to the Wanderers. This was a problem, because under the Group Areas Act, blacks were not allowed to take up tenancy in white apartment blocks; so I spoke to the owner and it was agreed that he could move in as long as we accepted responsibility in case of any problems. Fortunately, there weren't any.'

Ali also secured a rands-for-runs personal sponsorship for the West Indian from a company called Dashing Office Furniture whose managing director, Winky Ringo, asked the Johannesburg cricket writers to refer to his player as 'Dashing Kallicharran', a request that fell on deaf ears.

Ali and 'Kalli' became firm friends and they would meet for daily jogging sessions near the Wanderers stadium during which they would talk cricket. It was on one of these early morning runs that the seed was planted in Ali's mind to explore ways to recruit a West Indies Test-strength team to tour apartheid South Africa.

Chapter 15

'We're On Our Own'

SOUTH AFRICAN CRICKET was simply not big enough to afford the luxury of Ali Bacher working solely for Transvaal. In his former capacity as chairman of the Transvaal Cricket Council he had become a member of the SA Cricket Union board in 1981. Now, with his elevation to managing director of his provincial union, and thus being the only professional among part-time board members, his new role on the national body was redefined as 'special consultant'.

If individual provincial unions were jealous of the Transvaal success story, cricket as a whole saw great value in the way that Bacher had directed it.

Ali now joined Joe Pamensky and Geoff Dakin on their annual trips to London. Year after year, an SACU delegation would go there in the hope that the International Cricket Conference[1] (ICC) might give them a hearing and maybe a reprieve. Boon Wallace went, and Rashid Varachia too; now it became the turn of the new hierarchical trio – Pamensky, Dakin and Bacher – and the visits were as regular as clockwork, in June-July each year to coincide with the ICC's annual meeting; and each time they would be rebuffed by their friends with a 'sorry chaps, nothing doing at the moment, but keep on trying . . .'

---

[1] The International Cricket Conference was renamed the International Cricket Council in 1989. South Africa was a founder member in 1909 but ceased its membership when it left the Commonwealth in 1961.

They would then host their own media briefing – always courteously arranged so as not to conflict with the official ICC post-meeting press conference – at which they would bring the international media up to speed on cricket developments in South Africa, the dedication and sincerity of the cricket folk of their country and their disappointment at again being rejected by the international cricket community. Then they would traipse off home, empty-handed.

THEY WERE IN London now, having dinner with Doug Insole, Charles Palmer and George Mann, all of them top England cricket officials. They were all men of like mind but Insole felt his South African friends were lacking a crucial piece of understanding: the futility of coming to London each year to fight a losing battle.

Ali liked Insole[2] as an unambiguous man who played life like he played his cricket: in the words of a biographer,[3] he was 'a batsman with no frills but plenty of courage and resolution . . . his sense of humour and lack of pomposity kept the game in perspective'. Ali liked him because he spoke plainly. He told them that night: 'Until apartheid goes, you can forget about getting back into world cricket. England cannot support you. If we did, it would be the end of English cricket. The black nations would not play against us.'

Ali was depressed by this brutal truth and later that night he informed his two colleagues: 'I'm going home, we're wasting our time here.'

Dakin says that Ali would regularly pack up and go home when he felt things were not going their way but now, with straight talk from Insole, he could see the future . . . and the future was bleak. Nothing would change until apartheid disappeared and, in Ali's estimation, that would not happen in his lifetime. The grim reality for him was that there was not even a glimmer of light at the end of the tunnel.

The tragedy of the eighties in South Africa was that while President P W Botha was supposedly embarking on a reform programme of what he

---

[2] Doug Insole played first-class cricket between 1947-1963, captaining both Cambridge University and Essex. He played nine Tests for England and was vice-captain to Peter May in South Africa in 1956-57. He went on to become chairman of English cricket's ruling body, the Test and County Cricket Board, now called the England and Wales Cricket Board.
[3] Biographical source: *The Complete Who's Who of Test Cricketers* by Christopher Martin-Jenkins (Ernest Stanton Publishers 1980).

called 'power sharing'[4] by the races, he consistently excluded the black African from the bigger picture. His concessions to the other non-white race groups, however, were perceived by some whites to be so treacherous that the ruling National Party split and right-wing hawks flew off further to the right. In this theoretical climate of reform in South Africa, the reality was that Botha's security forces became a law unto themselves and more atrocities against anti-apartheid activists were perpetrated than at any other time. Most white South Africans would not have known this at the time, but they must have known that they were being governed by desperate people who were uncompromising in their ruthless subjugation of blacks. As much as Ali and like-minded people wanted apartheid dismantled, there was nothing he could do to change the status quo. Botha insisted that he would bring about change in the politics of his country, but he also showed signs of slinking back into his laager at the slightest hint of interference.

Bacher's beloved game was trapped in the middle of this calumny, and no one apart from him and his colleagues seemed to care if it withered and died. He and Joe and Geoff had tried to normalise the game as best they could in a divided country; they had tried to convince the world of their bona fides in promoting multiracial sport as best they could in a country shackled by its racial policies, but all they got was a slap in the face because, in reality, none of this was good enough.

'We can forget about getting back into world cricket through the front door,' Ali told the others. 'We're really on our own.'

It was in this climate that cricket's rebel era born; and through it Bacher would become both a loved and a hated man who was forced at times to compromise his principles in the name of his game; and in the midst of it all came his heartfelt statement: 'We are fighting for the survival of South African cricket, for the game that we love.'

As a full-time cricket administrator, it was his *job* to market and develop the game, and those who accused him of 'batting for apartheid' got it woefully wrong. The SACU operated on a system of checks and balances and, without exception, all the key people in the administration in those years would say that, whatever his failings, Bacher worked for one thing only . . . the well-being of cricket. There would come times when he would raise the ire of fellow officials by failing to follow protocol and the channels

---

[4] Botha instituted a Tricameral Parliament, in which there were separate governing Houses for Whites, Coloureds and Indians.

of consultation, and on one notable occasion act outside his mandate; but when the chips were down it was cricket that topped his agenda.

Mark Henning had observed Ali from the days when he taught him geography at KES to when they sat side by side on the Transvaal board. It was, says Henning, Bacher's drive and focus and pragmatism that were the reasons for his ongoing success. 'If he had political aspirations, he never showed them. Cricket was always the focus.'

THE SA CRICKET Union was single-minded in its objective, which Joe Pamensky spells out. 'We had to enable our cricketers who played in the domestic competitions to believe they could aspire to a higher level of competition and to provide them with opportunities to test themselves against international opposition. In our role as administrators we had to discharge our obligations to our players in this way and accept that the normal route of official tours was blocked. Admittedly, we were insensitive to the fact that there were people out there, people in South Africa, who did not want these tours to take place. We had no real understanding of their thinking and their situation because we were never in the political arena. It was sheltered from us.'

Henning's eloquence on the question of the politics is also revealing: 'We could hear Hassan Howa, but we couldn't understand. He and his colleagues were part of a bigger struggle, we were simply running cricket. What we lacked was a powerful liberal voice to say, "listen chaps, you're not thinking this through properly". We were good guys, we had respect for human dignity but . . .'

The unspoken part was a common problem among white South Africans: an insensitivity based on lack of understanding in the bubble they had created on the southern tip of Africa; and their reluctance to understand, perhaps the fear of finding out.

THE YEAR 1982 dawned with little new to offer on the cricket front other than Transvaal's dominance and the rampant provincialism of the domestic game. For most white South Africans, Test cricket between other nations held only limited appeal – except when Allan Lamb and the Smith brothers, Chris and Robin, were playing for England and Kepler Wessels for Australia – and there was some interest in the English county game where several South Africans were plying their trade.

A telling example of the frustrations was the resignation of Colin Bryden as senior cricket writer of the *Rand Daily Mail* (a plum job that was jealously guarded by its incumbents) after a fruitless and frustrating decade of covering cricket. There was nothing new to stir his blood by way of Tests or tours – and he had been waiting patiently for something to happen but, of course, it had not. He joined a public relations outfit run by an old friend Robin Binckes who, among other things, had the SACU account for promoting domestic tournaments.

Then, less than six months after quitting his newspaper job because he saw no future in cricket writing, Bryden[5] found himself one Sunday morning in February 1982 phoning the Johannesburg-based cricket writers on his media list. He invited them to attend a press conference that afternoon at the Balalaika Hotel, but would not say what it was about. This was most unusual because even Ali Bacher did not call Sunday press conferences.

An hour before the conference a local radio station broadcast a London report that a group of English cricketers were believed to be on their way to South Africa for what might be a ban-breaking tour. Details were very sketchy. The new cricket writer of the *Rand Daily Mail*[6] arrived at the hotel on schedule. As he parked his car, a kombi pulled up alongside. The doors slid open and several men spilled out. The journalist glanced in their direction, and then took a long and harder look. He recognised them as being among the England Test cricketers whose names he had heard mentioned on the radio an hour earlier.

The next day, every newspaper in South Africa reported the sensational front-page news that twelve English cricketers had signed to play three four-day 'Test' matches and three one-day internationals in South Africa.

Seven of the players – Geoff Boycott of Yorkshire, Alan Knott and Derek Underwood of Kent (the man they called 'Deadly' who was the unknown bowler that Ali could not remember playing against in 1965), Dennis Amiss of Warwickshire, Graham Gooch of Essex, and John Emburey of Middlesex – had arrived in Johannesburg on the Saturday and when the cricket writer saw them on his arrival at the Balalaika Hotel on the Sunday, they had just returned from their first net practice. The rest of the team, including the Kent and England batsman Bob Woolmer, would join them later. Four of the players – Boycott, Gooch, Emburey and Underwood – had been on the recent England tour of India and Sri Lanka.

---

[5] Colin Bryden returned to journalism upon South Africa's re-entry to international cricket and is currently cricket correspondent of the *Sunday Times* and editor of the *SA Cricket Annual*.

[6] Rodney Hartman succeeded Colin Bryden as *RDM* cricket writer in September 1981 and remained on the newspaper until its closure in 1985.

Alvin Kallicharran was initially part of the team although he never officially joined it. He had made his home in Birmingham and was England-qualified, but he was released before the first match because it was felt that his presence would diminish the team's all-English status.

In the wake of the immediate outcry from the rest of the cricket-playing world, Graham Gooch, the captain, declared: 'We stand by our decision to come and play here. We want to play and encourage multiracial sport in South Africa.'

Pamensky praised the players for 'the stand they had taken against the hypocrisy and double standards that have kept South African cricketers from taking their rightful place in the international cricket community'. The players, he said, had risked their future careers – a statement that was soon borne out when the Test and County Cricket Board (TCCB) banned them from international competition for three years.

The main opposition to the tour came from England where the team was immediately dubbed 'The Dirty Dozen' and Britain's shadow environment secretary Gerald Kaufman emotively suggested that the players were 'selling themselves for blood-covered Krugerrands'. The British prime minister Margaret Thatcher was inevitably drawn into the controversy: 'We do not have the power to prevent our sportsmen and women visiting South Africa, or anywhere else. If we did, we would no longer be a free country . . .'

The chairman of the TCCB was George Mann. He personally contacted Pamensky and asked him to call off the tour. In return, he promised that England would propose South Africa's re-admission to the ICC. Pamensky said no. He would not have forgotten what Insole had told him and his colleagues in Mann's company over dinner in London.

In South Africa, life proceeded as normal inside the bubble. All black political parties or movements who were opposed to the racist policies of the Nationalist government were banned, their leaders in prison or in exile, and influential black voices that would have objected were gagged by apartheid laws that prevented the media from quoting them.[7] A few SA Cricket Board officials made anti-tour statements that were largely ignored, and the white-owned newspapers, including the liberal *Rand Daily Mail*,

---

[7] The SA government had a 'banned persons register' that gained new entries by the day: it included everyone who had been prosecuted under the apartheid laws or who was under suspicion or on the wanted list. In essence, no one of any stature in the liberation struggle – members of the ANC, PAC or SA Communist Party – could be quoted in the media and editors and reporters faced jail if they risked doing so.

were generally supportive. Gooch and his men must have wondered what all the fuss was about.

Around the cricket grounds of South Africa there was great excitement and anticipation, but, in spite of the SACU's claim to being multiracial, the spectators remained largely white. This was not altogether surprising because the South African cricket team was exclusively white and the majority of black players were committed to the SACB and therefore had no stage on which to perform.

The SACU insisted that whatever it was doing had nothing to do with propping up the apartheid regime. Pamensky recounts being told in confidence by officials from black cricket nations during his visits to London: 'If we were South Africans we would either (a) not become cricket administrators or (b) do the same as you!'

Ali played no part in organising this tour. 'I was intrigued by it but I really had nothing to do with it – other than chair the national selection panel that chose the South African team.'

The chief organiser was Peter Cooke, a Lancashire-born league cricketer who had lived in South Africa for most of his life. He had befriended Geoff Boycott on his stopover in Johannesburg ahead of England's 1981 tour of the Caribbean. Their initial discussions inspired Cooke to travel to the West Indies where he met all the England players around the pool at the Trinidad Hilton in mid-February 1981. By the time he returned home he had firm written commitments – on Hilton Hotel letterheads – from virtually the entire touring party. The initial plan was that they should tour South Africa immediately after the West Indies visit but it was not until the next winter's tour of India and Sri Lanka that details were finalised. A fictitious company, Oxychem Ltd, was established prior to the India tour and the undercover plan was codenamed 'Operation Chess Match' and a system of chess-related codewords and names devised. By this stage Cooke had taken to making regular visits to England to negotiate with players and was in regular telephone contact with the cricketers touring India. Boycott took on the role as chief recruiting officer and nominal captain of the team but later, for a variety of personal reasons, he cooled to the whole idea and it took some considerable pressure from Cooke to ensure that he finally travelled to South Africa. In spite of this, and notwithstanding his decision not to captain the side, Boycott was the key to the tour. 'Without Geoff, it would not have happened,' Cooke admitted later; and Pamensky confirms that Boycott got paid more than any of his teammates.

After initial problems with would-be sponsors, SA Breweries agreed at the eleventh hour to underwrite the tour of the SAB English XI, as it was officially known. In addition to this, the Breweries made available R100 000 for the development of cricket which it defined as 'assisting the game on a non-racial basis at grass roots level in providing coaching and facilities for young cricketers'.

Ali's selection panel chose Mike Procter to captain South Africa and, for the first time in twelve years, the players were awarded Springbok colours. Before the start of the first one-day international at a packed St George's Park, Ali had a lump in his throat as he watched his old 1970 teammates – Mike Procter, Barry Richards and Graeme Pollock – walk out again in their Springbok caps. 'It was an emotional time,' says Ali, 'but after the initial excitement, that feeling disappeared as the tour progressed. It just wasn't the real thing.'

Gooch remained tight-lipped throughout the tour but at its conclusion he said: 'As an individual, I believe in freedom of choice and the right of professional cricketers to pursue their careers where they choose. I also believe that sport, and cricket, should be played on a non-racial basis. I would not have agreed to play in South Africa if I believed that in doing so I was in any way supporting apartheid. We have been inundated with messages of support from all over South Africa and from abroad, and as professional cricketers, we will be delighted if our tour has helped stimulate the game among cricketers of all races in South Africa.'

ALI BELIEVED THAT South African cricket would indeed stimulate interest among South Africans of all races if he recruited a team from one of the black cricket nations – and the object of his desire was the West Indies. South Africans had only heard of the exploits of the great players of the Caribbean nations, and to actually see them in action was the first prize. He reasoned that black South Africans, who mostly viewed cricket as a white man's game, would also come to appreciate the excitement of cricket if they could see the crowd-pleasing West Indians in action. After his talks with Kallicharran, he set out to establish contact with West Indies players. He reasoned that West Indies cricketers would be vulnerable to an offer because of job, financial and selection insecurities in the Caribbean. At around the same time, SACU received a letter from a Sri Lankan cricketer who spent his off-seasons playing and coaching in Holland. His name was Anthony Ralph Opatha, a medium pace bowler who had played for his country in the days prior to Sri Lanka's official recognition by the ICC as a Test-playing nation in 1981. Now well into his thirties, Tony Opatha had set himself up as something of a mentor for the younger cricketers of his country. His letter proposed that a Sri Lankan team, which he would assemble, undertake a tour of South Africa. In the winter of 1982, while the SACU delegation was in London on their annual visit, Pamensky, Dakin and Bacher took a small plane from Gatwick to Rotterdam to meet him. Five months earlier, England and Sri Lanka had played in the inaugural Test between the two countries in Colombo, a historic occasion in which England triumphed by seven wickets.

Opatha was clearly motivated by money. He had heard of the famous Krugerrand and was keen on earning lots of them for his players. Ali asked how much he wanted for each player, and he replied, '$30 000'.

Ali was taken aback, 'You say thirty thousand US dollars?'

'Yes.'

'Hey man,' exclaimed Ali, 'you're in cuckoo land!'

'Okay,' replied Opatha, 'then how many cuckoos in the dollar?'

Ali said he had a problem because he did not know much about Sri Lankan cricket and its players. The names that Opatha was bandying about were mostly unknown to him. He was concerned that the SACU would virtually be buying a team in the dark, with no way of knowing just how good they were until they were actually in action against the strong South African side.

'It was to Joe's credit,' says Ali, 'that he refused to accept that we should simply reject the offer. He felt we should investigate further and he then took it upon himself to do so.'

Ali's eye was on the West Indians – he was already talking to some leading players – but Pamensky's view was that, in the absence of a guarantee of a West Indies tour, the Sri Lankan venture should be pursued. It would also introduce South Africans to a black cricket team and act as a pathfinder for the 'big one' of the West Indies.

The three South Africans flew back to London early the next morning in time to attend a one-day international between England and Pakistan at Nottingham in which Allan Lamb scored 118 in a seven-wicket victory.

Two days later, Ali was in Portsmouth for a meeting with the West Indies fast bowlers Sylvester Clarke and Malcolm Marshall.

Pamensky took personal charge of the Sri Lanka operation and, after further negotiations, he sent an emissary to Colombo to finalise details. The emissary was Colin Rushmere, a member of the Eastern Province Cricket Union who had succeeded Dakin, his former provincial opening batting partner, as its president. It was reasoned that Rushmere, a lawyer, could go to Colombo without the danger of being identified as a cricket official. South Africa had strong trade links with Sri Lanka and it was not unusual for South African businessmen and lawyers to visit that country. Rushmere departed with the player contracts in his suitcase. 'Colin probably didn't realise that if he had been stopped and the contracts found, he would probably have been locked up,' says Dakin.

Word of the impending tour leaked out, however, and it was put on ice when the Sri Lankan government threatened to impound cricketers' passports. Later, Rushmere and June Gleason, SACU's in-house travel agent, returned to Sri Lanka.

On Saturday, 16 October 1982, the Sri Lankan cricket season opened with the first round of two-day domestic club matches on the island. Some key players were mysteriously absent. Gleason was at the airport busily writing out air tickets with a ballpoint pen on the lid of her briefcase, and the players flew out individually, dressed in business suits and without any luggage or cricket kit in order not to draw attention to themselves. Airport personnel had been told by authorities to be vigilant for anyone carrying cricket equipment. They arrived in South Africa four days after leaving Colombo on a deliberately circuitous journey via Hong Kong and Taiwan.

The team would be captained by Bandula Warnapura, the official Sri Lankan skipper, and Tony Opatha was the player-manager. They called themselves the Arosa Sri Lanka XI, the name deriving from the initials of Anthony Ralph Opatha being appended to the letters SA. They were banned from cricket for 25 years for participating in the tour.

Ali's concern about the strength of the team was not unfounded. The Sri Lankans were way off the standard of the South Africans and were soundly thrashed. This resulted in poor support from the paying public and big financial losses. From a cricketing perspective, the tour was a flop, but it strengthened Ali's hand in telling the West Indians that a black team could tour South Africa after all.

Chapter 16

Cloak and Dagger

THE MAKINGS OF the rebel tours lay in a series of convoluted cloak and dagger operations that might have been the creation of a pulp fiction writer. There were elaborate ruses, unexpected twists and turns, intricate decoys, coded messages, death threats, malicious leaks and double-crosses. The operations were fraught with problems; none of the tours turned out exactly as planned and each one, at various times, was in danger of not taking place.

The tours were not organised on an ad hoc basis; indeed, the negotiations for the Sri Lankan, West Indian and Australian tours ran concurrently. Even while Gooch's first rebels were playing in South Africa early in 1982, Ali Bacher was putting out feelers in Australia for a tour that materialised almost four years later.

SACU refuted suggestions that the rebel tours received backing from the South African government. It may be true that the regime did not take a collective decision to materially support these ventures, but there was certainly indirect assistance. An amendment to the Income Tax Act granted a double tax allowance to sponsors who backed events that were classified as 'international projects'. These rebates amounted to anything up to 90 per cent so, in effect, the taxpayer was footing most of the bill; and the sponsors were getting enormous commercial value for minimum nett cost.

There was also one occasion when a senior cabinet minister unilaterally offered a large sum of money to cricket from his department's budget. During the period of the West Indies tours, money in the SACU coffers was running low. Geoff Dakin says that it was pointless approaching the minister of finance, Barend du Plessis, because he would not have been helpful. An

184

appointment was made to see the foreign minister, Pik Botha.

'Joe Pamensky and I went to see him at 8.30 am at the State Guest House in Pretoria. We were short of a considerable amount of money. We had an hour of his time because at 9.30 am Senator Edward Kennedy was due to see him. I remember remarking on the extensive security support that the American senator had with him.

'Pik asked how much we needed. He told his director general, "you can give it to them out of the foreign affairs budget". It amounted to R4 million which was half of what the tour was costing us.'

According to Dakin, the foreign minister was supportive of the West Indies tour because he believed it would break down racial barriers and help the normalisation of sport. He was considered one of the more enlightened ministers.[1]

Ali did not attend this meeting and became aware of it for the first time when interviews were conducted for this book. As it turned out, the money on offer was never paid over to cricket because on the basis of the tax breaks that became available to sports sponsors, Pamensky was able to negotiate attractive commercial sponsorships that took care of the shortfall.

The amendment to the Income Tax Act came about, in fact, because of the heavy financial demands of the West Indies XI tour. To the 'normal' tax rebate claimable by sponsors was added a 'special' one; together they constituted the double tax allowance that became very palatable to would-be sponsors.

ALI CONSIDERED THE West Indies tour as the major coup of the rebel era. 'I was very excited about it,' he says, 'because the West Indies were riding the crest of the wave in world cricket and down the years they had produced some of the game's most outstanding cricketers, legendary players. I knew that if anything was going to fire the public's imagination and motivate our players it would be the West Indians. My abiding hope was that they would be an inspiration to our young black cricketers because I was convinced that in the townships we had our own Vivian Richards or Malcolm Marshall just waiting to be discovered. We believed the West Indians would provide the catalyst for representivity in the South African team.'

Ali, therefore, pursued the West Indians with great zeal in his new role

---

[1] Pik Botha was appointed minister of minerals and energy affairs in President Nelson Mandela's first democratic cabinet in 1994. He retired from politics in 1997 and announced in 2000 that he intended joining the ANC.

as the chief negotiator and tour organiser. When the SACU trio went to London in June 1982, they were the focus of a great deal of media and public attention in the wake of the Gooch tour; but this did not stop Ali from setting out on a top-secret mission. He slipped away from his colleagues and started talking to West Indian cricketers playing in England.

The first man he saw was the fast bowler Colin Croft. They had agreed to meet in Manchester at 5 pm, but the lanky West Indian was delayed in Birmingham where he was seeking treatment for a back injury from the well-known sports physiotherapist Bernard Thomas. Ali kicked his heels in Manchester, taking the opportunity to watch some county cricket at Old Trafford. He was due to catch a train to London later that evening, so time was running out. Croft eventually arrived at 7 o'clock and they talked in a pub near the railway station. It was the first time they had met and the chemistry was good.

As a frontline Test bowler, Croft was the kind of player SACU was after. He seemed eager to visit South Africa and, as a doctor, Ali took an immediate interest in his back ailment. Croft was struggling to find a cure for his problem. He had consulted various doctors and Harley Street specialists without success. Bacher was certain he could help. He knew specialists in Johannesburg who he believed would pinpoint the problem and perform corrective surgery if necessary. Croft, in fact, did join the tour, but he played only a handful of matches and was never a force. He received his tour fee plus free medical treatment, which included surgery. Ali was constantly at his side, spurring on his recovery, but he never regained the form necessary to command a place in the 'Test' team.

Ali's next stop was Portsmouth. Hampshire was playing Surrey in a county match, and both Malcolm Marshall and Sylvester Clarke were in action in the respective teams. He met the two fast bowlers, and they dined together that night. Both players responded positively about playing in South Africa. Ali told Clarke that, whatever happened, and even if there was no tour, he should consider coming to South Africa to play for Transvaal. He would be the black fast bowler that Ali had always wanted.

Ali then travelled to Gateshead, near Newcastle, where his youngest sister Sorrel lived with her large family. It was there that he had another important meeting. The West Indian opener Desmond Haynes was playing club cricket in the area, and he travelled the 50 miles to Sorrel's home. Haynes, like the others, was very interested, but there the matter rested.

The SACU trio returned home after yet another exercise in futility in the corridors of the ICC. The international governing body would not relent.

South African cricket was still outlawed.

From Johannesburg, Bacher telephoned Croft. Progress was slow. A recruitment drive was not producing results. The whole exercise had lost its initial momentum and the dream tour was in danger of falling apart. He decided at the very least that he should pursue Clarke to play for Transvaal in the new season. He drew up a contract but instead of returning to London himself, he called on Don Mackay-Coghill and Raymond White who were going to Europe on business. Ali gave the contract to Coghill and told him where and when to deliver it to Clarke. White would accompany him. Coghill got side-tracked in Paris, where he was doing business on behalf of Intergold, and was forced to change his plans. He would not be able to keep his appointment with the cricketer in London, so he sent the contract to White, managing director of a paper manufacturer, who was already in the British capital.

White went to Lord's for the NatWest Trophy Final between Surrey and Warwickshire on 4 September 1982. Surrey, in their fourth final at Lord's in successive years, were at last rewarded when they achieved a nine-wicket victory; and Clarke took two for 17 in 12 overs. White waited outside the dressing room. He sent a message, asking to see Clarke, but the victory celebrations were already under way. After an interminable wait, he was on the point of leaving when Clarke appeared. It was clearly not a good time to have a serious talk so he handed the fast bowler his business card in the hope he would make contact at a later stage.

Clarke, the card still in his bag, returned to his home in Barbados after completing his season in England. Several weeks later in Bridgetown, he was chatting to Gregory Armstrong, a retired fast bowler who had played for Barbados, and told him of the approaches from South Africa, of the envisaged tour, and of the possible Transvaal contract. Clarke produced White's business card. It was a pivotal moment.

Armstrong, sensing a unique opportunity, immediately telephoned White in Johannesburg. He in turn telephoned Pamensky who contacted Bacher, and Ali hurriedly booked a call to Armstrong. It was the start of an exhausting period for Ali as he began negotiating via long distance calls with players he had never met, let alone seen play.

'I approved a team by studying the Wisden Cricketers Almanack,' he says. 'It's an amazing book because in it I could look up all the details and statistics on all these players – the matches they played, what they scored against which bowlers, how many wickets they took against which batsmen. I was then able to get an idea of each player's strength; although it was hardly the ideal way to select a team.'

The Transvaal Cricket Council later claimed back R15 000 from the SA Cricket Union for international telephone calls made by Ali through its offices; but this was probably a grossly understated figure. He simply lost track of the international phone calls he made. The only person outside the inner circle who knew what was going on was the operator on the international exchange. There was no direct dialling, and calls to the West Indies had to be booked in advance. Ali told the operator never to disclose that the call was from South Africa when he connected him.

'How we doing, Doc, are we making any progress?' was the regular greeting from the man on the 090 exchange each time Bacher booked a call. 'It was the same man each time,' recalls Ali, 'and I never ever found out who he was.'

Spontaneously, Bacher and Armstrong developed a series of codes which they used to keep their telephone conversations as secret as possible. Players were never referred to by name. It was decided that Armstrong should come to South Africa for face-to-face talks. While the Sri Lankans were playing an international match at the Wanderers during November, he and the West Indian were holed up in a nearby hotel. For three days they were on the phone, Armstrong making the contact with players and then introducing them to Bacher. Over the weeks, Armstrong slipped in and out of Johannesburg without anyone knowing.

The team was taking shape but it was virtually changing by the week. Among the problems that Ali had to deal with was double-dealing by some players who said they would come but had no intention of doing so. Their ruse was to bait other players to join them in South Africa, and then stay behind and replace them in the official West Indies team.

'Haynes and Marshall were playing club cricket in Melbourne when, five days before the tour was due to start, they telephoned me to say that they were definitely in,' recalls Ali. 'Someone then leaked this information to an Australian newspaper and they were both immediately whisked back to the West Indies. That was the end of them.'[2]

An elaborate and complicated plan was drawn up to ensure that the

---

[2] After South Africa's re-entry to world cricket in 1991, both Marshall and Haynes became household names in the domestic game. Marshall played for KwaZulu-Natal where he shared his considerable experience and expertise with Shaun Pollock and Lance Klusener; and Haynes, at Western Province, nurtured the talents of Herschelle Gibbs.

players reached South Africa unhindered. Some came from Spain, others from New York and London and more from Australia. 'The pressure was relentless,' Ali said later. 'It affected my health, some said even my personality.'

The clincher was the signing of Lawrence Rowe as captain. The Jamaican batsman had a Test average of over 47 and boasted the unique achievement of having scored a century and a double-century on his Test debut against New Zealand. He was the 'man of stature' that SACU needed to give the team credibility. He came to South Africa amid death threats in the West Indies; and when it was time for him finally to return home, he gave Jamaica a wide berth and settled permanently with his family in the United States. He and his players were banned from representative cricket for ten years.

THE WEST INDIANS made two tours to South Africa over consecutive seasons. Capacity crowds watched them and there were some stirring contests with the South African team, which was initially captained by Peter Kirsten before he was axed in favour of Clive Rice. There were accusations that a Transvaal conspiracy had orchestrated this change of leadership; and it was interesting, if not significant, that where once the Bacher-Barlow rivalry had characterised the epic battles between Transvaal and Western Province, it was now the new captains of those two teams, Rice and Kirsten, who were the central characters in perpetuating the great north-south 'war' of provincialism.

During the first West Indies tour, Kirsten complained on behalf of the Springboks that they were being ignored by officials and media who seemed only interested in trumpeting the feats of the West Indians. This was demonstrably true but, as Ali points out, 'it was the first time we had ever seen West Indians in South Africa and obviously everyone got caught up in the euphoria'.

The South African players were also upset when they found out that the West Indians were being paid more than they were in the 'Test' series. They backed down, however, once it was explained to them that this was no ordinary series, and that the West Indians were being paid fees relative to their 'sacrifices' and not necessarily their 'ability'.

It was in this surreal climate that the first tour was thrown into crisis near its completion. It came during the one-day international series during which six matches were played over nine days. This unbelievably hectic schedule included back-to-back matches at the Wanderers, the first a day-night match on the Friday night and the second a day match on the Saturday.

Ali's phone rang at 5 am on the Saturday. It was Armstrong summoning him urgently to the central city hotel where the West Indians were staying. The players had heard reports of the capacity crowds clicking through the turnstiles and, more specifically, of the record gate takings of R600 000. They reminded Ali that they had sacrificed their careers by coming to South Africa and that the 'cricket mania' gripping white South Africa was due to their appeal and competitiveness. In short, they demanded more money by way of bonuses relative to the size of the crowds. If they did not get it, they would boycott the Saturday match.

Ironically, it was Ali who had been hyping up the entertainment value of the West Indians in the media, and it was he who had encouraged the national news agency SAPA to distribute news of the record crowd figures a day earlier. The rumblings in the team had begun in the dressing room immediately after their crushing seven-wicket victory the previous night. Joe Pamensky was called to the dressing room where a row broke out. 'It was the one and only time in my life that I heard Joe shout,' says Ali. 'He is a calm, measured man but he lost his cool with Lawrence Rowe and gave him stick.'

Paul Weiner, the lawyer representing the West Indians, also did not escape Pamensky's wrath. The SACU president turned on him, too. 'Call yourself a South African, where's your patriotism?'

Pamensky told Armstrong and Rowe that each party had accepted the goodwill of the other in agreeing to the tour contracts, and that if the team now thought they had a bad deal this was neither the time nor the place to raise it. 'They had a contractual commitment to play the (Saturday) match and we were prepared to negotiate only once they had completed the match. I told them that if they didn't like it, I would cancel the whole tour.'

The West Indians' disenchantment grew as the night wore on. 'At around five o'clock that morning,' recalls Weiner, 'Armstrong said he wanted to talk to Ali. It seemed that the West Indians wanted to deal only with him because they knew he wouldn't screw them.'

Ali arrived at the hotel and assured Armstrong and Rowe that he would ensure that they got a fair deal. He encouraged them to get to the Wanderers and play the match. 'It was only through Ali's reassurance that they backed down and agreed to play,' says Weiner, 'although the start of the match was delayed.'

At lunchtime that Saturday, Pamensky scolded Ali for bowing to demands under duress at the hotel earlier. 'You never, ever negotiate under duress,' Joe told him.

The West Indians lost the match by 51 runs, and Pamensky kept his word to reopen negotiations in calmer circumstances later. Dakin points out that a problem with the West Indies tour was that the players were contracted on a differential pay scale. This caused unhappiness when some discovered that they were being paid less than others. 'During that Wanderers row, Greg Armstrong also asked for more money for the team for the second tour. SACU had no option but to pay up because they had us over a barrel.'

As for Weiner, he came to Ali's assistance many years later when a malicious accusation was made by a Johannesburg attorney to the effect that Bacher had offered the West Indians more money on condition they lost the Saturday game. Weiner, Armstrong and Rowe all signed affidavits stating that this allegation was totally unfounded.

For the second tour, Ali insisted that he needed a few new faces in the West Indies team to reignite public interest, but in hindsight he concedes that SACU should not have done so. 'Players who were released from the first tour felt we had let them down because they had made the initial sacrifice, were banned from playing in the West Indies and were even ostracised by their own communities. Although we did pay them the second tour contract fee, I now believe we should have been more accommodating.'

Sylvester Clarke eventually did sign to play for Transvaal but not before an unsightly row erupted when Northern Transvaal claimed to have the fast bowler's promise to play for them. He went on to become one of the most devastating components of the 'Mean Machine', taking a record 58 first-class wickets for the province in only 10 matches in the 1984-85 season. He unleashed his fastest bowling against South Africa when his seven for 34 in the second innings of the Wanderers 'Test' won the match for the West Indies XI on their first tour.

'Garry Sobers later told me that of all the West Indies quick bowlers at that time, he was the most lethal,' says Ali. 'In the county championship there was Croft playing for Lancashire, Marshall for Hampshire and Clarke for Surrey – but Graham Gooch said that the county batsmen feared Sylvester the most.'[3]

---

[3] Sylvester Clarke collapsed and died of a heart attack at his home in Bridgetown, Barbados, in December 1999. He was 44.

Chapter 17

'A Most Insular Man'

THE 1983 CRICKET WORLD CUP was held in England. Ali Bacher attended some of the matches but most of the time he was in London, holed up in Natie Kirsh's flat in Charles Street, Mayfair, talking to Australians.

The first West Indies rebel tour was long over, the second one was still to come; but Ali's sights were now firmly set elsewhere. In March 1982, he had telephoned Tony Greig in Sydney to ask if he believed an Australian team could be assembled. Greig, the South African-born former England captain, apologised that he was not in a position to help. He worked for Kerry Packer and his boss would not take too kindly to it. He advised Ali to contact Bruce Francis, a former Australian batsman who became Greig's manager when he stunned the conservative English cricket establishment by throwing in his lot with Packer's World Series Cricket rebellion in the late seventies. Francis[1] was well disposed to South African cricket. He had toured the country as a member of the Derrick Robins XI and had developed a personal friendship with Joe Pamensky.

Three months later he visited South Africa. The Sydney marketing consultant and political science graduate said he had no moral problem recruiting a team because, in his view, the SA Cricket Union had integrated cricket in the republic. The one thing he would not do, though, was induce players to break their existing contracts with the Australian Cricket Board (ACB) and PBL Marketing, the Packer company that held the commercial

---

[1] In 1972, Bruce Francis played as an opening batsman in three Tests in England.

rights in Australian cricket. Bacher and Pamensky agreed.

A month later, Francis flew to London where he held further talks with the SACU trio on their annual visit to the British capital. He wanted to start recruiting immediately, but Pamensky insisted he wait until after the 1982 ICC meeting. It was important that they did things 'by the book'; and Francis went so far as to seek counsel from one of Australia's top barristers who advised that it would not be illegal to ask players to sign rebel contracts for a tour that would take place only after their ACB and PBL contracts had expired.

While not wanting to fall foul of the ACB, Francis was also mindful of the power that Packer wielded. In the wake of the cricket revolution he spawned in 1978, he had acquired the television rights he so coveted and was said to be the power behind Australia's cricket throne. Francis also did not want to ruin his personal relationship with the media mogul – for many years he had been the private cricket coach of Packer's son James.

Another reason that Francis was told to hold off for a while was that the Sri Lankan and West Indian tours were ahead in the queue but, in spite of all the subterfuge, the cricket grapevine soon began telegraphing rumours that an Australian rebel tour was in the offing. Charles Fortune, the veteran SACU secretary, received a phone call from a former Australian captain, Graham Yallop, who said he was interested in playing in South Africa and knew of many other Australian cricketers of like mind. Fortune passed on Yallop's number to Ali who told the cricketer to get in touch with Francis.

The following year, now in the Charles Street flat, Ali had the phone glued to his ear. The Australian team, under the captaincy of Kim Hughes, was in England for the World Cup and this would be an ideal opportunity to meet some of the players. At Leeds, he had dinner with Yallop and his South African-born teammate Kepler Wessels who had become a naturalised Australian and scored 162 on his Test debut for that country against England in Brisbane in 1982. 'Kepler was in (on the rebel tour) from the start,' says Ali, who immediately phoned Francis in Sydney and told him to get on the next plane to London.

'While the team was in London, Yallop and Wessels were told to meet me at the Cumberland Hotel where I was staying,' recalls Francis, 'and were warned to come incognito. Kepler pitched up in his Australian blazer and I jokingly asked him what he would have worn if he had not come incognito!'[2]

---

[2] Bruce Francis interview, November 2003.

One evening, Ali invited Francis to join him for a quick supper in Mayfair. What they thought was a fairly run-of-the mill café turned out to be a posh and expensive restaurant. They were very casually dressed and Francis recalls that Ali was not wearing socks. 'Sitting at a table close to us was Anton Rupert, the wealthy South African industrialist, who greeted Ali – and must still be wondering what kind of guy goes out for dinner in Mayfair without socks.'

The day after Australia had been knocked out of the World Cup by India, a meeting was arranged with the players at the Charles Street flat. Six turned up – Yallop, Wessels, Jeff Thomson, Rodney Hogg, Graeme Wood and David Hookes – but of these, only Yallop and Hogg eventually made it to South Africa on the first tour. An Australian lawyer also attended the meeting and produced a draft player's contract.

Within 24 hours of the Charles Street meeting, an Adelaide newspaper reported it on its front page – a 'leak' so serious that SACU weighed the growing risks and immediately informed the players that the tour was off.

Francis says that five months later he went to Brisbane on a business trip that by chance coincided with a Test match there against Pakistan. Before he left, he went to the Packer residence to advise James that there would be no coaching for the next few days, whereupon Kerry Packer took him aside and said, 'I understand you're going to Brisbane to sign up a few of my players for South Africa . . . don't waste your time, they're under contract to me; and even if you did sign enough players, you'd never get them out of the country.'

It was a chilling reminder to Francis that, even though SACU had aborted the project, suspicion was still rife.

It was more than a year later that Ali received a phone call from Yallop from Monaco. He was in the principality playing in a charity match and he wanted to stop over in Johannesburg on his way home. Francis was in South Africa at the time – he had been pestering Ali to restart the process and Ali says the Australian had become 'almost obsessive' about organising a tour – and the Yallop visit had the desired effect. Francis returned to Australia on a recruitment drive and the grapevine started leaking information like a sieve. In April 1985, two Australian newspapers published the names of players they claimed had signed rebel contracts; and the ACB and the Australian government began mounting a counter-offensive.

In late September 1984, the Australian team attended a training camp at the Australian Institute of Sport in Canberra prior to a short tour of India. It was an ideal opportunity for Francis to meet the players; and he

194

booked into an out-of-town motel and gave instructions that they should visit him in pairs so as not to arouse any suspicions. The next step was to get them to meet Bacher personally and Singapore was chosen as the venue. This was a popular stopover for shopping on the route between India and Australia and the rendezvous was set for early October.

In South Africa, Ali let it be known that he was going abroad to visit his sister. 'In Singapore, I booked into the Marco Polo hotel only to discover that Kim Hughes was staying in a hotel next door. I had to switch hotels hurriedly because Kim was still Australia's captain and did not know what was being planned.'

In the Paramount Hotel, the meeting began at 11 pm. Several players who had been in India were there, as were a few more who had flown in from Australia with two lawyers. Ali had told Francis that it was not possible to pay the players differential fees because of the unhappy experience with the West Indians; and it was agreed that the sum on offer would be $A200 000 each after tax for two consecutive tours. In addition to this, the players wanted a signing-on fee in the form of a loan. They felt they should be insured for possible loss of earnings if Australian authorities got wind of the project and the whole thing was scuttled. The fast bowler Jeff Thomson was not present but his lawyer made it known that his client expected more than $200 000. Ali said it was not possible; so Thomson was immediately out. It was then that the Australians got an insight into how Bacher operated in accordance with his credo of 'Do it now!' In need of a replacement fast bowler, he got on the phone and woke up Terry Alderman in Perth. It was the middle of the night but he thought nothing of asking his new recruit to get on to the next plane to Singapore. Alderman had a ready-made excuse; he had started a new job and could not possibly ask for leave of absence. He later joined the tour.

The meeting adjourned at 4 am, reconvened six hours later and finally ended at 6 pm to allow the players to return to the airport and avoid being seen by Hughes.

Prior to the meeting, Francis had a row with Ali over the players' remuneration, suggesting that the older, more experienced players should be paid more. Ali's argument was that once they were banned from representative cricket for going to South Africa, the younger players would in fact be worse off. Francis backed down, but there would be several other occasions when they clashed. Ali was not much interested in Francis's political theories – as a Sydney university student he had vigorously argued South Africa's case in debates with left-wing students – and Ali liked to call him 'Pik' after South Africa's foreign minister.

'He believed he was an authority on politics, whether they be Australian or South African,' says Ali, 'but as far as South Africa was concerned he certainly was no authority.'

Francis, on the other hand, could not understand Bacher's lack of interest in the logistical problems of organising such a tour. 'He had a vision, he opened doors and he said "now go and do it". He had no understanding of things like the floating dollar or the exchange rate; the details made no difference to him. All he was interested in was the outcome.

'A good example of his style of management was the way he dealt with the Australians' yellow playing uniforms when the tour was under way. He shared the players' view that the colour and material were unacceptable and promised he would have a new set of clothes in time for the next match two days later. He was not concerned about whether the manufacturer had an alternative material or whether his staff could produce a new set of clothes in such a short time. He was not even concerned about who would pay for them; he said Joe would sort it out.

'Ali was the original outcomes man and he was also the most insular person I've ever come across. His world revolved around the Wanderers.'

Ali admits that in personality and interests they were poles apart. 'I will say this for Bruce, though – without him the Australian tours would never have taken place.'

Although he had toured India, Wessels was advised not to attend the Singapore meeting lest someone spot him in Bacher's company. Later, whilst on holiday in South Africa prior to returning to Australia for the start of the 1984-85 season, he contacted Ali and asked if they could meet at the Burgerspark Hotel in Pretoria. 'It was here that I met a very serious Kepler Wessels who told me he wanted out. From the outset, he was always in, although he was never asked to act as an agent to recruit any players; but it was obvious at the Burgerspark meeting that Kepler had thought the matter through and realised the huge implications of joining the tour. He was backing off because I believe he knew that there would be serious repercussions against him in his adopted country if he went the rebel route. Australia, after all, had given him a chance to play Test cricket and he wanted to play for them in England in 1985.'

Ali had always had misgivings about Wessels taking part in both rebel tours. 'The South African players would have gone ballistic when they heard what he was earning. If he had come on both tours, he would have had to play provincial cricket in between and would have earned even more money. The one option, we felt, was for him to join the first tour only and then become re-assimilated in South African cricket. I felt that we could get David Hookes[3] to replace him for the second tour.'

The players' elected lawyer, the likeable Bernie Knapp, flew to South Africa early in November armed with his clients' power of attorney. For legal reasons, the player contracts had to be signed in South Africa; and Knapp did so on their behalf on the day before nine of them went into action in the first Test of the 1984-85 series against the West Indies. Of the official 12-man squad, only Kim Hughes, Allan Border and Geoff Lawson were not in on the deal, and none of them had been approached. Wessels signed a conditional contract in the unlikely event that he changed his mind. Unlike the other players, he did not receive a signing-on fee.

Australia were thrashed by the West Indies in the opening two Test matches; in the first match at Perth they were bowled out for 76 to lose by an innings and in the second at Brisbane they were beaten by eight wickets. Having lost a record five Tests in a row, Hughes broke down in tears at the post-match press conference in Brisbane as he announced his resignation as Australia's captain. Allan Border was named as his successor. Later, when the Australian selectors announced their team for the Ashes tour of England in 1985, Hughes' name was not there.

It was the gap SACU needed, and Francis quickly took it. Like Lawrence Rowe before him, Hughes was the player of stature SACU was seeking to captain the team. At first he declined, then later telephoned Ali to confirm his interest. Before signing any contract, however, he wanted to travel to Johannesburg with his wife for a face-to-face meeting with SACU.

The Australian media were on to him by now, but the couple travelled under a fictitious name, booking into their hotel as 'Mr and Mrs Greg Smith'. The media mistakenly believed they were travelling under the name of Scott; and, as luck would have it, a Mr and Mrs Scott from the United States were staying in the same hotel and were puzzled at the number of phone calls they received from Australian reporters.

Hughes duly signed on as captain and returned to Perth where he gave a press conference. 'I am going to South Africa with an open and, I hope, intelligent mind. I will be able to see for myself the truth of the matters which concern the politicians. I believe I have the ability to judge what is right and wrong. I also believe I will be able to comment and suggest ways

---

[3] Hookes was available for the second tour but he effectively priced himself out with a demand of $150 000.

in which the situation can be improved. Then it can be left to the politicians.'

Hughes was offered the same fee as the other players to tour South Africa although, according to Ali, he was likely to lose the most by joining the tour. 'By agreeing to come, he automatically surrendered a considerable amount of his money in the ACB's players provident fund.'

Ali liked Hughes, but this admiration was not shared by Dakin. 'He was our biggest problem, always asking for more money – even when the tours were over.'

The ACB moved quickly to seek a high court injunction to prevent Hughes from going to South Africa. It also sued several other players, Francis, Dakin and SACU for allegedly inducing players to break agreements. Dakin, who was now the SACU president with Pamensky the vice-president, retorted: 'The SACU wants no legal confrontation with the ACB over its projected tour. All we want is to play cricket again, but if the ACB declares war by taking legal action, then we will meet fire with fire.'

Lawyers began flying back and forth between the two countries amid the ongoing threats and counter-threats. The ACB was determined to take the matter to the law courts, and a date was set in early July 1985 for the case to be heard in the Melbourne High Court. The Australian government of Prime Minister Bob Hawke reluctantly granted Dakin, Pamensky and Bacher a 21-day visa to enter the country on condition that they did not talk to the media or 'propagate the cause of apartheid'.

Their arrival in Perth was like another twist to a spy thriller. 'We were taken under armed guard to a special lounge pending our connection to Melbourne,' recalls Pamensky. 'We were told not to stand or sit near any window because we might expose ourselves to some cranks. When it was time for the Melbourne flight to depart, we were taken through a back door and straight on to the plane.'

They were in Melbourne for almost three weeks, during which Ali was champing at the bit to return home, while lawyers from both sides were thrashing out complicated issues ahead of the scheduled court case. During this period Dakin received a call from Tony Greig with a message that Kerry Packer wanted to see him. 'So we went, Joe and I, and Packer was very irritated because he said we were poaching players that he wanted for the Australian team, including Mike Haysman.[4]

'He made his point in no uncertain terms, using very colourful language.

---

[4] Packer, in fact, bought three would-be rebels, Graeme Wood, Dirk Wellham and Wayne Phillips, out of their rebel contracts.

I reminded him that I had agreed to see him as president of SACU, and not in my private capacity, and I therefore suggested that he address me a little more courteously. He barked at me: "Listen, fella, you're maybe a rooster today, but tomorrow you're a feather duster!"

'I caught Greig's eye. I could see by the way he was looking at me that it would be unwise to take this any further, so I didn't.'

Later, the South Africans received an invitation to enjoy some Packer hospitality on his exclusive island retreat, but they courteously declined.

Pamensky says SACU believed it had 'the high ground' in respect of the court case. 'We met with the ACB chairman Fred Bennett and their executive director David Richards, and there was never any animosity. Fred and I had become very good friends when he managed the 1970 Australian team in South Africa, and Ali had a good relationship with Richards. We decided to leave everything in the hands of our legal teams.'

The SACU lawyers had done a thorough job and, what's more, the ACB was likely to be embarrassed if all the details of the makings of the tour were revealed. In addition, Australian officials did not want the contents of the ACB and PBL contracts to become public knowledge. The ACB backed down and agreed to settle out of court. The terms of the settlement obliged SACU not to contract any more Australian cricketers and to pay a contribution of $A120 000 to the ACB's legal costs. By this stage, SACU had already signed up the fourteen players it needed.

THE AUSTRALIAN REBELS were banned from official international cricket for three years. Kepler Wessels quit Australian cricket in 1986 after his ACB contract was downgraded from the highest to the lowest rung. He returned to South Africa for good, became a highly successful captain of Eastern Province, and joined the Australian rebels for their second tour. 'Graham Yallop had been very disappointing as a top-order batsman,' says Ali, 'and Kepler was the answer to take the pressure off Kim Hughes who had been shouldering the batting burden. There had, in fact, been a debate over who Kepler should play for – our team or the Aussies – but in the end they needed him more.'

The last thing the nation-hopping Wessels[5] could have imagined at that time was that one day he would be South Africa's captain in the official Test arena. In the mid-eighties, the political climate in South Africa was

[5] Kepler Wessels played twenty-four Test matches for Australia for a batting average of 42.95.

hardly conducive to the kind of change that was needed for the country to take its place in the international community.

Change in cricket, however, continued to make news. Don Mackay-Coghill came to the conclusion that Bacher had outgrown his job with the Transvaal Cricket Council. The province was now established as the most successful in the country – in fact Ali had carried through his chairman's original vision for the province beyond expectations – and Coghill suggested to Pamensky that the time had surely arrived for SACU to appoint him on a full-time basis. Dakin says he and Pamensky had, in fact, discussed this during the three weeks they spent in Melbourne; and, after his discussions with Coghill, Pamensky formally raised the issue at a SACU think-tank in Port Elizabeth in 1985. 'Joe was at the peak of his influence,' says Coghill, now a SACU board member, 'and Geoff saw the lopsided situation whereby Transvaal cricket was professional and SA cricket was not. What we needed, though, was a managing director. The analogy was Australian cricket versus the rest of the world cricket. The reason for their success was that they had the right guy at the top.'

Denis Carlstein, brother of the Springbok Peter, had already been given the full-time job as Director of Administration to effectively replace the retired Charles Fortune, but Bacher's allies felt that a place had to be found for him, too. There were, however, some misgivings on the board about appointing him – the fact that he would become the focal point of SA cricket and also the question of having to pay another full-time salary – but common sense prevailed and Ali was offered and accepted the position as Director of Cricket. When, a year later, Carlstein moved on, the board decided that Ali should be promoted to the all-encompassing position of Managing Director.

No sooner had he taken up this post than Coghill departed. He had accepted the offer to head up GoldCorp Australia and the Western Australian Mint and was leaving for Perth. 'The night before I left, Ali came to see me. He gave me a bedside radio alarm as a going away present and he broke down completely. It was very traumatic for both of us. I think he felt that I had left him exposed.' They had been the closest of friends and allies for some 25 years.

Chapter 18

A Brutal Country

THE EIGHTIES WERE turbulent times in South Africa. It was a knife-edge decade in which people walked tightropes of risk and fear and expectation. Politically, the country was in turmoil; it had become dangerously polarised across the colour line. President P W Botha's 'total onslaught' philosophy was met head on by the ANC's armed struggle and, on both sides, South Africans were being brutalised and murdered.

The struggle against apartheid was fast losing patience, becoming more brash and daring; and the activists were breaking out of the shadows, defiantly challenging the State. There was dissent in the ruling party, the hawks in parliament splitting with the National Party to bolster an ominously recalcitrant right wing.

The United Democratic Front (UDF) was formed in 1983, an extra-parliamentary organisation that opposed the government's constitutional proposals of that year. Until its banning under the terms of the emergency regulations of 24 February 1988, it served as an umbrella formation of anti-apartheid groups with its membership open to any organisation that endorsed the principles of the ANC's Freedom Charter; it was in effect the internal wing of the banned African National Congress. The 'Struggle' was spreading across the land, carrying with it a growing anger and impatience that could no longer be ignored by a regime looking more and more vulnerable.

After seven years as leader of the official opposition, Frederik Van Zyl Slabbert resigned dramatically from parliament in 1986. He would later say: 'For twelve years I tried to break down apartheid from an opposition stance in white politics. My resignation was the best commentary I could offer on my attempts. Parliament as an institution was increasingly rendered powerless through two conflicting, polarising political tendencies: the extra-parliamentary Struggle for the freedom of the ANC and the Total Strategy of an increasingly military autocracy under the leadership of P W Botha.'

The authoritarian Botha's idea of reform was to introduce the infamous Tricameral Parliament, with separate Houses for whites, coloureds and Indians, while all around him the black African townships were burning and becoming ungovernable. It was, says Van Zyl Slabbert,[1] a brutal country, caught in a cycle of repression and revolt.

By nature, Ali Bacher was an optimist; in fact, 'super optimist' would be closer to the truth. Problems for him were mere 'challenges' and he would seek out, and often find, the positives in seemingly hopeless situations. His children say they sometimes believed he was some kind of sage because he would often accurately predict an outcome that for them had seemed impossible. His cricket teams would be heading for certain defeat but he would say, 'don't worry, we'll still win this match', and lo and behold, they did.

In the midst of the 1980s, however, his unfaltering belief in the human spirit and unshakeable conviction that everything would turn out fine in the end was being sorely tested.

'It was the first time in my life that I started questioning the future of this country. I had always been a positive person, but now I wasn't sure.'

On what he describes as a blind impulse, he called a meeting in his office. He felt cricket needed to do something in a small way to improve race relations in the troubled land. It had to make a positive contribution. Those called to the meeting in Bacher's office were a media and communications consultant Chris Day,[2] a sports commentator Dumile Mateza, a Lenasia primary school principal and former fast bowler Hoosain Ayob, a Soweto teacher and cricket coach Lawrence Mvumvu and Ali's personal assistant Daphne Bradbury. They agreed to stage what they called a development clinic for the children of Soweto. The day of the clinic, Saturday, 20 October 1986, dawned bright and sunny but Ali and his friends got lost on their way to the cricket field.

---

[1] Interview with Van Zyl Slabbert, August 2003.
[2] Chris Day and Ali Bacher went back a long way. They were at high school together where, in the rugby team, Day played scrumhalf and Bacher flyhalf. Day was a leading newspaperman in Johannesburg before going into media consultancy.

'There we were in the heart of the townships, not knowing where we were and, at a time when no white person countenanced the thought of going into Soweto, we were greeted with some very puzzled looks.'

When they eventually reached the Elkah Oval they were greeted by the astonishing sight of a thousand children waiting for the fun to begin. Mvumvu was outstanding in explaining to the youngsters in their own language the basics of the game. The first township development clinic was under way.

For the next eight Saturday mornings further clinics were staged and the children kept coming back for more. 'I watched, and watched and was able to explode a myth. After three weeks, I could see that the old cliché that township kids can't play cricket because it is not in their blood was absolute rubbish. They had good rhythm and coordination and, like everything in South Africa at the time, all they were lacking was opportunity.'

Bacher was now on a mission and, as always, nothing was going to stop him. He telephoned Mervyn King[3] and said, 'Mervyn, I've seen something with huge potential, but we need money.'

Mervyn King was an ex-judge and prominent businessman who, through the foresight of Don Mackay-Coghill, had been brought on to the Transvaal Cricket Council board as an independent adviser, thus breaking the tradition of board members being nominated representatives of their clubs.

With Joe Pamensky and Professor Michael Katz, King formed what Ali called his 'Three Wise Men' to whom he would often turn when he needed counsel on a myriad issues. All three were exceptionally gifted human beings and showed the calibre of the people who he would carefully cultivate and cherish in his inner circle. It was a relationship that was built on absolute respect and trust, and it would endure throughout Bacher's many years in cricket administration, and even beyond.

At Ali's bidding, King set out to form the SA Executive Cricket Club of which he became the chairman. He recruited as its members the ten most

---

[3] Mervyn King SC, a specialist commercial advocate, served as a judge of the Supreme Court of South Africa between 1977-1980 before entering commerce to become a director and chairman of numerous companies. He became chairman of the King Committee on Corporate Governance in South Africa and was responsible for drafting the principles of Corporate Governance for at least 56 countries as the Commonwealth's top authority on the subject. He has received numerous awards for his business achievements and community work and has been involved for many years in 'various legal wrangles and angles' on behalf of South African cricket.

prominent captains of industry in the land. They would raise money within their industries at the rate of R100 000 each per year (a total of R1 million) over a period of ten years (a grand total of R10 million). With this funding, the national Development Programme became a viable reality – Ali pointed out that without King's efforts it probably would never have got off the ground – and it would take cricket into the heart of the disadvantaged areas in black townships around the country, Rockville, kwaMashu, Kagiso, Alexandra . . .

The programmes were driven by wonderfully dedicated black and white South Africans and performed the twin role of improving race relations and providing opportunities for disadvantaged children. Ali made bold to say that, for the first time, they were 'being given life' through the opportunities that this grass roots cricket was providing. It was an experience that opened his eyes to the terrible devastation of apartheid as witnessed in the living conditions in the townships. 'It distressed me to see the way people were forced to live. How the average family was able to survive, I just don't know.'

Around him Ali recruited some exceptional people: there was an Afrikaner woman, Bets Jansen, who would go alone into Kagiso near Krugersdorp, probably the only white woman ever to set foot in the place, and be welcomed by the township folk; and there were the retired Old Johannians club cricket stalwart John Jefferies and the former Border cricketer Robin Thorne, a provincial opponent of Ali's early in his provincial career, who together went into Alexandra township in the north east of Johannesburg each week. John would transport the Alex boys on the back of his bakkie to play at schools in the white suburbs and then afterwards take them home into the heart of the highly politicised ghetto. The boys called him 'Mister No Nonsense', and they had names that resonated with the aspirations of their community, the twins Peace and Justice Nkutha and their pal Harmony Ntshinka.

Among other outstanding people driving the project were Greg Hayes in the Border region, Adrian Birrell in the Eastern Province, the former Transvaal seam bowler Francois Weideman, a dedicated Afrikaner who would die tragically at a young age; and Lawrence Mvumvu, Hoosain Ayob and Imtiaz Patel,[4] a fine club cricketer and teacher at Pace College in

---

[4] Imtiaz Patel would later be appointed Development Director at the Gauteng Cricket Board and then become Bacher's protégé as National Director of Professional Cricket at the United Cricket Board. He left cricket in 1999 to take up an executive position at the TV sports channel Supersport.

Soweto. Such was the momentum of the process that Ali persuaded Hoosain to give up his job at Libra Primary School to go full-time into the development programme; and Lawrence, too, quit his teaching post to do the same. Of considerable importance, the irrepressible Kedi Sylvia Tshoma, a Soweto schoolteacher, became the most highly qualified women's cricket coach in South Africa. Her untimely death from a stroke in June 2003 would inspire Ali to say: 'Ours was a particularly warm and close relationship, and many was the occasion when cricket was experiencing troubled times that we would talk about the best way forward . . . an exceptional woman.'

These were Ali's people; and he cared for them, little knowing at the time that forces ranged against him in the UDF and its affiliates viewed his unilateral moves into the black townships not as a noble statement of solidarity but as an arrogant and impertinent intrusion.

Oblivious to this, Bacher and his people soldiered on relentlessly and enthusiastically. 'Thousands of kids were streaming into the programme and, as their numbers grew, so too did we realise that there were simply not enough coaches to go around. We therefore moved into the next stage of the programme, developing a concept by which we now set out to coach adults (and mainly schoolteachers) to become coaches. We launched a coaching academy with a donation of R1 million over three years from the Form-Scaff company and it was at this point that I prevailed on Hoosain Ayob to give up his headmastership to head up the academy. He did a fantastic job. His courses mainly accommodated teachers who, because they were in the majority, were black women. What was happening was a unique phenomenon in world cricket.'

If anyone could lay claim to straddling the race divide it was Hoosain Ayob.[5] His grandfather was a white Afrikaner and his grandmother a black African. They had three daughters who were, in skin colour, black, white and coloured. The coloured girl married an Indian and from this union was Hoosain born, a proud South African who always maintained that it was in his blood to understand all the divergent peoples of his country. Yet in his own community he would become stigmatised as a 'sell-out' for breaking ranks with the SA Cricket Board that he had represented as a

---

[5] Hoosain Ayob would later hold the positions of National Director of Development and National Director of Coaching at the United Cricket Board. In 1997, he became the ICC's Development Director for Africa and tirelessly spread cricket across the continent.

provincial player of some stature to join up with Bacher's SA Cricket Union.

The genesis of the township development programme lay in the Bakers Mini-Cricket initiative that brought school children together across the colour line for festivals of softball cricket. This began in 1982 in interesting circumstances when Pamensky introduced Ali to Clive Menell,[6] chairman of the mining group Anglovaal. At lunch, Menell said he was considering sponsoring a 'Golden Oldies' international cricket tournament, but Ali said he had a far better idea – why not introduce mini-cricket for the children? Menell agreed, and handed the project to Bakers Biscuits, who were part of the Anglovaal group. Bakers marketing director Barry Fowle was told to run with it. Without so much as a contract being signed, a sum of R50 000 for three years launched Bakers mini-cricket in the Transvaal. Three years later, Ali met Bakers managing director Lou Heilbron with a view to extending the project nationwide. In his office overlooking Durban harbour, the pipe-smoking Heilbron, a cricket fanatic, asked: 'So how much are we talking about here?'

'And I replied, one million rand.'

Heilbron said nothing. He paced back and forth across his office, biting on the stem of his pipe. 'At one stage I thought he was going to swallow it,' says Ali. 'I'm sure he nearly bit clean through it.'

A compromise was reached in the sum of R500 000 over three years but this was later upped to R750 000 when Heilbron saw the growing success of the project across the country. Again, all it took was a handshake to cement the relationship with Bakers, and at no stage during Ali's long involvement with the company was a contract ever discussed.[7] It underscored one of Bacher's basic principles: that good business was not about putting pen to paper, but about people, and relationships of trust. It was a rule he would apply throughout his life.

Fowle and Bacher forged a lifelong friendship and Fowle would later say of Bacher, 'whatever he did, he gave a hundred and plenty per cent'.

POTENTIAL NEW FRIENDS were emerging from unexpected quarters. At the end of 1986 Hassan Howa sent a message via a third party to Ali that he was

---

[6] Clive Menell, who died in 1996, made outstanding contributions to education, sport and the arts, and was invited by Nelson Mandela to organise and run the Nelson Mandela Children's Fund. With his wife Irene he also worked with composer Todd Matshikiza in creating the famous jazz opera 'King Kong'.

[7] In October 2003, Ali Bacher was the guest speaker at a function to mark the twenty-first year of the Bakers sponsorship.

ready to meet. It was a meeting that would create havoc, and ultimately cost Howa his position. His cricket constituency was the Western Cape, more militantly opposed to SACU than any other, and although he had been deposed by Krish Mackerdhuj as the SACB president, he still carried a huge amount of clout. Howa was a pragmatist who appreciated that both national bodies were in trouble – SACU with no international credibility and SACB with no money. While SACU still attracted big sponsorships, SACB had none.

Howa was interested in the development programme. The companies who were sponsoring the project did not specify that this was for SACU only; it was an across-the-board project to develop all young cricketers of South Africa, no matter what their affiliation. Howa was so keen to show Bacher the standard of his junior cricket that he invited him to join him at SACB's under-19 tournament that was being staged in January 1987 in Mitchells Plain on the Cape Flats; but the media coverage this meeting received unleashed a hornet's nest. Mackerdhuj and Frank van der Horst, hardline president of the SA Council on Sport (Sacos), launched a blistering attack on him. He was unrepentant. Of his meeting with Bacher, he said: 'We need each other . . . SACU cannot get into international cricket without us, we can't realistically think of going it alone without them.'

The knives were now out. At an acrimonious Western Province Cricket Board (WPCB) council meeting on 18 January 1987 a motion of no confidence in the president was tabled and Howa insisted on calling for an open vote. From the chair he watched the chaos as his supporters stood to one side of the hall, his detractors to the other and some remained in the middle and became the objects of ridicule. He was defeated by a narrow margin, and he was gone, amazingly driven out by his own people, this man whose name had become synonymous with the struggle against apartheid sport, the father figure of non-racial cricket; a giant, this Caesar, felled by men made lesser by the white regime's iniquity.[8]

Central figures in the anti-Howa faction were Ngconde Balfour[9] and Rushdi Magiet;[10] and a new interim committee immediately issued a statement in which it rejected all overtures from Bacher and SACU, and turned

---

[8] After unification with SACU, former SACB members refused to invite Hassan Howa to the launch banquet of the United Cricket Board of South Africa on 29 June 1991. He died seven months later, aged 69.
[9] Ngconde Balfour became South Africa's minister of sport and recreation in 1999.
[10] Rushdi Magiet succeeded Peter Pollock as convener of the national selection committee in 1999.

down the chance to share in the money to develop eager young cricketers.[11]

There was, however, one telling departure. The WPCB secretly did a deal with Barry Fowle to supply Bakers mini-cricket bats to their juniors. There was just one problem – all the bats were decorated with Ali Bacher's face and autograph. No problem: they simply scraped them off.

---

[11] Source: *More Than A Game, a History of the WP Cricket Board*, by Mogamad Allie (WPCA 2000).

During the rebel West Indian tour, Ali Bacher is pictured with the team manager Gregory Armstrong and Joe Pamensky **Photo:** Paul Bosman

Whereas the earlier rebel tours aroused no visible opposition in South Africa, the controversial Gatting tour of 1989-90 gave rise to unprecedented protest and demonstrations Touchline Photo/Getty Images

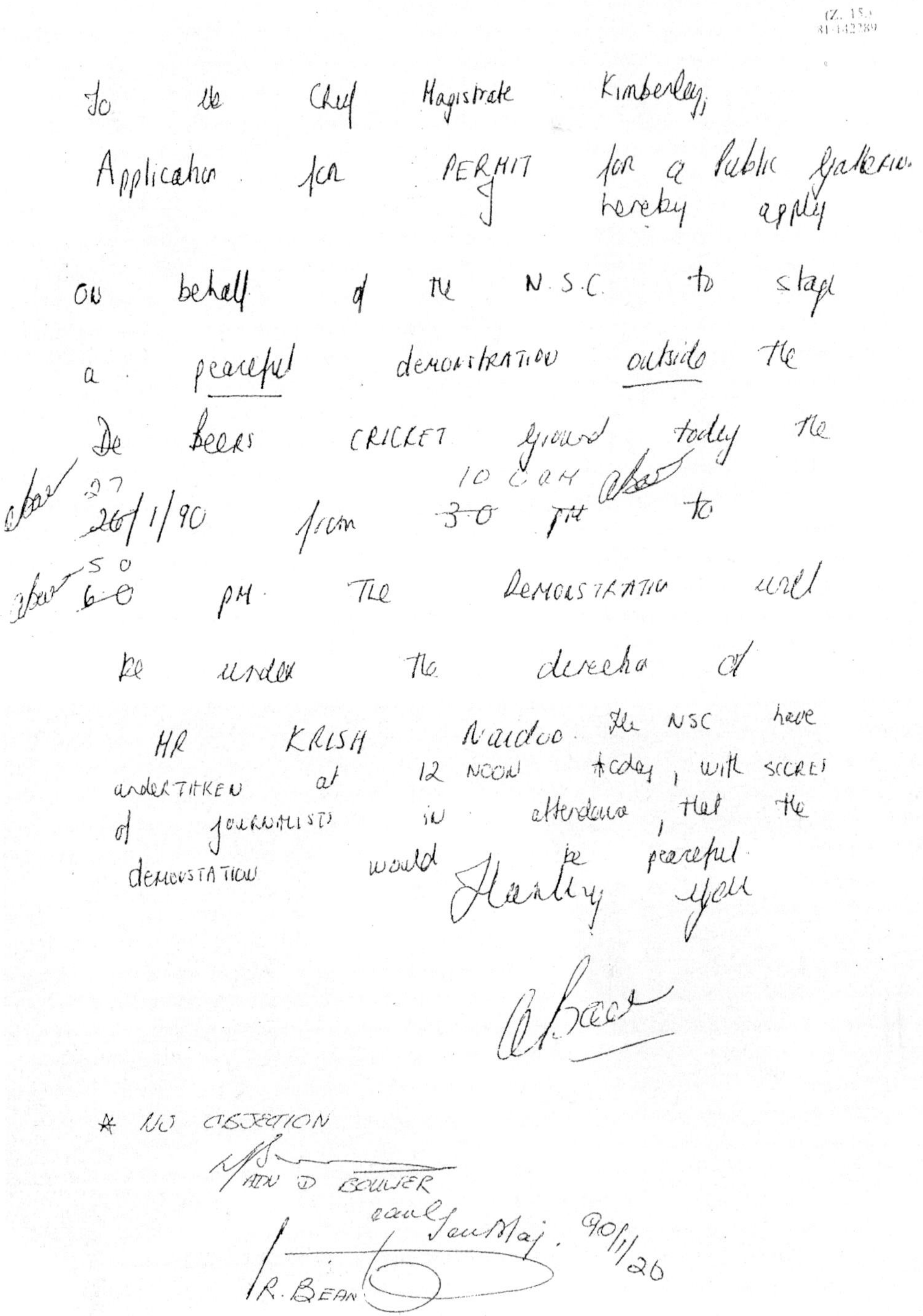

To the Chief Magistrate Kimberley,

Application for PERMIT for a Public gathering hereby apply

on behalf of the N.S.C. to stage

a peaceful demonstration outside the

De Beers CRICKET ground today the

27
26/1/90 from 3·0 PM to
10 CAM

5·0
6·0 PM. The DEMONSTRATION will

be under the direction of

MR KRISH Naidoo. The NSC have
underTAKEN at 12 NOON today, with scores
of JOURNALISTS in attendance, that the
demonstration would be peaceful. Thanking you

A Bacher

* NO OBJECTION
AIN D BOWIER
caul JaunMaj. 90/1/26
R. BEAN

Ali Bacher's handwritten note to the chief magistrate of Kimberley seeking permission for a peaceful demonstration against the tour he had organised

The SACU board that featured in a stormy meeting in East London in 1990 when Ali Bacher was under fire over the Gatting tour. Standing: Robbie Muzzell, Ewie Cronje, Fritz Bing, Alan Jordaan, Don MacLeod, Frank Brache. Sitting: Julian Thornton, Ali Bacher, Geoff Dakin, Peter van der Merwe, Raymond White

Ali Bacher flew back from the SACU showdown in East London to receive the Murray & Roberts Jack Cheetham Memorial Award at a banquet in Johannesburg. With him are members of his family, from left, Kevin Weisz, Lynn Bacher, David Bacher, Shira Bacher, Tuxie Teeger, 'Nana' Teeger, Ann Bacher, Darryl Weisz and Rose Bacher

AFRICAN NATIONAL CONGRESS. (LETTERHEAD).

MAY 20, 1990.

H.E. MR ...,
MINISTER OF FOREIGN AFFAIRS,
JAMAICA.

YOUR EXCELLENCY,

I HAVE THE HONOUR TO EXTEND TO YOU THE COMPLIMENTS OF THE
LEADERSHIP OF OUR ORGANISATION, THE AFRICAN NATIONAL CONGRESS.

AS YOU WILL SEE FROM THE ENCLOSED COPY OF A LETTER TO THE
CHAIRMAN OF THE INTERNATIONAL CRICKET COUNCIL, SIGNED BY MESSRS
DAKIN AND MACKERDHUJ, THE PROJECTED *UNITED CRICKET BOARD OF SOUTH
AFRICA* IS APPLYING FOR MEMBERSHIP OF THE ICC.

I WRITE TO YOU, SIR, TO INFORM YOU OF OUR SUPPORT FOR THIS
APPLICATION. AS YOU ARE UNDOUBTEDLY AWARE, THE ANC HAS FOR MANY
YEARS BEEN INVOLVED IN THE STRUGGLE TO END APARTHEID IN SPORT.

IN THE MORE RECENT PAST, WE HAVE BEEN INVOLVED IN EXTENSIVE
DISCUSSIONS WITH VARIOUS SPORTS BODIES IN SOUTH AFRICA TO
ENCOURAGE THEM TO FORM GENUINELY NON-RACIAL AND UNITED SPORTS
ORGANISATIONS REPRESENTATIVE OF EACH SPORTS CODE IN THE COUNTRY.

WE HAVE ALSO BEEN DISCUSSING WITH THEM PRACTICAL MEASURES AIMED
AT ENSURING THAT THE DISADVANTAGED SECTIONS OF THE SOUTH AFRICAN
POPULATION GAIN ACCESS TO ADEQUATE SPORTS FACILITIES, SO THAT
EVERYBODY HAS AN EQUAL OPPORTUNITY TO ENGAGE IN SPORT WITHOUT
DISCRIMINATION ON THE BASIS OF RACE OR COLOUR.

AS YOUR EXCELLENCY KNOWS, WE HAVE, IN THE CONTEXT OF THE STRUGGLE
FOR NON-RACIAL SPORT, ALSO INSISTED THAT ALL APARTHEID
LEGISLATION WHICH RESULTED IN RACIAL SEGREGATION IN SPORT MUST BE
REPEALED.

WE ARE SATISFIED THAT THE NECESSARY PROGRESS HAS BEEN MADE BY THE
RELEVANT CRICKET BODIES WITHIN SOUTH AFRICA TOWARDS THE
ESTABLISHMENT OF A NON-RACIAL CONTROLLING BODY. WE AWAIT THE
COMPLETION OF THE PROCESS OF THE REPEAL OF APARTHEID LEGISLATION
BY NEXT MONTH, AS HAS BEEN PROMISED BY THE SOUTH AFRICAN
GOVERNMENT.

IT IS IN THE LIGHT OF ALL THESE DEVELOPMENTS THAT WE REQUEST YOUR
EXCELLENCY TO USE YOUR GOOD OFFICES TO ENCOURAGE THE ADMISSION OF
THE PROJECTED *UNITED CRICKET BOARD OF SOUTH AFRICA* INTO THE ICC,
BEARING IN MIND THE CONDITIONS SPELT OUT IN PARAGRAPH 4 OF THE

ENCLOSED LETTER TO THE CHAIRMAN OF THE ICC.

A POSITIVE DECISION IN THIS REGARD WOULD PLAY A CRUCIAL ROLE IN
ENCOURAGING FORWARD MOVEMENT WITHIN SOUTH AFRICA TOWARDS THE
COMPLETE DESEGREGATION OF SPORT IN GENERAL. THIS, IN TURN, WOULD
HAVE AN IMPORTANT IMPACT ON THE PROCESSES IN WHICH WE ARE ENGAGED
DIRECTED AT MOVING THE MILLIONS OF SOUTH AFRICAN PEOPLE,
INCLUDING THE YOUTH, TOWARDS A NON-RACIAL AND DEMOCRATIC ORDER
AND A PEACEFUL AND STABLE SOCIETY.

WE TRUST THAT YOU WILL YOU WILL FIND THIS COMMUNICATION USEFUL TO
THE COMMON PURPOSE WE HAVE PURSUED OVER THE YEARS OF ENSURING
THAT THE APARTHEID SYSTEM IS BROUGHT TO AN END AND A NEW SYSTEM
OF EQUITY AND JUSTICE ESTABLISHED IN SOUTH AFRICA.

PLEASE ACCEPT, YOUR EXCELLENCY, THE ASSURANCES OF THE HIGHEST
CONSIDERATION.

THABO MBEKI.
SECRETARY FOR INTERNATIONAL AFFAIRS.

*The original draft of the 1991 letter from Thabo Mbeki to High Commissioners in London
which Ali Bacher could not personally collect from Mbeki's flat in a high-rise apartment
block in Johannesburg because of his fear of heights*

Steve Tshwete, Geoff Dakin, Krish Mackerdhuj and Ali Bacher face the media in the Long Room at Lord's Cricket Ground after South Africa's readmission to international cricket in 1991   Touchline Photo/Getty Images

The first board of the United Cricket Board that had equal representation from SACU and SACB. Standing: D Maku, C Docrat, E Cronje, F Brache, A Jordaan, G Karim, R White, B Leendertz, S K Reddy, D MacLeod, R Muzzell, S Swigelaar, Y Lorgat. Sitting: P Sonn, P van der Merwe, A Bacher, G Dakin, K Mackerdhuj, J Thornton and R Pillay. Absent: F Bing

Ali Bacher's first meeting with Nelson Mandela at ANC headquarters at Shell House in Johannesburg in late 1991 which resulted in South Africa competing against expectations at the 1992 Cricket World Cup. They are flanked by Steve Tshwete, left, and former West Indies captain Clive Lloyd **Photo:** *Bacher private collection*

In a graphic illustration of the healing process in South African society, Ali Bacher looks on as Steve Tshwete embraces Mike Gatting in the South African dressing room in Sydney following the victory over Australia at the 1992 World Cup *Touchline Photo/Getty Images*

In India in 1991, Ali Bacher struck up a good relationship (which later cooled) with Jagmohan Dalmiya, secretary of the Board of Control for Cricket in India (BCCI) who later became president of the International Cricket Council and BCCI. With them is UCB president Geoff Dakin

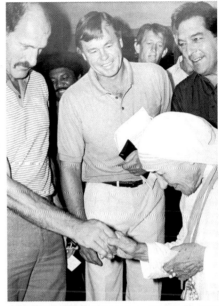

In Calcutta, South African team captain Clive Rice, coach Mike Procter and manager Ali Bacher meet Mother Teresa
Touchline Photo/Getty Images

Upon his arrival at Grantley Adams airport in Bridgetown, Barbados, in 1992, Ali Bacher is greeted by the Prime Minister L E Sandiford, far left, minister of sport and tourism Rev. Wesley Hall, far right, and Clyde Walcott, president of the West Indies Cricket Board
Photo: Bacher private collection

Old foes become comrades in arms: Krish Mackerdhuj, Geoff Dakin, Ali Bacher and Steve Tshwete after the extraordinary unification process in South African cricket
Touchline Photo/Getty Images

Ali Bacher and Krish Mackerdhuj wave the new South Africa flag on the dressing room balcony at Lord's to celebrate the 1994 Test triumph over England. Team coach Mike Procter is standing next to Bacher and manager Goolam Rajah is in front of Mackerdhuj. South Africa's future captain Hansie Cronje is top left
Touchline Photo/Getty Images

Chapter 19

The Gatting Tour

THE SOCIAL REVOLUTION of the tempestuous eighties gave rise to a growing feeling that a political breakthrough was imminent. Clandestine meetings were already being held abroad between groupings from across the political spectrum; and even enlightened Afrikaner businessmen and academics were cosying up to key ANC leaders in London and New York and on country estates deep in the English countryside.

The ANC was also very active within its own constituencies. At a meeting in Harare, in the presence of its president Oliver Tambo, the banned organisation targeted cultural activities as a sure-fire way to win hearts and minds. In December 1987, its Department of Arts and Culture staged a conference and festival in Amsterdam. It was attended by its director of Information and Publicity Thabo Mbeki who, unbeknown to many to this day, was a prominent influence in the sports movement. Among other things, the future of the cultural and sports boycott was examined during the four-day workshop. It was felt that it should be maintained for those who still resisted change, but that the time had come to make concessions to deserving causes.

Among the various debates raging at the time was the question of whether to start a new non-racial sports body or attempt to reform the existing SA Council on Sport (Sacos) which was established in 1973 but had lost favour with the ANC because it had become too politicised and had effectively taken its eye off the (sports) ball. It did not help Sacos that it had become a clique of coloured and Indian radicals with little black African involvement and, moreover, a total reluctance to accommodate whites. The formation of a new democratic body to oversee the normalisation of sport therefore seemed logical in line with three clear dynamics – the emergence of new political structures, the proposed revision of the cultural and sports boycott and the deteriorating relationship with Sacos.

Already in its infancy was a replacement democratic sports movement called the National Sports Congress (NSC), an offshoot of the so-called Sports Desk of the UDF. It would become a community-based organisation that also extended into the trade unions. It would be based on three pillars of endeavour in order of priority viz. Development, Unification and ultimately Preparation . . . for reacceptance on the world stage.

In the mean time, cricket was again causing waves. During 1989 the anti-apartheid groupings received word from Sam Ramsamy, the veteran London-based activist, that another rebel tour involving an English team was being secretly organised.

ALI'S INITIAL CONTACT was with John Emburey, the Middlesex and England cricketer who was a member of the original SAB English XI under Graham Gooch. Emburey was in South Africa on a private club tour and Bacher met him at Johannesburg airport and discussed with him the idea of another tour. There had been no international cricket in South Africa since the second Australian tour two seasons earlier and Ali believed it was time to launch another one. At no stage was he ever totally comfortable with the rebel route, but his job required that he keep the game alive in South Africa, and the only way he believed he could do this was to stage international matches involving teams of the highest possible calibre.

It was at this time that the former England captain and cricket writer Tony Lewis visited South Africa for the celebrations to mark the centenary of South African Test cricket. He wrote a series of articles for the *Sunday Telegraph* in which he found Bacher 'consumed by his mission to give South Africa a cricket future and his countrymen a future of racial freedom'. Furthermore, he wrote that Bacher's understanding of cricket and cricketers made him 'a wonderful leader against the most fearful opposition, a bullying government with a predilection for apartheid.'[1] Lewis' visit to South Africa was seen by the anti-apartheid movement as lending credence to an unjust system.

---

[1] From *Taking Fresh Guard, A Memoir* by Tony Lewis (Headline 2003).

BACHER WAS NOT blind to the fact that there was political upheaval in South Africa, and that the government was under increasing pressure to negotiate a full settlement with the ANC. So he set out to establish what, if any, time frames might have been set to bring about real political change and, in essence, the end of apartheid. He established that the general view in white opposition political circles was that it would probably take ten more years at best; and that as long as P W Botha remained in power, there was little prospect for change. Armed with this information, he concluded that cricket was still out in the cold, and that it had to continue to find its own way along the rebel road.

It is important to know that this assessment was made ahead of a pivotal event on the political front. In late January of 1989, P W Botha suffered a stroke that caused him to become an irrational and inconsistent leader. In the process, he began losing the support of many of his cabinet ministers and he decided to stand down as leader of the National Party – but not as President – a month later. F W de Klerk became the new leader of the ruling party and the wheels were then set in motion for him to oust Botha as President in acrimonious circumstances some seven months later.

IN APRIL 1989, Ali was invited to address the annual Wisden Dinner in London, a prestigious function on the English calendar. The invitation to be keynote speaker at such a distinguished gathering spoke volumes for the esteem in which Ali was held internationally, notwithstanding the fact that South African cricket had caused some considerable disruption in the international game since the start of the decade; and, what is more, although no one in the banqueting hall knew it at the time, another raid on English players was in process. In his extended speech to a rapt black-tie audience, he spoke eloquently of the changing face of cricket in South Africa and the remarkable inroads that were being made by taking cricket to 60 000 youngsters through the development programme. 'The complexion of our batting order is changing considerably, and already our junior provincial squads no longer contain mainly Anglo-Saxon names and a smattering of Afrikaners, but also names like Peace and Justice Nkutha, Harmony Ntshinka and Gift Mathe. Our team managers are no longer only the products of the South African equivalent of the British public school system, but include people like Akile Monate from Soweto, Masilo Mokhatla from Tembisa, Ezra Cagwe from Lange, Charles Kekana from Atteridgeville and Rodney Malamba from kwaMashu. Our coaches are not drawn solely any more from the ranks of white males, but also include outstanding female coaches from black primary schools, among them Sylvia Tshoma of Soweto, Thoko May of Mdantsane and Monica Mogodielo of Mamelodi. It is these people, and the others who make up the development cadre, whom I represent tonight – people who are doing things with cricket on and off the field that are bringing sweeping social changes which we believe will ultimately have a profound effect on South African society. It is these people who are at the coalface of apartheid inside South Africa, and it is them you have honoured by having me here tonight.'

Ali's speech was sincere and heartfelt, and was described as 'visionary' by those who gave him a standing ovation. In truth, however, it was completely out of step with the underground leadership dynamics of the apartheid-ravaged townships. It was also delivered against the background of a stringent, new International Cricket Council ruling that players going to South Africa merely to coach would be banned for five years. The ICC were made to believe that foreign cricketers might seek to play in South Africa in the guise of coaches, but Ali viewed this move as a terrible blow to the development programme – where expert coaching was essential – and it inspired him to find further justification for SACU's planned rebel tour. He sensitised his audience at the Wisden Dinner to this, without actually telling them about it, when he said: 'The development programme is extremely costly and the funds come only from the South African Cricket Union and the business community. As any cricket-playing country knows, most central funds come from tours; and if we are to keep the momentum going for our development and motivational programmes, we are going to have tours again soon . . .

'In the past we have had these tours in a vacuum, so to speak, with us paying out-of-proportion fees to international teams who take the money out of South Africa at a time when most of our people are very poor. We are still going to have to pay hurtfully high prices, but this time there is going to be a significant difference, as suggested by black community leaders. Players coming to South Africa as teams or individuals will be obliged by contract to assist in the township development programme. In addition, a significant percentage of all gate monies taken at matches involving international teams will be used for the township programme to provide coaching, equipment and facilities. This, coupled with funds generated by private enterprise and sponsors, will ensure that R3 million will be ploughed into black cricket at the grass roots annually.'

Of the ICC's desire to impose bans on overseas players who coached in

South Africa, Ali said: 'It is a terrible fact of life that the ICC decision hits the programme hard in two ways. It makes us pay more for fund-raising tours, which means less for the development coffers, and it acts as a deterrent to coaches coming to South Africa to help in the townships.'

IT WAS DURING this period that Bacher started 'leaning on' Van Zyl Slabbert, the former leader of the opposition in parliament, who he trusted and admired. Slabbert was a highly astute political consultant and bridge-builder who had already made successful attempts to engage the ANC leadership in exile and its underground structures in South Africa. Ali badly wanted people from the ANC to hear him out on the message of hope he had delivered to the Wisden Dinner. Slabbert viewed Bacher as a man with 'a good nose for politics . . . able to suss out when things were changing'.

In London in June 1989, Slabbert facilitated a lunch meeting for Bacher with Aziz Pahad, who was accompanied by Mendi Msimang, a stalwart of the liberation struggle who would in time become South Africa's High Commissioner in London and treasurer-general of the ANC. By this stage, Thabo Mbeki was head of the ANC's foreign affairs desk, and Pahad was his right-hand man. Over lunch at the Westbury Hotel, Ali spoke to them in earnest about the future of cricket and the good things that were happening in the development programme; and left them with a video of the township cricketers as evidence that what he was saying was genuine. He found Msimang[2] to be 'very cautious' throughout the meeting and also could not help but notice the watchful bodyguards who accompanied his two guests.

AT A SACU board meeting, the tour proposal was put to the vote, but not before its president, Geoff Dakin, had cast his own judgement. Dakin says he told his board: 'Gentlemen, P W Botha has had a stroke, the National Party is bleeding. People in this country are sick and tired with what's going on, the nation is depressed. If we have a tour now, we will uplift people's spirit because that's what international tours do. Let's not do that, let's maintain this state of depression and in this way put pressure on the government for political change.'[3]

---

[2] In 1999, Mendi Msimang's wife, Manto Tshabalala-Msimang, became South Africa's health minister.
[3] Geoff Dakin interview, October 2003.

It was put to the vote and the decision to go ahead with the tour was carried 9-1. The SACU board consisted largely of provincial presidents whose leaking cricket union coffers could do with the kind of cash injection that a tour would bring.

John Emburey had agreed to find out which players would be interested in coming to South Africa. He made contact with David Graveney, captain of Gloucestershire in the English county championship, who agreed to make the trip. It was decided that he would act as the team's player-manager and take over the administration of the project while Emburey continued to recruit players. Ali's best friend in English cricket, the former Warwickshire fast bowler Jack Bannister,[4] was also contacted to give his views on certain potential players. Dakin, who had bowed 'as a democrat' to the 9-1 judgement of his board, recalled going to London with Ali and Joe Pamensky and having dinner with Bannister. Dakin was surprised that Bannister was privy to the tour because he was secretary of the Cricketers Association which was the 'trade union' of professional cricketers in England. Ali makes it clear, however, that Bannister was never enlisted to personally contact any players or negotiate with them, but was merely used as a sounding board on the likely composition of the team. Moreover, Bannister could not be accused of a conflict of interests because, as Graveney would point out, he himself was on the executive of the Cricketers Association and recalled heated meetings during which the advisability of playing in South Africa was vigorously debated. Graveney was of the opinion that going to South Africa was a way of 'helping cricket out in a very difficult scenario'. The ANC would see it differently.

A faxed memorandum addressed to Graveney from Ngconde Balfour, NSC Interim Committee chairman for the Western Cape, stated in part: 'You are nothing more than a mercenary, and mercenaries should understand that they are not told everything by their employers, especially Mafia-type employers like Dr Ali Bacher.'

Furthermore, Balfour wrote: 'We are prepared to go out and be murdered and die on any field you will play on . . . and the blame will be squarely on the rebel doorstep, SACU and particularly Dr Ali Bacher.'

IT WAS AT a special Cricketers Association meeting at Birmingham in the

---

[4] Jack Bannister first met Ali Bacher when he played club cricket against him in Johannesburg during the early 1960s. He later became cricket correspondent of the *Birmingham Post* and a television and radio commentator.

late eighties that Bacher first met Sam Ramsamy.[5] They were invited by Bannister to present the case for and against the motion for English players to have contact with South African cricket. Ramsamy was a highly effective campaigner against apartheid sport. He had been in exile in London since the early seventies, succeeding Dennis Brutus as head of an organisation called Sanroc (South African Non-Racial Olympic Committee); and literally with a fax machine and a telephone in a tiny office in Finchley Road, Swiss Cottage, he waged a worldwide campaign to isolate apartheid sport. 'I anticipated that Ali would get a favourable hearing – and he did,' says Ramsamy, 'because he was talking to people who really did not understand the politics and only wanted to supplement their incomes by coaching or playing in their off-season. Everything at that time was about money and I really was on my own in that sort of company. What is more, I didn't trust Jack Bannister (his opinion of him would later change for the better) but he at least arranged for me to meet Ali and probably understood the political situation a bit better than the cricketers.'[6]

Ramsamy says he kept his distance from Bacher 'because I was highly suspicious of him' but Ali, in typical fashion, made all the advances. 'We eventually exchanged addresses,' says Ramsamy, 'and he would regularly write to me, send videos and documentation, but I would never write back or acknowledge receipt of them. I didn't want the wrong message to get back to my constituency, but I did admire him for never publicly mentioning our association.'[7]

The Cricketers Association meeting, however, did not alter the fact that Bacher, and not Ramsamy, was getting a far more sympathetic hearing from England's professional cricketers.

In looking back on those days, Dakin feels that he and his SACU colleagues were in fact practising deceit. 'Each year on our trips to London we would enjoy the wonderful hospitality of English cricket authorities; yet behind their backs we were busy pinching some of their best players.'

It must be said, however, that the rate of pay for the planned tour was

---

[5] In 1991, Sam Ramsamy was appointed president of the National Olympic Committee of South Africa and took South Africa back into the Olympic Movement to attend the 1992 Barcelona Olympics.
[6] Sam Ramsamy interview, August 2003.
[7] Bacher and Ramsamy are to this day the firmest of friends. When Ramsamy returned from exile in 1991, Ali arranged a flat for him in Johannesburg and invited him to make full use of his office facilities and staff two days a week until he acquired his own premises and staff.

calculated according to the players' earnings in county cricket, plus the loss of earnings for their inevitable ban. Pamensky made it clear that SACU was paying the 'going rate' in terms of the players' market value at that time, and was not going over the top by offering 'telephone number' cheques. In addition, in keeping with Ali's assurance at the Wisden Dinner, the players were required to sign agreements that they would coach in the townships during their tour.

SACU viewed as a coup the decision of the former England captain Mike Gatting, a major player in world cricket, to agree to captain the team in South Africa. Gatting was a tough and fearless batsman, a professional cricketer to the tips of his toes; and he was no political animal. For him, a cricket tour was a cricket tour, and he was ready to do the job in accordance with Graveney's rationale. The deal was a two-year contract for back-to-back tours in the seasons of 1989-90 and 1990-91.

It was this so-called Gatting Tour which hastened the formalisation of the NSC which would use the muscle of the 'internal ANC' to mobilise landmark demonstrations against the English team. In terms of the changing political landscape in South Africa, and by way of a concession from the reformist De Klerk, it was now possible for groups to stage 'peaceful demonstrations' by applying for magisterial permission to do so. Shortly before his inauguration as President on 20 September 1989, De Klerk gave the go-ahead for a march to be staged in Cape Town – the first of its kind – after local organisations insisted they be allowed to protest against killings that had recently taken place in a coloured township. Ali was in Gateshead at the time to attend the barmitzvah of a nephew. In his little hotel room, he watched on television as 30 000 people, with a militant Winnie Mandela in the vanguard, marched on the Cape Town city hall. 'I said to myself, "we've got trouble coming".'

Unbeknown to Ali at the time, the NSC had no plans to apply for permission to demonstrate. Why should it apply to a system it did not recognise as legitimate? No, its plan was to come out in force and, as Balfour suggested, face the consequences, but get the message out to the world that a tour of this nature was in flagrant breach of the three founding pillars of the NSC and, indeed, of all that they stood for under the banner of the African National Congress.

A SIGNIFICANT MOMENT in Ali Bacher's life came in October 1989 when the SACU executive committee agreed to meet members of the NSC executive at a central city hotel, the Johannesburg Sun & Towers. It was the first time these people would meet; the first time that Mthobi Tyamzashe and Mluleki George would have to negotiate an escalator in a five-star establishment; and the first time, to the horror of some SACU officials, that they would be in the company of men who addressed each other as 'Comrade' and 'Com Chair'. Ali recalls the worried look on the faces of some of his more conservative colleagues: 'It crossed my mind that they might even be thinking that the Red Army was at that very moment advancing down Eloff Street into the city centre.' That said, it should be remembered that white South Africans had been conditioned to believe that the ANC were involved in a major communist plot to take over their country.

The NSC had called the meeting after members of their executive had travelled to Lusaka, Zambia, to consult with ANC leaders in exile; and the purpose was simple. They were formally asking SACU to call off the coming Gatting tour as the start-up point in their quest to bring about true democracy. Dakin led the SACU delegation and the NSC party included Krish Naidoo, a human rights lawyer, and his fellow activists, Ngconde Balfour from Cape Town and Bill Jardine from Johannesburg. Ali and his colleagues had never even heard of these people before, let alone met them.

There was an interesting start to proceedings, which Tyamzashe recalls: 'There we were riding on an escalator for the first time, going up to the meeting room. When we reached the top, the whole of SACU was there, waiting to welcome us. We had called the meeting but they were welcoming us. Cricket was one up on us!'

Bacher addressed the meeting at length on the development programme and spoke passionately of the great benefits that township cricketers were already deriving from it, and how it was giving them and their teachers a new purpose in life. Balfour countered by saying that blacks had been playing cricket for a very long time and that their involvement with the game had not just started with Bacher's development programme. Ali's first impression of Balfour was of a forceful personality who spoke strongly on his subject. The grey-haired Jardine, who Ali viewed as the 'father figure' of the group, seemed more conciliatory and suggested that 'if we are not successful this time, and you have another tour, we will come back to you again'. Ali sensed from their body language that Jardine's comrades were not entirely happy that anything short of an immediate cancellation would be acceptable. A grim-faced Mluleki George, the NSC president and, unbeknown to the cricket officials, a member of the ANC underground, adopted a far more belligerent position when he warned that the consequences of the tour taking place would be 'too ghastly to contemplate' and that the NSC would not be held responsible 'for the blood that will flow'. This was strong rhetoric but it would have sent chills down the spines of cricket men who were now palpably out of their depth.

It was significant that the NSC delegation did not include Krish Mackerdhuj, arch enemy of SACU. He had flatly refused to attend because on a point of principle he was not prepared to sit in the same room as his adversaries. Mackerdhuj's particular involvement in the campaign would be to go to London with UDF leader Murphy Morobe to galvanise support against the tour from the British media, a mission that was obviously successful in the light of the subsequent war that some of the tabloids waged against Gatting. Balfour's presence at the meeting was therefore noteworthy. He was an executive member of Mackerdhuj's SACB but had decided to attend in spite of pressure from his board not to do so. His attendance, however, was important because he was the one member of the NSC party with some intimate knowledge of the Gatting tour. Some of his colleagues had little understanding of cricket and they admitted privately to being suitably impressed by his knowledge of the situation and the way he pulled faxes and memos from his briefcase. Only later would they learn that he had travelled to London with fellow activist Mi Hlatywayo to mobilise opinion against the tour and talk directly with Gatting and Emburey which, as it turned out, proved fruitless.

Ramsamy was involved in trying to gain access to the other rebel players but was unsuccessful because 'they regarded me as a British troublemaker'.

For the writing of this book, interviews were conducted in 2003 with some of those who attended the Sun & Towers meeting. Naidoo disclosed that allies had indeed been found on newspapers in England. 'There were two types of British media – and one of them was giving us information.' He also told how the NSC had contacted several leading South African players before the tour to try to persuade them not to take part, although this, as he put it, was 'probably too much for us to expect'. He said the NSC's strategy was to do a thorough job in advising key people of the likely consequences of the tour taking place; and this tied in with the visits to London by Mackerdhuj and Balfour, George's dire warning to the SACU executive and Balfour's fax to Graveney. 'We wanted everyone to be absolutely aware of our position so that they couldn't say later that they didn't know.'

Tyamzashe recalls how SACU pointed out that the English players had already signed their contracts and that these were not easily broken; and that most of the SACU delegation did not see the bigger picture on the political horizon and suggested that 'there was nothing in it for them' to call off the tour.

Tyamzashe insisted that the meeting was not simply about the tour, but was an opportunity for both sides to demonstrate their bona fides ahead of more important things to come. The SACU people, he felt, did not believe that the NSC had the political clout it claimed. This was not surprising because they knew nothing about the NSC and less about the ANC underground; what is more, previous rebel tours had met with little visible opposition at home.

The NSC officials also formed their own initial opinion of those facing them at the table. Tyamzashe saw Bacher 'as the one with the most information' and Dr Willie Basson (Northern Transvaal Cricket Union president) as 'showing early signs of understanding'. Bacher said that during the tea break he spoke 'amicably' with Tyamzashe which in itself was a breakthrough because, as Mthobi would later confide, 'where I came from you just didn't talk to people like Ali Bacher'.

Naidoo believed that 'Bacher bought into our argument, but he was too deep in it' (the tour), and that in his opinion 'the only two thinking people in the SACU were Bacher and Basson'. He could not know then that one of the more junior members of the SACU board, the Border Cricket Union president Robbie Muzzell, would emerge several months later as an important facilitator.

George was more sceptical about the people he was dealing with. He was the president of the UDF in the Border region and was therefore a very influential political player. For him, the question was simple: 'Can we trust Bacher?'

It was agreed in the Sun & Towers meeting that SACU would advise the NSC at nine o'clock the next morning of their decision on whether or not to proceed with the tour. The Comrades duly departed to leave the SACU men to continue with their own deliberations. The decision, reached late that night, was to proceed, but everyone was sworn to secrecy because the NSC would only be officially told the next day.

Robbie Muzzell boarded his flight back to East London. As fate would have it, he found himself seated beside Tyamzashe and George. Muzzell recalled: 'The flight was one and a half hours long, but it felt like six weeks. There the three of us sat in stony silence until George turned to me and asked, "So what's the decision?" I said, I'm sorry, I can't tell you; you

219

will receive formal notification as agreed. So George looked at me and said, "So what do you do in East London?" and I told him I ran a small factory. He said, "You know, I'm an activist. You'll regret it if you have made the wrong decision." At that point I could see my factory going up in flames.'

Sharp at nine o'clock, Bacher phoned Naidoo. 'I've been asked to inform you that the decision of my executive is that the tour will proceed.'

THE NSC WENT into immediate action, setting up anti-tour committees in all the provinces where the cricket matches were due to be played. Naidoo told newspaper reporters that they had R100 000 at their disposal to mobilise demonstrations. Tyamzashe laughed. 'We asked him where on earth he had got the money. He said he did not have it, but that pledges were coming in.'

'I was bluffing, of course,' says Naidoo, 'but the papers didn't know that.'

The anti-tour strategy included consumer boycotts, marches on the cricket grounds, trade union strikes in hotels where the team was staying and, where possible, damage to the cricket pitches.

The threat of demonstrations, of course, was something Ali did not anticipate when the Gatting team was recruited. At that stage of his deliberations, public protests of the kind described were forbidden by the apartheid regime.

ON 18 JANUARY 1990, Sam Ramsamy sent a fax from London to his comrades in Johannesburg. In advising them that the Gatting team was in the air, he concluded: 'They're all yours now!'

The NSC did not waste any time in mounting its first demonstration. Busloads of protesters set out for Jan Smuts Airport (now Johannesburg International) the next morning. Along the main route they encountered police roadblocks that prevented several of the buses from proceeding. Those buses that did get through on other routes were stopped at the airport and their occupants told to stay inside. Winnie Mandela arrived, her dark eyes flashing defiantly. She confronted the police and insisted the demonstrators be allowed to leave the buses. 'When they were, a lot of them were beaten up,' recalls Moss Mashishi, the NSC's publicity secretary, 'because the police claimed it was an illegal gathering.' As it turned out, the flight from London was delayed, and by the time the team arrived there were only traces of blood where the demonstrators had been. When the players checked into their Sandton hotel, however, more demonstrators and striking hotel staff confronted them. It was in this tense atmosphere that Ali arranged for Gatting and his team to attend a luncheon at his house two days later.

The Bachers' younger daughter Lynn was at that time studying architecture at the University of the Witwatersrand, Ali's alma mater from which all three of his children would eventually graduate. She did not count herself among the political radicals on the campus but she was 'arty and lefty' and belonged to some of the student groups. Like them, her stance was anti-tour. She recalls how, on going into a township on a road building project, she heard her fellow student activists singing protest songs in their language, and that the one word she could understand was 'Bacher'. It made her feel scared and, although she knew her father's heart was in the right place, she wished he had not become involved in this tour. She refused to attend the luncheon to meet the players and spent the day in the university darkroom working on photographs. In spite of her opposition to the tour, she would grow more and more upset in the days ahead when she saw the agonies her father would have to endure. 'He was so proud of me,' she says wistfully, 'that he would happily tell everyone, almost boastfully, that his daughter was against the tour.'

The first match of the tour was scheduled for East London. At the last minute, it was switched to Kimberley when SACU was advised that East London was a hotbed of ANC activity, and the threat of a major demonstration was very real. 'In retrospect, it was good that they moved it from East London,' says Tyamzashe, who was in charge of the anti-tour committee there. 'Political organisations were still banned so there was a danger that political people would be arrested. It would have turned very ugly.'

Bacher believed the switch was a shrewd move because Kimberley was an isolated city that was not known for its political activities. He got a rude surprise. Naidoo's contacts in the British media had tipped him off 48 hours in advance. 'Bill Jardine left Johannesburg immediately for Kimberley. He took with him Terror Lekota[8] who had just come out of jail. They mobilised the people there and we bused in people from Johannesburg.'

On the eve of the Kimberley match, Dakin received a call from the office of the lugubrious minister of law and order, Adriaan Vlok, summoning him

---

[8] Mosiuoa 'Terror' Lekota would later become South Africa's minister of defence.

to an urgent meeting in Cape Town. He took the next plane from Port Elizabeth. The meeting was attended by General Johan van der Merwe, Commissioner of Police. 'They told me that a huge demonstration was being planned for Kimberley and that I, as president of SACU, could make a request, apply for an interdict, to have it quelled. They would do the rest.' Dakin refused. 'Morally, I couldn't go along with them.'

The next day would reveal the true essence of Ali Bacher. First he gave instructions that rolls of razor wire around the field be removed and then, after Naidoo complained to him that a special police task force was blocking the demonstrators in their approach to the stadium, he effectively went to their rescue.

Kimberley had virtually come to a standstill; it was easy mobilising people in a small town. Black folk had stayed away from work and Ali was confronted with the sight of more than a thousand angry, chanting demonstrators facing the menacing barbed-wire police lines. Fair play had always been one of his guiding principles and, in a country where funda-mental human rights were non-existent, he would champion the cause of the downtrodden.

He had told the media that people were entitled to exercise their right to peaceful protest, and now, with an intimidating police presence blocking their path, the demonstrators were complaining: 'But *Ali Bacher* said it would be all right!'

To avoid any provocation on their part, the demonstrators were told by their marshals to sit down; and at this point Naidoo and Jardine found Bacher and demanded that he leave the cricket match and accompany them several kilometres down the road.

Moss Mashishi was in the thick of things. As the NSC's publicity officer, he had established a relationship with a medium-wave radio station in Johannesburg – Radio 702 – and was often enlisted by its producers to do on-the-spot reports. It was ironic that Bacher's brother-in-law, Issie Kirsh, was the founder-owner of the station.

Mashishi[9] recalls how Naidoo asked Bacher if he still believed the people had a right to peaceful demonstration. When he replied, 'Yes, of course

---

[9] Moss Mashishi became a highly successful businessman and chairman of several boards. After serving a spell as CEO of SA Tourism in the late nineties, he was appointed by the government as chief executive of the company that oversaw the World Summit on Sustainable Development in Johannesburg in 2002. In 2003, he was appointed First Vice-President of the National Olympic Committee of South Africa.

they have that right,' Naidoo said, 'Then please tell it to this police captain so he can hear it from the horse's mouth!'

Bacher told the captain that (a) peaceful demonstrations were perfectly acceptable to him and (b) he should move his men back because, armed with tear gas guns, they were provoking the crowd.

'I can still see that captain now,' says Mashishi. 'He looked at Ali and replied: "Listen, you do your job, and I'll do mine!" and then he turned on his heels and started barking commands to his men.'

There are varying accounts of what happened next, but what is certain is that the situation was explosive. 'I can still see the sheer horror in Ali's face,' says Mashishi, 'as he watched these demonstrators sitting down and the police contingent moving against them with *sjamboks* (whips) and batons. I think he had been of the view that we were the *agent provocateurs* but he now realised that the real provocation was coming from the police. It was the first time he had been in this situation and I believe at that point he saw at first hand the brutality of the system and he must have questioned the wisdom of trying to sustain the tour.'

Amid the growing tension, and a distinct feeling that all hell was going to break loose, the policeman told Ali that this was an unlawful gathering and that the march organisers needed to apply for a permit in order to demonstrate. They had refused, citing a democratic right; although, in truth, democracy was yet to come. Essentially the NSC had set out to show the fallacy of peaceful protest in South Africa; in their view it was an oxymoron.

'The situation was unbearably tense,' says sportswriter Edward Griffiths. 'There was, it was very clear, the potential for an appalling confrontation. At one stage when Ali spoke to the crowd, he had a police rifle barrel stuck across his chest.'

Ali, of course, believed that nothing was impossible at an operational level as long as he had the right people to pull the strings. He found a sympathetic ally in General Roy During, a riot police commander who had flown in especially from Pretoria, and together they resolved to start phoning around. Finally, after an hour of failed attempts to contact Gerrit Viljoen, the cabinet minister responsible for sport, he got hold of Roelf Meyer, deputy minister of constitutional development, who advised that a permit was required from the chief magistrate of Kimberley.

Under a blazing sun, the temperature was rising in the mood of the placard-waving demonstrators; and Ali, his tie knot undone and his damp shirt stuck to his back, was dripping sweat.

Michael Shafto, veteran sportswriter and newsman, dogged Ali's every footstep that day. He wrote:

> There's a particular stretch of road in Kimberley that will stay with me for the rest of my life. It's where Aristotle Ave becomes Regiment Way, long and straight with a railway line on one side and small boxlike houses on the other. It was here on the wide, dusty, shadeless pavements that demonstrators and police, with Dr Ali Bacher sandwiched between them, confronted each other for the first time over the controversial cricket tour. Riot police, smothered in heavy gear, faced the demonstrators across a space of 15 paces; and there were more police with restless, whining dogs. It was without doubt, however, that Dr Ali Bacher had the toughest day. At intervals when he emerged from apparently deadlocked talks with the police brass, he was harangued by frustrated demonstrators. "Just give me a little more time," Dr Bacher pleaded. A young black woman made an angry noise with her tongue. "It's another of your tricks, Bacher! You're just a liar, we can't trust you!"

It was into one of these boxlike houses that Ali and During were invited to use the phone. 'I'll never forget it,' says Ali. 'The owner of the house, a very nice man, turned out to be an uncle of the Howell twins who played cricket for Border. There we were, all hell breaking loose outside, Kimberley up in flames, me under siege, and all this man wanted to talk to me about was Hugh Tayfield and what I thought of him as a bowler . . .'

You're a liar, Bacher, we can't trust you, the words ringing in his ears as Ali experienced his own epiphany on Aristotle Avenue that day. He went to the chief magistrate, who was not in his office, and then to the town clerk and would later return clutching an undistinguished piece of paper that gave pause for thought in the ranks of the NSC and beyond. The most extraordinary thing had happened: the tour organiser had obtained permission for people to demonstrate against his tour.

At that very moment, says Mashishi, Bacher set the stage for establishing his credibility with the NSC leadership. 'When he got that permit,' notes Mthobi Tyamzashe, 'he took the wind right out of our sails!'

Tokyo Sexwale[10] was languishing in prison at that time but managed to watch the unfolding drama of Kimberley on television. With him was Walter Sisulu, acclaimed leader of the ANC, who turned to Sexwale when Bacher

---

[10] Tokyo Sexwale became the first premier of Gauteng province in 1994.

produced the permit legitimising the demonstration, and said, 'Hey, this chap's smart . . .'

Ali laid down one condition with which Naidoo agreed to comply. He told Bacher: 'You have my assurance that we will not interfere with the rights of people who want to watch the cricket.'

Some people did indeed want to watch the cricket but it all became rather secondary as the ill-fated Gatting tour stumbled on from one angry demonstration to the next. At Bloemfontein and Pietermaritzburg the demonstrations grew uglier, Gatting was pilloried in the tabloids and one of the English reporters, Paul Weaver, was deported, in spite of Bacher's call to the relevant minister to implore him to withdraw the deportation order. Gatting regularly found himself confronted by demonstrators, but he never once took a step back. Wherever he played, he agreed to go out and meet the protest groups and accept their petitions: *Honourable Captain, your presence at this time is frustrating our efforts to establish truly non-racial sport. Please go home and come back in three years.*

In Kimberley, the tone of the message had been far less polite. Thrusting a petition into Gatting's hand, the burly Jardine shouted angrily at the English captain: 'You have come here two years too soon . . . now get out of our country!'

Ian Wooldridge, celebrated columnist on the *Daily Mail* of London, summed up the situation perfectly: *Mike Gatting is in the wrong place at the very wrong time . . .*

It was an enduring nightmare for Ali who, unlike his colleagues on the SACU board, was constantly at the coalface, having to front-up to the demonstrations and the anger and the problems day after day. It had not helped that the headline on Shafto's lead story on the first day read *Round One to Bacher!* This had the dual effect of antagonising many people on the left of the political spectrum, who believed him to be patronising, and those on the right wing who marked him down as a man who caved in to 'terrorists'.

Not for the first time in his life, Bacher would find himself in a no-win situation; and he was out there alone because most of his fellow officials were running for cover. 'The Gatting tour was a minefield,' he recalls, 'and, with cricket under siege, I cannot recall receiving any phone calls from board members, including the SACU president (Geoff Dakin) or anyone else for that matter.'

In the circumstances, it was not surprising that Ali would later cross swords with members of his board who became incensed when he took decisions and made media statements without their prior approval. 'No one could really comprehend the pressures. At the start of the tour there were four matches where the demonstrations were at their most ferocious, and Geoff wasn't present at one of them. The media calls didn't stop, I couldn't pull the (phone) plug out, and I had to give instant answers. Once in the office after the staff had knocked off for the day, I sat at the switchboard and answered countless calls from the media. They needed answers, and I had to give them. I couldn't say, let's wait until after my next board meeting. The board met every three months.'

He also did not convey to his family the dangers that confronted him at every turn. 'He would always keep that side of things away from me and the kids,' says Shira. 'Sometimes only later I would learn from other people that his life had been in danger. He said nothing.'

At Pietermaritzburg, Bacher was genuinely scared. He and Gatting were forced to walk a hostile gauntlet of demonstrators who threw objects at them and which, he confesses, 'just finished me off'. He respected Gatting for never flinching because he was convinced the English captain was on the point of being assaulted . . . and all this against the background of F W de Klerk's epic speech to parliament the previous day in which he effectively signalled the end of apartheid by announcing that the ANC, the Pan Africanist Congress and the SA Communist Party were no longer banned, and that Nelson Mandela would soon be released from prison.

It was difficult enough for the average South African to digest the import of these staggering developments, let alone Ali, trapped in the veritable cauldron of the tour debacle. 'I was now afraid that someone might actually get killed if the tour continued.'

Little allowance was made for his own personal situation; the fact that his elder daughter Ann was to be married in a fortnight's time, and she wondering when her dad would return home because she was growing anxious about finalising the guest list.

Johan Esterhuizen, the highly diligent cricket correspondent of the Sunday newspaper *Rapport*, got a first-hand insight into Ali's state of mind during the Pietermaritzburg debacle. 'Each evening I would give him a lift back to Durban in my hire car. He tried hard not to show it, but I could see he was shattered. He was very quiet, always deep in thought; he tried to act like the same old Ali, always putting on a cheerful face, but he was really devastated and exhausted. He never thought the tour would end up like this and I got the impression he wasn't sleeping a lot. I'm sure if he had tried to drive back to Durban, he would have fallen asleep at the steering wheel.'

By the time the tour reached Johannesburg for the first 'Test' on Thursday 8 February 1990 – the rebel team had now been in the country for a fortnight – South Africa was in the grip of a crisis. City authorities refused to issue permits for demonstrations outside the Wanderers stadium and youths from Alexandra were tear-gassed and assaulted by riot police.

On the eve of the match, the parliamentary opposition Progressive Federal Party (PFP) facilitated talks with the NSC and the city traffic chief John Pearce at his home. The intention was to find common ground for a peaceful protest march around the outskirts of the Wanderers. 'We were afraid of going to this meeting because we thought it might be a trap and we'd be arrested,' recalls Mashishi. 'But we went and it was agreed that we could take a certain route from a nearby park and the police would make space for us. As it turned out, they locked us out of the park and some of our people were badly beaten up there. Krish Naidoo got tear gas in his eyes from close range and we were worried he might lose his eyesight.'

Naidoo was not aware that Bacher had also been invited to the Pearce meeting by the PFP. He was furious when Ali arrived because he claimed that this had nothing to do with the cricket boss. He insisted that Bacher leave immediately, and he did so – but not before an incident involving Mashishi. Ali knew who he was because of his high profile as the NSC publicity officer and his regular reports on Radio 702; in addition, Mashishi was in the same law class as Ann Bacher at Wits University, and she had met him on several occasions through his association with her fiancé, Darryl Weisz. Like Ann, Darryl was a top tennis player and was the chairman of the Wits All Sports Council, while Moss chaired the rival NSC-affiliated SATISCO Sports Council on the campus. In spite of this rivalry, they were on friendly terms.

When he arrived at the Pearce meeting, Ali walked straight across to Mashishi and greeted him with a big smile: 'Hi Moss, Ann says hi!'

This was all too much for Mashishi. In an instant, he saw his whole reputation as an activist going down the drain. 'It threw me completely,' he says, 'and my comrades looked at me as if to say, how come you two are so friendly? I was really very embarrassed.'

AFTER THE OPENING day of the Johannesburg match, Naidoo accused Bacher of rounding up unemployed blacks and busing them to the Wanderers to act as 'cricket fans'; but newspaper reports alleged that a mysterious pro-tour organisation called Freedom In Sport had taken groups of black hostel dwellers to the game with the promise that they would receive jobs and free food. Bacher surmised that this was a government-driven initiative. There was a huge police presence at the stadium and helicopters circled overhead. It was hard to imagine a cricket match was going on inside.

The next stop on the tour itinerary would be Ngconde Balfour's stronghold in Cape Town for the second 'Test' where it was said a militant lobby was planning to make the situation untenable. 'They had bought a thousand tickets for the Cape Town game and they planned to use flour bombs, ignite oil cans and throw tacks on the field,' says Naidoo. 'They really had it in for Ali down there; some even said they would kill him.'

The fact that the first 'Test' was a total mismatch on a villain of a pitch, and that Kepler Wessels withdrew from the South African team afterwards because some of his teammates opposed his selection, had little bearing on the bigger picture in which Ali was featuring. On the morning of the third and, as it turned out, final day of the Wanderers match, he was in his office at seven o'clock after sleeping fitfully. He wanted to be totally alone and to try to rein in his thoughts.

Unbeknown to him, the previous night a group of men in rural England had been busily involved in developing an intriguing sub-plot to the Gatting saga.

Chapter 20

A Call From Mells

Since 1987, groups of Afrikaner businessmen, members of the *Broederbond*[1] and men from within the inner circle of the ruling party had been meeting regularly abroad with the banned ANC. A lot of these clandestine get-togethers – and there were twelve in all – took place over weekends at an English country estate in Somerset called Mells Park House. It was owned by the British mining house Consolidated Goldfields, whose chairman Rudolph Agnew had agreed to put up the money to make this ongoing dialogue possible.

The object of these extraordinary exercises was to make friends, exchange ideas, examine relevant events at home and abroad, develop working relationships and influence forward thinking towards a meaningful settlement of South Africa's vexed political dilemma.

On Friday 9 February 1990, the second day of the Wanderers 'Test', the red carpet at Mells was again rolled out. The ANC delegation was as always headed by Thabo Mbeki and it included his foreign affairs colleague Aziz Pahad and Joe Nhlanhla, a commander in the ANC's Umkhonto we Sizwe (Spear of the Nation) guerrilla forces. Among the Afrikaners were top businessmen Marinus Daling of Sanlam, Attie du Plessis of Sankorp, who was a brother of the minister of finance, and Willem Pretorius of the Metropolitan group; as well as Mof Terreblanche, a broker who was a very

---

[1] A secret society of influential Afrikaners that included cabinet ministers, academics, policy makers and government advisers.

close friend of President de Klerk, and a Stellenbosch University professor Willie Esterhuyse, who was involved from the outset in making the secret meetings a reality.

Esterhuyse[2] recalls, 'Fridays were always set aside for socialising over dinner and good South African wine. Saturdays and Sundays we would get down to formal business. After dinner on this particular Friday, we went through to the huge library as we always did and it was there that Terreblanche raised the subject of the Gatting tour. He apparently was on some school committee in the vicinity of Newlands cricket ground and he said he was concerned because he felt the children might be endangered by the demonstrations.'

Terreblanche asked if it was not possible for the ANC to use its influence to 'postpone' the demonstrations but this was shot down. Mbeki and Pahad explained that international sport simply gave legitimacy to the apartheid regime and the official sporting bodies, and it was for this reason that demonstrations and boycotts were essential.

It was then, according to Esterhuyse, that Daling became very influential in the discussion. He pointed out that events around the Gatting tour were doing little to advance the conciliatory position adopted by F W de Klerk in his earth-shattering speech a week earlier. Daling proposed that they work out a way to negotiate a deal to defuse the issue.

Of significance that night was that only two people at the luxury manor house – and one was certainly Mbeki – knew that Nelson Mandela was to be released on the Sunday; and it was against this confidential background that he leapt at Daling's suggestion. It would be of inestimable value to the ANC if Mandela were released into a calm and relatively peaceful climate, and not into a country at war over the minor matter of a cricket tour. Around the hearth on a freezing February night, the library conversation grew animated . . .

AT 7 O'CLOCK on the Saturday morning, Ali Bacher was sitting alone in his office, across the road from the 'war zone' of the Wanderers stadium. He was deep in thought and introspection, staring distractedly at the wall in the manner that would sometimes inspire his son David to tell his sisters, 'Dad's in cuckooland again.'

---

[2] Interviews with Willie Esterhuyse and Allister Sparks and additional information from *Tomorrow is Another Country* by A Sparks (Struik) and *Die Burger* of 7 February 2003.

But this was not 'cuckooland'; this was grave business. Bacher was a worried man. From what he had seen from his first-hand experience in the frontlines of the cricket tour, alarming confrontations were looming.

Ali was wrestling with the conflict of being seen to be the enemy of marginalised blacks with whom he had great empathy; on the one hand, he supported their protests in abhorrence of apartheid but on the other he was a professional cricket administrator with a business to run. What to do?

Into the early hours of that morning, on the country estate in England, powerful men of divergent backgrounds were hard at work in search of solutions. Mbeki and his colleagues wanted the tour cancelled, but the Afrikaners were pushing for a compromise.

Esterhuyse recalls Pahad suggesting jokingly that when the time came the first official match by a South African team should be against India, because, in all seriousness, that country had been so supportive in the anti apartheid struggle; and Mbeki mentioned that Ali Bacher was the man to lead cricket out of the wilderness.

There have been suggestions that the businessmen actually worked out the exact details of how the Gatting tour should be curtailed but, given the extended negotiations that subsequently took place in Johannesburg, this is unlikely. What they did do, says Esterhuyse, was work out the broad framework of a compromise. It was decided that Du Plessis for the businessmen, and Mbeki and Pahad for the ANC, would take the lead in setting up urgent negotiations in South Africa. Esterhuyse was asked to organise telephones, and the calls began. 'I remember Mbeki telling Pahad to phone Sam Ramsamy in London and he himself also spoke to Ramsamy. Mbeki made several other calls. Marinus Daling, I believe, told Attie to phone Michael Katz in Johannesburg.'

According to Katz,[3] he was awoken by a phone call from Mbeki at four o'clock on that Saturday morning. 'He told me he was with fellow countrymen in England and informed me that De Klerk would announce later that day that Mandela would be released on the Sunday. He said the country would be euphoric but that there was just one unhappy blight: the tour was very divisive. He suggested I phone Ali Bacher and Krish Naidoo and facilitate a meeting with them urgently.'

Ali was still staring at the wall, silently praying for guidance, when his

---

[3] Michael Katz interview, October 2003.

telephone rang.

As we know, Michael Katz[4] was one of Ali's 'Three Wise Men'. They had known each other for a long time and shared a mutual respect and admiration. It was some 20 years earlier that they had first met, when Ali's father-in-law Tuxie Teeger telephoned Katz and asked him to help Ali with a legal problem. He had stood surety for a loan his late father, Koppel Bacher, had made, and was now being sued for the money. 'It was clear,' says Katz, 'that Ali should never have been asked to sign the suretyship and when he did so he did not have a full appreciation of the implications. Notwithstanding that, I was struck by his integrity and sincerity. He was determined not to let down the creditor and would stand by his father and his commitment.' Katz and Bacher resolved not to fight the case on a technicality, as well they might, but to concede liability, and arrangements were made for Ali to repay the money in instalments. 'I was left with a very good impression of him,' says Katz; and this was obviously mutual because Bacher in later years would enlist Katz's counsel on a variety of issues, and Katz would take his calls day and night and never ask a cent for his assistance.

On the morning of 10 February 1990, Katz told Bacher of the call from Mbeki and how he had agreed to contact Naidoo to set up a meeting. Calls were also made to Naidoo by Mbeki and Ramsamy, and Naidoo says he was simply told: 'If possible, bring this thing to an end because we don't want Mandela released into a climate of violence.'

At the Wanderers stadium, the 'Test' match finished prematurely with victory to Jimmy Cook's team but in the mean time a meeting, chaired by Katz, was under way in Bacher's office with Naidoo and Bill Jardine.[5]

'We failed to reach resolution,' says Katz, 'so we agreed to return the next morning. By lunchtime that Sunday we still had not reached an agreement and it was time to go home to watch Nelson Mandela's release on television that afternoon. That night I phoned both of them and suggested we meet at my home at 7.30 on the Monday evening.'

---

[4] Professor Michael Katz, senior partner of Edward Nathan & Friedland, is one of South Africa's most brilliant legal minds. Educated at Wits University and Harvard, he is his country's leading authority on tax law.
[5] Bill Jardine did not attend the subsequent meetings. Bacher says of him, 'Post-cricket unity he became one of my best supporters.'

Bacher realised that he was now involved in very serious business that would have huge implications for South African cricket. He started calling members of his board to attend an emergency meeting in Johannesburg on the Monday morning, 12 February, when it was agreed that he should continue negotiating within certain parameters. Naidoo says he went to Katz's house 'in an attitude of compromise'.

It was during the Monday night meeting that Katz says he proposed that SACU agree to scrap the Cape Town 'Test', curtail the seven remaining matches to four one-day internationals, and cancel the second leg of the tour scheduled for the next season. The NSC in turn should agree to call a halt to the demonstrations.

The meeting dragged on deep into the night because, at each new turn, Naidoo would leave the room to consult telephonically with his principals. The question now was where the four remaining matches would be played. In Katz's view, the first three answered the question themselves. 'The Wanderers, Newlands and Kingsmead were definites because of the potential financial success at those venues; the Eastern Cape would be (politically) difficult so Port Elizabeth and East London were out, so it was left to Bloemfontein or Centurion.'[6]

Katz recalls how Bacher had to phone each of the provinces in turn to advise them of the developing arrangements. In another room in the house, Naidoo was also on the phone to, among others, Mluleki George, who seemed to encounter some opposition before unilaterally listing the four venues that be believed were best suited. According to Naidoo, the NSC ruled out playing in Cape Town because Ngconde Balfour and his colleagues advised that they 'could not hold back the machinery' of their proposed protest action.

The deal was finally struck in the early hours of Tuesday morning. Naidoo says it was agreed that he would issue a statement to the media but that, at this stage, no mention should be made of the cancellation of the second tour. Later he was furious because Bacher spoke to the newspapers before him and, moreover, indicated that the second tour would still take place. Bacher explained that he spoke to *The Star*, only because a reporter had contacted him. The paper reported: 'When asked about the second leg of the tour, all he would say is that he hoped it would take

---

[6] The final agreement was that the matches would be played, in order, at Centurion Park, Kingsmead in Durban, Springbok Park in Bloemfontein and the Wanderers in Johannesburg.

place.'

He had reasoned, wrongly as it turned out, that he could keep its cancellation under wraps until his next meeting with his board.

Later that day, Bacher called a press conference. Gatting and Graveney, who had earlier been apprised of the sensational developments, were stony faced as they sat next to him to face the media. He told the conference that 'a third party' had influenced the decision to curtail the tour. The papers speculated that this was the government, but Gerrit Viljoen immediately denied it. *The Star* reported that 'a high ranking ANC official contacted both parties in the dispute last Saturday morning and, in anticipation of Mandela's release, urged them not to rock the boat at this delicate time.'

At the press conference, Gatting said: 'This spirit of compromise will hopefully take both parties a long way down the road towards complete understanding.' He was absolutely right.

The Freedom In Sport organisation withdrew its support for the remainder of the tour and accused SACU of 'bowing to threats'.

Ali was exhausted; and his daughter's wedding was now just five days away. Ann confided that she sometimes wondered if her dad was actually going to make it on time. Make it he did, but not before another shattering experience. The day before the wedding he was at prayers in the Waverley synagogue when Kevin Weisz, boyfriend of his second daughter Lynn, anxiously approached him clutching *The Saturday Star*. Ali saw the front page headline and went cold: *Now 2nd leg of rebel cricket tour is called off!* The report was sourced to Krish Naidoo.

'I did it,' says Naidoo,[7] 'because Ali broke our agreement on the original media release and then told the papers that the second leg was still on. I had to set the record straight.'

What he did do was set a huge cat among the hawks and doves on the SACU board.

ALI BACHER'S DILEMMA was of cricket's own making. To better understand this, it is necessary to examine how the game and its administration had evolved during the eighties.

In the seventies, the day-to-day running of South African cricket, at least the white version of it, was left to Charles Fortune, secretary of the

---

[7] Krish Naidoo interview, August 2003.

SA Cricket Association. He occupied a desk at one end of a long office in the grounds of the Wanderers Club; and at the other end of the room sat his secretary Aileen Ambler-Smith, or 'Mrs A' as she was affectionately known.[8] Fortune took tea each morning at the appointed hour; and when he did so, he would take the phone off the hook to avoid any disturbance. After lunch, he locked up his office, bade a courteous farewell to Mrs A, and went home. When a cricket reporter on deadline telephoned him at home early one evening with a simple question, Fortune berated him. 'How dare you phone me at this godforsaken hour? You Press Johnnies should stick to office hours!'

The secretary of the SA Cricket Association had more than enough time during his half days at the office to dictate letters[9] and fixture lists to Mrs A for mailing to the provincial unions and the umpires' association, take the odd phone call, and then at week's end meander off to his beloved Wanderers stadium in his other persona as the doyen of radio commentators.[10] Fortune by profession was a schoolmaster who had taught physics at St Andrew's College in Grahamstown; but it was his command of the English language that distinguished him, and the way he wove his love and appreciation of the summer game into his commentaries was one of the joys of the cricket season.

Fortune was a bit of a law unto himself, a man not to be trifled with; and although the presidents of the SACA under whom he served were men of stature, the likes of Jack Cheetham, Billy Woodin, Dennis Dyer and Boon Wallace, they allowed him to get on in his own particular way with managing cricket's affairs until everyone gathered for the annual general meeting, which involved a few formalities and a bit of chit-chat, and then

---

[8] Aileen Ambler-Smith could well lay claim to being the 'first lady' of South African cricket. She started in a part-time secretarial capacity as a young, bored housewife prepared to 'see how it goes for 18 months' and ended up working for SA Cricket for 42 years. When she eventually retired in 1995, she had spent the last nine years of her career as an invaluable admin assistant to Ali Bacher who greatly valued her expertise and advice, particularly for 'difficult' letters and correct language usage.

[9] Ali Bacher learned from Charles Fortune a rule that he would apply assiduously throughout his life: reply to every letter. He would adopt Fortune's stock letter template for hostile letter writers who might have not expected a response. It read: 'Dear Sir/Madam, I acknowledge receipt of your letter with thanks. We note the contents. Thank you for your interest in Transvaal/SA cricket. Yours etc . . .'

[10] The Charles Fortune Media Centre at the Wanderers stadium was unveiled shortly after his death at age 89 in 1994 and remains his monument.

they had a cup of tea and sandwiches and all went home again. The players were amateurs who took leave from their jobs in order to play cricket, there were no television rights to negotiate and, as a result, no major sponsorship battles to referee; and the big tours had dried up so international contact meant signing some cards at Christmas time for Mrs A to post off to England, Australia and New Zealand. This, then, was the Gentlemen's Game as it was played in isolated South Africa.

Don Mackay-Coghill was right when he said cricket had two choices at the start of the eighties: either remain as it was and probably lose its way, or grasp the nettle and become a big business in the entertainment industry. The Packer Revolution had unleashed 'Player Power' in which the cricketers were no longer afraid to air their grievances, the time of playing 'for the love the game' was gone, television was now a major factor, sponsors were demanding bang for their buck, and old-fashioned amateur administrators were being seriously challenged.

It was against this background that Bacher had moved into Transvaal and then South African cricket as the managing director of a vibrant new and exciting business. His personal evolution, however, did not necessarily match the pace of the boardroom trudge, and he soon found himself out of step with men still stuck in the ways of the old system.

'There was,' says the Western Province chief executive Arthur Turner – after Ali the longest-serving full-time cricket administrator in South Africa – 'sometimes a problem among board members who did not always appreciate the difference between *operational* decisions and *policy* decisions. I witnessed the clashes on the board when policy makers often questioned Ali for making operational decisions without their say-so.'

If cricket was indeed a business, then, like any other business, the MD was surely entitled to make operational calls in accordance with policy, and then report on his actions to the next board meeting.

Many board members agreed that Bacher was perfectly entitled to do this; most of them, after all, were top businessmen themselves; but it seemed to stick in their craw that they would read of new cricket developments in the newspapers which, in the true sense of the word, was 'news' to them. If anything, it was Ali 'stealing the limelight' in the media that seemed to irk them the most.

Against all of this, it is important to understand the man himself. Virtually all his life, Bacher was the boss. He assumed a leadership role as a small boy playing the neighbourhood backyard circuit and continued to be a leader in the fields of schoolboy endeavour that followed. Later, he captained representative teams in which he was the youngest member, he hardly played in a team that he did not captain; he captained his club at 20 and his province at 21, and although he was an 'ageing' 27 when he captained his country, he would surely have done so earlier if more international cricket was played in those days.

In his professional and business life, he was always the boss. In more than 20 years at the top in cricket he seldom served as anything less than chairman or managing director; and when he did, it was only for brief periods. He was very important to the game he served, and his colleagues recognised that; and although some of them would point out that he was not infallible, he survived every crisis and he outlasted every person who threatened his advancement.

Tiger Lance makes the point: 'Bacher would always win. I would tell the blokes "take him on, and you'll come off second best". Look at those blokes who took him on: they're gone but he's still there.'[11]

From the outset, Ali developed his own management style of old-fashioned common sense, absolute attention to detail, a steely discipline and what in the family is known as a hereditary thing they call 'Bacher stubbornness'. He was also a non-conformist and often unorthodox in his methods.

His most glaring failing was, in a perverse way, one of his strengths. His inability to recognise or understand the need to consult with his board meant that he often took decisions off his own bat which, given the urgency required, meant that awkward issues were often solved because of his swift action. Board members would argue that they were only a phone call away, but even that process, in his view, might have caused delays that could ultimately prove damaging to whatever issue he was addressing. When he decided on a course of action, he would be inflexible, almost obsessive; and it was as if he cultivated a naivety over inconsequential matters that endeared him to people. Brian Bath would say: 'It was as if in exposing his own vulnerability – in his self-deprecatory way – you automatically went along with him. If you look at the best management practice, he had it all instinctively.'[12]

He worked around the clock, through the week, throughout the year. He learned early in life where he came from and where he was going. He

[11] Tiger Lance interview, July 2003.
[12] Brian Bath interview, July 2003.

developed fierce loyalty to those who loved and supported him; he appreciated deeply the true meaning of survival. Coming from the roots of a people who had been brutalised in eastern Europe, he would become the ultimate survivor.

In March 1990, it was not just his own survival he was thinking about, but the very survival of South African cricket. The Gatting tour was over, the townships were closed to SACU, the development programme had ground to a halt and a coach like Francois Weideman was kicking his heels in the office. For the first time in his life, Ali was feeling utterly despondent and totally dispirited. For a man of boundless energy and enthusiasm, and whose chief working tool was the telephone, he found himself sometimes going home from the office at lunchtime, pulling the phone out of the socket, and lying down.

It was at this particularly low time in his life that he drew inspiration from the knowledge that, with moves for political change all around him, cricket had to strike out in a new direction. The next board meeting was imminent, and he started drafting his notes. He began writing, filling five foolscap pages with his schoolboy-like handwriting, a mixture of capitals and lower case, cursive and printing, but all the time neat, not like the average doctor, and always to the point. He read through his presentation, crossed out words and phrases, inserted new ones until finally he was satisfied that he had the right script.

The board[13] meeting in East London happened to be on the same day as a prestigious banquet in Johannesburg at which the annual Murray & Roberts Jack Cheetham Memorial Award would be made. Its recipients were men and women who were honoured for their contribution to the development of sport among disadvantaged people – regarded as the highest accolade of its kind in South Africa – and Ali Bacher was the man who would receive it that night. He arranged his flights so that he could go to East London, state his case, and return to Johannesburg in time for the banquet.

The meeting would not be easy. Even before the tour there had been rumblings of discontent on the board over his unilateral decision-making.

---

[13] The SACU board was Geoff Dakin (president), Peter van der Merwe (vice-president), Julian Thornton (treasurer), Frank Brache and Fritz Bing (both Western Province), Ewie Cronje (Free State), Willie Basson/Alan Jordaan (Northern Transvaal), Raymond White (Transvaal), Don MacLeod (Natal) and Robbie Muzzell (Border).

He had in fact received a personal letter from Geoff Dakin late in January bluntly setting out his grievances. These included the over-exposure of the tour arrangements in the media, particularly on national television, which SACU's president said was 'provocative and intimidating' to NSC people who were denied the same exposure to put their case. Then, when Dakin heard of *The Saturday Star* report on the cancellation of the second tour, he immediately denied that SACU had taken any such decision and reprimanded Bacher over the telephone. 'I told him it was a bloody disgrace that he was taking decisions without his board's knowledge and then running to the press.'

Given his initial opposition to the rebel tour, Dakin insists now that he would have backed Bacher on the cancellation, provided they had jointly piloted it through the board.

Looking back on those troubled times, Ali says: 'People must have been insane to believe the second leg of the tour was possible. It was sheer madness even to consider it. The anger and fury around that tour was something I had never experienced before and I was truly afraid that someone could die if it went on the way it began. It's true that I didn't have a mandate from the board to cancel the second leg, but I reasoned I'd give them all the reasons at the next meeting. I knew I had a justifiable reason to start a process to call off this tour; it was simply a case of looking for the right moment and the right reason.'

Bacher's notes for the East London meeting are instructive in many respects, not least for his acknowledgement that the board still had the option to bring the rebel tourists back a second time. The notes (on which he based the speech he made to the board) outline the nature of the negotiations with Naidoo and Katz and, in acknowledging their cancellation of the second tour, he wrote:

He (Naidoo) raised no objections for the (English) players to be brought back next summer on an individual basis should SACU wish this . . . he (Naidoo) even indicated he would motivate sponsors to help us find the money to pay the players – if we mentioned this in the press, it would be the kiss of death for him . . . the agreement by myself to cancel the second part of the tour was an inevitable consequence of those factors that made us curtail the first tour – i.e. police/demo confrontations, cutting off the townships from our cricket programme etc – which are certain to prevail on a more enhanced/exaggerated basis next summer . . . in theory, I went beyond my mandate and if (any) board member is offended by my action, I apologise here and now.

His notes acknowledge the authority of his board in suggesting that it still had two avenues open to it:

1) proceed with the second tour which, in my opinion for SA cricket would be disastrous, or 2) cancel the tour now. It will open the door for the first true discussions and negotiations . . . there are no guarantees, the road will very bumpy. However, by taking this route, for the first time in the past 20 years I see some light – even if it is a flicker of light at the end of the tunnel.

He then spelt out to the board the new realities in the changing political climate. Reading again from his notes:

The state of emergency will be lifted this year, notwithstanding the present unrest (in the black townships) . . . laws to restrain demonstrations are to be reduced . . . the police in the future will have to account to the courts if they attempt to stop massive demonstrations at the grounds . . . don't take the sponsors for granted, e.g. Nissan, if we alienate ourselves from the blacks of this country . . .

Finally, he read the following to the board:

In my opinion, the days of rebel tours are over. They served their purpose in the eighties but I personally would not want to get involved with them again.

It was a landmark speech and, in the heated debate that followed, Bacher was rounded on for thinking that he alone knew what was good for South African cricket; and indeed for entering into agreements that had not even been debated by his colleagues. Dakin was vociferous in his condemnation and he had strong allies in Don MacLeod, Raymond White and Peter van der Merwe who viewed Bacher's unilateral actions as a slight on the presidency and an affront to the board and all it stood for.

It was not so much that they necessarily disagreed with his vision, but that they believed he was conducting a one-man band. MacLeod said it was the first time he had ever heard Ali swear: 'He was under extreme pressure.'[14]

The meeting was still in progress when Ali realised it was time to leave to catch his plane. Dakin recalls the moment. 'He stood up and started

---

[14] Don MacLeod interview, October 2003.

packing away his notes, so I said to him, what now, are you resigning? and he muttered something about *"you people* can get on with running SA cricket", and left.'

Robbie Muzzell gave him a lift to the airport and then returned to the meeting. 'It was a tense time for sure,' he says. 'Geoff was in a difficult position because he had to drive the process and find common ground between the hawks and the doves. Ali worked on the basis of "don't worry, I'll fix it" and, yes, I did feel that he should have consulted much more with us. I was on the (SACU) sponsorships committee with him and sometimes he would do a deal without calling a committee meeting and I would read about it in the papers. If anything, that was his one failing: that he didn't consult enough and this is what cheesed off the board.'[15]

Muzzell himself was in a difficult position. He and Bacher were firm friends, and Robbie was a fine middle-order batsman who first played for Western Province before moving to the Transvaal where, in his first season under Ali's captaincy, they won the Currie Cup. Now he found himself trying to find the middle ground with men who were notoriously stubborn and proud. Having left Ali at the airport, he returned to the meeting where he spoke out on the impasse. He accepted that Dakin and Bacher were both strong characters who suffered clashes of personality, and he said, 'Let's be fair here; we need Bacher and he needs us. We've got to sort out this thing rationally for the sake of SA cricket.'

Dakin glowered at him: 'So whose side are you on anyway?'

Dakin remembers that moment well and admits that 'a lousy atmosphere' had developed between him and Bacher, but that he still had the utmost respect for his MD. 'As an organiser and a raiser of sponsorships, there was no one superior.' He knew that Muzzell had a point, and he says he made a conscious effort to call a truce as soon as possible with his managing director.

It was ironic that at the very time that Ali and his board were at loggerheads, the trustees of the Jack Cheetham Memorial Award were honouring him for his exceptional services to cricket development. The next morning, Raymond White wrote to him (a) to congratulate him in glowing terms and (b) to regret that 'hostile feelings' had developed between them. They had been teammates at Transvaal and sat together on the provincial board and, in his letter, White said he believed Bacher

---

[15] Robbie Muzzell interview, August 2003.

241

still had an enormous role to play in South African cricket. 'I do believe, however, that it would be wrong for me or any other board member to offer you unqualified support. I do not believe it would be healthy either for you or for cricket if the board were to regard you as infallible.'

White hoped they could go forward in a 'peaceful and constructive manner'.

TENSIONS AND TEMPERS had subsided a fortnight later when the board reconvened in Durban on the day of the Benson & Hedges Series floodlit final. They had had time to digest Bacher's words at East London and, in the explosive political climate that was gripping the country, the realisation had dawned that cricket could not isolate itself from an extraordinary process of change. To its credit, the board realised, too, that Bacher's lone wolf role in the trenches of the Gatting tour had taken him into a new dimension of political awareness. The board would not have known then that the NSC had taken note of Bacher's switch in direction and that, in their view, he had set the stage for gaining new-found credibility. 'The fact that he had championed that concession (to negotiate the cancellation of the second tour) enhanced him politically,' says Moss Mashishi.

At Durban, the board finally agreed officially to cancel the second tour and, what is more, they appointed Bacher as a one-man commission to investigate the way forward for South African cricket. The irony of that appointment would not have been lost on those who had been critical of the 'one-man show' he had become; and now he had an official mandate to be just that. Having tuned into the anger on the ground and established some rapport with NSC functionaries, Bacher was better placed than anyone in SACU to appreciate the imperatives; but in a media statement the next morning he made it clear that he intended canvassing a wide range of opinion within cricket to develop what he called 'a multi-person commission'.

His brief was to produce a blueprint for cricket in the nineties and he characterised it as 'the single biggest challenge in my career as a player and as an administrator.'

Dakin was in a good mood in Durban on Saturday morning, 31 March 1990. The previous night his Eastern Province, captained by Kepler Wessels, had beaten Natal[16] by one wicket in a nail-biting thriller, with the winning

---

[16] Natal was now under the captaincy of Kim Hughes, who signed for the province after the rebel Australian tours.

242

runs being scored off the last ball. The victory gave Eastern Province the 'treble' of provincial titles – the first time in their history that they had won the Benson & Hedges Series, the Nissan Shield and the Castle Currie Cup in a single season. Dakin was also relieved that a more positive mood had emerged from the board meeting that took place prior to the start of the final; although it is extraordinary to know that the motion, which he supported, to cancel the second tour was not a unanimous one.

In Johannesburg, the *Sunday Star* of 1 April ran a prominent story under the headline *Bacher's Blueprint: Cricket boss outlines his daunting brief.* In it, the reporter[17] quoted Bacher as saying: 'One cannot under-estimate the difficulties. There is such a well of resentment, bitterness and mistrust to be broken down . . . yet I am confident that all the obstacles can be overcome to create an atmosphere where we can forge a common future for all cricket in South Africa.'

The key goal was to 'create unity and an autonomous body for all cricketers in South Africa'.

Bacher copied the newspaper article to the SACB for its information. 'I believe,' says Ali, 'that once they read it, they said, "this guy's serious".'

As he had pointed out, though, the challenge was daunting, and this is best framed in the words of Mashishi: 'Up until then no one even wanted to meet with Ali Bacher. He was regarded as the architect of all the efforts to undermine our campaign to totally isolate South African sport.'

The time had arrived for Ali to deal with the despair and loss of confidence that was his own personal cost for the Gatting tour, and to do that he had to find a way to gain a semblance of respectability from his black countrymen.

'I made my peace in Alex,' he says wistfully. By that he meant he found comfort in re-establishing relationships in sprawling Alexandra township, the festering sore on the north-eastern outskirts of Johannesburg. It was there that he cemented a relationship with a former student activist and shop steward who had been fired by a major corporation for taking his workers out on strike. He was a popular street-smart figure in Alex, the place of his birth, and his name was Kapi Nkwana. On the dusty, litter-strewn streets of the ghetto he was known to one and all as 'Kapi the Goalkeeper' who had forsaken the chance to play professional football because his all-consuming passion was to work towards his dream of the

---

[17] Rodney Hartman, then sports editor of the *Sunday Star*, wrote the article.

unification of South African sport. During the Gatting tour he was the NSC co-ordinator for Alex whose task was to mobilise student and civic organisations in opposition to it.

It was through Solly Mashiloane – headmaster of an Alex primary school that had yielded a range of top youngsters to a development programme that had now ground to a halt – that Bacher made contact with Nkwana during that month of April. He explained the role he had played in the negotiations to cancel the second leg of the tour and suggested that they should let 'bygones be bygones' and build a meaningful relationship. 'My heart is in Alex,' Ali told him.

Far from rejecting Bacher's hand of friendship, the shrewd Nkwana viewed it as a possible means to achieve an end: the desire of his Alex All Sports Congress (the local branch of the NSC) to lead the way for the unification of sport at a national level. In discussing the best road to unification, there had been disagreement between Alex and the national office of the NSC; and it seems that Nkwana's people were keen to prove a point and take the initiative. 'We in Alex wanted to show the way in unification,' says Nkwana. 'We wanted to bring SACU and SACB together in an interim body.'

Normalising cricket, however, was not seen as such a simple matter; the ANC, for example, viewed it as one of the more difficult sporting ideals. When Steve Tshwete was first told by his comrades of their desire to explore the unification of South African cricket, he summarily dismissed the idea as 'a stillborn initiative'.[18] Ironically, this was not because cricket was seen as one of the more recalcitrant 'white' sports – particularly since SACU had forsworn rebel tours – but rather because SACB, with its strong Sacos background, was vehemently opposed to any contact whatsoever with SACU. The ANC line was that the normalisation of South African sport had to be approached very carefully and with pinpoint timing in order to avoid a white backlash on the one hand and black distrust on the other. It was reasoned that an 'easier' sport like soccer should be tackled first in order to sensitise the various race groups to this practice, and cricket would follow much later down the line. For cricket to normalise, unity would have to be achieved between two bodies that seemed light years apart.

---

[18] Interview with Mthobi Tyamzashe, August 2003. Tyamzashe became secretary-general of the NSC and later served as director-general to Steve Tshwete when he became South Africa's minister of sport in 1994. Tyamzashe later left sport to become a business executive in Johannesburg.

The NSC's role was to bring such people together around the table, but it first needed permission from the ANC leadership, of which Tshwete, a former Robben Island prisoner,[19] was an important figure. He was living in exile in Lusaka where he worked closely with Barbara Masekela who headed up the ANC's Arts and Culture Department. She had been instrumental in establishing the sport and cultural boycott and agreed with Tshwete that cricket talks were premature.

Nkwana made a telling point. In agreeing to build bridges with Bacher, he said it was obvious to him that the impasse in sport in South Africa 'was not Ali's fault, it was apartheid's fault' and that in different ways they were both victims. He suggested that, in trying to help Alex, Bacher should not only confine his efforts to cricket, but to all sports. There was a need in the township for a multi-sports complex and clubhouse.

Ali visited the giant Anglo American Corporation in downtown Johannesburg where he met its executive director Michael O'Dowd who was also chairman of the Anglo and De Beers Chairman's Fund. His request was simple – he wanted one million rand to build a sports complex. O'Dowd stared at the floor throughout the time that Ali spoke, then looked up and said, 'If you can get support for the project in Alex, come back to me.'

When Bacher returned, he was accompanied by Nkwana and Vusi Thabethe, respectively co-ordinator and chairperson of the Alex All Sports Congress. 'Normally a sponsor will ask, "what's in it for us?" before making a decision, but this time it was the other way around,' says Ali. 'My friends from Alex told their benefactor that they would accept the one million rand conditionally, but an Anglo American representative would first have to go to Alex to explain to all concerned why the company wanted to finance the complex. They wanted to make sure there were no ulterior motives!'

A meeting was arranged in a community centre in the heart of the township at which representatives from the trade unions, civic organisations, student bodies, women's league, youth league and sports congress gathered to hear Anglo American Corporation, the most powerful gold mining company in the world, state its bona fides. Anglo's Brian Freimond was given the task, and he arrived in his executive motor car and stated his case. The township leaders thanked him for coming and said they would be happy to accept the sponsorship. Freimond told Bacher afterwards, 'In

---

[19] In 1964, Steve Tshwete was arrested and charged with furthering the aims of a banned organisation, and with 16 counts of sabotage, and was sentenced to 15 years imprisonment on Robben Island.

all the hours I have spent working for the Chairman's Fund, that one was the best hour of my life!'

It was before this meeting that Nkwana showed Bacher photographs of youthful Alex demonstrators who had been beaten by police with *sjamboks* after they had been escorted away from the Wanderers stadium during the 'Test' match there. He could clearly see the welts and scars left by the whipping and the serious eye injury suffered by one of the victims.

'I was so upset with what I saw in those photographs that when a SABC television news crew conducted interviews after the historic meeting with Freimond, I used the opportunity to apologise to the nation for the Gatting tour.'

It was broadcast on the main news bulletin at eight o'clock that night.

It was not only into the black African communities that Bacher ventured in order to find a new direction. Indian and coloured South Africans were justifiably proud of their own cricket heritage; they boasted some of the most committed activists in the liberation struggle, and generally they held Bacher and SACU in utter contempt. Among those he now counselled was Ameen Akhalwaya,[20] a campaigning newspaperman, former Nieman Fellow at Harvard University, and a respected figure in the Indian community of Johannesburg. Ali had known him since the misguided days of 'normalisation' in the seventies and admired him for his political knowledge and deep love of cricket. He would visit him at his little office in Lenasia, the Indian area south of Johannesburg, where he edited an 'alternative' newspaper that vigorously challenged apartheid; and he became an important sounding board of the political mood in an influential Indian community that was SACB-aligned and militantly opposed to white domination. Throughout the eighties, these people regarded Bacher as Public Enemy No 1 but, in time, many would come to respect him once they accepted that his attempts to unify cricket on non-racial lines were genuine. In early 1990, however, the jury was still out on the question of his integrity.

ROBBIE MUZZELL WAS among those board members who wholeheartedly subscribed to Bacher's vision for the future. He had been thinking about the Sun & Towers meeting with the NSC six months earlier when he had first met Mthobi Tyamzashe. He regarded himself and Tyamzashe as mere

---

[20] Ameen Akhalwaya died from cancer in 1998 at the age of 52.

juniors in this important forum and felt the best way forward might be to initiate a process from the bottom up. He sensed that the people at the top of the pyramid were polls apart ideologically, and felt that he and Tyamzashe perhaps had enough in common to set the ball rolling. Tyamzashe worked in the human resources department of a pharmaceutical company in East London, and Muzzell was a good friend of its HR director, Wayne Munro. Off his own bat, Muzzell asked Munro if he could set up a meeting with Tyamzashe.

It was the start of an important initiative that saw the three of them meeting several times at the Curry Muncher restaurant. 'It was always the same restaurant and always the same table in the same cubicle,' says Muzzell. 'It crossed my mind that maybe the meetings were being bugged.'

More than a decade later, Tyamzashe laughs at the suggestion. 'I just happened to like curry!'

Together they thrashed through the issues of what cricket was facing in its quest for unification. Some issues they cast aside, others they re-examined. Some hurdles that had seemed insurmountable now looked fairly straightforward. They agreed they were only a small part of a much bigger picture, and that it would be a good idea to try to get their two principals, Mluleki George and Ali Bacher, together for more meaningful discussions. 'If you can get George, I'll have Ali in 24 hours flat!' enthused Muzzell. His intention was always to get to George because he, after all, was the NSC president and an influential figure in the ANC.

The problem, as Tyamzashe would later point out, was that 'where I came from you just didn't talk to Ali Bacher. It was tantamount to treason. He was hated for starting the development programme without the courtesy of consulting with us; and that's why it had to be stopped and later restarted through the proper channels.'

Among Tyamzashe's comrades, the playing of apartheid sport was so despised that it was forbidden even to watch games featuring all-white teams on television 'for fear of being contaminated'.

George insisted he would not meet Bacher alone but that he and Tyamzashe would do it together and hear him out. If this wasn't exactly supping with the devil, it was most certainly meeting with the enemy; and it did not seem to matter that as far back as 1987 Bacher had released a statement through the media which read:

The people of South Africa should be getting together to work out a common future based on mutual cooperation and mutual respect. Anything less than this is retrogressive and the consequences will be terrible. The SACU cannot urge the government strongly enough to rid South Africa of all laws such as the Group Areas Act and the Separate Amenities Act . . . until that happens apartheid will not be dead in South Africa and South Africa itself will die if apartheid remains.

MUZZELL TELEPHONED BACHER and told him that he had managed to broker a meeting with George. Ali was so excited that he then committed a serious blunder. During one of his many discussions with Van Zyl Slabbert, from whom he was constantly gaining political insight, he mentioned the coming meeting with the NSC president. Slabbert in turn made a passing reference to this to a colleague, Max Mamase, who came from the Eastern Cape. Word of it got back to George who was furious that confidentiality had been breached. He told Tyamzashe, 'Bacher is showing his true colours again!' and immediately cancelled the meeting.

It took a great deal of quiet diplomacy on Muzzell's part to get the process back on track and, once he had achieved this, it was agreed that the meeting would take place at Tyamzashe's house in an area known as Buffalo Flats.

At the agreed hour, Bacher and Muzzell arrived but they were asked to wait outside because their two hosts were busy conducting a rugby meeting. Like many blacks in the Eastern Cape, George and Tyamzashe were rugby men first and foremost. George[21] was the president of the non-racial Border Rugby Board and Tyamzashe had succeeded Steve Tshwete as its secretary when he went into exile. Here were rugby men concerned with cricket and, in the context of current developments, it was not out of place to recall that rugby reputedly began in England in the nineteenth century when one William Webb Ellis, a scholar at Rugby School, picked up the soccer ball and ran with it in flagrant disregard of the laws of the game. It was with a similar risky and unconventional spirit that these men now gathered in Buffalo Flats. Bacher, as we know, was not averse to running with the ball; but the two NSC men were running the real risk. They had no mandate from their political leadership, were indeed running counter to the Lusaka dictums regarding premature moves towards cricket unity, and would have incurred the serious wrath of their comrades if word of the meeting had leaked out. 'Those who were exposed as sell-outs,' says Tyamzashe, 'were written off and could never be redeemed.'

---

[21] Mluleki George would later serve on the executive committee of the unified SA Rugby Football Union and became Chief Whip of the ANC in parliament.

George told Tyamzashe, 'I only deal with people that I can see. When we met in Johannesburg (at the Sun & Towers meeting) Bacher came across as a committed and passionate man – unless, of course, he is a professional liar!'

George was a hardened activist who had been incarcerated on Robben Island and in and out of more apartheid jails than he cared to mention, and he had suffered horrific treatment at the hands of security police. He was known as a courageous man who challenged stereotypes and bent many of the conventional rules of the liberation struggle. He held no truck with the Sacos radicals and their 'no normal sport in an abnormal society', and would regularly clash with them. 'Are you waiting for someone from heaven to normalise society?' he would ask. 'No, the way forward is to talk and open negotiations.'

Tyamzashe would also recall Thabo Mbeki's advice to striking students that 'it is better to open the door from the inside than try to force it open from the outside'.

It was in this spirit that the two brave NSC men agreed to sit down with Bacher in Buffalo Flats.

Ali vividly recalls the secret meeting: 'It lasted 20 minutes. I spoke for 20 minutes. It was like talking to a wall. Neither Mthobi or George once looked at me.'

It was of course their deliberate tactic to make him feel uncomfortable and almost unwelcome; it was their way of testing his sincerity.

As always, Bacher spoke with passion and pride of the development programme. 'I always believed that this (programme) was the key to the door of mutual understanding.' And, like Mbeki, he would much rather unlock it from the inside than bang it down from outside.

George and Tyamzashe believed he did well enough to warrant a follow-up meeting; so a few weeks later they got together over an excellent dinner at the Muzzell home that effectively unlocked the door. In his understated way, Ali remembers it as 'a much warmer meeting than the first one' but Muzzell tells it somewhat differently. 'After dinner, as we sat in the lounge, George said he believed Ali's heart was in the right place and told him it was all right for him to carry on with the development programme provided he engaged the communities. Ali shot out of his chair and hugged him.'

Ali recalls, 'It was the first time that I could honestly say that a process had started to unite South African cricket. The selling point was the development programme, which was the way forward to redress imbalances. It was what they wanted. They particularly welcomed my suggestion that at national and provincial level there would be joint directors of development – one from each side as they existed then. That won the day.'

Bacher would later tell the two NSC men, 'I know the great risks you took in meeting with us without a mandate, and I really appreciate it. Please chaps, in future, no more risks!'

Muzzell is given the credit for getting cricket to this point. 'Without Robbie,' says Tyamzashe, 'the whole thing could have gone the other way. It was difficult not to trust him.'

Ali says of him, 'Robbie showed that he clearly understood the route that cricket needed to follow in the new political order. He started the unification process.'

Chapter 21

Secret Rendezvous

STEVE TSHWETE WAS among the first group of high-ranking ANC exiles to return to South Africa early in 1990.[1] There was danger all around.

Those opposed to political change knew that important people were being filtered in from outside South Africa's borders, and from the frontline states to the north, and the ANC was anticipating what it called an 'elimination campaign' targeting its leadership. The ANC might have been unbanned, but no indemnity had yet been issued for people on its 'wanted list'. ANC formations were warned to be on the alert and Tshwete was spirited away in a safe house in the East London area.[2]

He had been the Army Commissar in Umkhonto we Sizwe, the feared guerrilla forces known as 'MK' that right-wing propaganda categorised as 'terrorists'; and he was a member of the party's National Executive Committee. As a young man in the Eastern Cape he had joined the local branch of the banned MK, was involved in sabotage campaigns against minor installations, distributed a pamphlet he wrote on the coming 'bloodbath' and was finally arrested when a colleague informed on him. He was sent in leg irons to Robben Island at the age of 26 and was 41

---

[1] Steve Tshwete was a member of the ANC's delegation at the first round of talks with De Klerk's government in May 1990. These were held at the president's official Cape Town residence of Groote Schuur. The three-day summit drafted the famous Groote Schuur Minute which was the first joint document charting South Africa's course towards democracy.

[2] Hintsa Siwisa interview, August 2003.

when he was released. During those 15 years he suffered intolerable treatment that included nine months in solitary confinement and constant torture and beatings. He would say, 'You came to think of your survival not in days but in hours. You thought, if I can just survive for the next two hours, thank the Lord.'

While on the dreaded island, separated from the beautiful city of Cape Town by only a short stretch of treacherous ocean, he refused to buckle to his tormentors. He became Head of Political Education there, was described as a 'walking encyclopaedia of world revolutionary experience' and completed a BA degree in Education and Philosophy by correspondence from the University of South Africa in Pretoria. He had a great love of sport, especially rugby, and he established the Island Rugby Board (IRB), became its founding president and wrote a 19-page constitution. In his youth he had been active in the Eastern Cape in campaigns against racially segregated sport.

Upon his release from the island in 1979, he was served a two-year banning order that restricted him to his Eastern Cape village of Peelton, a former mission station on the outskirts of King William's Town. He could not believe that after 15 years' incarceration, during which he endured insufferable privation, he was now virtually in prison again without even the benefit of a trial. The restriction order claimed as its justification that he was involved in furthering the aims of communism. Its effect was to embitter him and inspire him to play a greater role in his fight against the apartheid regime.

He took up a teaching position and, once his banning order expired in 1981, he continued his political activities and suffered constant surveillance, harassment, detention, and further torture. He was a founding member of the UDF in 1983, became its first president in the Border region (Mluleki George would succeed him) and was immediately detained again for four months. His militancy and revulsion towards the apartheid system was by now intense; and it was not helped by the disappearance of fellow activists from his community and their subsequent brutal murder.

When 28 people were massacred in Duncan Village, East London, in August 1985, Tshwete was stricken with grief and hatred. He was advised by his comrades not to attend the mass funeral – which would mean him leaving the relative safety of his home in the Ciskei independent homeland, or Bantustan as such aberrations of apartheid were known – because the police would be there in numbers, but he insisted on attending. 'How can I not be with my people at this terrible time?' he told friends. When he arrived at the stadium where the funeral service was being held, the thousands of mourners acclaimed him. They knew the dangers he faced. With the police watching from a distance and unable to get near him because of the wedge that the mourners had deliberately driven between them and the podium, Tshwete broke down and wept at the sight of a child's coffin among the 28. In an atmosphere thick with tension, this great orator delivered an emotional and confrontational speech in which he whipped up passions by declaring that there had been enough burning in the township and that it was now time to burn the town. Afterwards, he sped out the back of the stadium in a waiting car to give police the slip.

Back in Peelton, the Ciskei homeland police were now on to him. They had been given instructions to arrest him and hand him over to their counterparts in the republic. 'They arrived at our home, maybe ten police cars,' recalls his widow Pam Tshwete, 'and a neighbour who was very drunk confronted these policemen and was shouting at them and telling them to leave us alone. Some of them came into the house and told Steve that they were taking him away. I think they were distracted by the drunk neighbour who was still shouting outside so they did not surround the house as they would normally do. Steve told the policemen that he was going to get his jacket and came through to the kitchen. He told me he was going to make a run for it. He left through the back door which was close to a railway line that was the border between Ciskei and the republic. It was December and the mealies (maize) were tall between our house and the railway line. He ran through the mealies without being seen. Once over the railway line he was met by a friend who took him to Mzi Nguni's house in Mdantsane where he was kept under cover.

'When the Ciskei police realised he had given them the slip, they began to threaten me. They told me that I would be killed, and my children too.'[3]

Tshwete shaved his head and disguised himself as a priest. When the time was right, he bade farewell to Nguni[4] and fled South Africa for Zambia in December 1985. He had been strongly advised by the ANC leadership to go into exile because his revolutionary pronouncements in South Africa were exposing him to grave danger from both the Ciskei police and the republic's security forces. Pam and the children followed him three weeks later. They had two children of their own, five-year-old Yonda and her

---

[3] Pam Tshwete interview, November 2003.
[4] Mzi Nguni is one of South Africa's most successful professional boxing managers who has trained several world champions.

three-year-old brother Mayihlome, and two 'adopted' children, Monde Zondeki,[5] born in 1982, and his younger sister Namhla, the offspring of Pam's late sister Nokwande. She was a teacher and SA Communist Party activist who was constantly harassed by police about her brother-in-law's whereabouts. She believed it was unsafe for her children to remain with her in Peelton so she sent them to join the Tshwetes in exile. She died later in a car accident.

In Lusaka, Pam attended the university teaching hospital where she took a diploma in primary health care.[6] Steve served on a number of ANC committees, went for military training and was co-opted on to the ANC's National Executive Committee.

Now, five years later, this man who had dedicated his entire life to the liberation struggle at great sacrifice to himself and his family had finally come home . . .

DURING THE 1980s, and largely with the help of Frederik Van Zyl Slabbert, groups of influential South Africans had travelled north to meet with the ANC in exile. On one such occasion in 1989, Flip Potgieter, a colleague of Geoff Dakin's on the Eastern Province cricket board, travelled to Lusaka. Of those he met, he was particularly impressed with Thabo Mbeki and Steve Tshwete.

Back in Port Elizabeth, Potgieter contacted Dakin. 'Tell Ali that Steve Tshwete is his man . . .'

The message was duly passed on, and Bacher made a note of it.

Since his appointment as SACU's one-man commission in April 1990, Ali had, as promised, been canvassing far and wide for advice and assistance. It was Van Zyl Slabbert who engineered the breakthrough. Early in 1990 he had attended a big dinner at the Carlton Hotel in Johannesburg where top businessmen met Nelson Mandela and other ANC luminaries for the first time in South Africa. Slabbert immediately telephoned Bacher. 'Here is a telephone number. Go to East London on Friday and meet with Steve Tshwete.'

---

[5] Monde Zondeki, a fast bowler, made his one-day international debut for South Africa against Sri Lanka in December 2002 when he took a wicket with his first ball. He was in South Africa's 2003 World Cup squad and made his Test debut against England at Leeds in August 2003.
[6] Pam Tshwete became an ANC MP in October 2002 and is a member of the parliamentary portfolio committee on health.

The name rang a slight bell with Ali, but he knew absolutely nothing about the man he was now due to meet. In truth, at that stage, there were very few white South Africans who had even heard of Steve Tshwete. Slabbert had been involved in facilitating so many contacts over several years that he cannot recall how that particular meeting was engineered.

Bacher flew to East London where Robbie Muzzell was at the airport to meet him. 'I've got a telephone number and a name, that's all,' Ali told him. 'Have you heard of someone called Steve Tshwete?'

'No.'

Neither of them knew that he was the head of the ANC Sports Desk, the man charged with overseeing the normalisation of South African sport.

Back at his home in the suburb of Clifton Park, Muzzell called the number. The woman on the other end of the line refused to talk to him. 'Give me your driver,' was all she would say. Muzzell handed the phone to his driver Freddy. He was given an address.

'Where is it?' asked Muzzell.

'It's in Mdantsane.'

Muzzell shuddered. Mdantsane was situated a mere five kilometres away but, for whites, it was a no-go area. It was the second largest black township, behind Soweto, in South Africa, and it was a hotbed of political activism. For a white man to go in there, particularly at night, was courting disaster. But it was there that Ali was headed, with Freddy at the wheel, in a little car belonging to Muzzell's wife Meryl. They drove off in the dead of night, and when they had not returned two hours later, Robbie glanced at Meryl and said, 'That's your car gone . . .'

Bacher meanwhile had been ushered into the front room of a township house. A woman invited him to take a seat. He sunk into the cushions of a large couch. There he waited alone for what seemed like an eternity. It was a very cold night.

In another room the woman, Nolundi Siwisa, was on the phone to her husband Hintsa, a human rights lawyer, activist and former detainee, who was working in his office. 'Ali Bacher is at our house and he wants to see Steve.'

Hintsa Siwisa says he then went to the safe house where Tshwete was staying and advised him of the visitor.

'What does he want?'

'I don't know.'

'Well, let's go and find out.'

Together they returned to Siwisa's house where Bacher and Tshwete

255

shook hands for the first time. Tshwete was a huge man who peered at Bacher through very thick, horn-rimmed spectacles. He spoke softly with a distinctive gravelly voice. 'He apologised for being late,' recalls Ali, 'and said he had been to visit his sick father.'

Tshwete pulled up a wooden chair next to the couch. 'He was a big man and I was sitting so low that he towered over me,' recalls Ali. 'All the time, he was peering at me through those thick glasses and chewing on his pipe.'

Ali spoke for 45 minutes. 'He just sat there and listened while I was fighting for cricket's existence.'

Till his dying day, Bacher will never forget what Tshwete said once the monologue was over. 'He looked at me, shook my hand, and said, "I'll help you". That was it.'

It was at that very instant that two men, poles apart, formed a bond that would change their lives, and a friendship that would flourish for the next 12 years.

As Ali would say, 'From that moment he never *stopped* helping me.'

According to Hintsa Siwisa, Tshwete's first move after the meeting with Bacher was to consult with the ANC leadership, and Mandela in particular, to take the cricket process forward.

At the same time, SACB officials were mulling over the article from the *Sunday Star* that outlined Bacher's brief to seek a new non-racial order for cricket. Mluleki George suggested the full SACB executive should meet in KwaZulu-Natal to discuss the way forward, but Krish Mackerdhuj seemed reluctant to do so. George asked him to list his objections. He replied, 'Distrust, history . . . and money.' The real problem, it seemed, was that SACB did not have the funds for all its executive committee members to attend the meeting. Financially, it was a cricket body that was forced by circumstances to fly by the seat of its pants; and the story goes that certain board members in Cape Town once staked the sparse money in the committee's account on a racehorse that a contact on the course had tipped as a 'certainty'. The horse duly won and the winnings allowed delegates to fly to the next meeting.

On this occasion, however, there was no suggestion of any crazy gamble. Tyamzashe telephoned Bacher to advise him of the situation. 'Don't worry, I'll fix it!' said Ali. 'Provided, of course, you find this acceptable?'

'Okay, but you dare not tell anyone that you're getting involved. I'll tell Mluleki George, but no one else.'

Bacher went to two of his sponsors, SA Breweries and Bakers Biscuits, and each of them chipped in R5 000. He put the R10 000 in cash in a bag and sent it to East London where an arrangement was made for Tyamzashe to collect it. 'I passed it on to George,' says Mthobi, 'and we didn't even count it!'

At their next meeting, George held out the bag to Mackerdhuj, 'Here's your money,' but did not say where it had come from. Tyamzashe had, in fact, contacted Sam Ramsamy in London – the only other person in the know – to suggest they say the money came from Sanroc. Ramsamy says he did not know how much money was involved but was prepared to go along with the ruse because he did not want the question of cash to put a spanner in the works of the exciting new developments.

LESS THAN EIGHT months after the Mdantsane meeting, the first session of unity talks between SACU and SACB took place in Durban. It was Tshwete who facilitated them and it was unanimously agreed that he be asked to chair them. All it took was three meetings under his exceptional guidance to achieve unification.

'Steve was brilliant,' says Ali. 'When things looked like they were going off the track, it was he who pulled everyone back into line.'

He was, indeed, a man among men; and he would play an extraordinary role in hastening a new life for all in the democratic South Africa that he had helped create through his blood, sweat and tears.

PART IV

UNITY

Chapter 22

Batting for South Africa

He was to us more than a comrade . . . He was to us more than a friend.
Of him we can say that he was part of our own mortal bodies . . .
He was a particle of our sun.
– President Thabo Mbeki on the death of Stephen Vukile Tshwete, 26 April 2002.

This book might never have been written had it not been for the sudden death of Steve Tshwete on the eve of Freedom Day in April 2002. He had been bedridden at his home in Pretoria with a debilitating lower back problem and was in constant pain and unable to move properly. Out of the blue, he developed acute respiratory distress and, battling to breathe, he was admitted to 1 Military Hospital in Pretoria where he was placed on a respirator. Ali Bacher visited him several times and twice he telephoned the President's office to advise Thabo Mbeki that his comrade was seriously ill. At 9 pm on Friday, 25 April 2002, Bacher took a phone call from Pam Tshwete. 'Please come and see Steve tomorrow morning, he's in a very bad way.'

Two hours later, he died. He was 63. Ali was shocked beyond belief when he received the news. His good friend was gone, and he searched for ways to express his true feelings and tell of their unique relationship; of their wonderful experiences together, their shared hopes and fears, and his deep admiration for the man.

He asked one of his communications directors at the ICC Cricket World Cup headquarters if there was perhaps a way he could put it all into a story and offer it to a newspaper for publication.

'Yes,' he was told, 'but you might also consider putting it all in a book one

261

day.'

That set him thinking. He felt that Steve's contribution to South Africa had to be told, otherwise it might never be told, and it was then that he made his decision to authorise a biography. This then is the story that he wanted to tell . . .

ALI BACHER KNEW from the start in Mdantsane that a special 'chemistry' existed between him and Steve Tshwete.

'Those three simple words "I'll help you" meant more to me than just about anything I had heard before. It was just the way he looked at me and said it. I left that township house with a deep conviction that, with him at our side, cricket could achieve its goal.'

Several weeks elapsed before anything happened. Then he received a call from Tshwete inviting him to Shell House, an austere, grey building in Johannesburg's inner city where the now unbanned ANC had set up its national headquarters.

Ali phoned Muzzell and asked him to fly to Johannesburg to be present with him. At Shell House, they were shown to Tshwete's office overlooking busy Plein Street where Muzzell met 'this big man in thick glasses with a gap in his teeth who smoked a pipe'. Tshwete made an immediate impression on Muzzell. 'He seemed to understand what needed to be done and he came across as a visionary.'

It was at this meeting, says Ali, that Tshwete agreed to facilitate the talks between SACU and SACB. According to Geoff Dakin, his SACB counterpart Krish Mackerdhuj was not initially amenable, but 'Steve spoke to him, and that was that!'

Tshwete's stature and influence were evident when the two bodies assembled in Durban in September 1990. It was the first time that Bacher had met Mackerdhuj and his SACB colleagues and the obvious tensions might have erupted had it not been for Tshwete's presence. The remark that best summed up that two-hour exploratory meeting came from Percy Sonn, the SACB vice-president from the Western Province Cricket Board. 'Hey guys, why aren't we fighting?' he asked when the meeting ended at lunchtime. Sonn was a hard-bitten lawyer who had been detailed by his comrades to be ready to 'take on' Dakin, a man they regarded as a firebrand. The confrontation never happened and, according to Dakin, Sonn said he found him 'a very pleasant person' to deal with.

The next round of talks was held in Port Elizabeth in mid-December 1990, and this time Tshwete's ability to put out fires – a role he was sometimes called on to play when internal strife emerged within the ANC – won the day. The problem involved a 'Charter' that SACB had tabled for adoption which required cricket to redress imbalances outside its sphere of influence. This, by way of example, included housing in disadvantaged areas. SACU insisted that this was not cricket's role, and tensions were running high.

The night before the meeting, Ali went to Tshwete's hotel room and apprised him of the problem. As usual, Steve bit on his pipe and listened. That same night, Dakin entertained Mackerdhuj and the SACB secretary, Ronnie Pillay, at his penthouse overlooking Algoa Bay and they agreed to put their differences aside.

That agreement, however, did not seem to extend into the next day's meeting where the two delegations immediately deadlocked over the contentious terms of the 'Charter'. Tshwete called for a ten-minute adjournment and took the SACB officials into a separate room. Ten minutes later the meeting resumed and suddenly there was agreement on the way forward.

At the end of the day's talks, Bacher took Tshwete aside. 'What did you say to them, Steve?'

'I told them they were not at the United Nations, and that if the talks broke down or failed, I would personally tell the ANC that it was their fault.'

It was not for nothing that Tshwete would be popularly portrayed in the media as 'Mr Fixit' for the central role he played in bringing sworn enemies to the negotiating table and sending them away as allies. It was not only in cricket that he achieved this; he went from one sporting code to the next and fixed the potholes on their roads to unity.

The third and final session of cricket unity talks was held at a Holiday Inn on the eastern outskirts of Johannesburg. This was going to be the big day when all loose ends would be tied up. It was there, however, that Tshwete found himself at a loss for the first time, and where Dakin would play the trump card.

The meeting was going well. A motion to merge the executives of the two national cricket bodies was about to be adopted when it was pointed out that there were ten SACU members and only seven from SACB. 'They were quite right to raise the objection,' says Ali, 'because they would have been at a 10-7 disadvantage. We were right at the finishing post, but suddenly the mood changed for the worse. Steve sensed that a breakdown was coming and was almost in tears. It looked like all the hard work and goodwill was falling apart.'

It was then that Dakin called a time-out with his SACU colleagues and proposed a solution: SACB would be invited to co-opt three more members, which they readily accepted, and the equitable deal was done.

There was just one detail that had been overlooked in the excitement, and the celebrations were about to start when someone asked, 'What about Ali?' As SACU's managing director, he was not among the ten board members from his union.

It was Sonn and SACU's Alan Jordaan, the two advocates in the room, who provided the answer: why, of course, he should continue as MD of the new united body. He had the know-how, the staff and the experience and it made perfect sense. So everyone heartily agreed, and Tshwete removed the pipe from his mouth, produced his huge gap-toothed grin, and warmly congratulated all the delegates. The 'stillborn initiative' that was once his view on cricket unity had become a bright new dawn; against all odds, cricket had beaten all other sports in the quest for unification. Although the formal constitutional launch of the United Cricket Board of South Africa was still several months away, on 29 June 1991, the game of cricket in South Africa, riven by racial divide for a hundred years, was now effectively one. It was hard to imagine that only 12 months earlier the men now embracing each other had been 'at war' over the Gatting tour. That wretched tour might have been a disaster, but it was surely the catalyst for this extraordinary breakthrough.

'Steve's role as chairman of those unity meetings was critical,' says Ali. 'He was greatly respected by both sides, he had a calming influence among cricket officials who had previously been sworn enemies and, of course, he was most influential among SACB colleagues who were part of his political constituency. Cricket owed him a huge debt of gratitude.'

Quite right, but Mthobi Tyamzashe offers a counterpoint: 'Ali Bacher was ahead of his time. The role he played is still not appreciated up to this day.'

'The unification of South African cricket,' says Ali, 'was the most important and memorable moment of my life in the game.'

The unity experience, however, would be just the start of a series of adventures that Bacher and Tshwete would share in the months and years that lay ahead . . .

In April 1991, Tshwete took Bacher to a house in the unfashionable Johannesburg suburb of Mayfair on a pivotal mission. It was Krish Naidoo's

264

house but he was out of the country studying in Scotland. The man there to meet them was Thabo Mbeki, whose father Govan Mbeki, an avowed communist, was sentenced to life imprisonment in June 1964 along with Nelson Mandela and others and would spend the next 25 years on Robben Island. There were other ANC National Executive Committee members in the house, among them Joe Modise[1] and Essop Pahad.[2] At Tshwete's bidding, Bacher outlined to Mbeki and his comrades the progress that cricket had made towards constitutional unification. He also told them that, with their blessing, the United Cricket Board wished to reapply to the International Cricket Council for membership.

'I told them we wanted membership of the international cricket family but that the aim was not immediate participation in international cricket. That would come later.'

Mbeki, clearly in charge in his position as ANC secretary for international affairs, listened and then said: 'Steve, you go with Ali to visit the high commissioners in London and get them to support the application for membership.'

Bacher knew that without the ANC's blessing there would be no return to international cricket; and he was overwhelmed by Mbeki's decisive response. Furthermore, the ANC's head of international affairs said he would write a letter of support, addressed to each high commissioner, that they should take with them.

Several weeks later, two of Ali's children, Lynn and David, agreed to take him to the airport to catch the London flight, but first they had to go to Mbeki's flat in Hillbrow to pick up the letter. The flat was on the 28th floor of the building and the lifts were out of order. The three of them started walking up the stairs which, to Ali's horror, had large outside windows through which he could see the street far below. It was well known to the Bacher children that their father suffered from a terrible fear of heights. By the seventh floor he was sweating profusely and was ashen. 'I thought he was having a heart attack,' says Lynn. He was on his hands and knees, frozen by the fear gripping him. 'It's an indescribable feeling,'

---

[1] Joe Modise was commander of Umkhonto we Sizwe and became defence minister in South Africa's first government of national unity in 1994. He died in November 2001.

[2] Essop Pahad, a member of the Central Committee of the SA Communist Party, attended Sussex University with Thabo Mbeki after going into exile in 1964, and was appointed minister in the presidency in Mbeki's cabinet in 1999.

says Ali, 'like a hidden force is drawing you helplessly to the edge.'[3]

'He was determined to get that letter but he couldn't move,' says Lynn. 'We got him to lie down on his stomach on the floor and David and I told him we'd carry on and meet him again on the way down.'

On the 28th floor, the door to the flat was opened by Joe Slovo.[4] Mbeki handed them the treasured letter. It read in part:

Your Excellency, I have the honour to extend to you the compliments of the leadership of our organisation, the African National Congress. We are satisfied that the necessary progress has been made by the relevant cricket bodies within South Africa towards the establishment of a non-racial controlling body. We await the completion of the process of the repeal of apartheid legislation by next month, as has been promised by the South African government. It is in the light of all these developments that we request Your Excellency to use your good offices to encourage the admission of the projected United Cricket Board of South Africa into the ICC. A positive decision in this regard would play a crucial role in encouraging forward movement within South Africa towards the complete desegregation of sport in general. This in turn would have an important impact on the processes in which we are engaged, directed at moving the millions of South African people, including the youth, towards a non-racial and democratic order and a peaceful and stable society . . .

With Tshwete, Ali visited the ANC's offices at Penton Street, North London, for the first time. It was there that he met Beryl Baker,[5] a white exile from the East Rand who was the secretary to the ANC's chief London representative Mendi Msimang. 'She was a most impressive woman and she diligently retyped Thabo Mbeki's letter for each high commissioner on ANC letterheads.'

She also produced a well-structured itinerary that, between 17 and 24

---

[3] In hotels, Ali Bacher requests a room as close to the ground floor as possible and on aircraft sits only in an aisle seat. On balconies at cricket matches, he sits only in the back row and will not go near windows or other exposed positions in high buildings.

[4] Joe Slovo was chairperson of the SA Communist Party, a member of the ANC's National Executive Committee and housing minister in South Africa's first government of national unity in 1994. He was born in Obelai, Lithuania, came to South Africa aged eight and attended the Jewish Government School in Johannesburg and Yeoville Boys School. He died in January 1995.

[5] Beryl Baker later returned to South Africa to join Nelson Mandela's staff in the Presidency.

May 1991, would take Bacher and Tshwete on a busy schedule of meetings in the British capital. First stop was the Commonwealth Secretariat where they were greeted by the secretary-general, Chief Emeka Anyaoku; then on to the high commissioners of all the key Caribbean nations – Barbados, Jamaica, Guyana, the Eastern Caribbean States, Trinidad and Tobago, Antigua and Barbuda – as well as Sri Lanka and New Zealand.

At Palace Court on the Bayswater Road, Ali walked into the high commission of Guyana to meet Sir Cecil S Pilgrim. 'The first thing I saw was this big picture of Fidel Castro hanging on his wall. I said to myself, hey, we've got problems here!'

Tshwete, however, stepped up to the plate to make an eloquent speech. The UCB, he said, was an embryo that would die if its blood and oxygen were cut off; but if given a chance to grow, he was sure it would mature into something very special. The high commissioner replied: 'When you (the ANC) asked us to isolate racist South Africa, we did so. Now you are asking us to support this initiative because the situation has changed, and of course we will do that!'

There was a meeting, too, with the ICC at Lord's. 'The *Sunday Times* took a photograph of Steve and me standing outside the Grace Gates (the main entrance to Lord's cricket ground) and it was a very special moment for both of us. Here, at the headquarters of cricket, I was being welcomed back – with a member of the ANC National Executive as my friend and ally.'

At Lord's, they were invited to lunch by Colin Cowdrey, the president of the ICC. Also present was the president of the MCC, Lord Hugh Griffiths. Tshwete and Bacher took turns to speak about the extraordinary developments in South African cricket and the case for readmission, after which Lord Griffiths said: 'Mr Tshwete, this is all very well and good, but do you not think it would strengthen your case if, in addition, you got a letter of endorsement from Chief Buthelezi?'[6]

'Steve went ballistic for five minutes,' recalls Ali. 'He explained forcibly why this was definitely not necessary, after which Lord Griffiths cleared his throat and said: "Gentlemen, in retrospect, that might not have been such a good idea!" '

In a welcome break from their hectic schedule of meetings, Bacher and Tshwete travelled by train to Birmingham to watch a one-day international between England and the West Indies at Edgbaston.

'That train trip took two hours and during it Steve told me – for the

---

[6] Buthelezi's Inkatha Freedom Party was an implacable foe of the ANC.

first and only time – of the terribly cruel treatment he had endured at the hands of his captors while in detention on Robben Island and elsewhere. He told me how he was in solitary confinement for nine months and for 18 hours a day was locked in a tiny cell with no light at all. He was then allowed to walk around in a tiny courtyard that was totally cut off from the sun. He virtually existed in darkness all that time and, when he eventually came out of solitary, he walked out into the blazing sunshine, which he had not seen for nine months. It was too much for him, and he swirled around like a drunken man and then keeled over.

'He also told me how, on several occasions after he had been arrested and was being transported in a police van to the cells in East London, the driver would stop the vehicle in an isolated area and the prisoners would be told by the policemen: "Okay, we're in a good mood today, we'll give you a chance; you can get out of the van and walk back home." Steve knew never to accept this invitation because it was tantamount to instant death. Any prisoner who walked away, in the happy belief that he was being granted unexpected freedom by compassionate police officers, would be shot in the back. The official death report would state that the prisoner was running away, attempting escape.

'When we reached Birmingham station, I went straight to the public toilets where I vomited. I never told Steve that this graphic account of his sufferings had made me physically ill.'

At the end of their mission to London, Bacher and Tshwete addressed a press conference that was chaired by Denis Goldberg, a treason trialist with Nelson Mandela, Govan Mbeki and the others who were sent to Robben Island in 1964. Goldberg was in prison for 22 years and, when he was released in 1985, he went to London as an ANC representative. 'Before the press conference I can remember Steve telling me that he was utterly relieved that there was someone who knew the London scene better than him; and that's why I was asked to chair the conference. I remember, too, being impressed by Ali Bacher. I could see that his views were not dissimilar to the ANC's policy of non-racialism. To me, his presence was a clear indication that the total mind control exercised by the regime was faltering. Here was a man who was using his celebrity status to challenge the absurdities (of the apartheid system). It was for this reason, I believe, that he was able to build such a close relationship with Steve Tshwete.'[7]

---

[7] Prof Dr Denis Goldberg *LLD, PhD, BSc Eng, BAdmin, BA, Bbibl* interview, November 2003.

LESS THAN A month later, Bacher and Tshwete returned to London with Geoff Dakin and Krish Mackerdhuj; the purpose of their visit – to be at Lord's to hear the outcome of South Africa's application for readmission, which the ICC's annual meeting would rule on.

The three cricket officials left South Africa together and Tshwete followed a day later. The first ANC Congress since the organisation's unbanning was taking place at the same time in Durban and some elaborate travel arrangements had to be made for him, including being driven to Johannesburg in ANC leader Walter Sisulu's car to catch the overnight flight to England.

The cricket officials had been in contact with their counterparts abroad in advance of the meeting. 'My first contact with international cricket was with David Richards, the executive director of the Australian Cricket Board,' says Ali. 'The Aussies were very supportive of our application and sensed our return would bring a breath of fresh air to world cricket. David opened the door for me to speak to Jagmohan Dalmiya, secretary of the Board of Control for Cricket in India (BCCI), and he recommended that if India would propose South Africa's readmission, Australia would second it.'

Dalmiya's title of 'secretary' was misleading; he was the president of the Calcutta-based Cricket Association of Bengal and had a very powerful influence in India, and indeed, world cricket. 'I must have phoned him 40 times before the meeting and we developed a close relationship that would last until 1996.'

On the eve of the ICC meeting, Ali received a phone call from an anxious Dalmiya who had just arrived in London. He was worried because there had been a snag and the situation had changed. The ruling Congress Party in India had contacted the BCCI to express concerns about the unseemly rush by South Africa to get back into world cricket. The party believed the BCCI was also moving at an unhealthy speed in their support of the UCB application. 'Dalmiya was clearly very concerned,' says Ali. 'He urged me to get someone (from the ANC) to phone Madhavrao Scindia, the BCCI president who was a leading member of the Congress Party and in some circles had been tipped as a future prime minister.

'We were staying at the Westbury Hotel and I went immediately to Steve's bedroom and woke him up. I explained the background to the crisis. Steve said, "Ali, get him on the line." I phoned Scindia in Delhi. It was the first time I had had any contact with him. I explained Steve's position in the ANC and asked him to hold the line for him.

'Ten minutes later Steve put down the phone. He put his arm around me. "Don't worry, Ali, they will support you!" '

Ten minutes later Bacher's phone rang. It was Dalmiya again. He was very excited. 'I have just had a call from Scindia. Everything's okay, he's instructed me to propose South Africa.'

The significance of this gesture was profound. When the National Party came to power in South Africa in 1948, India was the first country to close its embassy in Pretoria. Now, 43 years later, it amazingly led the way again in supporting the bona fides of South African cricket.

At the ICC meeting, the West Indies abstained from voting. Their delegate, Clyde Walcott, insisted he did not have a mandate from all the territories of the Caribbean. 'We couldn't budge him,' says Ali, 'but we understood his predicament.'

At the completion of voting, Colin Cowdrey announced that 'with immediate effect' South Africa was a full member of the ICC.

'I was amazed,' says Ali, 'not so much by the announcement but by Cowdrey's subsequent action: he immediately ushered us out of the room and we took no part in the 1991 ICC meeting. I thought that "with immediate effect" meant that we were now fully entitled to remain in the meeting but, be that as it may, we were all delighted that we were once again part of world cricket, that the days of us knocking on the back door were finally over.'

The amazing thing was that the politician who had played such a huge role in helping South African cricket reach this pinnacle did not even have the vote in South Africa, and was not even a member of its government. Ali was truly in awe of Steve Tshwete . . .

'Mr Fixit' became more and more influential in helping South African cricket find its feet in a world of challenge, confusion and opportunity. Suddenly, after years in the wilderness and not exactly up to speed with the pace of the real world, it found itself, like a newborn baby, overwhelmed by the attention visited on it by family and friends. It was in this almost bewildering environment that Tshwete's unruffled wisdom became a source of comfort to Ali. He became a ubiquitous presence in cricket circles, always prepared to give help and advice and open doors when called upon; but always content to stay in the background, allowing the UCB officials to deal with pure cricketing issues.

The South Africans were warmly received at the traditional dinner in the Long Room at Lord's that followed the ICC's meeting of reacceptance. Dakin privately expressed his surprise that, although South Africa was again a member of the ICC, the world body had decided against his country's participation in the 1992 World Cup, still seven months away, on the grounds of impracticality. At that time, Bacher was not particularly fussed by the World Cup issue. What was important for him was that South Africa was back in the international family; and international competition would surely follow when the time was right.

It was during the course of the evening that a message was delivered to Lord Griffiths. It came from No 10 Downing Street and it requested that the South African officials be brought to meet with John Major at 10.30 pm. Cowdrey went with them and they were well received at the home of the British prime minister. 'He even showed us around the house,' recalls Dakin, 'and he expressed in no uncertain terms his disappointment that South Africa was not going to the World Cup. He told Cowdrey that the situation was ridiculous and that every effort should be made for South Africa to take part. I even teased Colin in the taxi going back that he would get a knighthood if he carried out his prime minister's wishes.[8]

It was also at Lord's that Ali met Clive Lloyd for the first time. He immediately extended an invitation to the former West Indies World Cup-winning captain to come to South Africa to lend his support and encouragement to the children in the development programme. Soon after his arrival a month later, he called Ali to ask whether it was possible to arrange to meet Nelson Mandela.

'I immediately phoned Steve and within a few minutes he came back with the instruction "Bring Clive Lloyd to Shell House tomorrow".'

Ali vividly remembers the occasion. 'When we arrived at the reception room of Shell House, we found a big Swedish delegation there, including many media representatives, waiting to see Mr Mandela. The door to his office opened, and there he was. He immediately saw Steve and commanded, "Bring Ali and Clive in!" and the Swedish group followed and surrounded us. Mr Mandela said some very nice things about South African cricket. He had been informed that we were taking the game to the disadvantaged areas and encouraged our efforts. He then granted the Swedish media people a brief time for questions.'

Cricket, of course, is not a sport close to Swedish hearts but, no doubt influenced by all the cricket talk, one of the journalists was inspired to ask

---

[8] Sir Colin Cowdrey was knighted in 1992. In 1997 he was elevated to the peerage to become Lord Cowdrey of Tonbridge. He died in December 2000.

271

the ANC leader: 'Would you like to see South Africa taking part in next year's World Cup?'

'Definitely, yes!'

In a flash the news went around the world – that Nelson Mandela himself was backing South Africa's late inclusion in the World Cup in Australia and New Zealand in six months' time.

Tyronne Fernando, the president of the Board of Control for Cricket in Sri Lanka and later his country's foreign minister, had questioned the validity of the original ICC decision to keep South Africa out of the tournament. He also took note of Mandela's impromptu endorsement. 'Colin Cowdrey rang me several times and asked for my advice. He was trying to get South Africa into the World Cup by telephone consultations. I said that South Africa should come in with maximum goodwill and that the ICC should hold a special session. I telephoned Ali to assure him that I was backing South Africa's inclusion.'[9]

According to Fernando, he was inspired in his purpose by the resistance to South Africa's participation from Jagmohan Dalmiya and the Indian board's president Madhavrao Scindia, which strangely did not accord with their earlier decision to propose South Africa's readmission to the ICC.

On 9 October, Fernando faxed Cowdrey to confirm his request for a special session and, two weeks later, the ICC president asked the UCB to present its case at an emergency meeting of the world body in Sharjah, United Arab Emirates, where a tournament was taking place. The meeting took no more than 20 minutes – and South Africa's participation at the World Cup was assured.

Ali gratefully acknowledged the role played by Fernando in hastening this process, but did not underestimate the Tshwete-Mandela axis. 'If Steve had not reacted so promptly in facilitating the meeting for Clive Lloyd, the journalist would probably not have asked his question. It was a combination of Steve's quick response and Mr Mandela's reply to that question that finally got us to that tournament.'

AFTER THE SHARJAH meeting, a four-man UCB delegation of Dakin, Mackerdhuj, Bacher and Percy Sonn embarked on a whistle-stop goodwill tour to some black countries with which South Africa had never before had

---

[9] Tyronne Fernando interview, December 2003, and additional information from his book *Kings of Cricket* (1998).

cricket ties – Sri Lanka, India, Pakistan and Kenya.

Sonn's inclusion gives an interesting insight into Bacher's absolute attention to detail. 'Before our trip, I phoned Geoff in Port Elizabeth and told him that, because we were going to Pakistan for the first time, it would be a good idea to add a South African Muslim to our party. Geoff asked me who I would recommend, and I said Percy Sonn.'

Sonn said he accepted this 'to get the balance right', but he then pointed out that Jews were not exactly popular in certain countries that they would be visiting. His solution was to describe Dr Ali Bacher as 'a Turkish gynaecologist'.

They went first to Sri Lanka – where Ali invited Fernando to visit South Africa in 1993 with a Sri Lankan under-24 team – and then on to India. In Bombay, they were told that a scheduled tour of that country by Pakistan had been cancelled. Moving on to Calcutta they met up with Dalmiya, who made an impassioned plea to the South Africans to send a team to replace the Pakistanis – at less than a week's notice. 'We were all a bit taken aback,' says Ali. 'This wasn't on the agenda; in fact going to the World Cup in three months' time wasn't even on the original agenda.' Then in Delhi, Scindia made a similarly strong plea. He was a prominent man in Indian society, a man of royal lineage, a senior leader of the Congress Party and a long-standing cabinet minister whose portfolios included Railways, Tourism and Civil Aviation. It is worth noting here that, on his arrival in Delhi, Ali was met at his hotel by a local cricket official who advised him 'to play down Dalmiya in this part of the world'. In the complexities of Indian cricket politics, Dalmiya had been ousted as the BCCI secretary two months earlier and there were divisions within the Indian board.

After the meeting with Scindia, the South Africans said they would have to consult with their colleagues back home before responding to the request for their team to undertake a short tour.

On their return to South Africa, the delegation stopped off in Nairobi to meet Kenyan cricket officials. They stayed overnight at the Nairobi Gym-khana Club where Bacher and Sonn shared a room. 'I asked him how he felt about the Indian invitation,' says Ali, 'and he said it made him feel uncomfortable. Things were moving too fast for his liking. I thought it best to ask Steve, so I phoned him immediately, explained the nature of the invitation and the misgivings expressed by Percy. I then passed the phone to him and Steve told him emphatically: "You go!" and that was that.'

The day after the delegation arrived back, an emergency meeting of the UCB and the NSC was held at an airport hotel. The NSC hierarchy were all there – Mluleki George, Makhenkesi Stofile[10] and Mthobi Tyamzashe – and Ali was fascinated by the irony of the deliberations.

'The black cricket delegates were saying "let's go!" and the whites were saying "it's too early!" It was Steve's instruction, though, that won the day.'

Given its leading role in having South Africa reaccepted in international cricket, it was felt only appropriate that India should be South Africa's first opponents upon re-entry to the international arena.

AT THE WORLD Cup three months later Kepler Wessels' inexperienced team made a stunning start to their campaign by defeating the defending champions Australia at the Sydney Cricket Ground. Amid the wonderful celebratory scenes in the South African dressing room afterwards, photographs were wired around the world showing Tshwete, the tears rolling down his cheeks as he embraced Wessels and several other South African players.

Mike Gatting, still serving his playing ban but attending the World Cup as a commentator, came to the dressing room to express his solidarity with the South Africans. Tshwete was introduced to him by Ali and, in a telling commentary on the reconciliatory attitude of the ANC, he took the former rebel captain in his arms and hugged him. This, indeed, was a time for tears . . .

It was just as well that Tshwete was on the trip. The next game was against New Zealand in Auckland which provided another opportunity for 'Mr Fixit' to come to the rescue off the field; although, on it, the South Africans were brought back to earth with a bump in losing to the home team on the slow Eden Park pitch.

The drama began before the match. 'When we arrived in Auckland,' says Ali, 'I was told that HART (the Halt All Racist Tours organisation) was threatening to disrupt the match because, in their view, democracy had not yet come to South Africa – and until that happened they would ensure that no South African team was welcome in New Zealand. A delegation from HART arrived at the hotel where we were staying to make their views known and specifically to meet with Steve to outline their plans to

---

[10] Representing the UDF, Rev Makhenkesi Arnold Stofile went to New Zealand in 1984 where he led a successful campaign against the planned All Blacks rugby tour of South Africa. Upon his return home, he was detained for four months. A member of the ANC National Executive Committee, he was appointed premier of the Eastern Cape in 1997.

disrupt the game. The meeting took place, and an hour later they left quietly – and that was the end of HART!'

It was during the World Cup that white South Africans went to the polls in a vital referendum that sought their endorsement to end apartheid. Wessels' team, with Ali's support, issued a statement that they would be voting 'yes' in support of this, and urged their countrymen to follow suit. Anything less would doom all of cricket's efforts of reconciliation, goodwill, unity and reacceptance, not to mention the wider road that F W de Klerk had chosen to travel. It was a prospect too awful to contemplate, but white South Africans came out in numbers and the 'yes' vote prevailed.

Two years later, the 'Rainbow Nation' went to the polls in its first democratic elections. It was a time that all South Africans will never forget – blacks and whites standing happily together in long queues that snaked around the polling stations – and the ANC won a landslide victory with Nelson Mandela inaugurated as the new President. In keeping with his uncompromising policy to embrace whites in the new dispensation, he formed a government of national unity, with the Nationalists being granted proportional representation.

Ali was at Milpark Hospital having X-rays for a salivary gland swelling in his cheek when he saw the front page of that afternoon's *Star*. The paper was reporting on Mandela's likely new cabinet and, for sports minister, the report named the coloured Nationalist Abe Williams. Ali was astounded. Where was Steve Tshwete? His name was not mentioned.

'I immediately phoned Steve. How can we revise this; what's going on? He advised me to contact Lulu Johnson, the ANC's Youth League president. I did so, and two days later we met at Shell House. I impressed on him the outstanding work that Steve had done in unifying South African sport. I told him that it was unimaginable that anybody else could be appointed as the minister of sport.'

The question might well be asked why the ANC Youth League should have been involved. The answer lay in a debate within the ANC at that time on whether to establish a Youth Ministry or a Sport and Youth Ministry. According to Johnson, Tshwete's name was most certainly in the mix as a possible minister for either of these portfolios. 'The Youth League,' he says, 'had a very influential role on a range of issues that especially included this one.'[11]

Having met with Bacher, Johnson spoke with his predecessor, the

---

[11] Lulu Johnson interview, October 2003.

firebrand Peter Mokaba. 'We had to make time to talk to the president on a number of matters and Peter engaged the National Working Committee as well. I eventually went to see President Mandela and advised him that there were concerned sports administrators who had traversed a long road with comrade Steve. I can't say that I mentioned Ali Bacher by name but it was indeed he who had brought this to my attention.'

Johnson says that it was highly likely that Thabo Mbeki, then the national chairperson of the ANC, was also apprised of the situation. During the nineties, Ali had become fascinated with the politics of the ANC and regularly engaged Tshwete in discussions. He was particularly interested to know who the heir apparent was to Mandela – in the speculation, the names of Mbeki, Chris Hani[12] and Cyril Ramaphosa[13] were bandied about – and he saw then the 'fierce loyalty' that Tshwete had for Mbeki. 'In Steve's opinion, there was only one man who should succeed Mandela.'

Bacher's intervention on behalf of his new friend and ally paid off handsomely in 1994. When Mandela named his cabinet, Tshwete was minister of sport and Williams was handed the portfolio of Welfare and Population Development.

PAM TSHWETE HAS no difficulty in describing the relationship that existed between her late husband and Ali Bacher. 'Ali was like a brother to Steve. He invited us to his home for dinner, we went to two of his children's weddings and he even assisted us in finding schools for our children. It was not easy for us, coming out of exile, but he would intervene and go on our behalf to talk to the school principals. The kids became very close to him and in the summer holidays he would ensure that they attended the big cricket matches with us – our son and daughter, as well as Monde and Namhla Zondeki. They sometimes couldn't sit with us in the President's suites but Ali would get them good seats and make sure they had everything they needed. He really fussed over them. I am not surprised that Monde became such a good cricketer and went on to play for South Africa.'

ALI LOVED RELATING stories about his times with Steve Tshwete. Before the

---

[12] Chris Hani was MK Chief of Staff and general secretary of the SA Communist Party. On 10 April 1993 he was assassinated in the driveway of his home in Boksburg, east of Johannesburg, by a Polish immigrant Janusz Waluz.
[13] Cyril Ramaphosa was secretary general of the ANC and the party's chief negotiator.

New Year's Test against India in Cape Town in 1997, Tshwete phoned him to ask if he could bring the minister of labour Tito Mboweni[14] with him to the match.

They duly arrived and Mboweni was seated next to Bacher. This was his first cricket match and Ali proceeded to give him a crash course in the broad workings of the game. 'I was amazed. Half an hour later he had an excellent grasp of what was going on. I later mentioned this to Nelson Mandela who was not one bit surprised. He explained that Tito's intellect was well chronicled; and that he was one of the brightest members of the cabinet.'

During a break in play, Tshwete drew Ali aside. 'He told me how Tito had arrived at his home that morning, dressed up to watch his first cricket match – in shorts, sandals and a T-shirt. "Where do you think you're going?" Steve asked him. "Go home and get dressed properly, you can't come like that!" They were, after all, being invited to sit in the President's Suite.'

---

[14] Tito Mboweni later became Governor of the South African Reserve Bank.

Chapter 23

Making History in India

THE BIRTH OF the United Cricket Board of South Africa (UCB) was a time of great joy and sadness for Ali Bacher. On 29 June 1991, the 20-man executive met in an oak-panelled hall in the tradition-steeped Wanderers Club to formally constitute the new body. It was, said the president Geoff Dakin, 'a great day for cricket, but more than that, a great day for our beloved country'. During his address to the meeting, Krish Mackerdhuj turned to Bacher: 'Ali, if it wasn't for you, we wouldn't be here.' It was, said Bacher, a clear indication that goodwill among people would always triumph.

In the build-up to the great event, congratulatory messages had poured in, three of which bear repeating. The first was from Major-General Roy During, the policeman who was in the thick of things with Bacher on that fateful day of the Gatting tour at Kimberley. He wrote,

> *I wonder whether the significance or magnitude of your achievement is fully appreciated? You have accomplished what has seemingly been, for many years, the impossible. It is certainly at the very least indicative of your deep commitment and ethical insight regarding the extreme importance of normalising sport not only for the sake of cricket but also for South Africa.*

The second was from Sam Ramsamy, now chairperson of the Interim National Olympic Committee:

> *I have nothing but praise and respect for you and your colleagues in the sincere and responsible manner in which cricket unity has been achieved. This augurs*

well for South Africa in general and sport in particular.

The third arrived by messenger on a sheet of lined A4 notepad. It had no address and it was simply signed 'Ronnie'. In neat handwriting it said:

> *I don't know what the bearer has told you – but it is true I encouraged him to open up lines of communication with you, not only because I still possess a strong affinity with Yeoville boykies, but I somehow detected a certain keenness on your part to find 'the way forward'. Anyway, welcome aboard – not SS ANC – but aboard the broad movement for genuine non-racist, democratic change in this country. Whether you associate with the ANC is something else. Forge on with Steve for genuine change, Ali.*

The author was Ronnie Kasrils,[1] the Jewish *boykie* from Yeoville Boys School who had dedicated his life to the liberation struggle and was at that very moment being pursued by security police because indemnity had yet to come through for ANC operatives.

Another aspect of the birth of the UCB that was never fully explained was the derivation of its name. The 'United Cricket Board' seemed self-evident, but at the time of unification it was not the obvious choice. In April 1991, Bacher went to Cape Town to meet the German ambassador, Dr Immo Stabreit.[2] His objective was to ask for money for the development programme because he had been told that the German government was keen to assist in redressing imbalances caused by apartheid sport. Percy Sonn accompanied him to the meeting and, after stating their case, the ambassador asked: 'By the way, what's the name of your new organisation?'

They told him a decision had not yet been made but that the 'SA Cricket Council' was being mooted.

'I can't believe it,' he said. 'For 45 minutes all I have been hearing is *unification* and *unity* and *united* . . . surely your name should say that!'

And so the seed was sown and the United Cricket Board was duly titled.

The historic inaugural meeting of the new body was followed by a sumptuous banquet. The guest of honour was Sir Garfield Sobers[3] and the

---

[1] Ronnie Kasrils became deputy minister of defence in South Africa's government of national unity in 1994.
[2] Dr Immo Stabreit later became the German ambassador to the United States and France.
[3] Garry Sobers was knighted by Queen Elizabeth II in 1975.

keynote speaker was E W Swanton, the doyen of English cricket journalists who had reported on 281 Test matches either as a writer or broadcaster.

It was a time of great joy for Ali, unquestionably the highlight of his career in cricket, and it was followed immediately by the shock and pain of his mother's death.

The night following the celebrations, at the airport to bid farewell to Sobers, he had got the call that Rose Bacher had died. She had been ailing with a heart condition for some time, she had been admitted to hospital, she had seen her son reach the pinnacle of his game; she could die knowing that everything she had wished for him had come to pass. It was as if she had waited for cricket to be formally unified – and then she was gone, his great champion.

In a few simple words, the death notice from the Bacher family said it all: *Our most loving and caring Mother who dedicated her life to her children with total devotion. Your strength and courage was an example to all who were privileged to know you.*

As we have seen, the immediate weeks and months that followed the formation of the UCB was an exciting and exacting time – the ICC reacceptance at Lord's, the meetings with John Major and Nelson Mandela, the Sharjah agreement to proceed to the World Cup, the goodwill visits to Sri Lanka, Pakistan, India and Kenya – and, out of the blue, the invitation to send a team to India to play three one-day internationals.

For Ali, the passage to India would be an unforgettable roller-coaster ride. Simply getting there was no easy feat. There had been no formal links with India since 1948 and there were therefore no direct flights to that country. All the arrangements for the trip had to be made in four days; and here the UCB could be thankful it had decided that Bacher and his old SACU staff should remain in place. They sprang into action with Ali directing; again, ironically, they used all the experience that the rebel tour era had taught them in the areas of crisis management. The first thing that he did was charter an aircraft; and he then issued invitations to a range of officials, sponsors, media, friends and cricketing members of the local Indian community to come aboard. The convener of selectors Peter van der Merwe was told to select a team – South Africa did not have a national team at that time and the new season had only just begun – but the best possible side on past performance was put together with Clive Rice as captain and Mike Procter the coach. The team manager was Ali Bacher which, given the circumstances of the tour, seemed the right choice.

Immediately upon the announcement of the team, Ali received a phone call from Madhavrao Scindia, the BCCI president, advising him that the all-white team presented a problem. So he contacted Van der Merwe again and told him to select four 'development' cricketers – two black, two white – to be added to the touring party in a non-playing capacity, ostensibly to gain experience of conditions on the subcontinent. The four youngsters were Derek Crookes, Faiek Davids, Hussein Manack and Hansie Cronje, the latter having to obtain special permission to postpone his final exam for his B Com degree at the University of the Orange Free State in order to undertake the trip.

It was in 'a clapped out old Boeing 707 with no markings' – the words are those of one of the reporters on board, Chris Gibbons of Radio 702 – that the adventure began. 'The seats were decrepit, it was most uncomfortable, but Trevor Quirk[4] had a couple of crates of beer, so a big group of us smoked and drank all the way.'

The beer-drinking reporters did not know about the 3 000 cases of Castle Lager carefully stowed in the aircraft's hold – a donation from SA Breweries to provide some familiar refreshment in a foreign environment. It sounded as if they were headed for a massive party – and in a sense they were – but there was cricket to be played, work to be done, friends to be made, history to be recorded and some unexpected hurdles to clear. As the plane climbed into the air and headed east, this privileged group of South Africans in their happy aeroplane had not a clue of what lay in store for them; but the immense significance of the adventure would soon become apparent when Bacher's Boeing became the first South African-registered airliner to fly into Indian airspace and land at Dum Dum airport in Calcutta.

'I saw grown men weeping openly,' says Gibbons, 'and Ali was very clearly aware of the significance of this incredible moment. Some of us were jet-lagged and hungover but none of us could not have been totally overwhelmed by the sight of tens of thousands of cheering, shouting people lining the road from the airport to the city. A bus trip that normally takes 20 minutes took us four hours; we had to stop often to meet new dignitaries, to be festooned with garlands around our necks, and to hear lots of speeches with Bacher, Rice and Procter in the thick of things. Ali was at his diplomatic best but when we finally checked into the opulent Oberoi Grand hotel he

---

[4] A popular cricketer-turned-commentator who succeeded Charles Fortune as the 'voice of South African cricket'.

must have been emotionally wrecked. Behind the Bacher facade was a man, I am sure, who was totally gobsmacked at what he had experienced. We all were.'[5]

There was little time, however, to repair wrecked emotions because the next day would reveal the extent of the shattering poverty of a city of 11 million inhabitants – some 700 000 of them living, and dying, on the streets – and then the spiritual experience of meeting Mother Teresa, the missionary saint of these desolate people, a sparrow-like figure with a huge aura who serenely pressed hands and bestowed blessings on those who had arrived on Bacher's Boeing.

And then to Eden Gardens, where Jagmohan Dalmiya was king; and in this huge saucer of a cricket stadium, to see a crowd of 90 000 and to walk out on to the field before the match and bow and wave amid the deafening din of the drums and hooters. 'Always remember to acknowledge the crowd,' Ali had ordered his men ahead of the battle on 10 November; and this they did, with Rice leading by example, but they lost the match by three wickets which was hardly the issue. Andrew Hudson, opening the batting, out for nought, said he wasn't surprised because he had lost control of his emotions. 'If I had to do it all over again, it wouldn't be much different – I'd still be out for nought.'[6]

This then was the first taste of international cricket in India, this was what South Africans had denied themselves for all these years; and at the break between innings came a little piece of evidence that suggested that all was not as it seemed. An amazed Procter showed Bacher the match ball with which the Indians had bowled out their opponents for 177. The shine had been kept up on one smooth side – and also made heavier with the use of spit and sweat – but the other hemisphere was substantially roughened. With a ball in this condition, the fast bowlers could produce the phenomenon of reverse swing; in other words, the ball would swing through the air in the opposite direction to the norm. There was nothing wrong with this – provided the ball had not been deliberately tampered with on the one side.

'In my playing days, reverse swing was unheard of,' says Ali, 'but my information was that it had become common practice in Indian cricket – even in the schools – and was definitely not seen as cheating. It was simply a new phenomenon in cricket.'

[5] Chris Gibbons interview, September 2003.
[6] From *Hansie and the Boys* by Rodney Hartman (Zebra Press 1997).

Procter suggested that Bacher take up the matter on behalf of the team and so before the start of the next match at Gwalior two days later, he engaged Scindia, the suave and refined BCCI president who doubled as the Maharajah of Gwalior and whose Italian-style baroque palace – where the South Africans were lavishly wined and dined – commanded a view of the city from a sandstone bluff.

'Scindia and I had developed an excellent relationship and, in that spirit of goodwill and emotion prevailing around this tour, it was as if we were now ready to start a renaissance together in world cricket. India and South Africa would lead the way, and the first issue would be ball tampering. We simply discussed investigating this together to see if it was legitimate or not. It was nothing more than that; and at no stage did I ever suggest or even imply that the Indian team was cheating.'

Ali's mistake was that he did suggest that they visit the media box to inform some reporters that this was the way that India and South Africa would together take a new lead in world cricket. This was typical of his crusading manner, and Scindia seemed happy enough to go along with it, but the reporters did not see it that way; and neither did the Indian team after Scindia had paid them a call.

'His whole attitude immediately cooled after he came out of their dressing room,' says Ali. 'The warmth towards me was no longer so apparent.'

Amrit Mathur, an Indian cricket official who was Scindia's right-hand man, says the BCCI president was a great admirer of Bacher. 'He thought him to be a progressive, contemporary cricket leader who was committed to take the game forward. He knew him to be a man who would always retain and protect the game's traditional values and strengths.

'On the ball issue, there was a trace of annoyance in Mr Scindia's attitude for two reasons. Firstly, he could not believe that players, regardless of their nationality, could actually engage in any sharp practice. He was a cricket traditionalist who respected and loved the orthodox values of the game. For him, it was a shock that such things could even be contemplated, let alone actually happen.

'Secondly, he was a bit peeved that the matter was made public. He expected the issue to be discussed privately instead of the avoidable splash in the media. He thought the publicity surrounding the issue unnecessary and inconvenient, and considered it embarrassing for Indian cricket.'[7]

---

[7] Amrit Mathur interview, September 2003. Note: Mathur was the Indian team manager when they first toured South Africa in 1992-93.

Mathur puts it in nice folds, but Geoff Dakin is far more forthright. 'I was the guest of Mr Scindia and his hospitality was exceptional. At Gwalior, he approached me and I could see he was very upset. He said to me, "Your manager has made a statement and accused us of being dishonest. Unless you and your Board rescind the statement, there is no point in continuing with this tour." So I called the board together (many UCB board members were on Bacher's Boeing) and then I called a press meeting and I told them it would be short and sweet.'

Scindia was at Dakin's side when he made his press statement and offered profound apologies. 'It would appear that certain unfortunate remarks have been made. My executive was never approached in respect of this matter. To me there is no controversy, the matter is a storm in a teacup, and we find the statement most embarrassing. As president of the United Cricket Board and on behalf of my executive, I wish to say that we totally dissociate ourselves from the statement allegedly made by Dr Bacher. I apologise to Mr Scindia and the Board of Control for Cricket in India.'

Dakin was angry because he felt Bacher should have approached him immediately when Procter first raised the ball issue. 'We could have called a board meeting there and then and made a decision. I mean, this was a goodwill tour after all; we were just back in world cricket.'

Ali points out that it was not that simple consulting with his board members. 'We were staying in different hotels; I was with the team constantly and had to attend to them.'

He was also angry because he had heard that the board had met without consulting with him as the team manager; not only that, they had met within earshot of VIP guests and Scindia himself was present at the meeting. Robbie Muzzell, one of the board members present, said he had raised an objection to Scindia attending the meeting. 'How could we speak openly with him being there?'

'Ali went berserk,' is the way Dakin describes it. 'He said it was a disgrace that his board didn't stand by him. My response was that it was a disgrace that he issued a statement without the authority of the board. One of the board members actually proposed that we fire Ali. I said his value to cricket far exceeded this embarrassment.'

It was during this time that Ali started receiving death threats in repeated, anonymous telephone calls. For the rest of his stay in India he was given a 24-hour bodyguard.

AWAY FROM THE ball tampering controversy, the visit to Gwalior was an interesting and revealing experience. The team's arrival there confirmed Ali's high opinion of the character of one of the 'development' players, Hansie Cronje. 'We arrived there late at night and all our luggage was on the back of a big truck. There was no one to offload it and everyone was just standing around, tired and irritable. Hansie took the initiative, jumped up on to the truck and started offloading it by himself. Others then joined in. I could see his leadership qualities in the way he took charge.'[8]

For some of the passengers on Bacher's Boeing the arrival at the hotel was simply the next hurdle. 'It appears no one told them we were coming,' recalls Gibbons, 'and there were beds for about 30 out of 200 people. No one was being very helpful until Ali got on the blower to the Maharajah and then suddenly the mood of the hotel staff underwent an amazing change for the better. I wasn't feeling well so Ali suggested I have the spare bed in his presidential suite. Throughout the night his door kept opening as more and more members of the touring party, who didn't have beds, came in to find a place to sleep. By the morning there were about 15 people sleeping on the floor. I remember waking very early and there, in the early morning gloom, was Ali in his tracksuit. Nothing was going to stop him from going for his jog around the car park.'

Ali was careful by this stage to be properly dressed for his early morning runs. At Sharjah, in 44°C heat, he had gone running in the street without his T-shirt. He was puzzled at the strange looks people gave him; motorists, pedestrians, they all turned around and stared, and some even seemed a little shocked. He put it down to the 'Ali Shuffle'. Back in the foyer of the hotel, the manager, an Englishman, stormed up to him. 'Put your bloody shirt on quickly! This is a Muslim country, don't you know it's a jailable offence to go bare-chested in public?'

At Gwalior, Rice's team were run off their feet to go 2-0 down in the series; but they redeemed themselves in the final match at Delhi where they sprinted home with an eight-wicket victory.

THE QUESTION OF the team manager demands further scrutiny. It was over coffee at Dubai airport – following the Sharjah meeting when Colin Cowdrey announced that South Africa would be going to the 1992 World Cup after all – that Dakin, Mackerdhuj and Sonn told Bacher that he was

---

[8] Hansie Cronje succeeded Kepler Wessels as South Africa's captain in November 1994.

their choice as the World Cup team manager. 'The appointment of the team manager had not yet crossed my mind, but I readily accepted their vote of confidence.'

It was clear, however, that between Dubai and Gwalior, attitudes changed.

A few weeks after the return from India, Dakin phoned Bacher. He invited him to meet with him and Mackerdhuj. They were coming to Johannesburg for a board meeting on the Sunday and he suggested they meet with him on the Saturday evening. Dakin was obviously extending the olive branch, but Bacher declined. He told the UCB president that whatever he had to say he would say it to the board.

'I made a mistake,' concedes Ali. 'I should have accepted his invitation because I'm sure that everything would have been resolved.'

He was anxious about the board meeting, the first one since the ball tampering row in Gwalior. He had been told by a friend close to certain board members that the knives were out for him; and, feeling the need to judge the temperature, he telephoned Alan Jordaan, the Northern Transvaal Cricket Union president, who he saw as a friend and ally on the board. He told him confidentially what he planned to tell the meeting the next day and asked Alan how he felt he might shape up. He says Jordaan told him, 'Just stay cool, the coolest one will win.'

Unbeknown to Ali, on the Saturday night some board members – including the president – decided to nominate another candidate for the manager's job. When the subject came up at the meeting the next day Dakin announced that there were two nominations – Ali Bacher and Alan Jordaan. Ali was taken aback. Alan had not told him this. The two of them were asked to leave the room while the others voted.

'Outside, I took one look at Alan and immediately walked back into the boardroom. I told them I was withdrawing my nomination. He could have the job.'

Ali was extremely upset because Jordaan had not told him that he had been approached. 'I accept that when we spoke on the Saturday morning he had probably not yet been approached, but he could have phoned me back later once he had been asked to stand.'

There was another related issue that clearly exacerbated the problem. Three days before the board meeting, Bacher was contacted by John Bishop, sports editor of the *Natal Witness* in Pietermaritzburg with a speculative query: would he be available to manage the World Cup team? Ali said yes, because at the time he believed that senior UCB officials wanted him to do the job.

At the board meeting, Peter van der Merwe from Eastern Province used the *Witness* article to suggest that Bacher, as an employee of the board, had no right to put forward his case in the media. This pronouncement rang true with the prior warning that some board members were 'out to get him' in the aftermath of Gwalior. It was also yet another example of board members concluding that Bacher was 'using' the media for his own purposes, while his argument was that a reporter had contacted him with a straightforward question to which he had given a straight answer.

As for Jordaan, Ali was not prepared to stand as a paid official against a board member and it was for that reason that he withdrew his name. He would still be able to attend the World Cup for a shorter period in his capacity as MD, but his original expectation that he would manage the team was not to be. Moreover, his belief that Clive Rice would captain the side did not materialise. In an atmosphere of acrimony and bitter bold headlines, Van der Merwe, in his role as convener of selectors, dropped Rice from the South African team and appointed Kepler Wessels as the new captain.

It was around this time, too, that Tony Lewis, the former England captain and cricket writer, reported in the *Sunday Telegraph* that moves were afoot in South Africa to get rid of Bacher. Ali was infuriated. He demanded that Lewis reveal his source. The Welshman declined with equal annoyance. Their friendship, however, endured down the years, and Lewis would later write of him: 'Ali Bacher was a seeker of advice but single-minded once he had decided on the way ahead. He had no time for waverers and, although he was sometimes wounded by the inevitable criticism of those who opposed his instinct to be in control, the vision of his ultimate goal always took him through. He played politics because only the politicians could create the rainbow country ahead. Like his batting, his administration bristled with grim determination and durability.'[9]

---

[9] *Taking Fresh Guard, A Memoir* by Tony Lewis (Headline 2003).

Chapter 24

Dinner with 'The Don'

IT WAS DURING the World Cup in Australia that a dream would come true for Ali Bacher. At last he would get the chance to meet his boyhood hero, Donald Bradman, the man whose books he had devoured, the great batsman with whom he had once been compared – much to the budding young batsman's acute embarrassment – and the cricketing sage whose wisdom and teachings he had always revered.

Many others, of course, had been compared to him but they were mere pretenders; in the final reckoning, there was only one Don Bradman whose Test batting average of 99.94 stood alone like a shining beacon at the pinnacle of cricketing excellence.

In Adelaide, Ali and Shira were invited to his double-storey home. 'He gave me a beer and we chatted for over an hour. I was struck by the depth of his knowledge of South African cricket. He rattled off the names of players that I had barely heard of, and he knew the history of our cricket inside out. He also showed a strong interest in South African politics, and was keen to find out how strong Chief Buthelezi was on the political scene.

'He and his wife Lady Jessie then took us to dinner. He drove the car and we went to a restaurant that he frequented. He was a very private man, and I suppose he had to be, and I recall he used another name when he booked our table. Sir Donald was sometimes portrayed as a rather dour man, but he certainly enjoyed his wine and was the life and soul of the dinner party. He spoke to me about the back-foot no-ball law that he wanted reintroduced. He was very strong on this and asked me to champion its cause at the ICC. I did raise it at a meeting, but it was immediately shot down by the English.'

Among the dinner guests that night was Dr Donald Beard, one of Bradman's closest friends and, for many years, the surgeon to the South Australian Cricket Association. 'I lived only a couple of kilometres from Sir Donald,' says Dr Beard. 'In his last few years I always called on him at his home in the late afternoon and we would enjoy a sherry and talk on all sorts of national and international issues. Always the conversation would come round to cricket and cricketers. I well recall on several occasions Sir Donald speaking of Ali Bacher and his devotion to the game. He had a great admiration for Ali, not only for his achievements as a player and captain, but particularly for his tremendous efforts in overcoming the boycott of South African cricket during a period of political turmoil. We enjoyed an excellent dinner that night in 1992. The conversation was enlightening, and Ali and Sir Donald stimulated laughter and friendship around the table.'[1]

It was the only time they would ever meet, although they continued to correspond with each other and speak on the telephone.[2]

IT WAS ALSO during the World Cup, in March 1992, that Geoff Dakin was befriended by Kerry Packer's people at the Channel Nine network who were keen to do a television rights deal with South African cricket. Lynton Taylor, one of Packer's key executives, wined and dined the UCB president in a style befitting royalty, once taking him to an offshore meeting in a private seaplane. He told Taylor he would take up the matter with his board immediately upon his return home.

At the next board meeting, he duly raised the matter for discussion, but his managing director immediately interjected: 'I've already done the television deal.'

Dakin and the board did not know that Bacher had conducted successful talks with the London-based CSI and had contracted the company to represent the UCB in the sale of television rights outside of South Africa.

Dakin was furious; once again Bacher had not consulted his board on an important issue.

It was the previous year, 1991, that the action began. Taylor, who was

---

[1] Dr Donald Beard interview, September 2003.
[2] Sir Donald Bradman died peacefully at his home on 25 February 2001 at the age of 92. Lady Jessie Bradman died, aged 88, in 1997.

cast as Packer's right-hand man in the World Series Cricket rebellion in the late 1970s, came to South Africa with another Packer lieutenant, Tony Greig, on a rights-securing mission. Ali drove to the airport to meet them on their arrival in Johannesburg. As far as the brash Taylor was concerned, the TV deal was a mere formality, probably because of Greig's South African connections. Bacher later told Taylor that CSI had been appointed by the UCB to sell the rights abroad and promised that they would give the Nine network the first option for the Australian series in South Africa in 1993-94.

'I later received a letter from him offering $50 000 for those rights. I did not consider that kind of offer worthy of a reply.'

In the mean time, Ali had met a very interesting character. His name was Michael Watt who, unlike Packer, was relatively unknown in the public eye. He was the charismatic founder and chairman of the television rights company CSI, and, although he deliberately maintained a very low profile, he was a major player in the lucrative world of sports marketing. He had built his company on a simple principle: having not had the courtesy of a reply to two letters he wrote to Mark McCormack in the 1960s – in which he sought employment at the great man's International Management Group – he built his own company around those sports that McCormack ignored. Aware that IMG concentrated their efforts in tennis and golf, Watt pursued rugby, soccer and cricket to prove to those sports that they were being 'swindled by the national broadcasters'. In time he became successful enough to worry McCormack 'who came after me with a big stick but I didn't give a hoot'.[3]

It was this man then who arrived in South Africa with exactly the same purpose as the Packer people, and Ali took an immediate liking to the personable New Zealand-born globetrotter. So, too, CSI's chief executive officer, an Australian Jim Fitzmaurice, with whom he developed an excellent and enduring business relationship.

The Nine network believed it had an automatic right to beam cricket across Australia and, as such, it offered what were clearly token payments for the rights to do so. CSI saw it differently. Having been appointed by Bacher to represent the UCB in securing rights deals in the global marketplace, the timing of their arrival was perfect. The mighty Australian cricketers were about to tour South Africa for the first time in 24 years, so

---

[3] Michael Watt interview, November 2003.

Fitzmaurice stuck to the agreement and offered the Nine network the first option for the television rights. When no offer was made, he informed Taylor that he would have to approach another channel. 'Good luck,' he was mockingly told.

Fitzmaurice immediately approached the Channel Ten network, one of Packer's major rivals, who at the time were going through a change of ownership. They agreed to pay $2.5 million in order to beam the 1993-94 series into Australia.

Bacher could be well pleased that he had decided to use CSI to do the television rights deal rather than negotiate directly with a single channel that offered a paltry $50 000.

The turnabout would clearly have angered and embarrassed Taylor, and consequently Packer, because this was a cricket series that would undoubtedly attract a huge television audience in a market that the Nine network had cornered. Interestingly, 'Ten' now got back to Fitzmaurice to put forward the view that the station's new owners, CanWest Global Communications Corp, 'doubted' that they had a binding contract for the cricket tour. They clearly wanted out.

Fitzmaurice told them that they did, indeed, have a contract and that CSI expected them to honour their commitment. He then flew from London to Australia to meet the new owners, and thereafter CSI initiated legal action against the Ten network.

The case was due to go to court in Sydney and in advance of it there was the usual 'discovery' process during which the opposing lawyers revealed all their documentation. It was here that they came upon a 30-page affidavit from Fitzmaurice, detailing his dealings with 'Ten', which had the effect of rather startling their lawyer. Now aware of the amount of evidence weighed against them, and realising that this was no bluff, he suggested that a settlement might be reached.

Bacher by this stage had gone to Sydney for the court case. In five minutes of talks with Fitzmaurice and the lawyers, he agreed after consulting with his treasurer and friend Julian Thornton that the UCB would compromise on a figure of $2 million with the proviso that 'Ten' could on-sell the rights to 'Nine'.

So Packer got a series that was rather more expensive than he had bargained on, the UCB banked a considerable amount of money in South African rands, and the Ten network's new owners could conclude that they had been given a most agreeable 'out'.

In essence, television history in respect of Australian networks had been made and it was hardly surprising therefore that the UCB board members, once they had been given all the details, backed Bacher with an 18-2 vote on the way he had done the TV deal.

As Fitzmaurice tells it: 'The television sport market in the early nineties undertook an incredible upward spiral, hugely accelerated by the advent of Pay-TV. We did the rights deals for any number of tours into South Africa; and once the dollars and pounds were converted into rands, it is true to say that we represented a major source of income for the United Cricket Board. I enjoyed working with Ali. The more I got to know him, I came to realise that he was the kind of man who did not necessarily waste words. We had what I would call quick exchanges, and it all worked out rather well.'[4]

THERE WERE OTHER memorable, and often unorthodox, deals and contracts that Bacher orchestrated during the nineties, and it was hardly surprising when he was nominated as South Africa's Marketing Man of the Year for 1992. If there was a single monument to him, however, it was surely cricket's development programme and all that was enshrined in it.

Alexandra township had got its multipurpose sports complex, but what its cricketers now needed was their own cricket oval.

In the early nineties, the British foreign secretary Sir Douglas Hurd paid a visit to Alex to hand over cricket equipment on behalf of his government. Ali's friend Kapi Nkwana did not miss the opportunity. He took the foreign secretary aside and told him that the township parents could not afford to go to the Wanderers every week to watch their kids play, and he hoped that the British government might help to build them their very own oval.

Kapi discussed the issue with Ali and it became apparent that the only possible place for a cricket field in the overcrowded township was on the site of an old rubbish dump on a steep incline known as East Bank. It would require expert engineering and a lot of hard work to level the ground.

As the proud recipient of the 1989 Murray & Roberts Jack Cheetham Memorial award, Ali invited Nkwana to go with him to visit David Brink, chief executive of Murray & Roberts, one of South Africa's biggest construction companies. 'I told him we needed a little bit of levelling work to be done and he agreed to lend a hand at no cost. He then sent out his

---

[4] Jim Fitzmaurice interview, October 2003.

engineers who told him that the "little bit of levelling" was actually a major engineering operation that would cost Murray & Roberts R750 000.'

Brink recalls, 'He didn't tell us that his piece of ground was actually a massive donga (ditch) and that we now had to convert a ravine into a cricket field, a very big job. Still, it was a job worth doing.'

Bacher was impressed. 'David kept his word and they completed the project as he had promised.'

Brink's parting shot was, 'I think he conned us, and I pulled his leg about it later. When he asked us to do similar work on fields in the Eastern Cape, I wasn't going to get caught twice. I made sure we made a thorough investigation before making any commitment.'[5]

As for the Alex project, the British government agreed to grass the field and erect the practice nets.

After the completion of the massive project, John Major, on his first official trip to South Africa in 1994, paid a visit to Alex for the opening of the oval. His government had taken a particular interest in the development of sport in the township and the British prime minister was given the honour of opening the new nets by bowling the first ball to Steve Tshwete – and dismissing him.

'Within a minute of Mr Major's arrival,' recalls Ali, 'I told him that we now needed a clubhouse and I strongly recommended that the British government put up the R250 000 that it would cost. He got very cross at my effrontery, did not respond and looked at me in such a way that I just froze. For the rest of his morning's visit, he gave me the complete cold shoulder. I felt very uncomfortable.'

That evening, Sir Anthony Reeve, the British high commissioner, hosted a dinner in Major's honour. 'It was held in a big marquee and at about 11 o'clock, Sir Anthony approached me to say that his prime minister wished to see me immediately.

'I walked over to his table, fully expecting to be given a blast. "Ali," he said, "how much money do you need for that clubhouse?" I told him, and he then turned to the guests sitting at his table. One by one, he addressed them. "You will give 10 000 pounds, and you will give 10 000 pounds, and you will give 10 000 pounds . . ." '

---

[5] After levelling one of these grounds, a complaint came in that there was still too much of a slope. Peter van der Merwe, who was working for Murray & Roberts in the Eastern Cape, was sent by David Brink to make an assessment with a surveyor. He reported back that the famous slope at Lord's was more severe.

The prominent captains of industry he was *telling*, rather than asking, were Basil Hersov, chairman of the Anglovaal mining group, Julian Ogilvie-Thompson, the chairman of the Anglo American Corporation, Joe Stegman, the chairman of the Sasol petroleum company, Adrian Day, the managing director of Rascal Radio, and Andrew Witty, the chief executive officer of Glaxo – all of them companies with major British interests. Through their donations, an amount of R275 000 was raised and the new clubhouse became a reality.

Sir Anthony later wrote to Ali: 'The prime minister was quite delighted with his morning in Alexandra (not least, his first ball at Steve Tshwete!) and he was also particularly pleased that he was able to persuade the five British companies to stump up the money for the clubhouse.'

Kapi Nkwana was forever grateful to the British government for their willing assistance in developing cricket in his township. During a six-month stay in England to study sports management, he paid a special visit to the House of Commons to say thank you. When he was told that the foreign secretary was speaking in the House, he contrived to send a message into the debating chamber to advise Sir Douglas Hurd that 'Kapi from Alex is here to see you'.

This, needless to say, caused some degree of confusion and consternation but when the identity of Kapi was finally established, the foreign secretary did indeed come out to shake him by the hand. It was all in a day's work for the man from Alexandra.

As can be seen, Kapi Nkwana was an interesting and forthright fellow. Ali was constantly amused at the way he addressed Michael O'Dowd, Anglo American's executive director who had agreed to fund the R1 million Alex multi-sports complex. 'Everyone, including myself, would always address him as Mr O'Dowd. We wouldn't have dreamed of calling him by his first name. But not Kapi. He would greet him with a "Hi Mike, howya doing Mikey!" as if they were long lost pals. We would all be in fits of laughter.'

Years later, when this was pointed out to him, Kapi squarely laid the blame at Bacher's door. 'It was all his fault! When I first met him, I called him Dr Bacher but he insisted that I call him by his first name. I thought that was the white man's custom, so when I said "Hi Mike" I believed it was a sign of respect.'[6]

---

[6] Kapi Nkwana later became Regional Manager: Sport and Recreation in Johannesburg.

Bacher rejoiced in the success of the development programme in Kapi's township, because it was here that the first black youngsters from the development programme would be selected on merit to play in a national tournament. When Walter Masemola – who Ali nicknamed 'Wes Hall'[7] because he was the fastest kid around – and his cousin, the seam bowling allrounder Billy Mabena, were selected for the Transvaal under-13 team it was proof positive that black kids *could* play cricket. Those cynics who described this as 'window dressing' knew very little of the true meaning of development, and how a lifetime of existing in separate worlds could not be solved by simply distributing free cricket bats and balls and offering a bit of coaching. The mere five kilometres that physically separated Sandton from Alex was the equivalent to light years in emotional dysfunction. Even a man who had studied medicine, and had a basic understanding of psychology, was shocked to discover the extent of the damage that apartheid had caused.

Bacher first saw this in the strange behaviour of Masemola. Identified at the time as the best of the young black talent, he was fast-tracked into the Wanderers club by Bacher in order to play league cricket in the best company on the best fields. When for three weeks in a row he failed to turn up for matches, a Wanderers official reported his absence. The following Sunday morning Ali went himself into the township to find Walter, ticked him off for his behaviour and took him personally to the club. His absences, however, did not abate. He now started making excuses that he had to attend funerals at the weekends; but Ali had learned by now that the hoary old 'funeral story' was a popular excuse among shirkers. He could not understand it: an underprivileged boy living in the harshest of environments was being offered the chance to spend his weekends in the leafy suburbs, at the best of clubs, on the loveliest of cricket grounds, with top players, at no charge, all for his own benefit . . . and he wasn't taking it.

Slowly the truth emerged: Walter was scared stiff. He had never before rubbed shoulders with such affluence and been on first name terms with young men who drove flashy cars and dressed in designer clothing; he had nothing of his own to compare . . . no status, no trappings, no communication skills with people he did not understand. He preferred to stay away, at home with what he knew and understood . . . in the ghetto.

---

[7] After the great West Indies fast bowler of the 1960s.

Bacher immediately enlisted the aid of a sports psychologist to help the township cricketers come to terms with their past, and their future.[8]

He was particularly fond of the boys from Alex. On many a Sunday, he would invite them to his home in Sandton where he would share with them his cricketing experiences and knowledge. He judged it vital that they experience life away from the narrow confines of their upbringing.

IF THE DEVELOPMENT programme was all about relationships, so too was the basis of Bacher's dealings with sponsors. They liked him because he was a straight man to deal with, his word was his bond, he hated long meetings, and he always ensured that the sponsors got maximum mileage.

His toughest moment came when he felt compelled to tell Benson & Hedges that the time had come to part company after an excellent association lasting 15 years.

'We were back in world cricket, Benson & Hedges sponsored the one-day domestic game and the national limited overs team and it started to worry me for two reasons. It didn't seem right for someone like Jonty Rhodes to be out on the world stage wearing cigarette branding. It was just not the sort of image we wanted to project to the youth. Also, I had an inkling that the government would soon legislate against sports teams and events being sponsored by tobacco companies.'

Bacher conceded that Benson & Hedges had been 'fantastic sponsors' in the eighties when they backed the popular night cricket series – the first provincial tournament of its kind in the world – and also helped to erect floodlights at various grounds. In the nineties, however, this continued involvement was of concern to him. Their contract was coming up for renewal and he knew he had to tackle the issue. He also knew he had a potential new sponsor in Standard Bank after he had informally spoken to their chairman Conrad Strauss. 'I told him briefly that something could become available in South African cricket, and he expressed an interest. However, there were no guarantees from either side.'

Ali got on particularly well with the B&H managing director Stuart Sutherland and felt terrible about going to see him. 'I took Ian Smith (UCB

---

[8] Walter Masemola toured England with national age-group teams in 1993 and 1995 and went on to play senior provincial cricket for Gauteng, formerly Transvaal. He died in his sleep aged 26 in 1992 in Guildford, England, where he was playing club cricket in the Surrey League. His memorial service was held at the Alex Cricket Oval.

financial director) with me and all the way in the car I was tense and couldn't say a word. In Stuart's office I had the worst two minutes of my life in cricket sponsorship. I felt so bad that I couldn't get the words out; I was stuttering. Stuart was shocked when I finally told him that I believed it was time for us to part.'

In further discussions with the company, B&H pointed out that they contractually had the first rights to renew the contract. As he would often do in tricky situations, Ali went to see Professor Michael Katz, the astute commercial lawyer.

Katz told him that they should not be tempted to place any onerous demands on B&H in an attempt to persuade them not to renew; but to be totally sincere and transparent. He says it was agreed that Bacher should level with the company and not 'play games'.

'I took Michael to the next meeting as the facilitator and we got the company to understand where we were coming from. We happily parted on good terms. I then met with Strauss and the new deal with Standard Bank was finalised in ten minutes.'

IT WAS IRONIC that a match sponsored by Benson & Hedges would inspire Bacher to make one of modern cricket's great discoveries. It happened on a Sunday in July 1992 while he was sitting at Heathrow airport watching cricket on television. The previous day's Benson & Hedges Cup Final between Hampshire and Kent at Lord's had been affected by rain; and the match was now continuing into a second day. Ali was on his way home after a succession of overseas trips following South Africa's whirlwind re-entry to the international scene; and on TV in the airport's departure lounge he was watching Graham Cowdrey batting. The Kent batsman set off on a quick run and the fielder at backward square leg, David Gower, hit the stumps with a direct throw. 'Not out,' thought Ali, and the umpire agreed. Cowdrey looked to have grounded his bat behind the popping crease before the wicket was broken.

'It was then,' recalls Ali, 'that the BBC showed a replay from a camera square on to the wicket. I couldn't believe it, he was clearly out by about a metre. Then it just hit me. Surely we should enlist the aid of television to judge run out decisions! It was clear to me that the naked eye could not be relied on in such close calls.'

On the plane journey home he thought more about the exciting new concept. He would need to speak to the television people in Johannesburg to see if they could rig up special cameras at the correct height in positions directly in line with the stumps. Talks followed with Mike Demaine, South Africa's top cricket television producer.

When India came to South Africa on their historic first tour later that year, Ali went to one of their net practices at the Wanderers. There he spoke to the captain Mohammad Azharuddin and their coach Ajit Wadekar about introducing television-based decisions during their tour. 'They were both very nervous about supporting the innovation but Clive Lloyd, who was the match referee for the Test series, leant on them and they finally agreed.'

Thus it was on 14 November 1992 – almost four months to the day since Ali had come up with the idea while sitting at Heathrow airport – that the first decision was made in international cricket by using the 'third umpire' television system. The batsman given out in this fashion was Sachin Tendulkar after a quick throw by Jonty Rhodes to Andrew Hudson.

In terms of the new set-up, the umpire could make a 'referral' to the television umpire if he was in any doubt; and this would be underlined in the next Test at the Wanderers when umpire Steve Bucknor of the West Indies ended up with egg all over his face. When the Indians appealed for a run-out against Rhodes, he judged him 'not out' without bothering to make a referral. The television replay, however, clearly showed that Rhodes, with 28 runs at the time, was out by a good 15 centimetres. He went on to score 91.

Bucknor's embarrassment clearly proved that the new system was essential. He admitted as much when he and Lloyd attended the post-play press conference. 'That was the turning point,' says Ali.

The ICC backed South Africa in its ground-breaking invention but it would take two more years before all the Test-playing countries were obliged to introduce the 'third umpire' or 'television umpire' system.

In the mean time, South Africa continued to refine and expand the concept. The famous Pana-Eye was introduced in which four fixed and automatic cameras were used to cover both ends of the pitch; and the costs, running at more than R1 million, were underwritten by Panasonic. Again at Bacher's instigation, the system of referrals was broadened beyond the 'line calls' of run-outs and stumpings to include 'boundary decisions'. This elicited a huge debate in cricket as to how far the game should go in using technology – the traditionalists claimed that the on-field umpires' role as the final judge was being marginalised – but in time it would be proved, with the umpires' support, that Ali's idea whilst sitting in the departure lounge at Heathrow was a major breakthrough for the international game. In time, too, Bacher would make strong recommendations to include lbw decisions in the television replay referrals.

Chapter 25

'Where's a Dakka Bakka?'

WEST INDIES CRICKET held a certain mystique for Ali Bacher. In his playing days, he was denied testing himself against some of the game's finest players whose names he sometimes read in newspapers and whose dazzling images occasionally flickered on the newsreels at the cinema. He might have played Test cricket against them, but he could not. The evocative names of Frank Worrell, Conrad Hunte, Garfield St Aubrun Sobers[1] and Rohan Kanhai; he knew of their feats but they were not part of his world; Wes Hall and Charlie Griffith, Lance Gibbs and Seymour Nurse; and those two little spinning pals, Ramadhin and Valentine.

This was the region of Worrell and Walcott and Weekes and of the 'black Bradman' George Headley; and later still came the wave of fast bowlers – Holding and Garner, Marshall and Roberts – the openers Greenidge and Haynes, their illustrious captain Clive Lloyd, and the master himself, Vivian Richards.

It was to the Caribbean that Bacher finally went in his 50th year – to countries once violently opposed to the racist policies of the country of his birth – and at the airport in Bridgetown, Barbados, they shook him warmly by the hand, these men from the old newsreels, Cammie Smith, Sobers and Nurse, the Rev. Wesley Hall and Clyde Walcott . . .

They were men who empathised with efforts to create a new order in

---

[1] He did, of course, play briefly with Garry Sobers in Rhodesia but double-wicket cricket hardly counted and, to prove this, the great West Indies allrounder had to take a back seat to Ali's bowling prowess.

South African cricket, and Reverend Hall, at that time the Barbados minister of sport, would later articulate these feelings. 'There are special moments in the history of all societies that are shaped by the extraordinary contributions of individuals,' he writes.[2] 'One such moment was post-apartheid South Africa and the special contribution of Ali Bacher. In seeking the realisation of a new day, (his) society continues to benefit from the unrelenting commitment of this outstanding citizen. As a West Indian cricketer and one who has long been involved in the political craft of nation building, I fully understand the project to which Ali committed himself. In the West Indies, cricket culture also played a critical role in the search for social cohesion in which justice, equality and fair play could flourish. In creating a context for social interaction across classes and races . . . he seized the opportunity to ensure that he would bring significant and lasting benefits to the disenfranchised masses. In my playing days, the West Indies team was the only multiracial outfit in the international arena. We were the rainbow coalition, in a world that had not yet begun to understand this. Ali's contribution to post-apartheid South Africa showed clearly his understanding of the beauty of ethnic diversity.'

Sir Frank Worrell was one of those who understood. When he became the first black man to captain the West Indies in 1959, he united disparate forces within the Caribbean and turned them into a proud and successful outfit. Sadly, an exemplary life was cut short prematurely when he died of leukaemia at the young age of 42 in 1967; and it was early one morning in Barbados that Ali visited his tombstone. And who would not go to pay their respects to one of the game's legends on a first visit to a little island measuring just 166 square miles that had given cricket so many of its truly great players? Well, for a start, none of the South African cricket journalists went – heaven forbid, were they already becoming cynical? – but Shaun Johnson went, the only political writer among the South African contingent; and he would record the behind-the-scenes stories of South Africa's first short tour of the West Indies in April of 1992 with bold and colourful strokes of his talented pen.

To go to the Caribbean immediately after the World Cup in Australasia required some political manoeuvring. Enter, yes, Steve Tshwete who, in Ali's words, 'phoned the ANC's key bloke at the United Nations in New York and told him to go and look after our boys over there because some

---

[2] An appraisal, written exclusively for this book, November 2003.

of the territory might still be hostile'.

So he came, Tebogo Mafole, once of Alexandra township, to tell a press conference that 'our presence here is testimony to the fact that South African cricket has taken leaps and bounds towards the new South Africa.' His statement was strengthened, of course, by letters written by Nelson Mandela to the Caribbean prime ministers in which he voiced his support for international contact with South African cricket. There was, of course, some scepticism on the islands because true democracy had yet to dawn in South Africa and even Mandela still did not have the vote; and Jamaica's prime minister P J Patterson told Bacher and Krish Mackerdhuj that 'we were only persuaded at the last moment to go along with this (visit) because of the position taken by Mr Mandela and the ANC. I must tell you it has been a decision that has not received uniform acclaim.'

In Jamaica, images of Mandela were everywhere; graffiti aplenty and a highway named after him between Kingston and Spanish Town. One of apartheid's greatest foes, the retired Jamaican prime minister Michael Manley explained: 'Here, Mandela is regarded as a hero of a proportion that I wonder if people inside South Africa can even begin to understand. So when he tells me he is ready to co-operate . . . this is good enough for me.' In *The Daily Gleaner*, the sports editor Tony Becca wrote: 'If by opening our doors we can allow them to experience the beauty of people living together, then we will be making a contribution to the death of apartheid.'

Financially, the tour made good sense to the West Indians. Having suffered losses on every tour into their region since 1976, they could be well pleased that Bacher had persuaded BP South Africa to pick up the tab for the South African team – something the hosting country is traditionally obliged to do – as well as funding the first telecasts of local matches throughout the Caribbean.

With the formalities now out of the way, the cricket could begin and, in Port of Spain, Trinidad, the intrepid Johnson found the average cricket fan very keen to see the South Africans. One of them asked him quite pointedly, 'Where's a Dakka Bakka? Where's a Whistle?' and here we have to trust his translation of 'Where Doctor Bacher? Where's Wessels?'

Furthermore, said the political writer, Ali's acceptance was emphatically assured when, at Trinidad's airport, he was acclaimed by a popular Calypso artist with the name of Black Stalin.[3]

---

[3] Shaun Johnson interview, November 2003.

As for Tebogo Mafole, he was learning fast; this big, jovial man who had once regarded cricket as 'a white man's imposition' was now comfortable in the knowledge that there were eleven players in a team and that you gripped the bat by the thin end. He became a very popular member of the touring party and defused some tricky political situations by engaging prime ministers and politicians in discussions, and taking part in radio and television talk shows. According to Johnson, there was no doubt that without his presence the tour would have been marred by nasty incidents. Ali agreed. 'Mr Mafole's diplomacy, his softness, his pragmatism and his feel and vision for our country give me every confidence in the new South Africa.'

In a shrewd move by the UCB, a South African under-19 multiracial development team was also sent to the Caribbean to undertake a simultaneous tour. Ali watched them play a match at Spanish Town, black and white together, and remarked: 'I think we are watching the beginning of the future of South African cricket.' He was certainly right in one respect, at least, because among the batsmen was a coloured boy named Herschelle Gibbs.

The senior South African team, however, was not happy. Some of the players claimed they were being used as pawns in a political exercise without proper consideration to the challenges that were being thrown at them on the field. After being thrashed in three successive one-day internationals, and fearing that they were now being viewed as failures back home, Wessels asked Bacher to address his players on the eve of the one-off Test at Bridgetown. Ali conceded that the players had been 'knocked around a bit'. He told Johnson in an interview, 'In the past few months they have been shunted around the world in this cricket diplomacy exercise. A week in India was no preparation, and there was no preparation here. It's been a difficult time for them.'

He told the players about the wider benefits of the tour for South African cricket. 'I don't think they fully understood the broader context of what we were doing to gain total acceptance in the international community – and particularly in the West Indies where the anti-apartheid struggle was taken very seriously.'

It would not be the last time that Bacher would conclude that South African cricketers did not fully appreciate the wider context of their return to world cricket in the nineties . . .

Also, in an exclusive interview with Johnson, he justified the UCB's decision to affiliate with the NSC, a body now relaunched under its new title, the National and Olympic Sports Congress. 'The decision,' he told the political reporter, 'may well be controversial among white sportsmen, but our priority is the development programme and the redressing of imbalances in cricket. This is the reason why we are here in the West Indies. It is the only moral way forward.'

Because the NSC was mass-based, it was deemed to be the best vehicle for addressing the problems of the disadvantaged in South African sport. Furthermore, said Bacher, it had given an agreement not to interfere in cricket's administration – 'The ANC has never tried to run cricket, and I don't believe they ever will.'

It is very interesting to know that even before the constitutional unification of South African cricket in mid-1991 Bacher was already helping the NSC raise sponsorships. He carried with him a letter on NSC letterhead, dated 20 February 1991, addressed 'to whom it may concern', and signed by Mluleki George, the president, and Mthobi Tyamzashe, the general secretary. It said, in part:

We have come to know of Dr Ali Bacher's relationship with local sponsors and his track record in the development of sport, and (have) accordingly commissioned him to endeavour to help us receive the kind of funding that would enable us to continue with the job we have started. Our brief to him is to identify, approach and present our case to prospective national sponsors, for the purpose of developing and preparing South African sport for the post-apartheid era.

When one considers that this letter was written exactly a year to the day after the penultimate one-day match involving Mike Gatting's team – when Adrian Kuiper bludgeoned a 49-ball century at Bloemfontein – it is almost unbelievable to realise how quickly the turnaround happened. From the point of seeing Bacher as an 'evil man' not worthy of engagement, the NSC hierarchy was now embracing him; so much so that he eventually received the ultimate accolade from his former foes when he accepted a top-table invitation to become an executive member of the NSC . . . 'and when Steve (Tshwete) heard about it, he just laughed and laughed'.

Tyamzashe had become a firm friend, which is all the more extraordinary if one considers that when he was a student in 1970, he was unaware that South Africa was playing a Test series against Australia, or even that Ali Bacher was the Springbok captain. Now, however, his respect for Bacher's sphere of influence was such that he would often jocularly address him as the 'Deputy Minister of Sport'.

There was also another interesting story about their relationship. After their initial secret meetings in 1990, and still at a time when contact with people like Bacher was forbidden, Tyamzashe flew from East London to Johannesburg for a NSC meeting. When Ali heard of this, he extended an invitation to him to sleep over at his home. The NSC did not have a lot of money in those days, but Tyamzashe was wary of this offer so he checked first with Tshwete. 'You go and spend the night at Ali's place,' was the reassuring advice. Bacher picked him up at the airport, where they were obviously spotted together, and ten minutes after their arrival at the Bacher home the telephone rang. Lynn Bacher answered it and thought nothing of it when the caller asked: 'Is Mthobi Tyamzashe there?' She answered in the affirmative, and handed the phone to him. 'Read the *Sowetan* tomorrow morning,' warned the sinister anonymous caller, and then hung up.

'I could hardly sleep that night,' he says. 'When Ali got up for his jog at five o'clock, he found me packed and ready to leave. I was very jumpy, and he suggested we go out and buy the *Sowetan* newspaper. There was nothing in it about me. I breathed a huge sigh of relief, but to this day I still don't know who made that call.'

THE 1992 WEST Indies tour ended in a nail-biting climax. At the Kensington Oval in Bridgetown, South Africa started the final day needing 79 runs for victory with eight wickets in hand. Two nights earlier, after the third day's play and ahead of the rest day, Ali had watched the players partying on the deck of a Caribbean cruiser called the *Beijun Queen*. 'I had never seen players like Kepler Wessels and Hansie Cronje so relaxed, and I didn't like it. The West Indies fast bowlers Ambrose and Walsh saw them too, and I'm sure they decided there and then to take the smiles off the South Africans' faces.'

On the fifth and final day, they did just that, taking the last eight wickets for just 26 runs.

'I told Peter Kirsten afterwards,' says Ali, 'that it would have been wrong had we won. It would have given us a false sense of our own ability. It would have been bad for our cricket because we were considered the world champions in 1970 and now, 22 years later, we would have thought that nothing had changed, despite more than two decades of isolation.'

The tables would be dramatically turned almost seven years later when West Indies made their first full tour of South Africa. In a low point in their history, they were thrashed 5-0 in the Test series by Hansie Cronje's team and lost the limited overs matches 6-1. The tour, it must be said, did not get off to a settled start and it was only through Bacher's eleventh hour intervention that a major crisis was averted.

In a bizarre chain of events, the West Indian players were due to arrive in South Africa from various destinations, but they made their way to London instead and holed up in a hotel at Heathrow airport. From there, they let it be known that they were effectively on strike in a dispute with the West Indies Cricket Board over their tour payments.

Bacher, of course, had had previous experience of recalcitrant West Indian cricketers, and he decided to enlist the assistance of President Mandela by asking him to record in writing the importance of this West Indies tour to South Africa. 'After a telephone link-up between (UCB president) Raymond White, myself and the West Indian officials Pat Rousseau and Steve Camacho, it was agreed that I should fly to London with Clive Lloyd and end the dispute.'

Lloyd was the manager of the West Indies team and had arrived ahead of them in South Africa; but now he and Bacher boarded the London flight and Ali had Mandela's letter safely tucked away in his jacket pocket.

By this stage, the West Indies board had not helped matters by announcing that the captain and vice-captain, Brian Lara and Carl Hooper, had been fired.

'On arrival at Heathrow, I took up position in another airport hotel, with Lloyd and Joel Garner (a West Indies board member) to time the moment for my intervention. I asked a reporter from South Africa's Independent Newspapers to alert me as soon as the international media arrived at the players' hotel and, duly alerted, I walked the short distance between the two hotels and, in the foyer, I bumped into Courtney Walsh, the players' representative. In front of the television cameras and the international media I asked him to convey to his teammates that I had a message for them from Nelson Mandela, and handed him the letter. I also made a copy of it available to the international media.'

Rousseau, the West Indies Cricket Board president, had also been advised to fly to London, whereupon the dispute was resolved after a meeting with the players' representatives. Lara and Hooper were reinstated, and the team arrived in Johannesburg, albeit a few days later than expected.

'There was no way that they would have not come,' says Ali, 'having received an impassioned request from Nelson Mandela to tour his country. The West Indies people would have killed them.'

It is also worth pondering how many other cricket administrators, from whichever countries, would have gone to the lengths that Bacher did to help solve the dispute. Indeed, his life in cricket contains a litany of potential failures that were turned to success through his simple logic and innovative thinking.

Chapter 26

'Call Me Madiba'

THERE CAN BE no denying that Ali Bacher enjoyed the best of both worlds. By his own admission, he lived a privileged life as a white South African, and then after the advent of black majority rule he was embraced by the new order. This, of course, did not come about through chance or good fortune. It was his willingness to admit to the wrongs of the past and to work tirelessly to redress them in his own particular sphere of influence that endeared him to those who had been oppressed by apartheid; and estranged from those who became suspicious of his motives.

Such was the zeal with which he approached the task of creating an equitable deal for South African cricket that some people were convinced that he was an active member of the African National Congress. This was not true – he was never a card-carrying member of any political party – and although in the nineties he received invitations to attend ANC election meetings, he was advised by Barbara Masekela, a prominent member of the party's National Executive, to stay away. 'In your position, you must serve all constituencies,' she told him.

In serving all constituencies, Bacher's life in cricket became a series of adventures. As soon as he had completed one, he would move on to the next. There was always a new challenge, a new adventure, and the only snag was that each involved a different set of people who, enchanted by his magnetic personality and commitment, began to regard him as indispensable to their cause. Because of this, they sometimes felt abandoned when he moved on; a good example was the people of Alex who joined him wholeheartedly in the incredible adventure of virtually launching formal sport in the township and lifting kids out of the gutter.

This perception of abandonment also applied to players from bygone eras who would ask, 'What has happened to Ali, why doesn't he contact us any more, are we no longer important in his life, did we do something wrong in his eyes?' but of course he was now up to his ears in another adventure, with a new set of people. He had not forgotten or abandoned anyone – he was just moving on to the next challenge.

It is extraordinary that virtually every major 'adventure' in South African cricket, from the moment he took up his full-time appointment in 1981, was either planned, masterminded, managed or driven by him. A lot of people did a lot of wonderful things in cricket – the individuals who became involved selflessly in the development programme are shining examples – but he always directed the big picture.

More than anyone else in the history of South African cricket, he was always at the coalface. In South African sport as a whole, only the legendary rugby administrator, Dr Danie Craven, could lay claim to a similar achievement.

Apart from directing and delegating with consummate ease, another of his attributes was his willingness to get his hands dirty. Nothing was too much for him and he would readily perform chores that most managing directors would have considered demeaning. When he travelled to Delhi from London in 1996 to watch South Africa's third Test at Kanpur, the UCB's managing director not only carried his own luggage but also toted another large bag that contained kit and accessories that his players had requested: new boots for Klusener, batting helmets, various other bits and pieces. The errand was exacerbated by a nightmare trip. This included an aircraft that, unbeknown to its passengers, burst two tyres on take-off at Heathrow, the captain later announcing 'we have a problem and are being diverted to Bombay', the man sitting next to him – a Coca-Cola executive, as it turns out – praying inconsolably throughout the trip, and the alarming sight of a reception party of ambulances and fire engines with flashing lights awaiting them on the tarmac. Having then caught a flight to Delhi where he was too late to make the connection to Kanpur, he went to the railway station. There we find him running frantically with a confused 'guide' through literally thousands of people in the teeming labyrinth to board a moving train as it was leaving the platform for a hair-raising rail trip all by himself to Kanpur – 'the most frightening experience I ever had'.

And all this in the service of cricket . . .

He had always been a man driven by his ambitions and passion for the game but in the nineties he developed an extra dimension that was inspired by his almost obsessive determination to make a real contribution to the new South Africa through the power and influence that he wielded in cricket. His wife Shira suggested a motto that best described him – ' A life is not a life except for the impact it has on other lives' – and it is undoubtedly true that he committed himself to doing only those things that made a difference. Unconsciously, perhaps, he was inspired in this purpose by the example set by the man he most respected – Nelson Mandela. He was proud to say that he admired certain ANC luminaries for their vision and humanity but, without question, the greatest privilege of all was to know Mandela and to be called his friend. The defining moment in their relationship would come when, shortly before the start of the 2003 ICC Cricket World Cup in South Africa – the tournament he so diligently directed – Bacher took a telephone call in his office.

'Ali, Madiba[1] here.'

The former president was calling to wish him good luck for the tournament.

'Thank you very much, Mister Mandela.'

'Ali, my name is Madiba to you.'

'Thank you, Mister Mandela, but where I come from I always address people for whom I have enormous respect as Mister.'

'Ali, where I come from, unless you call me Madiba, I will not regard you as a friend of mine.'

It was, for Ali, the ultimate compliment and one he graciously accepted. He was, after all, from the old school and he treated his elders and those in higher office with due deference. He held Mandela in the highest esteem and was always visibly proud when seen in his company. In his life in cricket he had met and socialised with many important people – from saints to queens to princes and prime ministers – but never did he look so proud than on those occasions when Madiba was his guest.

The word 'Madiba' had entered white South Africa's lexicon quite unobtrusively. It was only in the mid-1990s that people began hearing the word and, in many cases, wondering what it meant. Understandably for the majority of white people it meant nothing at all. They all knew who Mandela was but the name Madiba was not in their frame or reference.

---

[1] Madiba is the name of the clan to which the Mandelas belong. For anyone to be known by that name is a sign of great respect.

This certainly applied in August 1993 when Ali was admitted to hospital to undergo an angioplasty[2] procedure. According to his aides, it was part of Mandela's daily routine to pick up the phone and contact an ailing friend, a bereaved family, someone in need of comfort or a kind word and a little reassurance . . . each day without fail.

This particular morning he phoned the Bacher residence because he had been told that Ali was in hospital. Shira was at the hospital so he left a message, 'Madiba rang. Please call him.'

The name Madiba meant nothing to Shira. 'I thought he might be one of the development coaches,' she says awkwardly. Over the next few days there were more calls from this Madiba but she missed him each time because of her visits to the hospital. She would dial his number when she returned home at night and there would be no reply. Then one day as she was about to leave the house, she answered the phone. 'Hello, it's Madiba here . . .'

Shira acknowledged the greeting but remained puzzled at the man's identity. It was only after he had been chatting away for a couple of minutes that the realisation dawned on her. 'My face must have been tomato red,' she says, 'and he asked me if Ali *would mind* if he visited him in hospital.'

Unfortunately this visit did not materialise because of more pressing business, but the sentiment was enough to cheer up the patient.

HE HAD MET Mandela for the first time in 1991, the year in which cricket's equivalent of the Berlin Wall came crashing down and South Africa was readmitted to international cricket. It was at the meeting with Clive Lloyd at Shell House that he first made his acquaintance. In the passage of time, Mandela would lend his support to cricket, as indeed he did for many other sports. He did it willingly, spontaneously and with great sincerity, but he was not averse to call in a favour. The UCB discovered this in the late nineties when, shortly before two o'clock one afternoon, Ali was informed by his telephonist that Nelson Mandela was on the line and wanted to speak to him. He had never received a call directly from him before and it was with a sense of pride that he took the call. Mandela asked if they could meet at his residence in Houghton in 20 minutes, but Ali had an important appointment looming and he politely requested that

---

[2] The technique for restoring normal blood flow through a narrowed or blocked artery by either inserting a balloon into it or by using a laser beam.

311

the meeting be delayed until four o'clock.

At five minutes to four, he arrived at the Houghton mansion. For about half an hour they chatted informally about cricket, then Mandela said, 'Ali, I think you will acknowledge that I have played a role in helping cricket get to where it is today.'

'Yes, sir, absolutely.'

'Good, my Foundation needs to complete an important social responsibility project and I would like cricket to donate a million rand towards it. Can you arrange that?'

Ali cleared his throat. 'I'm sure there will be a lot of support for your proposal, but I think you will understand that I must first seek support from my board.'

'Of course,' said Mandela, and they shook hands.

A fortnight later the UCB board met under the chairmanship of Raymond White and Ali told them of Mandela's request. Not all of the board members were happy. One was adamant that cricket could not afford to part with this sort of money, another maintained that they were not a charitable organisation, a third said if they agreed to this, where would it stop? Every charity organisation would come knocking on their door.

'Okay,' said Ali, 'if your answer is no, then you tell him. I'm not going to do it!'

He was impressed with White's quick follow-up. 'Look,' said the UCB president, 'let's have a show of hands. All those opposed?'

No hand was raised.

Ali personally delivered the cheque to Mandela and got permission to take his family with him. There were ten of them in all, suitably dressed for the occasion, and a memorable visit was highlighted when Mandela plonked Ali's two eldest grandchildren, Jesse and Daniel, on his lap and sang *Twinkle, Twinkle, Little Star* to them.

Later, whenever Bacher mentioned the one million rand request in casual talk at dinner tables or to business associates, he would get knowing smiles. Quite apart from all his other attributes, Mandela was apparently *the* fundraiser supreme. Ali discovered that there was not a single CEO or captain of industry who had not had a Mandela phone call or a personal visit. In this way, he personally raised hundreds of millions of rands to build or renovate schools and other community facilities in the rural areas. He would invite these top business people to join him on helicopter trips into the country to see for themselves the value and necessity of his requests. Ali knew for sure that in the Eastern Cape alone the Mandela Foundation had built more than fifty schools.[3] The UCB had been asked to provide cricket equipment for them.

When invited to attend international cricket matches, Mandela's routine was to arrive in the VIP area and head immediately to the kitchen where he would first greet the working staff and spend some time with them before going to his seat. His opening line when he shook someone's hand was 'You might not remember me . . .'

The first time he attended a match at the Wanderers stadium was in February 1993 when West Indies and Pakistan contested the final of a triangular limited overs tournament. It was arranged that he would visit the dressing rooms during the break between innings to meet the teams. After this was done, Ali suggested to him that there were two routes back to the Long Room, either down a thoroughfare behind the stands or along the boundary in full view of the crowd. Mandela opted for the latter and, as the entourage made its way slowly around the perimeter, the ANC leader waved to the spectators and was cheered all the way. Whichever route he followed, it was always going to be a security risk. Bacher was walking behind him and, as they passed in front of the south-western embankment, his eye caught sight of a man with an orange in his hand. He threw it as hard as he could at Mandela, it scorched past his ear and Ali stuck out a hand and caught it. Mandela did not blink an eye. He simply continued his walk, waving at the crowd. Nothing was said.

Later that day, Ali spoke to the close protection officers. Yes, they said, they had seen the incident. And yes, they added, so had Mandela. They all knew not to react or acknowledge in any way the perpetrator's deed. That would have been his victory.

On another occasion, Ali looked forward to welcoming his special guest of honour to the seventh and final one-day international against England at St George's Park in January 1996. Mandela arrived on schedule dressed in cream trousers and shirt, white takkies and a striped green and gold South African blazer and team cap. It was a totally unsolicited gesture of solidarity with cricket and Ali never did find out where the President acquired the kit.

During this match the television cameras focused on Mandela sitting

---

[3] By the fourth quarter of 2003, Nelson Mandela had opened more than 90 schools that were built through his initiatives since 1994 and are now being looked after by the Nelson Mandela Foundation.

out on the Presidential balcony. Ali's mobile phone rang.[4] It was his daughter Ann. 'Hey, Dad,' she enthused, 'I'm watching you on television sitting next to Mr Mandela. Wow, you're lucky!'

'Hello Ann, yes darling, it's terrific . . .'

'Who's calling you?' interrupted Mandela.

'It's my daughter Ann. She saw us on television and . . .'

'Give me the phone!'

The President of South Africa proceeded to chat to her like a long lost friend.

Later that afternoon, a Mandela aide scolded Bacher for having the audacity to ask the President to take a phone call. The aide had been watching from a distance and was not aware of the circumstances. It was a fact that those around him – security people, close protection officers, aides and advisers – often could not keep track of his movements because he would ignore their advice and 'do his own thing'. Rory Steyn was the former security policeman who headed up Mandela's close protection unit and later worked with Bacher on the 2003 Cricket World Cup project. He acknowledged that Madiba was a security nightmare, often acting with total disregard for the advice of those attached to him. Ali did not tire of the stories that Steyn would tell so amusingly about his unforgettable days with the President; how the great man would sometimes behave like a naughty schoolboy.

Mandela's common touch and dignity distinguished all that he did. Famously, before the Rugby World Cup Final at Ellis Park in 1995 he walked out to meet the players, the Springboks and the New Zealand All Blacks, dressed in a replica No 6 jersey worn by the Springbok captain Francois Pienaar. At the time of this tournament, in which the South Africans triumphed against the odds, he also came out publicly in support of the Springbok emblem. This had always been a political hot potato regarded by most black South Africans as a symbol of the old apartheid order.

Cricket under the new order shunned it and, again conveniently, many white South Africans blamed Ali because it had become fashionable to blame Bacher for everything in cricket. How on earth, they wanted to know, could a man who had not only been a Springbok but also the Springbok cricket captain turn his back on his heritage and this great

---

[4] Ali concedes that it is a strict rule in these VIP enclosures that all mobile phones should be switched off at all times – but his cellphone, of course, was his chief business tool.

314

tradition? The answer was quite simple. He considered it a very small price to pay for the largely painless unification process that had opened the doors for South Africans to play on all the cricket grounds of the world. Cricket's unification had been facilitated through the good offices of the National Sports Congress to which it later affiliated, and the NSC saw the Springbok emblem as representative of everything it had opposed and resented during the apartheid years. It would have been a churlish white cricket administrator who put up a fight to retain the emblem and, as it turned out, there was no fight whatsoever and the King Protea was adopted as cricket's new badge. In Ali's view, the most important thing was that South Africa was back in international cricket; doing away with the Springbok was in keeping with the need to have new symbol for a new era and not cling to one that was associated with the past. He was aware of course of the huge white outcry. A lot of South Africans wanted the best of both worlds but they were battling to come to terms with the need for some give and take. They were living through one of the most extraordinary social revolutions of the twentieth century yet, and perhaps understandably, they could not see the wood for the trees. It was all happening so fast. These were amazing times, and the pace of developments was just too much for some people to comprehend. They were being dragged along in the slipstream of the pace-setters and, like most amazing roller-coaster rides, not everyone was particularly happy on the journey.

Rugby had its own reasons for clinging to the Springbok emblem and for being allowed to do so. But when Mandela came out publicly in support of it, the UCB's officials were not impressed. They had shown their bona fides by discarding the emblem because they believed it reflected the apartheid era; and here was Mandela himself, the greatest icon in the fight against apartheid, supporting it in his position as the president of the country. In a television interview, Bacher said, 'We respect Mr Mandela enormously but our constituency does not accept the Springbok emblem . . .'

The interview was screened as the main item on the SABC's 8 o'clock news.

The next morning his phone rang. It was Mandela. 'Now, Ali, you and I have been friends for a long time[5] but I think we need to get together to talk about the Springbok emblem.'

Lunch was arranged at the Union Buildings in Pretoria. Raymond White

---

[5] Ali thought this statement very endearing, as if they had spent years together on Robben Island!

and Krish Mackerdhuj were out of the country so Ali asked Percy Sonn and Julian Thornton to join him. It was shortly before Mandela's birthday and they had an excellent lunch. He opened a bottle of fine white wine that was a gift from an east European country. He did not drink but he wanted his guests to enjoy it.

Then Mandela explained his position on the Springbok rugby emblem, the premise of which was that rugby was the game of the Afrikaner. Yes, it was a game keenly followed by English speakers too, but first and foremost it was the passion of the Afrikaans community. His support for the Springbok was his way of thanking them for the role they had played in the peaceful transition to majority rule and their support for him as South Africa's first democratically elected president. Secondly, he had been told by intelligence agencies that he should not discount the threat of an attempted right wing coup[6] from the far right wing. South Africa could ill afford this, and again the concession to the Springbok was his way of holding out an olive branch.

Anyone who was fortunate enough to be in South Africa during the 1995 Rugby World Cup will testify to the wonderful mood and spirit that permeated all communities during that magical month; and how big rugby men chanted 'Nelson! Nelson! Nelson!' when he walked on to the Ellis Park pitch on the day of the Springboks' greatest triumph . . . this man of no bitterness and no vengeful anger, this man who had devoted his life to a free South Africa and sacrificed 27 years of it behind bars.

IF THE EIGHTIES were turbulent, the mid-nineties were tumultuous. The country was awash in what became known as 'Madiba Magic' and for South Africans it was a time of hope and reconciliation and confidence in the future. The new democracy was being held up to the world as a shining example – with Mandela fêted wherever he went – and South African sport looked in excellent shape.

But as the nineties wound down, new realities began to emerge that would signal the end of the honeymoon and with it a whole new set of challenges.

---

[6] This threat was not far fetched. After Mandela's retirement and during the presidency of his successor Thabo Mbeki, a group of right-wingers were arrested and charged with treason for their alleged bid to overthrow the government.

Chapter 27

The Second Unity

HANSIE CRONJE WAS like a favourite son. Of all the young cricketers in South Africa, he was the one who seemed best able to understand Ali Bacher's vision.

He did not need persuading to coach and motivate disadvantaged cricketers in the townships. He once drove alone from Bloemfontein to Sharpeville at 4 am on a Saturday morning to attend the opening by Steve Tshwete of a sports complex there; and after having some fun with the kids he then drove back again, a round trip of some 600 kilometres. He did a lot of promotions like this and, unlike some other people, he did not need television cameras to convince him to do them.

During his reign as South Africa's captain, he would often have to travel to Johannesburg for promotional work. If he had an hour or two to spare, he would voluntarily go into Soweto to do a spot of coaching. The media were never aware of these activities. He was the kind of self-motivated young man who Bacher greatly admired as the perfect captain and role model. It was little wonder that he was so well liked by the black youth of South Africa, voted as the third most popular sportsman in the country behind two black football idols. He was a young Afrikaner who carried no discernible baggage.

Bacher had known the Cronje family for many years. He and Hansie's father had played provincial cricket in the same era when Ewie had captained Orange Free State; they had served together on the boards of the SA Cricket Union and the United Cricket Board; and Ali had much respect for 'a down to earth, salt of the earth man' who proudly headed a

317

warm and loving and successful sporting family.

In terms of his pedigree, Hansie was not unlike Ali. The Bloemfontein boy had captained school and club teams from an early age, and like Bacher he was 21 when he was made captain of his province. Ali was delighted when the young man was appointed South Africa's captain in succession to Kepler Wessels in November 1994; at the age of 25, he was a couple of years younger than Ali when he became the national captain. Bacher had long ago judged him a born leader who was blessed with all the right stuff in terms of leadership qualities. As he grew into the captaincy, so too did he get more freedom, responsibility and power. 'I gave him room to operate with as little interference as possible. I gave him power within reason.'

Did he perhaps give him too much power? The coach to Cronje's team, Bob Woolmer, said so, but only with the benefit of hindsight after he had left the job in 1999 and when reasons were being sought for Cronje's motivation in the match fixing scandal. 'We might have,' says Ali, 'but we had such confidence in him as the captain. And it should not be forgotten that in cricket the captain, not the coach, is the boss.'

As Cronje's term of office continued so too did he begin challenging authority. When Bacher privately remarked on this in a critical way, Shira reminded him that he too had sometimes questioned officialdom as a young captain; and that he and Cronje were quite similar in this respect.

On tour, Cronje would be involved in team selection, along with the coach and vice-captain, on a match by match basis; and there were occasions when Bacher felt that his captain was straying from the vision they seemed to share. The first of these occurred in January 1998 during the one-day international series against Australia and New Zealand. Having already qualified for the finals, the South Africans arrived in Perth for two matches in three days. Before the first of these, against New Zealand on the Friday, Ali received a phone call from Cronje. 'You'll be pleased to know that we've selected Makhaya Ntini!'

Bacher was indeed delighted, and even more so when the 20-year-old black fast bowler made an impressive international debut in which he took the important wickets of the captain Stephen Fleming and the hard-hitting Adam Parore in a convincing victory. It seemed obvious to Ali that Ntini should be given another outing on the Sunday against Australia, and during the course of the Saturday he considered phoning Cronje to confirm that this would happen. In the end, he decided against it because he did not want to interfere. When he turned on his television set the next morning, he was extremely disappointed to see that Ntini had been left out.

Four months later, when the team toured England, Bacher was again dismayed when an all-white team remained unchanged for all three one-dayers at the start of the tour. The South Africans had secured the series by winning the first two matches and Ali was expecting that Ntini would be selected for the third. What made it worse was that a big transformation seminar was being held in South Africa that very weekend where about a hundred coaches, development officers and other officials were gathered. During a subsequent telephone discussion with Cronje on various other issues, Ali told him, 'You should also know, Hansie, of the overwhelming sense of disappointment at the seminar when you did not play Makhaya in that third match.'

Cronje was contrite. 'His explanation to me,' says Ali, 'was that the senior players felt strongly that the frontline fast bowlers Allan Donald and Shaun Pollock should play in the last match as both were contenders for the Man of the Series.'

This award, of course, carried a monetary reward but, as it turned out, neither bowler was voted Man of the Series, an award that went to Jonty Rhodes.

It is significant to note that whenever Bacher contacted the South African team on tour to discuss an issue, it was always Cronje, and not the coach Bob Woolmer, that he called. As a former successful Test captain, Bacher was unwavering in his belief that the captain was in charge; in fact, he would always believe that the importance of the coach in international cricket was, and is, over-exaggerated. The position was a relatively new one in a game that for more than a hundred years – during which most of its greatest players graced its stage – had done very nicely, thank you, without team coaches. It was only in the 1990s, when the game got caught up in the technological revolution, that players who were part of the computer generation came to regard coaches, who knew how to work laptops, as valuable allies.

Woolmer was one of these – in fact, he had turned cricket technology into something of an art form – and he was engaged to succeed Mike Procter as the national coach in September 1994. The other candidates for the job were Eddie Barlow and Duncan Fletcher.

Procter's dismissal came in unfortunate circumstances. Shortly before the UCB reached their decision to fire him, he was admitted to hospital with chest pains, which was diagnosed as inflammation of the tissue around the heart. It was in the intensive care unit that he received Bacher's phone call to advise him that his contract had not been renewed.

Ali had tremendous respect for his old teammate. 'I know he was deeply hurt by the decision and that I contacted him at the wrong time. Mike was a great player and a good coach but he was not one of those who bothered about the technical side of the game. He was just such a naturally gifted player that it did not concern him.'

Procter later wrote a heartfelt letter to Ali, thanking him for the flowers he had been sent in hospital, and adding, 'On a personal note, I am really very sorry that I let you down with my job as the cricket coach.'

Ali's summation of Woolmer was that he was a good coach and did well during his five years in the job. 'I was a supporter of him at the time.'

As for Bacher's relationship with Cronje, certain officials, again with the benefit of hindsight, believed it to be too exclusive. Also, although it was in Ali's job description to take responsibility for the national team, he was sometimes seen as too much of a one-man band in this regard. It was him and the team, to the exclusion of others, and most of the time it was just him and the captain. Bacher was also in a complicated position in that he was first and foremost a players' man – a cricketer at heart – yet he was committed to ensuring that cricket met the broader needs of the new South Africa. Bruce Francis made the observation back in the mid-eighties that 'I have not known anywhere in the world another cricket official so genuinely concerned for the players in his care'.

What was very clear, however, was that the majority of the cricketers, like so many administrators, did not understand the political issues and sensitivities. Should they have? They were players, after all, and not politicians. Their brief was to win for their country. They were in the same camp as the selectors whose brief was to select teams that could achieve victory. The selectors had empathy with the players because they held their careers, and their livelihoods, in their hands and they did not underestimate this weighty responsibility. They were representing the interests of young professional men and were naturally nervous that political interference could seriously retard a player's career. At the same time the selectors were very aware of the need to find black players worthy of selection and, when they did, to give them as much opportunity as they could to gain experience. In every argument and debate, 'merit' was the word they held up as their shield; yet black people were wondering why it was taking so long to get from point A to point B, and why the journey from 'disadvantaged' to 'merit' seemed without end.

What was clear towards the end of the nineties was that a stand-off was looming that could be very damaging one way or the other. There were signs of dangerous polarisation. On the one hand there were players, selectors and officials who complained of political interference without always understanding what it was all about and, on the other, there were key cricket officials (led by Bacher) and prominent politicians who had become allies but, in the cold light of day, were finding it difficult to look each other in the eye. It was now simply unacceptable that, seven years down the road from international reacceptance, the national team was still virtually all-white and, according to information that would later surface, had become an exclusive little club that was a law unto itself. The joke that it was harder getting out of the team than into it was actually not so funny.

The crunch came before the first Test against Brian Lara's West Indies team at the Wanderers in November 1998 when an all-white South African team was selected. At the centre of the crisis was the young fast bowler Makhaya Ntini. Just three months earlier on the occasion of his 21st birth day, he had taken four England wickets in the Test match at Headingley, Leeds, and was only denied a fifth through a dropped catch. He received glowing notices and, in a book on that tour, it was noted:

> In only his fourth Test, Ntini looked like a real Test match bowler. He maintained a disciplined line and length, giving batsmen just enough width to tempt them into indiscretion, and he maintained his pace and aggression in spite of having to bowl uphill and into the wind. Considering that this was the second time in the series that he had removed Mike Atherton,[1] and that earlier in the year he had twice dismissed the great Sri Lankan Aravinda de Silva, there was everything to suggest that a wonderful Test career lay ahead.[2]

It was not as if they would be throwing him in at the deep end; he had already taken ten wickets in the four Test matches he had played against England and Sri Lanka. It was not as if they were being asked to select a player who was not good enough. It was just that they were being asked to select a player because, heaven knows, payback time had come and gone and there was now a moral obligation.

'A few days prior to the selection of the team,' recalls Ali, 'I was discreetly

---

[1] In the third Test at Old Trafford, Manchester, a month earlier, Ntini dismissed Atherton, England's outstanding batsman, for 41.
[2] From the book, *Hansie & The Boys: A Year On* by Rodney Hartman (Zebra Press 1998).

321

informed that Makhaya would not make the Test side.'

He immediately phoned Peter Pollock who explained that Ntini was out of form and that this had been confirmed to him when he called colleagues at Border, the province where Ntini played. 'I asked Peter if he could propose the following: that the selectors name Makhaya in the squad, bring him to Johannesburg earlier for intense coaching and attempt to get him back into form in time. I then gave Peter the assurance that if, after all that, the selectors and coaches still considered him not ready for action, I would publicly support him and his fellow selectors by issuing an appropriate statement.'

This would run along the lines that 'despite every effort to get Ntini into tip-top form, he was not ready; and that to select him could only jeopardise his career'.

Pollock did not like the idea. He argued that if Ntini was named in the squad and then left out of the Test XI, no amount of Bacher rationalisation would be heard above the inevitable outcry. It was a Catch 22 situation because when Ntini was not included in the squad later that week, there was an outcry anyway.

'I was very disappointed,' says Ali. 'I wrote a strong letter to Raymond White and asked him to circulate it to all members of the UCB General Council.' White strongly urged his MD to withdraw his request. He told him that if the letter was circulated, it would inevitably be leaked to the media. Bacher heeded the warning and the letter was not distributed. Instead, he unilaterally prepared a media statement which, on the morning of the first day of the Test, 26 November 1998, he took to the press box at the Wanderers. It read:

I have had numerous requests from the media to comment on the composition of the South African team selected to play against West Indies in the first Test match. At the outset, let me say that I am disappointed that no players of colour have been selected to represent South Africa in this historic Test match. The national selectors have informed me that due to loss of form and injury to players of colour who were in contention for the team, they were unable to select these players. I have discussed the matter with the UCB president, Raymond White, and we have agreed that the issue will be fully debated at the next meeting of the Board on December 5. In addition, I am confident that a clear selection policy with parameters that the national selection panel must adhere to will emerge from that meeting. I reaffirm the United Cricket Board's commitment to making cricket a truly national sport, played and supported by all South Africans.

Bacher was under extreme pressure on the political front. Steve Tshwete was saying publicly that he could no longer support a team that was 'lily white' and that he might have to introduce legislation to forcibly correct this. Mvuso Mbebe, chief executive officer of the NSC, met with Bacher and Tshwete immediately after the first Test. He wanted to know what was going on, and Tshwete emphasised that an all-white team was unacceptable.

Later, during the fourth Test at Cape Town, Bacher sat for a time with Alec Erwin, the (white) Minister for Trade and Industry. 'I'm just warning you as a friend,' he told Ali, 'that our constituency is growing impatient.' Gibbs and Adams were in the team, but Ntini had still not convinced the selectors of his form.

Those people who conveniently argued that Tshwete's public pronouncements were simply political points-scoring in the run-up to the 1999 General Election were, at best, blissfully ignorant or, at worst, utterly contemptuous of the fact that they owed their continued existence in cricket to the very people whose authority they were now ignoring. In order to get South Africa back into world cricket, Tshwete had gone in person to visit high commissioners in London to tell them that the time was right for them to establish sporting ties with South Africa; and that great things were happening for young black cricketers in the township development programme. That was in 1991. More than seven years later the West Indies, representing so much that was considered great about black men rising above poverty and mediocrity through the power of their sport, were in South Africa on their first five-Test tour; and there was not one black player considered good enough to play against them in the opening match. Tshwete would not buy this, and neither apparently would Nelson Mandela. It was his custom to accept invitations to attend the Wanderers Test matches but now the President declined. This caused great consternation in the UCB where, ironically, the finishing touches were being put to the so-called 'Transformation Charter' that was due to be presented during the Wanderers Test. Now with 'transformation' under serious threat, the ceremony was put on hold. It was sad but true that the trust that once existed between Peter Pollock and Ali Bacher was being eroded and neither man felt comfortable with the other's approach.

Pollock was a players' man, which was altogether understandable and acceptable. The players asked that the only criterion for selection should be merit; and that was right, too. But what the selectors and the playing staff did not understand – and this ultimately was the fault of the UCB –

was the bigger picture of what needed to happen in cricket in post-apartheid South Africa. What the UCB might have done at the time was to ask people like Mluleki George and Mthobi Tyamzashe[3] to articulate the expectations of black people to those whose role it was to select and play for South Africa. In the author's discussions many years later with Tyamzashe, the following emerged as the kind of message that should have been conveyed to Pollock, Cronje, Woolmer and Co and, indeed, to certain high-ranking officials on the UCB:

> When unification of South African cricket was in its infancy, people like Tshwete and George and Tyamzashe took considerable risk to enter into negotiations on the basis of trust and face value against men who their constituencies not only distrusted but also despised. Again persuaded by Tshwete and George and Tyamzashe, it was these black communities who made sacrifices that were far greater than any the whites were asked to make; they were asked to scrap their own 'national teams'[4] of which they were very proud – and whose players were greater heroes to them than any Springbok – in return for the promise of a 'united national team' in which all communities would be properly represented. They were told by Tshwete and George and Tyamzashe not to expect this to happen overnight – because whites under apartheid had obviously prospered in the inside track – but that they should know that it would happen before long and then everyone would rejoice. These were big sacrifices that were asked and given – in return for which the whites were asked only to understand, and act according to their conscience.

Bacher would add a rider to this when he pointed out that, unlike many other African governments, the ANC never once sent him a letter or made an official phone call to give him instructions. He would constantly remind his colleagues of the extraordinary roles played by Mandela, Tshwete and Thabo Mbeki in 'getting us back into world cricket'. As he pointed out, 'They accepted our bona fides, they backed us, they acknowledged us and never once did they exert any pressure.'

It was unwritten and unstated but Ali knew that his role in the nineties

---

[3] These stalwarts of the now defunct National Sports Congress had moved on to higher office: George was an ANC Member of Parliament and Tyamzashe the Director General in Tshwete's Department of Sport and Recreation.
[4] Until 1991 Africans, coloureds and Indians had their own separate associations and national teams which were passionately supported.

was to hasten the process of transformation in cricket. It was the least he could do; and he was unyielding in that purpose.

As for Ntini, he was seen by many as having become a lone pawn in a rather shabby game; and whether or not that was true, it spoke volumes for the young man's character that through any number of setbacks he would emerge in time as one of the world's leading fast bowlers. The saddest aspect of this particular period was that there was only one black African in the national frame; and he therefore attracted all the attention.

The upshot of the Wanderers debacle, and ahead of the 5 December board meeting, was that Bacher met with the UCB lawyer Clifford Green to draw up a selection policy on behalf of the UCB executive. After the meeting, White issued a statement which said in part:

> The UCB is committed to taking cricket to all communities and to support the Government's objectives in bringing players of colour into the highest echelons of the game. The UCB believes that standards of excellence in the national team should not be prejudiced nor compromised to achieve these objectives. The national selection committee shall, with immediate effect, be given clear directives that players of colour should be selected for all future squads chosen to play international matches.

It added that if the selectors ever judged it impossible to do this for reasons of form, injury or illness, they should refer their selection for the approval of a new four-man committee whose members were White, vice-president Percy Sonn, Bacher and Gerald Majola, a member of the UCB executive.

Ironically, Bacher's insistence on the new policy claimed as its first 'victim' his nephew Adam Bacher. The opening batsman was dropped for the second Test at Port Elizabeth to accommodate Herschelle Gibbs. The official line was that Adam, with two single figure scores in the first Test, was out of form; but the truth was that Gibbs had to play in order to provide the 'player of colour'. Adam, the son of Ali's eldest brother Issy, had played 17 Tests for his country.

In what others saw as the second 'victim', Pat Symcox was also dropped during the series to accommodate Paul Adams. It would later emerge that this selection had the effect of tipping Hansie Cronje over the edge, which came to a head when the South African captain walked out on the team after they had completed a 5-0 rout of their opponents.

THE DAWNING OF 1998 had ushered in a difficult and eventful 12-month period for South African cricket. First came the arrival of the Pakistan team, under the captaincy of Rashid Latif who had retired from international cricket three years earlier because, as the then vice-captain, he had fallen out with the captain Salim Malik[5] who he accused of match fixing. When Pakistan, the overwhelming favourites, lost a one-off Test by 324 runs in Johannesburg in January 1995, talk in the press box, if not in the Long Room, centred on rumours of corruption. After the South African leg of their tour, the Pakistanis went to Harare where they lost to Zimbabwe by an innings. Because no one could actually prove them, the persistent rumours were treated as something of a joke. When Salim Malik was relieved of the captaincy and subsequently drummed out of the game after the controversies of 1995, Rashid Latif came out of retirement and was now the captain in South Africa. There was a view in world cricket that trouble dogged Pakistan touring teams, and the team that came to South Africa in 1998 was no exception.

A couple of days before the start of the first Test at the Wanderers, newspapers carried front-page reports that two of the Pakistani players, Saqlain Mushtaq and Mohammad Akram, had been mugged the night before in Sandton. They claimed they were walking to a restaurant across the road from their luxury hotel when a car pulled up and two occupants jumped out, assaulted them and robbed them at knifepoint. Latif described his players as ambassadors of their country and said their safety was paramount. South Africans were mortified. What sort of message would this convey to the world about the new democracy?

Ali leapt into action to help placate the Pakistan team. 'I phoned Steve (Tshwete) and he got Mandela to phone the two cricketers concerned and to apologise to them for the incident.' Ali also sent a message to the Pakistan Cricket Board expressing heartfelt apologies and promising tighter security for the players.

In the confusion, some reports claimed the Test was cancelled and others said the Pakistanis were about to go home. What Latif actually did was request a postponement and Ali agreed that the match would start 24 hours late.

Then came the next bombshell. The SABC's 8 pm television news

---

[5] Before the best-of-three limited overs series finals against Pakistan, Hansie Cronje was offered $10 000 to lose the first match. The offer, by a man known to Malik, was rejected. Source: *Evidence from the King Commission into Match Fixing, June 2000.*

reported that the 'mugging' was in reality a brawl with bouncers at a strip joint called *The Blue Orchard,* which was several miles away from the Sandton hotel and certainly not 'a restaurant across the road'. According to the report, there had been quite a bit of drinking and an argument had ensued. The new story was all over the front pages of the morning newspapers, but the team's management strongly denied it. Ali phoned Allister Sparks, one of South Africa's most celebrated newspaper editors who was now running the SABC television news department. He asked him how sure he was of the facts of the strip club fracas. Sparks replied that he would never have aired the story 'without solid information'.[6]

Interestingly, with no witnesses coming forward, and *The Blue Orchard* management maintaining a stony silence, the final word on the story was never written.

The Test match ended in a draw. It was marred by bad weather and, in another South African innovation inspired by Bacher, the floodlights were switched on in the middle of the day for the first time in a Test match; but this did not seem to help much in the ambient light. It was, however, a practice that would in future be used many times at different Test match grounds with a greater degree of success.

THE GLARE OF controversy, meanwhile, moved away from the Pakistanis and on to the pale complexion of the South African team. A parliamentary portfolio committee raised the issue of the 'lily-white' nature of the side and some politicians simply disregarded the inclusion in Test squads of coloured, or mixed race, players like Adams and Gibbs and began demanding black African representation, like Ntini.

The sport that had beaten all others in its unification was now under the cosh. Ali himself urged change. 'In 1998, we cannot have an all-white team,' he said in a media statement. 'Our constituencies will not allow it. They are pressing for change and they want to see it reflected in the national team. South Africa is not a normal country at the moment and it is something we must all understand.'

In a subsequent article in the *Sunday Times,* he added: 'We must not compromise standards . . . the UCB is opposed to quotas at the national level and would be unhappy if government legislation interfered in the running of our sport . . . but we do need to select a national team of colour.'[7]

---

[6] Allister Sparks interview, September 2003.
[7] Source: *Hansie & The Boys. A Year On* (Zebra Press 1998).

BACHER'S THREE LIEUTENANTS at the UCB head office were Imtiaz Patel, Khaya Majola and Hoosain Ayob, who as an entity, in the words of Patel, 'gauged the pulse in the country'. By this he meant that Ali relied on them to judge the mood of the people on the ground and convey it to him. They would sit on the couch in the boss's office after normal business hours when Patel claimed the real work was done.

Patel and Ayob were old allies from the SACU days of the development programme and Majola, the brother of Gerald, was an excellent black cricketer under the old SACB banner who came to Johannesburg from New Brighton township in Port Elizabeth to join Bacher as co-national director of development – an appointment in keeping with the original assurance given by Ali to Mluleki George and Mthobi Tyamzashe when they had their secret dinner at Robbie Muzzell's home back in 1990. Soon after that dinner, Bacher met Majola for the first time when they had a quiet drink together in Port Elizabeth. He had already been identified as the co-director but word got out about their meeting and the SACB voiced its displeasure. In spite of this, SACB agreed that Majola should take the job. That he and Ali developed a particularly close relationship is more remarkable for the fact that, during the Gatting tour, Majola threatened 'to kill Bacher' if he should ever set foot in New Brighton.

'When he arrived at the UCB offices at the Wanderers in 1991, Khaya was enthusiastic, inexperienced and lacking in confidence,' says Ali. 'We developed a wonderful relationship, one of mutual respect, and I was desirous to impart to him everything I knew. Not a day went by when he was not in my office – sometimes ten times a day – which was what true mentoring was about.' Majola would often refer to Bacher as 'my father'.

Now in the role of the UCB's director of amateur cricket, Majola and his two 'pulse gaugers' advised Bacher that a new strategy was needed. They warned him that 'nothing was changing' and that black people were growing restless at the apparent lack of transformation in the national team. Not for the first time in his life, Ali called a meeting under the general heading, 'We need something to happen, chaps!'

What did happen was that they met with Phillip Glaser, a 'transformation consultant' from Cape Town, who already had a good track record of helping various groups and companies transform the old apartheid mentality into one of sustainable human development.

They convened an all-day workshop at the Aloe Ridge conference centre outside Johannesburg, and the challenge on the table was to 'reunite cricket'. For 12 hours they thrashed out the new strategy. Glaser and his colleague

Gideon Steyn fired questions and took turns at the whiteboard writing down the answers. It was an exhausting but exhilarating experience and it signalled the start of what became known internally as 'the Second Unity'.

Based on the founding principles of the Aloe Ridge workshop, transformation seminars were staged throughout the country, province by province. Patel, who had assisted in the development programme for a decade, was given the task of 'driving' the project. He was on the road for 40 days on the trot; as he put it, he was 'living the cause' on a mission that went beyond being merely a job. As he recalls, 'We were all in it together, on an incredible high in an unforgettable time.'[8]

The Transformation Charter was drawn up during November 1998 at a 'national vision conference'. It was now Raymond White's duty to present it publicly during the tea interval of the fourth Test against West Indies at Newlands on Sunday 3 January 1999. To a packed stadium and a VIP enclosure that included several cabinet ministers, the UCB president read out South African cricket's 'Pledge to the Nation'. It reaffirmed the UCB's absolute commitment to non-racial principles and the development of cricket among the disadvantaged people of South Africa as a moral duty. Having read out the Pledge word for word, White then departed from the script. He declared that cricket did not want or need interference and that the team deserved support. He was given a rousing cheer from the capacity crowd, but within the VIP enclosure all hell broke loose.

Having delivered his message, White was immediately called into an impromptu meeting of UCB officials and members of its newly formed Transformation Monitoring Committee. He was roundly castigated for changing the wording of the script which was interpreted as an attack on the government. 'They wouldn't listen to me,' he recalls. 'You were either for them or against them. In the UCB there was no longer room for robust debate or articulated opinion. If you were against them, they marked you and conspired to get rid of you.'[9]

Demands were made for White's immediate resignation but he compromised by agreeing to make a public apology. 'I apologised for changing the wording of the Pledge, and only that.' He steadfastly refused to apologise for the sentiments he expressed.

'I had said that we didn't need interference. I did not say "political

---

[8] Imtiaz Patel interview, September 2003.
[9] Raymond White interview, November 2003.

interference". I was referring to the NSC and to every newspaper editor who was telling us how to manage cricket. When I said the team deserved support, it was a clear reference to Tshwete saying that he could no longer support them. I also wanted to send a very clear message to the South African cricketers that they had my full support.'

Tshwete held talks with Bacher and other UCB officials during the course of the fifth Test at Supersport Park, Centurion. It was a meeting that Ali would describe as 'very difficult'. The sports minister told them bluntly: 'We need greater representivity. The people are losing patience.' Gibbs and Adams were still in the team, but Ntini was not.

It was at this point that Bacher came up with the solution that saved the day. He proposed, and Tshwete accepted, that the South African squad for the seven-match Standard Bank International limited overs series should be expanded to 16 players – and that four of them would be 'young up-and-coming' cricketers who would remain in the squad for all seven matches. The UCB executive committee ratified this, 'bearing in mind the current situation regarding our ongoing discussions with government regarding representivity'.

Ali's next step was to talk to the players, but he did not inform White or Peter Pollock that he was going to do so. He went to the team's hotel once the Test match was over and South Africa had completed its 5-0 series triumph. His notes, on which he based what he told the players, are again instructive:

The key to the success of this country is transformation; and it is inevitable and right. There can be no specific policy to achieve this. We have to be pragmatic, it can only be a philosophy. When the opportunity presents itself, we should give preference to peripheral players, both black and white. This will require vision and initiative of the selectors and I hope support from the team. We shan't do silly things. I am confident that the selectors and administrators will carefully handle the process so as not to drop standards.

Bacher called the new philosophy 'merit with opportunities' and emphasised that 'we are not transferring the existing constituency to another'. He knew that the Transformation Charter would be dead if South Africa fielded all-white teams. Already during the Test series, a majority of black VIPs had declined invitations to watch the cricket.

He also conceded that the problem lay at provincial level where there were no black cricketers in the top 20 batting and bowling averages; but that during the past decade several white players had performed indifferently at national level. 'So what if the same fate befalls players of colour? Does it mean to say that we can only win matches if all eleven players perform well? No, it doesn't happen like that.'

After the meeting Hansie Cronje packed his bags and effectively walked out of the team. More than anything, he was angry that the historic 5-0 whitewash had been almost ignored by officials intent on changing his team. Bob Woolmer phoned Bacher to tell him the captain had gone back to Bloemfontein, and Ali then called Peter Pollock. 'Just let him cool down for a bit,' was the chief selector's advice. Pollock, however, contacted Ray McCauley, the team's unofficial pastor who had first been invited to perform this function by Kepler Wessels in 1992 and continued tending to the spiritual needs of the team when Cronje, a reborn Christian, took over the captaincy. If anyone could talk rationally with Cronje, he could.

McCauley was a prominent figure in South African public life. Once a champion bodybuilder, he founded the Rhema Bible Ministries, a charismatic church with a congregation of thousands. He had a forceful personality, a persuasive preaching style and a total commitment to transformation and reconciliation in the new South Africa. He was a man of the cloth, but he was also a man of the world. And he had great respect for what Bacher was doing in terms of the game's transformation.

'I went to Bloemfontein to see Hansie. He had actually written his letter of resignation. We had a long talk and I tried to help him understand the process that was needed. South African captains didn't always understand their political functions. I told him that what cricket was being asked to do was a small price to pay.'

So Cronje withdrew his resignation and rejoined the team. He also committed himself, says McCauley, to spending time getting to know Ntini, at times living with him, and coaching him. This was an example to his teammates because, as McCauley confides, 'Hansie was not the only one who wanted to leave the team. There were a few others as well . . .'[10]

The upshot of all of this, however, was that the Cronje-Bacher relationship cooled. 'It remained cordial,' recalls Ali, 'but from that moment the very warm and close relationship that we once had was never the same again.'

---

[10] Ray McCauley interview, November 2003.

Chapter 28

The Anonymous Benefactor

THERE IS A question that cricket people like to ask: who would you select to bat for your life? What this means in essence is who do you consider to be the one batsman who would go through a wall if the situation demanded it. It would be fair to say that in the modern era a cricketer like the Australian Steve Waugh would be a popular choice to bat for someone whose life depended on it; and the same could be said in a different way about Ali Bacher. If he considered the cause worthy enough, he would stay with it around the clock in relentless pursuit of his objective. Like Waugh at the crease, he would simply not give up – provided, of course, he was convinced of the authenticity of his mission.

Thus it was with the 21-year-old Makhaya Ntini. Bacher asked him three simple questions to establish whether his was a cause worthy of his support.

'Makhaya, do you respect me?'

'Yes, Dr Bacher.'

'Would you ever lie to me?'

'No, Dr Bacher.'

'Did you rape that woman?'

'No, Dr Bacher!'

Off the field, the cricket season of 1998-99 was a most difficult and challenging time. To the political anger, the obstinacy of the captain and certain officials, and the discontent among the players was added the shocking news that Ntini – the player at the very centre of the trans-formation row – had been charged with rape.

'I was convinced he was telling the truth,' says Ali, 'and because of that I was prepared to support him all the way.'

Others thought him naïve and misguided. At least one senior UCB colleague told him to walk away from the case. Rape was a heinous crime and, should Ntini be convicted, Bacher's credibility would be destroyed in the eyes of a public who quite rightly placed rapists in the same category as murderers.

News of the charge broke on the eve of the fifth Test against the West Indies. It was alleged that Ntini had raped a 21-year-old woman at his home cricket ground, Buffalo Park in East London, six weeks earlier. He was subsequently not selected for the limited overs series, nor for the tour to New Zealand because the trial date was set during that period. The UCB announced its 'moral support but not financial support' for the player, and Ali was relieved that Raymond White had backed him on this decision. 'I have discussed this matter with Makhaya on numerous occasions. He has always remained adamant that he is completely innocent. On that basis, I support him fully,' Ali told the media. 'We realise that this is now in the hands of the courts and we hope that the case is disposed of as soon as possible. We will endeavour to assist him wherever possible with moral support.'

There was a huge outcry from individuals and organisations who were fighting for women's rights. Ali received highly critical telephone calls and letters, and the newspapers reflected this backlash.

Ntini, of course, had emerged on the cricket scene as if in answer to Bacher's prayer. It was always Ali's belief that black cricketers would emerge from the development programme to play Test cricket – and Ntini was a shining example. He came from Mdingi, a little village in the rolling hills near King William's Town, where he was spotted by development coaches when they held a mini-cricket clinic in the township in 1993. The same year he was selected for the Border under-15 team, and two years later he was in the South African Schools XI for their tour of England and India. He made his senior provincial debut for Border against England in their 1995-96 tour, was later selected for the South Africa A team, and then his big break came when he replaced the injured Roger Telemachus on South Africa's tour of Australia in 1997-98.

Ali went to East London for the first day of the court case in April 1999, and came away feeling uneasy. 'I just didn't have a good feeling about the way the case was being conducted. I left the courtroom questioning whether or not justice would prevail.'

A few days later he received the news that the magistrate, Deon Roussouw, had convicted Ntini of rape and handed down a six-year jail sentence.

In another media statement Bacher said: 'The UCB supported Makhaya because we believed him, as did his and the UCB lawyers, to be innocent of the charge. We are obviously disappointed by the judgment handed down by the magistrate. We have not had an opportunity to study the judgment but, having spoken to Makhaya's lawyers, we understand that there are definite grounds for an appeal. The UCB will continue to support Makhaya until the legal process has been completed. He will be withdrawn from the South African Squad for the 1999 World Cup and his replacement is Alan Dawson from Western Province.'

The outcry now reached fever pitch. In spite of his conviction, Ntini was still receiving Bacher's support. The criticism did not deter him; and he continued to bat for the youngster's life. 'I always believed that he told me the truth, and I never doubted him. I also studied the testimony from his trial. As a medical doctor, I know the kind of evidence that is found when a rape has been committed. The report of the medical examination of the woman showed absolutely no evidence of this kind – no abrasions, lacerations, contusions, pubic hair or semen. I asked myself how on earth he could have been convicted.'

What is more, there were no witnesses to the alleged crime and the woman's testimony seemed flawed and contradictory. Ntini's lawyers immediately served notice that they would appeal against the verdict and sentence, and a date was set for October 1999 in the Grahamstown High Court.

Bacher counselled the UCB lawyers and they recommended that the Cape Town-based advocate Jeremy Gauntlett, one of South Africa's most highly respected senior legal counsel, be approached to head the appeal. He agreed in principle. 'I had read the judgment and I knew there was a very good prospect of succeeding in the appeal.'[1]

In the mean time, the people of Ntini's community – led by the Border cricket official and East London businessman Ray Mali – were also convinced of Ntini's innocence based on private investigations they had conducted. Mali had enjoyed a good relationship with Bacher since the day in 1991 when Ali went to the highly politicised Eastern Cape for a Bakers mini-cricket festival involving 600 children at Fort Hare University.

---

[1] Jeremy Gauntlett interview, October 2003.

334

He continued to pay visits to the area where he oversaw the establishment of the Ntselamanzi cricket ground that would be accessible to 12 nearby villages, and became a very popular figure with the young cricketers of those parts. They would never forget the day that he gave each and every one of them, all 600, a cricket bat at the mini-cricket festival. 'That gesture remains in the minds of many of those cricketers,' says Mali. 'It was too wonderful for them and they never forgot Ali.'[2]

Now, however, Bacher and Mali were approaching the Ntini case from different angles. Ali was, as always, looking for the best man for the job to lead the legal team, and Mali was consulting with his constituency to establish the best approach from their perspective. Ntini was like a son to Mali and his wife Peggy and they wanted to do the right thing by him. What particularly upset them was that officials at the Border Cricket Union kept them in the dark at the outset. It was a full six weeks after the alleged rape at Buffalo Park that the Malis were told about it for the first time. He and his people also had no say in the initial defence team that was assembled and that ultimately failed.

Ironically, a fortnight before the alleged rape, Mali gathered what he described as a small committee of cricket people to go and meet with Ntini. He had not been selected in the South African team against the West Indies and was unwittingly caught up in the transformation controversy. Mali felt the young player needed help. 'I saw that his cricket was slipping and that he was not putting in enough effort, missing practices and so on. I discovered that he was staying with his grandmother and that his mother was actually in Port Elizabeth. He seemed to be lacking a support base.'

The rape case put a whole new slant on Mali's priorities. 'Until this stage our main interest and expertise was in cricket development, now suddenly we were faced with something out of the ordinary that was affecting the very face of development. Makhaya was a role model in our area and this case was critical to the future of development. It was important for us to make decisions by engaging the community, and particularly the women who had formed a support group.'

Bacher told Mali that he wanted Gauntlett to handle the appeal, but Mali's choice was another Cape Town advocate, Peter Hodes, with whom he had had previous dealings.

Mali's people were adamant that they would have to meet first with Gauntlett before deciding if, indeed, he was the right man for the job. It

---

[2] Ray Mali interview, September 2003.

was arranged that they meet him at Johannesburg International airport immediately following his return from a case in London. It was the first time that Bacher would meet him, this learned man who had done his postgraduate studies at Oxford University.

The meeting was anything but easy and the advocate was totally non-plussed when faced by Mali and eight members of his community, who included his wife and other representatives of the women's support group. 'It was extraordinary,' recalls Ali. 'Here was this top senior counsel, who would normally pick and choose his cases, virtually being asked to sell himself.'

The meeting went on for four hours and at one stage Gauntlett was so visibly irritated that Ali had to take him outside and implore him not to walk away. Gauntlett confesses to being a bit 'puzzled and bemused' by being confronted by a delegation of people representing a community with its own dynamics. He felt he was not there to market himself, but he could see that 'Ali was busy trying to sell me'.

A sticking point came in the insistence of Mali's group that a lawyer named Dali Mpofu be included in the legal team as the junior counsel. The local community deemed his appointment 'politically important' because, although his practice was in Johannesburg, he was one of theirs and the community trusted him. Mpofu's selection was apparently non-negotiable; indeed, Mali was prepared to drop his claim for Hodes in a compromise to ensure Mpofu's presence.

Gauntlett was only prepared to accept the brief on his own terms. He was at first concerned about Mpofu assisting him, and Mali interpreted this as meaning that he was 'not in the same league' as the learned counsel.

'No, I knew Dali and we got on well,' says Gauntlett. 'The reason I was concerned about us as a team was the public perception: an all-male line-up in a rape case might not be good. On top of that Mpofu was based in Johannesburg and I was in Cape Town.'

Gauntlett acknowledged, however, that there were political imperatives from the community group for Mpofu's appointment.[3]

The meeting ended without agreement, and Clifford Green had to fly to Cape Town later, ironically on the express instructions of Mali, to persuade Gauntlett to take the case. Once this had been achieved, the senior

---

[3] Dali Mpofu was once romantically linked with Winnie Mandela when they worked together in the ANC's social welfare department. This relationship was cited in court papers when Nelson Mandela divorced his wife in 1996.

counsel assembled his team. 'I ended up having two juniors – the Cape advocate Nazreen Bawa, who had clerked to Justice Richard Goldstone at the Constitutional Court, and the community's choice of Dali Mpofu.'

What impressed Gauntlett about Bacher was that he was under huge pressure to distance himself from the case, but the loyalty he had for Ntini, who had always professed his innocence to him, prevented him from doing so. 'He wouldn't budge and I found it quite moving.'

Ali recalls: 'I was coming under intense pressure for continuing to back Makhaya, but I was determined to see justice done. I felt the original trial left too many unanswered questions, and I felt it imperative to go to a higher court.'

There was just one more question to answer: who was going to pay for what was clearly an expensive exercise? Bacher insisted it was not the UCB and, in time, the most he would reveal was that it was 'an overseas benefactor'.

IT COULD BE said that Michael Watt had led a full and interesting life. He was educated at New Zealand's poshest school, Christ's College, where he was expelled at the age of 15 for being 'absent out of uniform' to attend jazz concerts. He then became a nomad, bumming his way around the world and, while in the United States for fours years, becoming what he calls a 'jazz groupie' by way of following the big name musicians and band leaders in and out of clubs around the country; working illegally as a bellhop in Las Vegas, a dishwasher in New Orleans; living with black folk in New York's Harlem district, and then moving on to Canada. 'I guess you could have called me white trash', he says; although 'street smart' would probably be a more apt description.

Until the age of 30 he was a blue-collar worker, a labourer in the docklands, a lorry driver, a young man living a life of spending and running with a fine disregard for money and possessions. Later he took on greater responsibility and started an oil-drilling business in Spain where he began making what he considered a fortune of money, enough in fact to go into partnership with a company that was looking to do some marketing around the Winter Olympics in the mid-seventies. When the marketing company could not honour its debts to him, he took it over and, now into his thirties, he became a white-collar worker for the first time in his life. 'I guess I was just sick and tired of rednecks.'

We know, of course, that he became the founder-chairman of the global sports marketing and television rights company, CSI, and how he met Ali

337

Bacher in the early nineties and signed the television rights contract with the UCB. Since then he had sold CSI to Octagon; and Octagon-CSI became the sports marketing company for the cricket boards of Australia, England, South Africa, Zimbabwe and New Zealand. In 2003 it would be appointed as the broadcasting production company that was responsible for the worldwide television coverage of the 2003 Cricket World Cup.

Approaching retirement, Watt spent his time producing musicals on Broadway and the West End . . . and, with as much anonymity as he could muster, giving away money to deserving causes. He financed the cricket academy in New Zealand and when they wanted to name the ground in his honour, he threatened to drop the project. It is called the Bert Sutcliffe Oval after one of that country's most famous players.

He also showed a great interest in South Africa where, with his usual anonymity, he sponsored a music school in the black township of Daveyton and got involved with what he calls 'another operation' in Soweto. He has spread his wealth so generously into disadvantaged areas that he says that he does not always remember the exact identity of the projects and has empathy with black and white alike.

'He once told me,' says Ali, 'that he came from nowhere, he had made a lot of money and he didn't want to die knowing that he had not helped people in need. Now all he wanted to know was whether I was convinced that Makhaya was telling the truth and, having established that, he contributed the 12 000 pounds that covered the major costs of the case.'

Ntini himself chipped in all the money he could, but even he was not aware who the chief benefactor was. 'I wanted to be anonymous,' says Watt, 'because grandstanding the fact at the time would have been crass. I suppose now, with the passage of time and for the historic record, it's all right to tell the story.'[4]

JEREMY GAUNTLETT AND his team flew to East London the day before the High Court appeal before a Full Bench of two judges in Grahamstown to inspect the site of the alleged rape. It was during this inspection of the scene by the legal team that he could see for himself the conflicts in the statements of the complainant after she herself had been taken to the scene. For example, in her original statement she claimed that Ntini had locked the toilet door before raping her. On inspection it was found that there was no

---

[4] Michael Watt interview, November 2003.

338

lock inside the door, but a padlock on the outside. Also, the toilet was not in the main pavilion as she had claimed but in another area about five to seven metres from a security guard. The rape, she said, had taken place standing up against a wall; and Gauntlett concluded that for two people of the same height to indulge in non-consensual sex in the manner described, five metres from a security guard would have been tricky at best. In the magistrate's court trial, the female prosecutor had called as an expert witness a district surgeon, a 23-year-old houseman named Dr Green, to say that this was possible. The defence counsel on that occasion asked him how he knew this and he replied 'from personal experience'; whereupon Gauntlett took great delight in referring to him during the appeal as the 'appropriately named Dr Green'.

The appeal took place in an old colonial style courtroom, hot and stuffy, packed with people. What Gauntlett performed was a demolition job on the unsatisfactory nature of the woman's evidence in the trial record. Robbie Muzzell watched Gauntlett's performance from the public gallery. It was, he said, like a surgeon slicing through the evidence, dissecting and destroying it point by point. The crux of Gauntlett's argument was whether she, as a single witness, uncorroborated, with several contradictory statements, could be believed in every respect.

The presiding judges, Justices Joss Jones and Chris Jansen, concluded she could not and upheld the appeal.

THREE MEN, THEN, made it possible for Makhaya Ntini to spend the next six years on the cricket field instead of inside a jail.[5] Ali Bacher batted for his life, Michael Watt[6] generously provided the much-needed wherewithal, and Jeremy Gauntlett SC set the record straight.

'I backed Makhaya,' says Ali, 'because he told me the truth from day one. You cannot walk away from someone whose life is on the line. How could I accept his conviction when I knew he was innocent – and when the lack of critical evidence ultimately proved that to be true?'

---

[5] On 8 August 2003, Makhaya Ntini telephoned Ali from the UK to thank him for everything he had done for him. This followed his remarkable ten-wicket haul in South Africa's victory at Lord's earlier in the week. He ended 2003 with 59 Test wickets, placing him No 1 among the world's Test wicket-takers in the calendar year.

[6] On South Africa's 2003 tour of England, Michael Watt was introduced to Makhaya Ntini for the first time at Arundel in an emotional meeting. Upon learning the identity of his benefactor, Ntini was so grateful that he broke down and cried.

Chapter 29

Fallout in the UCB

SOUTH AFRICAN CRICKET approached the twenty-first century like a tail-end batsman facing the new ball. Relationships in general remained strained and there was a feeling among some players that Ali Bacher was restricting their individuality and rights of choice. During the Second Unity process, he had refused Phillip Glaser permission to engage in one-on-one interviews with the players – designed as highly confidential opportunities for them to confess their fears and insecurities – that were seen as a key requirement in transformation. Bacher's view was that the players carried enough responsibility without having to engage in what he perceived as mind games. He himself declined to undergo one of these interviews.

Also, at UCB headquarters some black members of staff began tugging at his apron strings. They acknowledged that he had empowered them, but they wanted more independence; and it was as if, as with his players, he found it difficult letting go. It is worth recalling here what Bruce Francis said of him: 'I have not known anywhere in the world another cricket official so genuinely concerned for the players in his care' . . . and this could well be extended to 'everyone in his care'.

Relations were also becoming strained between him and senior white officials on the UCB, which was something that Ray McCauley did not find one bit surprising. Like Bacher, he too was walking the tightrope between the right and left wings of his constituency. It was McCauley, after all, who had stood up at the Truth and Reconciliation Commission on behalf of the Evangelical Pentecostal Charismatic Churches and 'confessed the sin of apartheid and silence'.

He explained: 'We (the whites) had to take on the corporate sin of apartheid. A minority of whites had undergone a Damascus Experience – and Ali Bacher was one of them. It was as if the scales dropped off your eyes and you could suddenly see what a terrible system it was. For cricket to survive, it had to have someone with tremendous commitment, insight and drive – and he was the man.'

It was a particularly difficult time for Ali. He was performing a balancing act between his own 'left and right wings'; and it was perhaps significant that in a confidential scientific Personal Profile Analysis conducted on UCB staff at the time, the assessment found that 'he may be reporting to more than one superior, possibly resulting in conflicting loyalties; and he may have a personality clash with his superiors resulting in a strained relationship'.

Even though he was in faraway Perth, Don Mackay-Coghill was keeping close tabs on the transformation challenges facing South African cricket. 'Ali was more sensitive than most to the needs. He was living the situation morning, noon and night, but there were troublemakers behind the scenes for sure. The stakes were so high and no one could come out of it unscathed. I can only imagine how difficult it must have been; I mean, this was not just cricket, this was the dynamics of an entire society.'

These were difficult times; and it was sad that relationships were souring between men who had walked a long road in cricket, from their carefree playing days into the hornet's nest of sports administration in South Africa. Bacher's relationship with Raymond White was just one them. 'Ali was not the easiest of people to deal with,' says White. 'He didn't seem to have a philosophical or political compass to guide his decision-making. It was hard to know where he was coming from. I was president of the UCB but no one bothered to inform me that the captain had walked out on the team. I sat with Ali during the first one-day match (against the West Indies), and he never said a word about it. When he asked me to intervene to get Makhaya Ntini picked for the first Test, I refused because I could not interfere with the selectors. I was told that Ntini was having psychological problems and that he was nowhere near his best. To simply put him in the team would have been no good for him and it would have sent a bad message to the other players. It was interesting to me that the outcry over that all-white team only emerged four days later. I believe it was orchestrated by various men within the UCB; and then all hell broke loose once they had informed the NSC.'

In White's view, the UCB had itself to blame for succumbing to what he believed was political pressure; and it seems he did not much care for the moral issue that was clearly foremost in Bacher's mind. White's regret was that the UCB did not 'draw a line in the sand' against the politicians. 'If I had been able to, I suspect things might have taken a different path. Steve Tshwete and Ngconde Balfour (Tshwete's successor from June 1999) were always threatening legislation. How could they have done it? It would have taken South Africa back to race qualification. No, there was a lot of bluster that South African cricket should have resisted for the good of the game.'[1]

The Cambridge-educated White said he had always been guided by 'classic liberal principles'. Mackay-Coghill said he had attended White's wedding during the apartheid era and that the groom used the opportunity to make a political speech condemning the system. Ali says of him, 'Raymond had the best cricketing brain on the board in the nineties. He was a cricket man, strong on traditions and values and culture, the ethos of the game. He was a highly intelligent person but he spoke down to people which cost him a lot of support and unfortunately in my opinion he lacked leadership qualities. We had many run-ins – particularly on the pace of transformation – but deep down I believe there was an underlying mutual respect.'

White was unyielding in his perceptions of political interference in cricket, and by mid-1999 even his erstwhile allies on the board were privately giving notice that they could no longer support him.

THE SITUATION GREW worse. When Hansie Cronje's team travelled to New Zealand in February 1999, they lost the first one-day international; and immediately dropped Gibbs to revert to an all-white team for the next game. On tour, it should be remembered, the selection panel usually consists of the captain, the coach and the vice-captain.

'I phoned Peter Pollock,' recalls White, 'and suggested this was not a clever move by Hansie Cronje and that he should have a word with him. After all, we had agreed at the last board meeting that there should be at least one player of colour in the side. Peter told me that if I felt that strongly about it, I should speak to him.'

Because of the time difference with New Zealand, the UCB president could not contact the captain before the team had started their third game

---

[1] Raymond White interview, November 2003.

– again with an all-white team.

'When I eventually got through to him at 7 am, he was still fast asleep. I tried to explain very gently the selection policy because I was aware how volatile he could be. He just went off pop.'

Cronje was angry on two counts: (a) that no one had bothered to give the team a copy of the new selection policy after the 5 December board meeting; and (b) that the team selections reflected the experimentation that was under way to find the best combinations for the World Cup in England in three months' time.

White recalls 'a ghastly board meeting' at the time. 'The mob were baying for blood – Pollock's, Cronje's and mine. John Blair made the nonsensical suggestion that we should bring Cronje home. All sense had gone out of the window.'

THE BACHER-WHITE relationship now entered a paradoxical phase in which the UCB president went in to bat for his old captain. He did so ostensibly to protect cricket's future, but also because he got wind of a plot that reminded him of the fate that befell Julius Caesar in the Senate chamber on the Ides of March in 44 BC.

In mid-1999 White came to the conclusion that events round the West Indies tour had taken a terrible toll on Bacher. The 2003 World Cup in South Africa was looming and White felt that the time was right for his managing director to ease out of his position to concentrate on organising that important tournament. He went to see him. 'I told him that the time would come when he could not do both jobs and that in the interests of his health we should develop a medium-term plan in which he would relinquish the MD's responsibilities. I sensed he was relieved by my proposal. I then started contacting board members to suggest that he was the right man to run the World Cup. The board agreed, although there was no time frame set on the changeover. Ali and I spoke about who should take over as MD and we both agreed it had to be the best man for the job. One man who was definitely mentioned was (Western Province CEO) Arthur Turner.'

Later, at the UCB's annual meeting Percy Sonn stood against White for the presidency and was defeated. 'After that meeting,' says White, 'four board members got hold of me and asked if I was aware that there was a plot by a black clique in cricket to get rid of Ali. I was absolutely horrified and I realised it was very important now to clearly determine his future.'

He again went to see him. 'He was looking much better, more relaxed and under far less pressure. I suggested that he should stay on as MD until at least the middle of 2001, that we should set a clear date and get a contract drawn up immediately. I didn't think the board would have any difficulty in agreeing. Every board member I phoned agreed. The only one I could not contact was Gerald Majola. I left a message and he got back to me. He was vehemently opposed to Ali.

'Within an hour of that call,' says White, 'I received phone calls from three board members who said they wanted to reconsider their decision. The telephone line was now buzzing from board members who were dependent on the ANC. They were all changing their tune.'

It was not so much that they were opposed to Bacher running the World Cup, but they did not want him to play a dual role as MD of the UCB for any longer than was necessary. He later told the board at his own initiative that he had set a date of 1 January 2001 to move across full-time to the World Cup.

In November 1999, the England team, now touring South Africa, played a match at Supersport Park against a combined Gauteng-Northerns XI. The day before the combined team was due to be announced, White was sitting with Gerald Ritchie, the Gauteng Cricket Board chairman, watching cricket at the Wanderers. Ritchie told him that Geoffrey Toyana, a black batsman, had been selected ahead of two white players, Andrew Hall and Sven Koenig, who were considered better prospects. When White asked him why, Ritchie replied, 'The UCB said so.'

White reminded him that he was president of the UCB and that, to the best of his knowledge, the national body did not have a selection policy for combined provincial teams. 'Gerald then implied that Ali had said so.'

White phoned Bacher. 'He conceded that there wasn't a policy but that things were going so well that we should just leave it.'

I replied: 'No soft decisions, Ali.'

Bacher says he told White that he would phone Sonn and Blair to sound them out. 'They said they didn't have a problem (with an all-white combined team) based on the information that I gave them, and when I told Percy that the press would murder us, he said, "Refer the media to me." I then phoned Raymond and Gerald to tell them.'

To this day, Ali cannot figure out why he did not take a stand. 'I just knew it was wrong and that we were heading for another showdown. People know that I don't yield when I feel strongly about something, so why I didn't assert myself, I just don't know. It was one of my worst administrative decisions.'

The newspaper reporters had a field day in highlighting the selection of the all-white team, with White and Bacher taking the flak. 'Percy Sonn and John Blair ran a mile,' is the way White describes it.

In the row that followed, there was more confusion. When one of the fast bowlers, David Townsend, withdrew from the team, his replacement was named as another white player, Rudi Bryson. The UCB insisted that a black player should get preference because Bryson was not in the running for national honours. So Bryson was dropped, and Walter Masemola brought in. 'I later phoned Rudi Bryson and apologised to him,' says Ali.

Toyana never did get a game, but Koenig did, and he failed in both innings.

Early the next week, in an interview with the *Cape Times*, Sonn attacked Bacher for interfering in selection affairs.

WHITE'S TENURE AT the helm of South African cricket was growing more and more tenuous. During the New Year's weekend in January 2000, while South Africa was playing England in a Test at Newlands, the UCB board convened what he described as 'an awful meeting'.

'I got blamed for my role in the combined provincial team selection, Percy Sonn denied any involvement and Ali was also blamed. One of the ring leaders was Gerald Majola who before the meeting handed me a letter which I stuck in my blazer pocket.'

Bacher did not attend the meeting because it was called ostensibly to discuss his future, but White says it broke up without any resolution on this issue. It was only later that the UCB president opened Majola's letter. It called for his resignation.

'At first I chose to ignore it, but then changed my mind. There was another board meeting in Johannesburg in January and it was there that I told them of the letter, suggested that they might like to discuss it, and recused myself.'

White went home, leaving Sonn in the chair, and waited for a phone call. It came more than three hours later from Ali. 'Things haven't gone well,' he told the president. 'I need to see you, Raymond.'

The board had decided that he should vacate the presidency with immediate effect, and that he should be given the opportunity to resign. Ali volunteered to break the news to him, but White sensed what was afoot. By the time Bacher arrived at his house he had decided to quit. 'I had nothing more to contribute because I was being frustrated at every turn. It would be better for cricket and for me if I left.'

He resigned the next month, but not before he had accompanied Bacher

345

to Singapore for an important ICC meeting on marketing for the 2003 World Cup.

After he had resigned, and in a telling aside, White says he received information 'that during the Test match against England at Centurion, Hansie Cronje had been involved in some sort of corruption and that this might not have been the first such occurrence'.

Did he pass on the information to anyone in authority?

'No. I was now out of cricket and I just didn't want to get involved.'

IT WAS NOT only the challenges of transformation and politics that beset Bacher. There were also personal crises and tragedy. In the first of these, he came within a whisker of losing his life.

In September 1999, on the eve of travelling to Nairobi for a four-nations tournament, he had dinner with family and friends at a restaurant in Sandton. As usual, he ordered chicken. Halfway through the meal he began feeling discomfort in his throat and, when it got worse, he came to the conclusion that he had swallowed a chicken bone. He went to the Sandton Clinic for X-rays but they showed up negative.

In Nairobi, he was due to make a speech at the welcome function for the four teams, but by the time he got there he began feeling acute pain in his throat, and his neck became locked at an angle. In spite of this, he made his speech and members of his audience remarked how odd he appeared because not once did he look straight at them or move his head.

'By this stage, I was unable to swallow and couldn't bear the pain any more. I went to Nairobi Hospital where I had further X-rays and the radiologist, a Dr Malik, again told me they were all clear.'

Ali and Shira were now due to go on safari and stay overnight at a famous game lodge. 'We drove there and it felt like there was a knife through my throat. It was becoming so bad that by now I couldn't even swallow liquids.'

After living for three days with his problem, Ali knew he had to return to Johannesburg as a matter of great urgency. He telephoned his friend Dr Harry Phillips, and arrangements were made to see a gastroenterologist at the Morningside Clinic. Dr John Jamieson, an oesophageal surgeon, was also called in and saw him at 8 pm. After a barium swallow, Jamieson diagnosed that a foreign body (an impacted chicken bone) was lying embedded obliquely across the oesophagus. In the operating theatre, Bacher was given a general anaesthetic; and Jamieson removed the wide flat bone that had lodged in the walls of the oesophagus, causing a total blockage in the throat and on top of which had dammed up anything that Ali had swallowed. 'You're lucky to be alive,' Dr Jamieson told him, and later explained: 'It should have been pretty standard procedure to detect the bone at the outset. To have missed it had placed his life in jeopardy. Had it perforated the walls of the oesophagus, all the food and liquids would have seeped into his chest cavity and the bacteria would immediately have caused an abscess and the potential for a very nasty outcome.'

Jamieson said it was extraordinary that Ali had endured the pain for so long. 'This was extremely rare because normally within 24 hours of this sort of blockage occurring the patient simply cannot endure the pain any longer. He had a very, very close shave.'[2]

Bacher would be eternally grateful to Dr Jamieson for saving his life. 'If he hadn't taken that bone out, and it had perforated the walls of the oesophagus, there's no question – I would have died.'

Having fortunately averted that tragedy, Ali was faced with two others. Khaya Majola had been diagnosed with cancer of the colon, and Conrad Hunte, his old friend and ally from the West Indies, died suddenly from a massive heart attack while playing tennis with friends in Sydney.

Hunte was an extraordinary man. He was regarded as one of the great opening batsmen of West Indies cricket, vice-captain to Garry Sobers, and after his retirement from the game in the sixties, he dedicated his life to helping others. Becoming a member of the worldwide Moral Rearmament Movement, he visited South Africa in the 1970s and first met Ali Bacher when they opened the batting together for a social team that visited South West Africa (now Namibia) in 1977. A cheerful man with great passion for his calling, he later offered his services to Ali in the development programme and after a time settled in South Africa with his family. His development work took him deep into Africa, and he became the 'father' of women's cricket in South Africa.

He eventually resettled in Barbados in 1998 and was knighted by his country two months before his death at the age of 67. Ali travelled to Barbados to speak at his funeral and it was there that he referred to him as 'the Nelson Mandela of cricket'.

He added, 'Sir Conrad's contribution to the transformation of South African cricket and its consequent ripple effect into our society as a whole is inestimable. He inspired thousands of young people, boys and girls from

---

[2] Dr John Jamieson interview, October 2003.

the black townships, to throw off the shackles of the apartheid past and to go forward, through cricket, to a brighter and happier future. He preached reconciliation and unity ... and became one of South Africa's greatest adopted sons. He has shown us the way, and we will not waver.'

KHAYA MAJOLA NEVER wavered. 'I have never seen anyone,' says Ali, 'handle a terminal illness with so much courage and character. He never stopped working and he never complained. I would sometimes take him to the clinic for chemotherapy and during one of these visits the oncologist told him that the cancer had spread to his lungs and liver. He then told him straight that he was at death's door. In the car afterwards, he broke down for the first, and last, time and cried. This lasted less than a minute, he pulled himself together and went back to work again. He knew he was dying, but he simply carried on.'

His father, Eric Majola, was a famous rugby player who starred in black teams in segregated sport, and died in a car accident while still in his thirties. Steve Tshwete told Ali that Eric was as good, if not better, than the Springbok flyhalf of those times, Keith Oxlee. It was because he had no father that Khaya adopted Ali as 'my father', although this sentiment was not shared by his brother Gerald.

At a major dinner to launch the Transformation Charter in 1998, the once bitter Khaya Majola who had threatened to kill Bacher over the Gatting tour walked across the room and put his arms around Ali. 'He apologised to me for that threat and asked my forgiveness.'

Khaya died at the age of 47. His team of development coaches would remember his words: 'If it's not in your heart, don't even try.'

Another of Ali's colleagues who demonstrated such qualities of bravery and dedication in the face of terrible adversity was June Gleason, the Rennies in-house travel consultant at UCB headquarters who had been a faithful ally since the rebel tour days. She too contracted cancer and, like Khaya Majola, she lived with it uncomplainingly for almost seven years, reporting for work on the day before she died in mid-2001.

THE DAY AFTER he came out of hospital minus the chicken bone, Bacher received another shock. Imtiaz Patel, his national director of professional cricket, came to tell him he was leaving the UCB. 'I couldn't believe it,' says Ali. 'He was good, I had groomed him, he was blossoming ... and now he was going.'

Bacher saw a bright future for Patel in cricket and it was as if all the hard work he had put into their relationship had been undone. Patel had great respect for him. He regarded him as 'a man ahead of his time', and called him 'a child of the universe'; but he had received an offer of an executive position at the Supersport TV channel and, after a lot of soul searching, he reckoned it was time to move on. He found it difficult breaking the news to Bacher, and concedes that, with him still convalescing from a life-threatening experience, it was probably not the right time.

'I was shocked and very cross,' recalls Ali. 'Firstly, I was in bed convalescing and Imtiaz presented me with this fait accompli. It was the first I had heard of it. Secondly, I had an excellent relationship with Russell MacMillan (MD at Supersport) and I thought he could have picked up the phone to put me in the picture. But neither he nor Imtiaz had any prior discussion with me. Russell later contacted me and I bluntly told him how I felt.'

Supersport was one of South African cricket's major sponsors and Bacher had high regard for both the company and MacMillan. 'In the South African television sports industry, he was in a league of his own; and based on where I had travelled in the world, Supersport was the best sports network I'd seen, and Russell was responsible for it.'

He and MacMillan had once done a R59 million deal in Ali's office in a meeting lasting – and Bacher timed it – seven minutes. 'I sent out a memo to my executive committee to inform them of the deal, and both Raymond White and Krish Mackerdhuj phoned me immediately to point out that I had mistakenly added an extra nought to the figure. They thought it was 5.9 million but I said no, 59 million is right.'

It was against this background that Ali thought he deserved better by way of some prior knowledge of Patel's planned move. He did not speak to his departing director for the next couple of weeks; later, when he attended a sponsorship meeting at Supersport, he objected to Patel being part of it. MacMillan was furious. He wrote to Bacher: 'You have no right to decide who represents Supersport at meetings or events of which we are the sponsors. We will decide for ourselves who represents us, and if this not to your liking, then I suggest we cancel our involvement in the Supersport Series[3] with immediate effect.'

MacMillan also contacted White to make his feelings known, but the

---

[3] South Africa's premier first-class competition that replaced the Currie Cup (later Castle Cup) in 1996.

UCB president calmed him down and the relationship was patched up.

There were other harrowing moments during the nineties, but Ali would look back on two of these with great mirth. The first was in 1994 when he was held at gunpoint by police at Gatwick airport: wearing a nut-brown tan, a big panama hat, and a colourful floral patterned shirt after a few days' break in Portugal, he was mistaken for an Arab terrorist. Earlier that day, a bomb had gone off in a Jewish area in London and extra security had been mounted at Gatwick because of a large contingent of religious Jews who were using the airport to connect to Leeds. Ali was also on his way to Leeds for the second Test match, but was clearly identified as a suspicious character. Police, pointing automatic rifles, swooped on him when he took out his cellphone to switch it on. 'I think they thought it was a remote device,' says Shira who admits that she told her husband he looked like 'a member of the Mafia'.

'I started joking with them,' recalls Ali, 'but I realised they were serious when one of them stuck a gun in my face. They asked me my name and I said "Ali" but they looked in my passport and it said "Aron".'

Shira says the police were eventually placated when other passengers identified Ali. 'It was quite funny really. Only two weeks earlier, we'd had lunch with John Major during the Lord's Test.'

In the second harrowing, yet hilarious, incident, Ali walked into the ladies room adjacent to the MCC President's Box at Lord's at lunchtime during the 1998 Test match. He went into one of the cubicles, closed the door and was taken aback when he heard women's voices. 'Just when I wanted to escape, more women came in, chatting away. I was opening and closing that cubicle door like crazy for about half an hour, growing more and more anxious.'

And all the time his luncheon host, the MCC president Colin Ingleby-Mackenzie, was growing more and more puzzled by his absence. 'I was petrified that the women would see my shoes through the gap at the bottom of the cubicle door and at one point I even imagined the headline in the British tabloids:

Bacher arrested in ladies loo at Lord's!

'Eventually, the ladies room went silent, and I made a dash for it. I was proud of those women. They were all wives or partners of cricket officials from the adjacent England Cricket Board suite or the President's Box and at no stage did they engage in any malicious gossip!'

IN THE WAKE of the political and transformation upheaval since 1998, Bacher began seeing a change in Hansie Cronje; and he was not alone. A sports writer interviewed him over a cup of coffee shortly before he took the team to India in February 2000 on the last tour he would ever make. When the reporter pulled out his notebook, Cronje said, 'I trust what you write. You needn't take notes.' It was a strange thing to say and the reporter wrote a perspective in which he suggested that Cronje seemed ambivalent about his future in cricket. A long hard tour was about to start, but the captain seemed distant and preoccupied. One of his great characteristics, an intense focus on the job at hand, was missing. The reporter's conclusion was that the South African captain had become disenchanted by the politics and also seemed in doubt of his own form and ability to retain his place in the team. He seemed ill at ease, even a little depressed; he spoke of studying for a new business degree.[4]

Bacher's view was not dissimilar to the reporter's. It was his contention that the transformation priorities in the South African team had got to the captain. Cronje's teammates also saw it that way. They knew how proud he was to have 'earned' his South African cap the hard way and how he saw it as a privilege for any player to represent his country. In his mind, the danger now existed of South Africans caps being 'handed out wholesale'.

A very strange thing happened several weeks later. During the course of the India tour, the UCB managing director received from his counterpart on the Sri Lanka Cricket Board of Control a draft itinerary for the forthcoming South African tour of Sri Lanka. This was standard practice and Ali's next move was to ask the South African captain for his comments before, by mutual consent between the competing nations, the itinerary would be finalised. He faxed the draft to team manager Goolam Rajah in India, requesting that he show it to the captain and then revert to him. Rajah phoned back to say that Cronje had told him: 'Give it to Shaun Pollock, he'll be captaining the team to Sri Lanka.'

---

[4] Hansie Cronje interview with the author for the *Sunday Times* of 13 February 2000.

Ali Bacher introduces Sir Garfield Sobers to Walter Masemola, right, the fast bowling gem of the development programme who would die prematurely in England in 2002 at the age of 26
Touchline Photo/Getty Images

The exuberant Archbishop Desmond Tutu takes part in the 'Mexican Wave' during an international match against England at Newlands, much to the amusement of Ali Bacher and Test and County Cricket Board chairman Dennis Silk, right

Photo: *Bacher private collection*

President F W de Klerk, centre, is introduced to the first Indian team to tour South Africa in 1992-93. To his right is the Indian manager Amrit Mathur and behind him, centre, is the captain Mohammad Azharuddin   **Photo:** Bacher private collection

Watching cricket at the Wanderers in 1993, ANC leader Nelson Mandela is seated between Ali Bacher and the ICC President Sir Clyde Walcott. On the far right is ANC stalwart Walter Sisulu   **Photo:** Bacher private collection

The greatest legacy that Ali Bacher left to South African cricket was its development programme. Here young stars in the making surround him during a Bakers mini-cricket festival **Photo:** Bacher private collection

Nelson Mandela waves to the Wanderers crowd as he and Ali Bacher walk around the perimeter of the field during the lunch interval of the 1993 triangular one-day final between West Indies and Pakistan. It was during this walk that a spectator hurled an orange at Mandela which narrowly missed him, and which Bacher caught
Photo: Paul Velasco

Since 1981, the famous 'Ali Shuffle' became part of his daily routine

During his playing days, Ali Bacher meets Rhodesian prime minister Ian Smith in Salisbury (now Harare)   **Photo:** *Bacher private collection*

On the occasion of the inaugural Test between Zimbabwe and South Africa in Harare in October 1995, Ali Bacher is pictured with SA captain Hansie Cronje, Zimbabwe president and patron of the Zimbabwe Cricket Union (ZCU) Robert Mugabe, the host captain Andy Flower and ZCU president Peter Chingoka

Ali Bacher keeps step with Queen Elizabeth II of Great Britain while South Africa's minister of sport Ngconde Balfour gives directions during a visit to the Alex Cricket Oval
Photo: Bacher private collection

In London in 1994, Ali Bacher meets Prince Edward, son of Queen Elizabeth II, after addressing the Lord's Taverners banquet. Centre is Thabo Mbeki
Photo: Bacher private collection

Ali Bacher and British prime minister John Major enjoy the cricket from the balcony at Lord's in 1994
Photo: Bacher private collection

Ali Bacher, right, testifies at the King Commission of Inquiry into match fixing in Cape Town in June 2000. Judge Edwin King is in the foreground   *Photo: Mujahiel Safodien/Trace Images*

Dear Ali,

Congratulations & best wishes on your 60th Birthday. You have been a real inspiration to various sections of the sport fraternity.

Madiba

May 2002

Ali Bacher, his family and domestic staff visit President Mandela at his home when Ali delivered a R1 million donation from the United Cricket Board for one of Nelson Mandela's community projects; right, a note from Mandela on the occasion of Ali's 60th birthday

President Thabo Mbeki delivers his address at the opening ceremony of the 2003 ICC Cricket World Cup at Newlands in Cape Town. With him on the podium from left are compère Tumi Makgabo, ICC CEO Malcolm Speed, ICC President Malcolm Gray, UCB President Percy Sonn, UCB CEO Gerald Majola, Sports Minister Ngconde Balfour, the CWC 2003 Board chairman Prof Jakes Gerwel and CWC 2003 Executive Director Ali Bacher

Touchline Photo/Cotty Images

Ali Bacher is pictured with three legendary cricketers, from left, the West Indians Sir Everton Weekes and Sir Garfield Sobers and former India captain and record run-scorer Sunil Gavaskar. All three were International Ambassadors to the 2003 ICC Cricket World Cup in South Africa

Photo: Courtesy Tim Hutchinson

The proud grandfather with his fifth grandchild, Jarren, who was born to his son David and Cindy Bacher in November 2003

Ali Bacher and the author during a development clinic in Soweto, circa 1993

PART V

DE PROFUNDIS

Chapter 30

Into the Darkness

IT WAS SHORTLY after 11 o'clock on Friday, 7 April 2000, that Ali Bacher was told something that was beyond his comprehension: the United Cricket Board's communications manager Bronwyn Wilkinson had received a call from a journalist in England to inform her that the South African captain Hansie Cronje and three of his teammates were under investigation for match fixing on the recent tour of India. *Agence France-Presse*, the international news agency *AFP*, was running a story sourced to Delhi police.

Later reports indicated that K K Paul, Delhi's joint Commissioner of Police, had chaired a press conference in the Indian capital at which a transcript of alleged conversations between Cronje and a bookmaker, Sanjay Chawla, was revealed as the fuse that fired the bomb.

Bacher was angry that the Indian police had made public statements concerning South African cricketers without first notifying the UCB of its intentions. He told Wilkinson to phone the Delhi police department to find out what was going on. She recalls: 'Ali seemed to have absolutely no doubt in his mind that there was nothing in the allegations. He repeated the words "absolute rubbish" so many times that day – to colleagues, to the media and to Hansie himself. It was clear to me when I first took him the story that he didn't think there could be any truth in it, but he still called Hansie and asked him. Once he had spoken to the captain, and later the other players who had been named, he had absolute faith that he was being told the truth. Our strategy became one of trying to find out how the hell this had happened, and even to go on the attack against the Indian authorities for holding the press conference about our players

355

without informing us first. I tracked down K K Paul in Delhi and asked him how he could have had such an important press conference, with such massive implications, without first informing us or the South African authorities. He reply was a pretty curt: "Madam, and why on earth do I need to inform you of my criminal investigations?" '

The phones at the UCB offices were ringing off the hook amid the media frenzy. 'I never knew it was possible for two people to take as many calls as Ali and I did that day,' recalls Wilkinson, 'although we learned on the following Tuesday that it was possible to take even more.'

Bacher and Wilkinson met with the UCB's lawyer Clifford Green at his offices in the Sandton business district to discuss the way forward. Wilkinson was new at the UCB, having only recently joined Bacher's staff from the newspaper world. At heart, she was a reporter. 'Having come out of the media, I was very cautious about issuing blanket statements declaring anyone's innocence and I told Ali that in the meeting. I suggested to him that in order to be seen to be doing something it might be a good idea to have an investigation or inquiry. This could even be a good way for the players to clear their names. He exploded. "Bronwyn, you back your captain!" When I pursued the issues, he repeated over and over again, "You back your captain!"

'We spoke to Hansie several times that evening, and over the weekend, and Ali told him each time that we were all behind him and we would sort out the mess. Ali really believed in him and was absolutely certain he was telling the truth. I don't think it occurred to him at all to doubt that.'

Green recalls that Bacher was 'absolutely livid that someone had dared threaten his captain'.

Two MONTHS AND five days later in Cape Town, Bacher took the oath upon entering the witness stand in a judicial commission of inquiry into 'cricket match fixing and related matters'. Before the commission was Hansie Cronje following his initial denial and subsequent confession. The Commissioner was a retired judge named Edwin King, a former Judge President of the Cape of Good Hope Provincial Division of the High Court, and the so-called King Commission was in session in the large reading room of a reference library called The Centre of the Book. This was the culmination of the shocking events that had unfolded in rapid succession after the initial alarm bell was sounded on 7 April.

The eyes of the cricket world were fixed upon it; because it was the first time that anything like this was taking place. Judge King drew on a biblical reference when he advised Cronje that 'the truth shall set you free'. He did so to remind him that the National Director of Public Prosecutions, Bulelani Ngcuka, had offered Cronje full indemnity against prosecution if, in the opinion of the judge, he made full and frank disclosure to the commission.

Jeremy Gauntlett's success in freeing Ntini from his rape conviction eight months earlier made him an obvious choice to captain the UCB's legal team at the King Commission.

On the eve of his testimony on day four of the hearings, Bacher was battling to contain the raw emotion. Under scrutiny was a young man who for many years had been 'his boy', the object of his affection and trust and support; and in the public gallery sat the boy's disconsolate father, Ali's friend and former colleague, Ewie.

Here, the erudite Gauntlett offers a lyrical description: 'Each day throughout the hearings sat this tall, grey spectral figure, alone and silent, his head bowed; the King Commission was haunted by Ewie Cronje.'[1]

It was an incredibly difficult time for Bacher. The Cronjes were as close to him as any other family in cricket and, in a sense, he was now ranged against them in all their vulnerability. Early in his testimony on Monday 12 June, he was asked by Gauntlett to describe his relationship with the Cronjes. What follows hereafter in italics are excerpts of the commission's transcript, edited only in minor detail for the sake of grammatical clarity.

DR BACHER: I have known the Cronje family for decades. His father, Ewie, has done wonderful work for sport in the Free State. During the 1980s, it emerged very quickly that there were two rising stars in South African cricket, Hansie Cronje and Jonty Rhodes. In the South African Schools team, they were captain and vice-captain. My memories go back to 1987 when for the very first time we took cricket to the township of Rocklands in Bloemfontein. It was mid-winter, it was a very cold wintry day, I shall not forget that day. Ewie was there with Hansie . . . to start the process of taking cricket to the disadvantaged people. My immediate impression of Hansie Cronje was that here was a natural leader, a born leader who would ultimately captain South Africa. I don't think that you can, as it were, manufacture leaders. You are either born with that inherent motivation and leadership quality, and he always had it.

MR GAUNTLETT: Now could you describe for the Commissioner over the period of

[1] Jeremy Gauntlett SC interview, October 2003.

357

the 13 odd years, as I understand it, that you have known Mr (Hansie) Cronje, how would you summarise his qualities as South Africa's team captain?

DR BACHER: An extraordinary asset to South African cricket, committed to South African cricket, dedicated to South African cricket, a role model for the youth of this country, an extraordinary ambassador for the game of cricket internationally.

MR GAUNTLETT: You have obviously worked very closely with him over a long period of time. How did you come to know him as a person? How would you assess him as a person and would you describe to the Commissioner your own relationship with him?

DR BACHER: A very committed person, a deep person, a very serious person. He took his responsibilities as captain of South African cricket very, very seriously. In fact when he lost the odd game, and all international teams lose the odd match even if they are a very good international team, he would almost punish himself for a couple of days, reflecting on, as he said it, having let down his country.

MR GAUNTLETT: What was your experience of his personal integrity in your relationship?

DR BACHER: Never ever questioned his integrity, never ever.

On the evening of 10 June – two nights before Bacher entered the witness stand – he was taken out for supper by Gauntlett. The object of the exercise was to calm down a man who, in Gauntlett's words, was 'hugely stressed and distracted'; and deeply caught up in the emotions of the terrible circumstances in which cricket found itself. By his own admission, Gauntlett had no compelling interest in the game of cricket and the supper was arranged as an informal distraction in the company of Mrs Gauntlett, and his fellow senior counsel Michael Fitzgerald and his wife. Gauntlett described Bacher as a deeply conflicted man who spoke of Hansie Cronje with warmth and a deep sense of loss. Yet the astute advocate noticed that just as Ali had stood resolutely by Ntini to the very end, ignoring pleas to walk away from the rape case because he believed implicitly in the player's assurances to him, he now adopted a somewhat different position because of Cronje's betrayal of honour and for what Gauntlett called 'his captain's truth in instalments'. Above all, Gauntlett sensed that Bacher could not forgive Cronje for targeting 'development players' – and by these he meant the coloured players Herschelle Gibbs and Henry Williams, as his naïve and failed accomplices – while 'carefully avoiding his fellow fundamentalists' and other senior teammates.

Ali did not see the King Commission as a forum in which to exact revenge on Cronje; but nor was it the place to help find excuses for his captain's behaviour. As always, it was the future of cricket that he cared about, and it was a great sadness for him that someone so close to him would have to take the fall. 'The judicial commission of inquiry was set up by the government, and when that happened it was out of our (the UCB's) hands. We also had to abide by the rules and regulations of the ICC, so people were incorrect to think that this was the UCB's area of responsibility and that we were targeting Hansie.'

Ali would steadfastly refuse to acknowledge that he was betrayed by Cronje. 'I was let down, yes, but not just me; cricket was let down.'

The harshest thing he could ever bring himself to say about the disgraced captain was that 'he had erred grievously'.

At supper that Saturday night, Gauntlett did his best to steady Bacher's hand. On the morning of Monday 12 June, the elegant Senior Counsel, leading evidence, asked him what he told Wilkinson to do when she advised him of the *AFP* report on 7 April.

DR BACHER: *I asked her to get hold of Hansie which she did immediately and to convey to him the allegations that were now emanating from the police in Delhi.*

MR GAUNTLETT: *What was your own personal, immediate reaction when she communicated these reports to you, first of all?*

DR BACHER: *I just wouldn't believe it.*

MR GAUNTLETT: *What happened when you spoke to Mr Cronje then, for the first time?*

DR BACHER: *I said 'Hansie, you have been informed about these allegations, is there any substance to these allegations?' His response was immediate, decisive, 'rubbish, absolute rubbish'.*

MR GAUNTLETT: *And your reaction to that?*

DR BACHER: *I . . . as I have in the past . . . accepted his word immediately.*

MR GAUNTLETT: We have it that thereafter both you and Ms Wilkinson advised Mr Cronje to switch his phone off and that you would continue to contact him on his wife's mobile phone and that you told him that you would deal with the media and you would arrange for a brief statement to be sent to the media. Would you just read it out, the first press statement, April 7, 2000.

DR BACHER: '. . . The United Cricket Board of South Africa is certain that no South African cricket player has ever been involved in match fixing. Its managing director, Dr Ali Bacher, has spoken to South African captain, Hansie Cronje, who is adamant that the allegations contained in press reports in India are completely untrue. Cronje is known for his unquestionable integrity and honesty.'

When, at one point, Wilkinson had suggested to Bacher that perhaps he should hold an inquiry before issuing such statements, he replied, 'Let this be my worst mistake if I support him in his hour of need.'

MR GAUNTLETT: We have heard that later that same afternoon, that is Friday the 7th of April, you met with Mr (Clifford) Green, who is a legal adviser to the UCB, Ms Wilkinson and Mr Goolam Rajah, the team manager, and that was in Sandton, is that correct?

DR BACHER: Correct, Mr Gauntlett.

MR GAUNTLETT: You discussed the content of a statement which you had released and about asking Mr Cronje to come up (to Johannesburg for a press conference). You say here '. . . Mr Cronje was reluctant for the very understandable reason that it was their wedding anniversary' . . . is that correct?

DR BACHER: That is correct. He said to me the following day which was Saturday was their fifth wedding anniversary and to me it was a reasonable request not to come up to Johannesburg on that day for the press conference and to await his arrival in Durban on the Sunday.

The South African team were assembling in Durban that weekend for the start of the three-match limited overs series against Australia – the first time the two countries would meet since their heart-stopping tied semifinal of the 1999 World Cup which eliminated South Africa from the tournament and took Australia through to a triumphant final over Pakistan. On Sunday 9 April the South Africans were due to play a practice match at Kingsmead.

Bacher was also heading to Durban and then into northern KwaZulu-Natal where he and Percy Sonn would be entertaining their Australian counterparts – Denis Rogers, the ACB's chairman, and Malcolm Speed, the former barrister who was the ACB's chief executive officer – for a few days at the exclusive Phinda game reserve. 'We had a braai (barbecue) on the Monday night (10 April) and Malcolm said to me, "Ali, why do you think the Indian police have gone public if they don't have evidence?" I said I didn't know.'

AT THE KING Commission on 12 June, Gauntlett continued leading Bacher through his testimony of what transpired on 7 April.

MR GAUNTLETT: *The names of three other players allegedly involved had started to come out of the media reports . . . Nicky Bojé, Herschelle Gibbs and Pieter Strydom. What did you do when those reports started to break?*

DR BACHER: *It was Friday afternoon, April the 7th. I first phoned Herschelle Gibbs and the conversation went like this '. . . Herschelle, do you respect me? Yes, I do, Dr Bacher. Would you ever lie to me? No, Dr Bacher. Is there any substance to these allegations? He said, definitely not, Dr Bacher.' I then phoned Nicky Bojé and the same sequence evolved. I was unable to get hold of Pieter Strydom, his mobile phone was off, so I left a message and he duly phoned me at my home at approximately 6.30 that Friday night. I asked him very simply whether there was any substance to these allegations and he emphatically denied that there was any substance to them.*

MR GAUNTLETT: *Now, on Saturday, April the 8th, you spoke to the South African deputy foreign minister, Mr Aziz Pahad. Why were you speaking to the deputy foreign minister, could you explain?*

DR BACHER: *I was so confident and so certain that there had to be a mistake, that there could never be any substance in these allegations. I have known Mr Pahad for about 10 years, I took the liberty of phoning him as a friend and to convey to him that honestly there had to be a mistake here, there had to be an error and please could he use his Department to be in contact with his counterparts in India and try to get to the bottom of these allegations.*

MR GAUNTLETT: *Did you convey it to Mr Pahad as a deputy minister in the South African government the kind of assurance that you had had from Mr Cronje that this was all in his words 'absolute rubbish'?*

DR BACHER: Most definitely, Mr Gauntlett.

MR GAUNTLETT: Did Mr Pahad doubt that or engage with you on that topic, or did he accept that assurance?

DR BACHER: He accepted the assurance from me.

MR GAUNTLETT: Now later that Saturday morning, the 8th of April, you received a call from Cronje, would you tell the Commission in your own words what happened in that call?

DR BACHER: Yes, he phoned me and, you know, the allegations were coming fast and furious. I was being inundated with media (from) throughout the world of cricket and I felt strongly that more than ever this was the time to strongly convey to him my support for him in his hour of need, on the basis that, as I have said previously, I couldn't believe that there could be any substance to these allegations.

MR GAUNTLETT: Did you convey to him that you had, specifically, spoken to senior government officials to try to clear his name?

DR BACHER: Yes, I did and I also conveyed to him my strong support for him as our national captain (as) he had had a very tough season. I think he was very disappointed that, after the success against the West Indies in the 1998-1999 season and getting through to the semifinal of the 1999 World Cup in England, he was only made captain for the first two Test matches (against England in South Africa in 1999-2000). I just felt more than ever that this was a time to express from a personal point of view my support for him as captain. I said to him very clearly on that phone, 'Hansie, you are our captain, we are going to back you and you are going to lead us to success in the 2003 World Cup (in South Africa).'

MR GAUNTLETT: Then Sunday, 9 April 2000 came, the South African team played a practice at Kingsmead and a press conference was scheduled for 7pm during the dinner break. What did you do immediately prior to the press conference?

DR BACHER: We arranged to meet with Hansie at 6.30, I asked Clifford Green to be there, Goolam Rajah, Bronwyn Wilkinson, Nicky Bojé and Herschelle Gibbs. In essence three issues emerged from Hansie. He said that firstly he had never been involved in a match where he had thrown a match, secondly that his banking accounts were open and available for anybody to scrutinise and thirdly that he had never, ever approached any of the players.

MR GAUNTLETT: Gibbs and Bojé, what did they convey to you?

DR BACHER: They confirmed to me that there had been no approach by Hansie Cronje to them.

MR GAUNTLETT: Dr Bacher, in that press conference, do you recall a particular question being raised by Mr Colin Bryden of the Sunday Times?

DR BACHER: Yes, I can recall . . . that in the Sunday Times in the morning there was detailed exposure to the transcripts (issued by the Indian police) and Mr Bryden, who is the cricket correspondent for the Sunday Times, asked Hansie his response or his reaction to those transcripts and Hansie said that he hadn't seen them.

MR GAUNTLETT: What occurred to you at the time, did something occur to you?

DR BACHER: It is difficult to assess now, there is no question on that Sunday night that Hansie was very, very tense. I thought at the time (it was) understandable as it had become a major international cricketing issue.

MR GAUNTLETT: Now, you went on to the Phinda Game Park with the Australians that you were hosting, the senior officials of the Australian Cricket Board. Then on Tuesday, the 11th of April, 2000, you received a telephone call at three o'clock in the morning from the team manager, Mr Rajah, would you tell the Commissioner about that?

DR BACHER: Yes, Mr Gauntlett, it was three o'clock in the morning, the phone rang, the call woke me up. In trying to get the receiver, I knocked over the phone, it fell to the floor, I picked up the phone and it was Goolam Rajah who said the following to me: 'Doc, the captain wants to speak to you'. Hansie came to the phone and he said to me: 'Doc, I haven't been honest with you'. I said immediately, Hansie, have you taken money from a bookmaker, and he said yes. I said to him, what is the amount, and he said between $10 000 and $15 000. The second point that emerged in that telephone call is that he said to me very firmly that none of the other players were involved.

Ali will never forget that moment. 'I felt like I had just experienced a terrible nightmare. I immediately phoned Percy Sonn at his bungalow (in the Phinda camp).'

The UCB president, who had also been contacted by Rajah, told Bacher he would join him immediately, which would involve walking some distance in the dead of night. Even with his mind in turmoil, Ali was not beyond thinking of Sonn's welfare.

'I remembered that a few months earlier a guest at the camp had been mauled by a lion while she was walking to a bungalow late at night, so I insisted that Percy stay indoors and we talk a bit later on the phone. I lay down again on my bed, and my mind was racing. I forced myself to think clearly and logically and then, having devised a plan, I picked up the phone again at 3.30 am and called Percy. We agreed on a three-pronged course of action: (a) to remove Cronje from the team to play Australia (b) request the government to institute a judicial commission of inquiry (c) apologise to the public and the Indian police for the UCB's defence of Cronje.'

MR GAUNTLETT: I wonder if you could just explain what your thinking was as to why the United Cricket Board should offer a public apology in the circumstances?

DR BACHER: Mr Gauntlett, we had been sadly so misled. We had defended Hansie to the world, we just believed it appropriate to tell the world in fact that we had not been given the right information and it was necessary to make a public apology in this regard. With regard to the question of asking our government to institute a judicial inquiry, accepting money from a bookmaker is a very serious issue in world cricket, a very serious issue. As we progress with my testimony today, I will with your permission bring to the attention of this forum my serious concerns about what is happening in international cricket at this point in time.

IF EVER PROOF were needed of Ali Bacher's fortitude, it was provided on the day that began with Hansie Cronje's seismic confession at 3 o'clock in the morning and gained its awful momentum 12 hours later when he fronted a televised press conference that had the effect of unleashing a tidal wave of shock and incredulity on a nation that sought refuge in either outrage or denial.

At 5 o'clock in the morning, Goolam Rajah had phoned again to tell him that Cronje insisted on immediately leaving the Elangeni Hotel in Durban where the team was staying and being provided with a driver. His intention was to go to Pretoria to meet with Aziz Pahad. Bacher again reached for his phone.

MR GAUNTLETT: You then, I understand, immediately phoned Mr Pahad. What did you say to him?

DR BACHER: Well, unfortunately I woke him up, but he accepted that in the right spirit. I indicated to him the contents of Mr Cronje's conversation to me at three o'clock in the morning. I also indicated to him that Mr Rajah had said to me that Hansie was going to leave the hotel immediately, that nobody was going to stop him leaving the hotel, and he wanted to go to Pretoria to see Mr Pahad personally. Mr Pahad then said to me that in fact he was leaving early morning for Cape Town and that if Mr Cronje wanted to see him, he should travel to Cape Town, which he duly did.

MR GAUNTLETT: Then at six o'clock Mr Rajah faxed to you at Phinda a copy of the statement which Mr Cronje had handed to him. Did you yourself read it through as you stood there?

DR BACHER: No, Mr Gauntlett, both Advocate Sonn and myself were in a hurry to get back to Durban, to handle this crisis as best we could. At six o'clock I telephoned my counterpart in Australian cricket, Mr Malcolm Speed. I said to him 'Malcolm, I am sorry, we have a crisis, there is a serious issue involving our national captain.' I briefly conveyed to him the contents of Mr Cronje's phone call to me and we immediately then left for Durban. I did not during that morning read the contents of that fax that was sent to me at six o'clock in the morning.

MR GAUNTLETT: You also then called the convener of the national selectors, Mr Rushdi Magiet, is that right, what did you ask him to do?

DR BACHER: That is correct, Mr Gauntlett, at half past six in the morning, I phoned Rushdi Magiet who was still in Cape Town. I informed him that there was a need to find a new national captain. I didn't give him the details, I said I would communicate the reasons to him in Durban that afternoon. I asked him to consult with his co-selectors, that there would be a press conference at Durban at three o'clock that afternoon and that he should give the new captain's name to Advocate Percy Sonn to announce to the country at that press conference.

MR GAUNTLETT: You then contacted Ms Wilkinson and asked her to tell the media that Cronje had been withdrawn, that you then telephoned all the Executive Committee members as you were driving from Phinda down to Durban, except one who you couldn't get hold of, and brought them up to speed. Is that correct?

DR BACHER: That is correct, Mr Gauntlett.

Percy Sonn drove the car to Durban and Bacher, the ubiquitous cellphone glued to his ear, phoned his executive committee members one after the other. One of them, Julian Thornton, a close cricketing friend and the long-time treasurer of both SACU and the UCB, listened and then asked, 'Ali, you backed Makhaya Ntini; should you not back Hansie too?' Bacher replied, 'No, Julian, he's confessed. We've asked for a judicial commission of inquiry. It's out of our hands now.'

MR GAUNTLETT: Then at 1.15pm comes the meeting that you attended with the South African team at the players' team room at their Durban hotel together with Mr Sonn, Ms Wilkinson, Mr Rajah, Mr Green. Could you just briefly run through that meeting, how you conducted it?

DR BACHER: There was tension in the room. I think the players knew there was a very serious problem. I spoke first at the request of Advocate Sonn. I conveyed to the team and the management of that team what had transpired at three o'clock in the morning. I indicated to them that this was a very serious issue. I then asked for every member of the team to inform us on two issues: firstly, had they ever been party to match fixing, and secondly had they ever been approached by anybody to get involved in this practice. My first question was directed at Herschelle Gibbs. I asked him to stand up and in front of his players to indicate to me where he stood and he said very clearly that he had never been party to match fixing and that he had never been approached by any player. I then asked Nicky Bojé to do likewise and he responded in the same manner. And then I went around the room and asked every member to tell me where they stood. Everyone responded negatively. The only additional fact that was forthcoming at that meeting (was) when it came to Jonty Rhodes, he alluded to a game in 1996, the tour of India, where the team had been offered money to throw a match.

MR GAUNTLETT: And after the meeting, did he elaborate on this, did he take you to one side, could you tell the Commissioner what happened?

DR BACHER: Yes, there was a side room; he said, 'Doc, I would like to speak to you'. He took me aside and he said very briefly, 'Had it not been for Andrew Hudson that offer may have been taken far more seriously'.

MR GAUNTLETT: Dr Bacher, this event to which Mr Rhodes referred, had you heard about this before, (in) the media or from anybody else?

DR BACHER: *This was the first time that I personally was aware that in 1996 in this benefit game in Bombay that an offer had been made to our national team to throw the match.*

MR GAUNTLETT: *Had you, however, had a conversation shortly before the events we are talking about, in which Mr Cronje had said something to you which you considered later tied in with this?*

DR BACHER: *About a few weeks before these revelations emerged in South Africa, in discussion, but not initiated on this particular issue, for about 5, 10 seconds, out of nowhere, Hansie just said to me 'there was a match, an offer, we turned it down immediately'. There was no mention made to me of the year, the country, the amount of money. It was dismissive, it was almost reflex(ive), and I don't think it lasted more than five seconds.*

MR GAUNTLETT: *What was your reaction at that time, to this brief reference without any details?*

DR BACHER: *I thought nothing of it because that would have been the response that I would have anticipated from the national captain, and at that point in time it would have been unthinkable to me for our national captain to even remotely consider that type of offer.*

MR GAUNTLETT: *Dr Bacher, this incident, if it is the incident we understand, surfaced in the international media, I think in late 1998. Were you aware of these reports, did you yourself read them?*

DR BACHER: *I have been shown the report from Colin Bryden (and) it was (published in) the latter part of 1998. I cannot recall ever reading that report.*

MR GAUNTLETT: *Your attention is also being drawn to statements in recent weeks by (the then team coach) Mr Bob Woolmer. Did you ever receive any report from Mr Woolmer in 1996 relating to any such offer in his capacity as reporting officially on the tour?*

DR BACHER: *That tour of India was a tough one, it took two months. It ended with this unhappy match taking place in Bombay and I think I should tell you about it.*

The players were decidedly unhappy about participating in this benefit match for (veteran Indian player) Mohinder Amarnath. My counterpart in Indian cricket at the time (was) Mr Dalmiya, who is now the president of the ICC. It was a late addition to the itinerary; the players were unhappy and quite rightly so. It is unheard of in my opinion to have a benefit match between two countries regarded as an official one-day international match. I phoned Mr Dalmiya and I expressed to him very strongly our unhappiness about this match. He implored me to speak to the players to go through with the match. The match had been advertised, it had been promised to Mr Amarnath, there were television sponsorships, and reluctantly I spoke to the team and asked them to proceed with the match. I think that background is important. It was a very unhappy team that proceeded to Bombay for that particular match. One week after the return of the team to South Africa, it was December the 17th, Mr Woolmer in his capacity as national coach, as he would do normally, sent me a very detailed and very comprehensive report of that tour to India. Mr Woolmer is a very meticulous coach, his notes are always very copious and detailed, and he described in detail to me the tour, the positives and negatives, the carriers they took, the hotels they stayed in, the food, the liaison officers, the practice conditions, the pitch conditions, the umpiring, from A to Z. But in the report there was no mention whatsoever of this offer to the South African team.

WHEN, IMMEDIATELY PRIOR to the King Commission, media reports suggested that there had been an offer to throw the match, Bacher was puzzled because this was the first time he had heard of it. He immediately phoned Robbie Muzzell, the South African team manager in India in 1996, and asked, 'Robbie, what's going on here, what's this I'm reading?'

Muzzell told him that the players had had an informal discussion in the team room in Bombay during which an offer was briefly discussed but that he heard no particular match mentioned. The players had joked with him about it, but he cautioned them against indulging in such talk. Later, unbeknown to him, there was a meeting of some of the senior players when an offer on the match in question was discussed and rejected. A written statement from him was tabled at the Commission.

Bacher again phoned Muzzell during a recess in his testimony to clarify the issue. Gauntlett recalled him to the witness stand the next day.

MR GAUNTLETT: Now, Dr Bacher, in the presence of your legal representatives did you speak to Mr Muzzell and try and clarify what the position was?

DR BACHER: Yes, Mr Gauntlett. During the latter part of yesterday, in the presence of the United Cricket Board lawyers, I phoned Robbie Muzzell in East London. He concurred that I had phoned him when it emerged a few weeks ago in South African newspapers that there was a serious offer to our players to throw the last one-day international in India . . . and that he had said at an informal meeting in the team room (in Bombay) . . . 'Chaps, don't think about it, don't talk about it, don't laugh about it, in this room, in the corridors'.

ACCORDING TO MUZZELL, his caution to the players was made in a general sense in relation to a very brief informal discussion about match fixing in the subcontinent that did not warrant inclusion in his official report on the tour. It was a full three years and four months later – on 14 April 2000, when he visited the South African dressing room at Newlands during their one-day international against Australia – that he learned for the first time that the senior players had met again prior to the Mohinder Amarnath benefit game on 14 December 1996 to discuss the offer. He was shocked to learn this, but knew nothing about the meeting of senior players in Bombay.

MR GAUNTLETT: So do you accept what Mr Muzzell . . . how he has it in his statement . . . that there was no specific incident he was talking about. It was some general discussion, and the first time he learned of this specific incident was on the 14th of April (2000)?

DR BACHER: Yes, Mr Gauntlett.

A LOT WAS made of the original report on the match-throwing offer in the (South African) *Sunday Times* that Bacher said he had not read. In the wake of his testimony to the King Commission, questions were asked about how he could not have read the report when it appeared in 1998. It was said that there was no cricket report that he did not read; and some of the innuendo attached to this – suggestions that he knew of the match-throwing offer but did nothing about it – hurt him deeply.

This speculation in the media frenzy was baseless: Cronje had mentioned to Bacher 'in five, ten seconds' that an offer had been rejected without going into specifics,[2] Muzzell did not know about the senior players' meeting, and Woolmer first made mention of it four years later around

---

[2] In his testimony to the King Commission, Hansie Cronje confirmed this: 'It (the offer) was often spoken about in the team and joked about and . . . I had said to Dr Bacher that there was an offer, but we refused it from a very quick point of view, (and we) didn't go into detailed discussion.'

the time of the King Commission.

In the context of the drama surrounding the King Commission, the *Sunday Times* article of 1998 seemed very important indeed; but in the context of the day on which it was published, how important was it? The sports editor[3] of the *Sunday Times* was not called by the King Commission but, had he been asked to do so, he would have testified that part of his job was to decide where stories were placed on the sports pages. The most important ones went on to the back page and the really important ones were taken by him to the editorial executive conference for consideration upfront i.e. in the news section of the paper and perhaps even on page one. He decided to run the story on an inside sports page in a position known as the 'top strip' which is to say that it ran across the top of the page, with a scaled down headline, but was not the main story on the page. As always the sports editor used his best news judgement which on this occasion was neither challenged by his own production staff nor the executive conference. The story said the SA cricketers had turned down an offer to throw the Mohinder Amarnath benefit match. The sports editor expected nothing less from them. If the story had said that the SA cricketers had decided to fix the match, he would have taken it upfront immediately; and it would have made banner headlines. The *Sunday Times* judged the story to be in the 'dog bites man' category and not of the 'man bites dog' variety. It was a story of significance but not an attention-grabber and the sports editor could not recall any great discussion around it among *Sunday Times* staff or readers, neither on the day of publication nor thereafter; until, that is, in the immediate weeks prior to the King Commission.

'The claim that I read every cricket report is grossly exaggerated,' says Bacher. 'It has always been my practice to read reports where I have been quoted to make sure that I have been accurately reported, and check interviews with reporters who I don't have confidence in. There were days when, due to pressures within South African or international cricket, I wouldn't read any newspapers.'

In a subsequent article in a London newspaper at the time of the King Commission, Woolmer made brief reference to having told Bacher of the 1996 match-throwing offer. If he did mention it to him, it is odd that he did not consider the offer serious enough to warrant recording it in his meticulous, official written report on that tour. Bacher to this day has no

---

[3] Rodney Hartman was the sports editor at the time.

recall whatsoever of any such conversation with a coach who had a reputation for leading with his chin; and Bacher's reputation for memorising anything of even a mildly serious nature or, alternatively, of 'switching off' to idle chatter suggests that Woolmer, at best, said nothing to him of any great import.

MR GAUNTLETT: *Now, Dr Bacher, one thing that you haven't actually described to the Commissioner . . . as these events unfolded fast from that early morning call. What was your state of mind, how did you react to what had happened from three o'clock on that day, what were you thinking?*

DR BACHER: *Devastated. It devastated this country, and I don't think this country has recovered.*

Bronwyn Wilkinson recalls: 'Ali was in a complete state during the press conference at the Elangeni Hotel, which went out live on several worldwide networks. He could not believe any of this was happening to him or to the man he had believed in so completely and who he had stood by through so much – especially over the previous four days. Clifford and I had to prompt him at times because he lost his words completely or he would start saying things that could cause legal problems later. His skin was grey, his hands were shaking and he was sweating. Towards the end of the press conference I wondered if he was going to make it.'

At the 3 pm televised press conference in Durban that day, Bacher would declare: 'Let us say unequivocally that we in South African cricket are shattered, unequivocally. We want to say unequivocally that the United Cricket Board and the government have been deceived.'

After the press conference, Bacher asked Wilkinson to accompany him to the hotel's reception desk. 'He told me to switch off my cellphone; he switched his off (one of the few times I ever saw him switch his phone off without being in a big meeting) and he asked me to take him for a walk. We handed over our jackets and phones to the receptionist and stepped outside on to the beachfront, turned right and walked south through the crowds. Ali was gutted. He kept repeating: "How did we get to this? How did this happen? I've known Hansie since he was a youngster and he became like a son to me. I thought we were so close that he could tell me anything – and he lied to me."

'Ali felt utterly bewildered. He cried.

'I think if Hansie had told the truth from the start instead of allowing

Ali to back him so publicly and so absolutely while being lied to over something so important, the outcome may have been different. He would still have been removed from the captaincy and there would still have been an inquiry, but Ali's approach to it may have been gentler in the sense of working with Hansie to sort the issues out. But he had gone so far to defend him, including involving our Department of Foreign Affairs and their counterparts in India – and it had all been a lie over an issue that was to bring the game to its knees.

'While we walked, several people greeted Ali with a lot of sympathy in their voices. It must have been a strange sight to them to see the man who had been so strong through so much looking so completely devastated, with tears on his cheeks. But as we walked back to the hotel, he turned to me and said: "Bronwyn, we are going to have to be so strong now. I am going to need you and we are going to face a lot of pressure – we will have to work together for cricket." It was our worst day yet.'

THE NEXT DAY South Africa went into action in the first of the three matches against Australia with a new captain, Shaun Pollock. The shock of the previous day was all around but the South Africans still won by six wickets at Kingsmead. The previous afternoon, when each player was asked to declare his innocence, Bacher told them, 'We all need to rise above this crisis.'

At that afternoon's press conference, he described the new captain as a player with an immense future ahead of him, 'a very good cricketing brain on him and his feet on the ground'.

Steve Waugh, the Australian captain, recalls how Ali had taken the trouble to go to Johannesburg airport to meet his team on their arrival in South Africa. 'The news of Hansie Cronje had just broken. He was devastated and shocked at the allegations and one hundred per cent sure that Hansie wasn't involved; or could not possibly be linked to such corruption. His loyalty was admirable and just as strong as the emotion of devastation the following day when the truth began to surface. It was a difficult period, not only for South African cricket, but also for world cricket. Serious issues needed to be confronted and overcome.'

When Bacher went to Cape Town for the second game, Ngconde Balfour summoned him and Sonn to his house in a fury. The minister of sport was in a rage. The UCB officials sat silently while Balfour berated them for holding the press conference in Durban to announce that Cronje had lied and been removed as captain; while he himself, in a bizarre set of circumstances, was holding a press conference in Cape Town, with Cronje at his side, and referring to him as 'My Captain'.

'Ali was astounded,' recalls Wilkinson, who was present, 'but he spoke very quietly and very firmly to tell the minister everything that had happened and the meeting eventually moved on to discuss a Commission of Inquiry. It was incredible that, even in his state, he was able to contribute to a meeting that had started on such a bad note and work towards turning it into something positive.'

Cronje, of course, had gone to Cape Town to meet with Aziz Pahad. He was joined there by Pastor Ray McCauley who had also received a phone call from Cronje in the early hours of Tuesday, 11 April. 'He was crying and he told me he wanted to fax me a letter, the same one that was copied to Ali. He wanted to go to Pretoria to meet Aziz Pahad. He was already on his way there when I found out that Pahad was in Cape Town so I told him to turn back and catch a plane to Cape Town. I did the same. Minister Balfour was recuperating from an operation but we met with Pahad, and Balfour later called the press conference.'

SHAUN POLLOCK, MEANWHILE, had made a regal start to his reign as Cronje's successor. Although his team lost the second match by five wickets in Cape Town, the new skipper took four wickets in the decider at the Wanderers, and South Africa clinched the series with a four-wicket triumph. A crowd of over 31 000 was in the emotion-charged ground to celebrate the final victory, and in many cases to wave banners of support for the fallen captain – and such was the growing antagonism against the UCB for its perceived hardline stance against Cronje that Bacher was booed when he emerged on the podium for the presentation ceremony. With him was the Gauteng premier, Sam Shilowa, who expressed extreme disappointment at the crowd's behaviour. Why was he booed? Perhaps the answer lay in the fact that the cricketing public had descended into a state of denial on the alleged activities of their beloved former captain; and in the high-profile Bacher they found their scapegoat. Was he now getting the blame for not protecting the former captain from his own devices?

As for the team, the one consistent failure was Herschelle Gibbs who in three innings faced 29 balls in all and scored a total of nine runs. The otherwise high standard of performance provided a brief elixir to the pall of gloom that had been hanging over the game; but it was not to last. The fallout from Cronje's confession was still thick in the air when another bombshell burst three days after the Wanderers victory.

Bacher's phone rang. The caller was Goolam Rajah.

MR GAUNTLETT: And what did he tell you?

DR BACHER: He said to me that he had received an anonymous phone call that morning that Herschelle Gibbs, Pieter Strydom and Nicky Bojé had in fact been approached by Hansie Cronje. I immediately phoned Clifford Green who also indicated to me that Goolam had been in contact with him with regard to this information. I asked the two of them to come to my house that afternoon. We discussed our strategy. I then phoned Pieter Strydom and said to him 'Pieter, I have been informed by Goolam Rajah that in fact you were approached by Hansie' (and) he said 'Yes, that is true now'. I said, 'I think it is important and imperative that you come to me tomorrow morning, which was the Thursday morning, the day before Good Friday. I phoned Herschelle and he said to me that, yes, he had been approached by Hansie, and I said to him, 'I think it is important that you come to my house tomorrow morning'. I phoned Nicky Bojé and he once again conveyed to me that Hansie Cronje had never, ever approached him. I said to him, 'Nicky, the other two are coming to my house tomorrow. Think about it, and if in half an hour's time you have changed your mind, please phone and come to see me tomorrow morning.' He never phoned me and he never came to my house on the Thursday morning.

The reason why there was ongoing interest in this trio was simple: they were the three players named with Cronje in the original statement by Delhi police on 7 April. Their names had been mentioned in the alleged conversation between Cronje and Sanjay Chawla in the transcript released by Police Commissioner K K Paul. Another player mentioned in the transcript was Gibbs' roommate Henry Williams but his name was not contained in the police statement.

MR GAUNTLETT: Then the meeting went ahead on Thursday at your house with Strydom and Gibbs . . .

DR BACHER: That is correct . . . in regard to Pieter Strydom, firstly he told us that two days before the first Test match in Mumbai, Hansie had asked him to come to his hotel room (and) the meeting lasted between five to ten minutes. Initially it was in a joking manner (that) an offer had been made for the South African team not to get more than 250 runs and that, if the team complied, Pieter would receive R70 000. Pieter – and he was honest to us on this occasion – he said to Hansie, 'Look, it's early in my career; I have only played a couple of Test matches. Possibly in a few years' time, if I have played 70 Test matches, who knows how I will respond to this, but I really cannot give it serious consideration because of my early appearance in the national team.' As I said, it lasted between five to ten minutes. Then the following morning, Hansie had come to him and said that the offer was now R140 000. I, in fact, was at that Test match and it was a magnificent win for South Africa on a very difficult and turning pitch and young Mark Boucher and Jacques Kallis did this country proud under extreme pressure. At the end of the game, Pieter said he went to Hansie in a joke and said, 'Well, I could have made a lot of money!' and he said Hansie didn't respond to it (Note: South Africa's totals were 176 and 164 for six). Pieter told me that when he got back to South Africa there were a few phone calls with Hansie. He wanted to know from Hansie what was happening, and then (in) the last call Hansie said the following to him, 'Tell them about the approach, but don't tell them about the money side.' With regard to Herschelle on the Thursday morning, he said that on the morning of the fifth one-day international (in Nagpur), Hansie had come into their bedroom. Henry Williams was there, I think he said he was packing his suitcase or he was having a shower. The conversation lasted 30 seconds, it was joke-joke, 'I've had an offer, ha-ha, no, we won't be party to it', and that was Herschelle's response to our question on that Thursday morning of whether in fact Hansie had made a serious approach to him.

Under oath at the King Commission, Gibbs and Williams admitted that they had accepted an offer of $15 000 each from Cronje to underperform in the Nagpur match. The deal was that Gibbs should score fewer than 20 runs and Williams concede more than 50 runs in his 10 overs. Gibbs, in fact, scored 74 runs in 53 balls and Williams left the field through injury after conceding 11 runs in 11 balls. Bojé and Strydom consistently denied any wrongdoing. In his testimony, Cronje said he had untruthfully mentioned their names to Chawla. Gibbs, Williams and Strydom would later appear before a UCB disciplinary hearing, chaired by former judge Mervyn King.[4] Gibbs contacted Bacher and apologised for lying to him.

OF ALL THE people who testified before the King Commission during its eleven days of public hearings none revealed so much so willingly as Ali

---

[4] At the hearing on 19 August 2000, Gibbs and Williams pleaded guilty to a charge of accepting an offer to underperform. Gibbs was also charged with bringing the game into disrepute by lying to Bacher, at the behest, it transpired, of Cronje. On 28 August, the UCB banned Gibbs and Williams from international cricket until 31 December 2000. In addition, Gibbs was fined R60 000 and Williams R10 000. The penalty took into account the influence Cronje had over them, that they did not deliver on their undertaking to underperform and they were never paid. Pieter Strydom was acquitted.

Bacher; and none did so at so much risk. Most of the others who gave evidence seemed to do so either reluctantly, or under protest, duress and, at best, with a severe case of stage fright.

Not so Bacher. 'Transparency' had become his middle name. For example, for several years he had insisted that the salaries of his contracted players be made public and, yes, he was prepared to divulge his own if anyone in the media wished to know; and he saw the King Commission as the ideal place for unfettered disclosure of an evil that had beset the game he loved, even if it meant exposing himself to serious danger.

Frederik Van Zyl Slabbert, who had grown to know Ali over the years, would say that one of the man's qualities was that he was never afraid to tackle an issue head-on; and that 'this was best described during the Hansie Cronje saga'.

Bacher was adamant that there should be no cover-up, particularly in the light of the Australian Cricket Board's handling of the case of Mark Waugh and Shane Warne when, almost by chance, world cricket heard that these two players had given basic information on aspects such as weather conditions and the state of the pitch to an Indian bookmaker; and that the matter had effectively been swept under the carpet after the players had been fined.[5]

'Our strategy was very clear,' says Ali. 'It was highly improbable that only one person could be involved and that this was surely a global problem. It wasn't possible that Hansie Cronje was the only cricketer involved; there clearly was an international involvement and, unless we exposed that, nothing good would come from the Commission. Our strategy then was to internationalise the malpractice and to rectify it in the interests of the game.'

The last thing the UCB wanted was for corruption to be seen as only a South African problem. And so Bacher volunteered to tell all he knew about match fixing in the international game, even if some of it was based on hearsay. This, Gauntlett warned him, was dangerous business and that the stakes were high. If he insisted on following this course he might not

---

[5] Waugh was fined $Aus10 000 and Warne $Aus8 000 by the ACB. Other than a reference to the incident in the minutes of an ACB meeting of 28 February 1995, no mention of this was made public until 1998. According to a report published in April 2001 by Sir Paul Condon, Director of the Anti-Corruption Unit of the International Cricket Council, this cover-up 'would accord with the then feelings of the ICC that, in the best interests of cricket, such matters should not be released into the public domain'.

enjoy full legal protection in other countries and could expose himself to counter-action. 'He was taking the largest risk because this (testimony of widespread match fixing) could have turned on the UCB and he could have been burnt.'

As the UCB's senior legal counsel, Gauntlett was compelled to advise his client accordingly, but he nevertheless admired Bacher's courage for 'not hunkering behind the parapet' but coming out boldly and taking the fight into the open. Gauntlett admits he liked the strategy.[6]

During the Easter weekend in late April of 2000, Bacher prepared a report on the information he had been given in relation to the international aspect of the match fixing allegations. His intention was to hand this to the chairman of the ICC's Code of Conduct Commission, Lord Hugh Griffiths, but it was decided by the UCB that he should rather use it in the first instance in his testimony to the King Commission.

At the heart of it was a sensational claim that two matches in the 1999 World Cup were fixed. Bacher told the Commission that the former Pakistan Cricket Board chief executive Majid Khan had told him that the matches involving Pakistan against India and Bangladesh were fixed in favour of Pakistan's opponents. The loss to lowly Bangladesh, in particular, astonished the fans because Pakistan, after all, were eventual World Cup finalists.

Bacher then read to the Commission a letter he had received from Majid Khan in support of his testimony:

> In the interests of world cricket, I have no objection if your statement, including my discussions with you about malpractice and corruption in Pakistan cricket is made public. In my capacity as Chief Executive Officer of the Pakistan Cricket Board, I requested the President of Pakistan, in January of 1998, to institute a Judicial Commission to investigate these malpractices.

DR BACHER: Mr Commissioner, the next sequence of events relates to an acquaintance who I've met on five or six occasions during the past five to six years. He's an Indian bookmaker, and can I refer to him as Mr R, because I do fear for his safety?

COMMISSIONER: Yes.

DR BACHER: Thank you, Sir. During the 1995-96 season, England toured South

---

[6] Jeremy Gauntlett interview, October 2001.

Africa. On the flight from Johannesburg to Port Elizabeth for the Boxing Day Test match . . . I sat next to a cricket supporter from India. He knew his cricket inside out, and informed me he was a bookmaker. A long-standing friend of mine is Jack Bannister, and I would say on the international cricket scene he would probably be the best friend I've ever had over many decades. He's an ex-Warwickshire county player, a former BBC commentator, and a former bookmaker. Jack Bannister met up with the Indian bookmaker during the fourth Test in Port Elizabeth. He had asked him to review the contents of a book that Jack was about to publish in 1996, entitled 'Tampering with Cricket'. I can recall asking Jack Bannister whether he believed that the Indian bookmaker was above board, and he replied in the affirmative. He did not believe he was involved in inducing players to fix or manipulate matches. During the next two cricket seasons, 1996-97 and 97-98, I met him on approximately three occasions, twice in South Africa and once in Sydney.

COMMISSIONER: When you say 'him', Dr Bacher, is this the bookmaker you're talking about or Jack Bannister?

DR BACHER: No, the bookmaker. Thank you, the bookmaker. I suppose, Sir, you could ask me why did I have this contact with this bookmaker? Firstly, he knew his cricket very well he knew facts and figures and the history of the game. Secondly, I was guided by Jack Bannister's assessment of him, and nobody in international cricket, I can vouch, would ever question Jack Bannister's integrity. And I just wanted to keep the door open, because what was surfacing in world cricket now were allegations of match fixing, corruption in the game of cricket. During these infrequent, I wouldn't say 'meetings', they were generally over dinner, he told me in no uncertain terms that match fixing, match manipulation, takes place on the subcontinent. The modus operandi, and it was the same story every time, was that it generally involved one-day international matches, it generally involved matches played outside of the home country, that with some of the countries they were playing between 40 to 50 one-day international matches per calendar year, that it generally involved three or four players, and that instead of winning 28 out of 48 one-day matches per annum, they'd only win 24 and it wouldn't be the end of the world.

MR GAUNTLETT: And Dr Bacher, while you're on that, could you just tell the Commissioner what you also learnt about remuneration of players comparatively between South Africa and I think one or two of the countries you're trying hard not to mention?

DR BACHER: I don't want to mention the countries, but he indicated to me that a *starting point for enticement was the very fact that some of these players don't have contracts, that they only get match fees and that their payment in relation to their status in their society was not properly rewarded.*

MR GAUNTLETT: Thank you. I think you were at the point of describing how you travelled to Leeds for the fifth Test match.

DR BACHER: I travelled to Leeds for the fifth Test match, this is 1998, England versus South Africa. It was a decisive match, the series was one all. It was a Test match that was won by England, but history will also record that many dubious decisions were made by (Pakistan) umpire Javed Akhtar. Mr Commissioner, if I can tell you that during that Test match there were 10 lbw decisions given, 9 were given by Mr Akhtar, 8 were given against the South African team and 7, according to knowledgeable critics of the game, were considered to be dubious. After returning to South Africa, I phoned the Indian bookmaker in Bombay, and enquired of him whether the umpire concerned could have been bought. His answer was, 'possibly', but he did not have any evidence to substantiate this. In February of 2000, I departed for Mumbai for the first Test match between South Africa and India. I arrived there on the Thursday morning and on the Friday morning he phoned me at my hotel where I was staying with the team. He asked me if I had an evening free, and I said, 'Sunday night'. We won the game on Sunday afternoon. It was a wonderful win by our South African team. He came to my hotel, we walked about four blocks and we went to a restaurant. During the course of the dinner, I asked him again whether match fixing, match manipulation, was still taking place in the subcontinent. He replied, once again, in the affirmative. He specified some Pakistan players, some Indian players. I said, 'Sri Lankans?' and he said, 'No'. I said, 'South Africans?' and he said, 'No'. Then, during the latter part of the dinner, he startled me with the following: 'Ali, you remember you phoned me after the Leeds Test about the possible manipulation of an umpire during that match?' I said, 'Yes.' He then said to me: 'The umpire concerned was on the payroll.' And he added that he had acquired this information subsequent to my telephone call, and that he had been subsequently informed that one of the biggest bookmakers in Karachi had left Karachi for Leeds a couple of days before that Test match to ensure that his client complied. Startled, I decided on my return to Johannesburg from Mumbai that I would request a meeting with Lord Griffiths in June of this year, during the annual ICC conference, to inform him what had been relayed to me on February the 27th.

Bacher then introduced another important international aspect into the record.

I met Javed Burki for the first time during the 1994 South African tour of Pakistan. He is a former Pakistan Test player, and was at that time the president of the Pakistan Cricket Board. He is also currently in no official position with the Pakistan Cricket Board. In January of 1999, he visited South Africa as the Match Referee for the South Africa versus West Indies one-day international matches. During an evening at the Sandton Sun Hotel in Johannesburg, he told me at dinner in the presence of Tony Cozier, the West Indies journalist, Brian Basson, the UCB's Director of Playing Affairs and Umpiring, and Mr Rajan Madugalle, ICC Match Referee for the South Africa-West Indies Test matches, that match fixing involving the Pakistan team had happened in some instances, and some players were involved in this practice. I phoned him in Pakistan on the evening of April the 22nd 2000, once again this was over the Easter weekend. He reaffirmed to me that the above was a true reflection of what he had said to me at the Sandton Sun Hotel, and that he was happy for me to incorporate this in my letter to Lord Hugh Griffiths. He also said to me during this telephone call that during his term as president of the Pakistan Cricket Board, the Patron of the Board, that is the President of the country, had asked him to look into allegations of corruption within Pakistan cricket. During his one-year term he found one cricketer to be culpable. He took appropriate action. The cricketer was subsequently banned in February of 1995, but the new (Pakistan) Board reinstated him. On the 13th of May of this year, I received via e-mail from Majid Khan the following: 'Javed (Burki) says he has no problem with you submitting his discussion with you to the judicial inquiry, and if necessary, for them to be made public.'

Bacher's strategy of 'internationalising' the problem of malpractice in cricket gained strength as his testimony continued to captivate his large televised audience on that long and trying day of 12 June. Gauntlett confides that Ali 'used the most of the opportunity' from the witness stand, and the experienced senior counsel guided him on his course. Gauntlett was impressed by Bacher's willingness to place a huge trust in him; and together they sallied forth into the tortuous labyrinth of the match fixing underworld which, by its very nature, was fraught with perils for anyone bold enough to expose its machinations in a public forum.

MR GAUNTLETT: Dr Bacher, you prepared a report with some very serious statements in it for Lord Hugh Griffiths and for the ICC, and you've explained how you thought it important that, because the facts with which the Commission is concerned straddle continents and you're not dealing with a domestic disease, that you should talk about these matters. Have you been in contact with your international counterparts about giving this information? Could you just tell the Commissioner, briefly, what is their attitude?

DR BACHER: *Yesterday I put aside to – I wouldn't say to consult – but just to put (them) in the picture what was going to be in my statement today. I first phoned David Richards, the Chief Executive of the ICC. I then phoned two very important players in world cricket. One is Mr Jagmohan Dalmiya, who is the president of the ICC. He is based in Calcutta. I've known him for more than a decade. He in fact was the driving force in 1991 to get South Africa back into international cricket. So we have a long, long association. He is under siege at the moment, which is sad. There are question marks about his integrity, and I made it very clear to him on the phone that he has my support (as) I would not question his integrity. Fundamentally and essentially he said to me he was very, very happy with the processes taking place in South Africa (and that) it must be open, it must all come out and we must unite together to be effective in eradicating once and for all this practice from world cricket. I also phoned Mr Ehsan Mani,[7] who is a Pakistan accountant based in London and is the Chairman of the ICC Finance and Marketing Committee. He is a very important player in world cricket, and he too was supportive of this process, and very supportive that what must come out must come out once and for all in the best interests of the game of cricket. I had endeavoured in the last 24 hours to make contact with Mr Chowdhury, who is the president of the Bangladesh Cricket Board, a good friend of mine, to indicate to him that I was going to inform this inquiry what Majid Khan had said to me about the Pakistan-Bangladesh match during the World Cup. I was unable to contact him. Also my counterpart in Pakistan cricket is a Mr Saeed, and I've endeavoured on seven occasions to make contact with him, to bring to his attention the information which I felt was in the overall interests of world cricket.*

MR GAUNTLETT: *Dr Bacher, would you tell the Commission as to when you first, looking back, would think that there were indications emerging of some kind of contamination in international cricket starting to wash into South Africa?*

DR BACHER: *If I reflect back . . . I would say that the first time that I became suspicious of this possible malpractice in world cricket would be the 1994/95 season. We had a quadrangular one-day international tournament here. We got permission and support from our most distinguished President Mandela at the time to allow his name to be associated with this tournament. We invited New Zealand, Sri Lanka and Pakistan*

---

[7] Ehsan Mani succeeded Australia's Malcolm Gray as ICC President after the World Cup in 2003.

381

to come to South Africa and participate in this quadrangular tournament to pay tribute to President Mandela. We now have the final, and it was a two-legged final between South Africa and Pakistan. The first leg was in January of 1995, in Cape Town at Newlands Cricket Ground. Prior to this match, a week before, I had received correspondence from the United Arab Emirates Cricket Board, and they are an associate member of the International Cricket Council, requesting that the United Cricket Board provide VIP treatment to two of their cricket administrators. The Cricket Board and South Africans are warm, hospitable people, we like to entertain people from abroad, and I responded only with pleasure. The match took place and the two alleged administrators came to the ground and . . . I invited both these administrators to be my guests at my particular table at the dinner break. After dinner, Qamar Ahmed, a Pakistani (journalist) living in London who has covered more than 250 Test matches, a man well known in world cricket, a great friend of South African cricket, and a great personal friend of mine . . . he called me aside, because I had also invited him to one of the tables for dinner, and he said to me, 'Ali, what's going on here?' And I said, 'Well, I've got this letter from the United Arab Emirates Cricket Board.' He said to me, 'Ali, nonsense, they're bookmakers, man!' The second point that happened during that particular match is that (Pakistan captain) Salim Malik won the toss and decided to allow South Africa to bat first. Now everybody in international cricket and South African cricket knows that, for whatever reason, when you have a day-night match at Cape Town, if you win the toss, you bat first because in the evening the ball swings and seams. So that was a second, call it, signal, that just kind of alerted me, just something's not right here. The second leg of the match went to the Wanderers Stadium. He won the toss again . . .

MR GAUNTLETT: That's Malik?

DR BACHER: That's Salim Malik. He won the toss again, and again he did the same as in Cape Town. He asked South Africa to bat first. Now at the Wanderers Stadium there could be cricketing reasons to bat second. But the important fact is, as told to me by Doug Russell, the South African liaison officer with the Pakistan team, that the Pakistan team were angry, were furious with him (Salim Malik)[8] and it required the considerable efforts and persuasion of Intikhab Alam, their coach, to get them on to the field. The third signal, or alert signal . . . we had agreed with the Pakistan

---

[8] Salim Malik and paceman Ata-ur-Rehman were banned for life in July 2000 upon the recommendation of the protracted Qayyum Commission of Inquiry into match fixing in Pakistan. Among those who gave evidence against Malik were the Australians Mark Waugh and Mark Taylor.

Cricket Board to have a one-off Test match against Pakistan at the Wanderers Stadium in January of 1995. That was after the completion of the Mandela Cup Final. We batted first, were 30 for three, and I can recall like yesterday saying to one of my colleagues in the Long Room. 'We'll get 350 plus.' And he said to me, 'Why?' and I said, 'Look, I've played Test cricket, I've captained international teams. Something's not right out there.' Their adrenalin wasn't flowing. It just appeared to me that the Pakistan team were just going through the motions . . . there just wasn't urgency out there, and I think anybody who has played international cricket could sense that. And the fourth, call it, signal, alert signal, is that the Pakistan team from there went to Zimbabwe. Rashid Latif, the vice-captain, and Basit Ali didn't complete that tour, they didn't go to Zimbabwe. And for the very first time it started to emerge, through the media, that during that particular tour there was a possibility, the likelihood that three or four matches were thrown by the Pakistan team during that tour.

Bacher informed the ICC at a meeting of Full Members in June 1997 of the allegations of match fixing in world cricket. He remembered it well because it was the last meeting chaired by Sir Clyde Walcott. During the course of the meeting a discussion on match fixing came up and Bacher said he had information that suggested it was probably taking place. He did not belabour the issue but simply made his point known; it was not as if he was mounting some crusade. The debate lasted between five to ten minutes and he could recall Sir Clyde saying, 'There's no smoke without fire', and the discussion was never minuted.

MR GAUNTLETT: Dr Bacher, how do you assess what has been the impact on South African cricket of the events of the past couple of months?

DR BACHER: The revelations, as I've said previously, have shattered this country. I can't recall ever in my long association with sport in this country, which goes back to the 1960s, any particular sporting issue to have ever dominated the news as persistently and strongly as this one. But I see a positive side to it. I am not a policeman, but I am as confident as one can possibly be that match fixing, manipulation, has taken place in world cricket and for the very first time in my experience as an international administrator the world cricketing authorities are taking this practice very, very seriously. I think previously administrators have been very defensive and there's a stock phrase 'where's the evidence?' but I think in an inquiry of this nature where we get the information, it must be taken seriously, it's got to be taken seriously.

MR GAUNTLETT: Dr Bacher, do you believe – and I know hindsight is an exact science – but do you believe that the UCB is beyond criticism in relation to these events? Do you have a sense that in some respects at least the UCB may have failed (the) players, may have failed the public and failed international friends?

DR BACHER: Yes, Mr Gauntlett. On reflection, I honestly believe that we have underestimated the inducement factor on cricketers. You've got young cricketers, inexperienced cricketers, some of them very talented at their sport but (they) may not have had the best possible education, for political reasons, in South Africa. They now get exposed to this international forum where inducements are substantial, are real and have been happening. So I think we need to look at that factor very, very seriously. We also need, in my humble opinion, to ensure in the future that for our young cricketers – and there are some wonderfully talented cricketers in this country – we put in place structures, systems in place, to ensure that the inducement factor does not come into play. I think too – and I hope this is received in the world of cricket not as an attack by the United Cricket Board on any particular Board – that this is a problem which goes beyond cricket administrators. In my humble opinion you're talking about a Mafia-type operation, underground, illegally acting (and) manipulating players in some matches. It's a very serious issue. Cricket administrators on their own cannot solve all these problems; it will need the co-operation, liaison and support of governments and the police forces in those respective countries.

According to Gauntlett, there were various aspects of Bacher's testimony that might have exposed him to attack by Cronje's legal team, but nothing of the sort was forthcoming. In fact, he was asked only five questions in the cross-examination by senior counsel John Dickerson. Included in his answers was his confirmation that he had received threats of physical violence and that he was not surprised to learn that Cronje had also received similar threats, including death threats; as he had said, he believed the match fixing menace went to the heart of the criminal underworld.

Bacher also acknowledged under cross-examination that he had never felt that the South African team under Cronje's leadership was not trying its best to win.

Dickerson's final question gave rise to an interesting revelation:

MR DICKERSON: Lastly, Dr Bacher, were you not aware, or was your Board not aware earlier this year that a series of benefit matches were to be played in India in April of this year by a Hansie Cronje XI?

DR BACHER: I can record that in March of this year Hansie phoned me (from India) to indicate to me that some of the players had been invited to go to India for a few benefit matches (after the completion of their official tour). I can recall very clearly saying to him, 'Hansie, have you chaps not had enough cricket?' He said to me, 'Doc, it's only for about seven to ten days. It will only involve a few matches', and I said, 'In that context, all right, if you don't feel that you've had too much cricket, I do not have a problem.' I've learned subsequently, which was never brought to my attention unfortunately, that these arrangements were being made in January of this year, that it wasn't purely just a few players, in fact it involved about 13 South African players who would go across to India to play in benefit matches under the Hansie Cronje XI banner, and also that it would be played against, in all probability, a team selected by (Indian captain) Mohammad Azharuddin.[9] That was not conveyed to me by Hansie Cronje, unfortunately.

As a mentally exhausting 12 June 2000 drew to a close, Jeremy Gauntlett posed one final question.

MR GAUNTLETT: Lastly, Dr Bacher, for you as you step back and you look at all that's happened in these events and the revelations that there were and the devastation that you've described, is there for you any final lesson which emerges from all this?

DR BACHER: I would sum up my feeling as follows, that if the bookmakers can get to Hansie Cronje, they can get to anybody in world cricket.

As HIS ELDER daughter Ann would later say, 'The Hansie Cronje case changed my father's faith in humanity. He had always been very idealistic, always looking for the optimistic viewpoint, the good side ... and this just shattered him.'

---

[9] In his testimony to the King Commission, Hansie Cronje said that it was Mohammad Azharuddin who had introduced him to a bookmaker, 'MK' Gupta, after the third day of the third and final Test in Kanpur in 1996. Gupta asked Cronje to ensure that South Africa lost the Test and gave him $30 000 in cash. Cronje said he took the money but did not act on the request, although South Africa did lose the match.

In December 2000, Azharuddin was banned for life by the Board of Control for Cricket in India.

Chapter 31

Summoned by Lord Griffiths

JEREMY GAUNTLETT'S PRIOR warning to Ali Bacher that he might open a can of worms in 'internationalising' his testimony to the King Commission was borne out by the widespread and often hostile reaction that came in the wake of it.

Pakistan umpire Javed Akhtar vowed to take legal action against him, saying, 'I am sure he is biased against Pakistan and that is why he is making such baseless allegations, all figments of his mind.' A summons was later served on Bacher at the UCB offices requiring him to appear in court in Karachi. He was being sued for 100 million Pakistan Rupees or the equivalent of R10 million. 'I advised Ali not to do anything about it,' says Clifford Green, and there the matter rested.

A C Muttiah, president of the Board of Control for Cricket in India (BCCI), said that since Bacher had not shared information with the International Cricket Council on his 'long-standing links with a bookmaker in India', he was liable for action under the ICC's Code of Conduct. 'It is unfortunate that in the testimony before the King Commission of Inquiry, he made various statements which he ought to have brought to the notice of the ICC as and when he became aware of the incidents. As a member country of the ICC, we shall be writing to notify the ICC Executive Board to carry out an investigation in the matter.'

According to reports at the time, Muttiah wrote letters to the president of the ICC, Jagmohan Dalmiya, and its chief executive David Richards.

BCCI secretary Jaywant Lele denounced Bacher's assertion that the India-Pakistan match at the 1999 World Cup was fixed. 'How can a match between India and Pakistan be fixed when both teams are out to get at one another?' Anshuman Gaekwad, India's World Cup coach, said he did not believe his team's win was not genuine. 'It was a very competitive game, Pakistan fought hard before going down. I went into the Pakistan dressing room after the match and the players were very depressed by the defeat.'

Former Pakistan Cricket Board (PCB) chief Arif Abbasi claimed Bacher had named Pakistan in his testimony in order to divert the world's attention from South African cricketers 'as his own house is not in order'.

Majid Khan was not at all fazed by what Bacher told the King Commission. 'Ali phoned me before he testified and said that only if I agreed that he could divulge what I had told him (about the two 1999 World Cup matches) would he do so; otherwise he would not. I told him to go ahead and divulge it.'[1]

Ali's opinion of Majid is that 'he was the bravest man of them all' for being prepared to go public with allegations against his own country. It was, in fact, at Majid's instigation that a judicial commission of inquiry into match fixing was instituted in Pakistan; but he refutes that he was the 'bravest of them all', conferring that honour instead on various Pakistan players, most notably Rashid Latif, Aamir Sohail and Rameez Raja, for first speaking out publicly about alleged match fixing practices in Pakistan teams. He also awards a very high degree of bravery to a female Pakistan cricket reporter, Fresti Gatai, for consistently reporting on match fixing allegations within Pakistan cricket.

On the question of the alleged throwing of their 1999 World Cup match against Bangladesh, Majid says: 'After the tournament the whole team was summoned to appear at a Pakistan Senate probe. It was there that one of the senators asked how it was possible that the odds on a Pakistan victory could suddenly go down from 44-1 to 29-1 on the morning of the match. In fact, a friend of mine told me the odds had gone from 66-1 at the start of the World Cup to 9-1 on the match day. I didn't say it, but a senator did.'

It was noteworthy that Imran Khan, the famous former Pakistan captain and cousin of Majid, was scathing in his condemnation of Ali. 'Bacher is a man of double standards and should never be trusted,' he charged. 'He should be sued for damages for the allegations he has made on hearsay. I

---

[1] Majid Khan interview, December 2003.

personally watched the India-Pakistan match at the 1999 World Cup . . . and only a silly man can say that it was fixed.'

Ali was puzzled by this attack from a man who was always above suspicion during his highly distinguished playing career as one of the world's great allrounders. In fact, there is a documented case of Imran telling his teammates that he planned to bet the equivalent of the runners-up cheque on a Pakistan victory in the final of a tournament in Sharjah; in other words, if any of his players was considering throwing the match, as was rumoured, they would be paid nothing.

If anyone should have welcomed moves to stamp out corruption, it was Imran, so why the attack on Bacher? The answer could be twofold: following South Africa's re-entry to international cricket in 1991, Asif Iqbal, a former Pakistan captain, visited South Africa before the 1992-93 season in an attempt to persuade the UCB to host a Pakistan-India series in South Africa as a fund-raiser for the cancer hospital that Imran Khan had established in Karachi in honour of his late mother who had died of cancer. Ali says that 'one can only compliment Imran for his philanthropic vision in building this hospital but I immediately turned down the offer. Firstly, because of India's support for our readmission to world cricket, we gave them the assurance that they would be the first international team to tour South Africa after our return to world cricket and we weren't going to break our word. Secondly, how would South African cancer victims feel if we raised money for cancer patients in another country?'

A few years later, Imran arrived in Johannesburg unannounced and a development clinic was organised in his honour in Soweto. The petulant superstar reluctantly agreed to go there; and it was during this clinic that he berated Bacher in front of a large gathering of media for turning down the proposal for the Pakistan-India series in South Africa.

Also, Ali's friendship with Majid Khan[2] might have annoyed him. It was claimed that the two cousins had not been on speaking terms since 1982 when Imran, the captain, dropped Majid, a renowned attacking batsman, from the Pakistan team during a series against India.

Be that as it may, the uproar in the subcontinent following Bacher's testimony to the King Commission was deafening. When he and Percy

---

[2] Majid Khan was a successful captain of Cambridge University and Glamorgan and also played for Queensland. He represented Pakistan in 44 Tests, three of them as captain, and scored 7 Test centuries.

Sonn attended an ICC Executive Board meeting in Paris in June 2000, Ali knew he would come under intense fire.

'Before the meeting I warned Percy that the UCB and I could expect a broadside, and he replied, "leave it to me". As anticipated, within three minutes of the meeting starting, there was a blistering attack on me by General Zia of Pakistan and Dr Muttiah of India. Percy kept his word and immediately responded in support of me; and the words came out of his mouth fast and furious.'

Sonn says: 'I pointed out to them that the UCB had told Ali to tell the truth and that if they attacked him, they attacked us, and that we would remember it in future. I said that here was a man who was being honest, in keeping with the objectives of our new democracy, and all they could do was attack a man who was telling the truth. I took a moralistic line and it was hard for them to come back at that kind of truth.'[3]

Nevertheless, both the BCCI and the PCB formally asked the ICC to charge Bacher with bringing the game into disrepute. The BCCI seemed particularly concerned by the headline of a newspaper report *Indian subcontinent source of problem,* which appeared the day after the Durban press conference at which Cronje's admission of dishonesty was revealed.

The ICC acted on these complaints and asked Lord Hugh Griffiths to investigate whether there was any basis for them. He wrote to Bacher and requested him to substantiate his claims to the King Commission and answer the subcontinent's disquiet at being identified as the source of the problem. Ali immediately called Clifford Green to ask his advice on how to address the latest issue.

Green had grown accustomed to calls from Bacher at all hours of the day and night. 'The pressure was incredible; it was one thing after another. There were the transformation problems in the UCB, then the Ntini affair, then the Cronje crisis and the King Commission; it never seemed to abate. In public, Ali might have looked reasonably calm, but behind the scenes he was really feeling the strain. I would religiously get phone calls from him at 6.30 in the morning – I'd be in the shower and my wife would shout, "It's Ali", without even answering the phone – and he would say "You won't believe what's happened now!" and we would sometimes wonder if it was ever going to stop. We were living on our nerves.'

On Green's advice, Ali wrote to Lord Griffiths. He reminded the chairman

---

[3] Percy Sonn interview, December 2003.

of the ICC's Code of Conduct Commission that he had raised the question of match fixing at an ICC meeting in June 1997 – when Sir Clyde Walcott had remarked 'there is no smoke without fire' – and that this had not been minuted. Furthermore, he wrote: 'At an ICC Executive Board meeting in June 1999, which took place immediately after the Cricket World Cup final, I reported that I had been informed that two World Cup matches were thrown. Sir John Anderson, the chairman of the New Zealand Cricket Council, will confirm that I relayed this information to the meeting. Once again, it was not minuted.'

He also reminded Lord Griffiths that while under oath at the King Commission he was obliged to openly and honestly disclose all information at his disposal.

'During the period leading up to my appearance at the King Commission,' wrote Ali, 'I took great care not to identify particular countries, matches or individuals. We were aware that inaccurate reporting was aggravating our attempts to handle the situation in a controlled and considered manner. It may have been that, during this intense period of media activity, I made the statement about the subcontinent, which would not have been made with any malicious intent, but rather during my frequent and stressful meetings with journalists. Although this statement was vindicated at a later stage, it was not made with the intention of undermining the King Commission, any ICC inquiry or Cricket Board.'

IT IS GENERALLY accepted that the three biggest crises in the history of cricket were the Bodyline fast bowling controversy that marred the Australia-England series in 1932-33; the Kerry Packer rebellion of 1977-78; and the match fixing scandal of 2000.

'Of these, undoubtedly the greatest crisis that international cricket had ever faced was the match fixing,' says Ali. 'Yet amazingly, I cannot recall from the moment it started ever getting a call from the president of the ICC (Dalmiya); or him ever making an appearance in Cape Town to attend the commission of inquiry on which the eyes of the entire cricket world were focused.'

AFTER AN EXCHANGE of letters with Lord Griffiths, Bacher was eventually summoned to London in 2001 to meet with him and a former High Court judge, Oliver Popplewell QC, in what was effectively a hearing on the complaints by India and Pakistan.

'I phoned Lord Griffiths a couple of times,' recalls Green, 'because I didn't want Ali to walk blindly into anything. We needed to know what the forum was, what the format of the meeting would be, should he have a lawyer with him and should he also know what questions were going to be put to him. Lord Griffiths was very courteous and I came to the conclusion that Ali would not need a lawyer. I suppose we took a bit of a chance, but he went there alone.'

The meeting with Griffiths and Popplewell at the Royal Garden Hotel in Kensington had been in progress for only a few minutes when Bacher asked, 'Gentlemen, can I be honest?'

'Yes, go on.'

'You've got the wrong person!'

'Who are you suggesting should be here?'

'The leadership of the ICC.'

Following further discussion – and after a member of the ICC staff had contacted Sir John Anderson on behalf of Lord Griffiths to verify Bacher's recollection of the 1999 Executive Board meeting – they concluded that there were no grounds for charging him with bringing the game into disrepute. The ICC, however, did caution him to be 'more circumspect' in future in his dealings with the media. As a member of the ICC, he was obliged to discuss all issues with the world body before talking to the press, and they were concerned that he had not followed this protocol.

IF ALI HAD one regret about his testimony to the King Commission, it was something that hit him between the eyes, quite unexpectedly and most disturbingly, whilst he was in Paris for the Executive Board meeting in 2000. During the tea break, he turned his cellphone back on. Almost immediately, it rang and the voice on the other end said, 'Why, Ali, why, why, why?' It was 'Mr R', the Indian bookmaker. 'He told me,' recalls Ali, 'that the testimony I gave about him being one of my sources – and even though I didn't name him, and to this day I still don't know his surname – had forced him to take his whole family out of India because he feared for their lives. I felt terrible. I never, ever thought that I was endangering him. And that's the last I heard from him.'

ON 26 JUNE 2000, the ICC established its Anti-Corruption Unit under the direction of Sir Paul Condon, former Commissioner of the London Metropolitan Police and recipient of the Queen's Police Medal for distinguished service. His task was to conduct an exhaustive investigation into match fixing in world cricket; and thereafter, with the help of his small team of hand-picked former Scotland Yard detectives and regional anti-corruption officers, to monitor the game very closely to ensure that it remained free of this menace. During a visit to South Africa about a year before the 2003 Cricket World Cup, Lord Condon requested a private meeting with Bacher through a third party. Ali had no idea why he wanted to see him, and felt a bit anxious. He had no cause to worry, however. The Anti-Corruption Unit director wanted to let him know that what he had told the King Commission about match fixing in world cricket was true.

'I can confirm,' says Lord Condon, 'that during this confidential meeting I informed him that my unit was receiving information from around the world that tended to confirm the allegations made by Dr Bacher inside and outside the King Commission.'[4]

---

[4] Lord Condon QPM DL interview, October 2003. Note: Paul Condon became the youngest London Metropolitan Police Commissioner at the age of 45 in 1993. He was knighted in 1994 and created a Life Peer in 2001.

Chapter 32

The Final Tragedy

ALI BACHER WAS at the ICC meeting in London in June 2000 when Hansie Cronje testified. He watched some of it on television. It broke his heart when, at the end of it, the young man collapsed in tears and left the packed room in the arms of his brother.

In the court of public opinion, the judgement was that he was being victimised; and in many homes around South Africa, people shed a tear. Ali could understand why the majority viewpoint, in South Africa at least, was one of sympathy for Cronje. 'The people saw an inconsistency between his case and that of the Australians Mark Waugh and Shane Warne. He told the truth and was crucified for it. The Waugh-Warne affair was swept under the carpet and when it was eventually revealed, there was only a slap on the wrist for them.'

That was the charitable view; the converse was that the outpouring of sympathy for the fallen idol was symptomatic of a nation that, probably as a result of its cynical past, had become accustomed to corrupt behaviour from some people who occupied high office. On the one hand, there was a lot to be said for a nation prepared to forgive as it embarked on a fresh start; on the other was the awful truth that a deep-seated trust had been betrayed.

The people who backed Cronje represented a cross-section of society and were not, as some cynics suggested, just misguided white folk with a laager mentality. There is a telling example of this. At the *Sowetan*, then the biggest daily newspaper in South Africa servicing black readers, an editorial and advertising meeting was arranged to plan a new cricket supplement ahead of the 2003 World Cup. In discussing elements of its content, the meeting was interrupted by a senior editorial executive who had a brainwave. He asked excitedly, 'Can't we get Hansie Cronje to write us a column each week?' There were no dissenting voices but, as it turned out, the column idea, and the supplement, was stillborn.[1]

After the King Commission, Cronje phoned Bacher a couple of times. The UCB had banned him for life and, in dismissing his appeal to reverse this decision, High Court Judge Frank Kirk-Cohen said Cronje seemed to demonstrate a lack of appreciation for the extent of his wrongdoing. 'He cast aside the honour of leading his national cricket team for the shadowy pleasures of bookmakers' money,' he said in his judgment.

When Cronje phoned Bacher, he was particularly upset by a statement by UCB president Percy Sonn that 'if the UCB had its way, it would not even allow Cronje to play beach cricket'.

He asked the UCB managing director whether that statement reflected the majority view of the UCB. It most certainly was not Ali's view, and he told him so. People who heaped blame on Bacher, and still do, for not supporting him do not know the full extent of the pain that he felt for his fallen skipper.

Don Mackay-Coghill makes the point that the Cronje affair 'took years off Ali's life', and that he showed too *much* sympathy, not too little. 'In my view, and I have argued this with him, he was far too soft on a player who had betrayed South African cricket.'

At the end of one telephone conversation with Cronje, Bacher remembers asking him, 'How is it going with you?' and his replying, 'It's bad, it's bad . . .'

Ali made the point that the life ban was not of the UCB's making. South African cricket was compelled to fall in line with the ICC, which had drawn up a code of conduct with various penalties or sentences for different levels of transgression. In banning Cronje, the UCB was simply complying with ICC requirements. Bacher's view was that 'as the custodian of the game, its values, its history, its culture and its future, the ICC had every right to impose stringent penalties on Hansie Cronje and other international cricketers who had indulged with bookmakers in international cricket.'

---

[1] Although the supplement did not get off the drawing board, the *Sowetan* did produce some excellent sections on the 2003 World Cup in South Africa and were duly acknowledged for the support they gave the tournament.

Having said that, he adds: 'I still felt that a couple of people in the UCB were quite heartless in their attitude towards him, but when I left the national body at the end of 2000, I no longer was able to play any meaningful role in influencing their thinking.'

By nature, Bacher has a soft heart and he felt that a more humane approach towards the disgraced former captain would have been better. It was a position that had not gone unnoticed among some cricket officials. A UCB executive meeting at the Centurion Lake Hotel towards the end of 2000 began with one of the board members slyly turning to him and asking, 'Are you being blackmailed by the other side?'

'I was very angry, and I said so. What did he mean? Was he implying that the Cronje camp had something on me, or something on the UCB, or South African cricket or the board, or whatever?'

This boardroom exchange was very significant because many Cronje fans found it convenient to blame Bacher for being 'too hard' on their old hero; whereas the hawks in the UCB were disappointed that he was being too soft.

The one issue on which Bacher and the UCB did, however, agree was that Cronje should not be given media accreditation for the 2003 World Cup. There were reports that media groups were interested in contracting him to provide expert opinion, and there was nothing in his banning to prevent him from pursuing journalistic work. 'I took a pragmatic view,' says Ali, 'and reasoned that his presence in the media box during the most important cricket event ever staged in South Africa would only succeed in taking the focus away from the World Cup. Sachin Tendulkar might have been scoring a century, but all the visiting international journalists would be trying to get an interview with Cronje.'

Nevertheless, Bacher indicated his conditional support for Cronje. 'He had erred grievously, and he knew that – but I conveyed a message through his brother Frans that if there was any way I could help or guide him, he should come and see me.'

Hansie Cronje never did, and Ali would never see him again.

'If he had come to see me, I would have told him to take a back seat, be low profile, sort out his life and be patient. My view was that after the World Cup, he and I could get together and work out something where he could start coaching the township kids, as he always had done so well in the past, in a low-key way, gradually building up his confidence and self-esteem through cricket again. Who knows what could have happened in time if he had done things one step at a time? People can be very forgiving;

just look what happened in our own country when democracy was achieved through oppressed people forgiving their oppressors.'

To this day, Ali still shudders to think what Cronje went through and the agony and pain he suffered. 'When I saw the change in his personality during 1999, I put it down to the transformation priorities that he was battling to come to terms with. Now I believe I know why he changed. It is said that once the bookmakers have got you, they've got you for life. He must have been noosed by these bookmakers and he was desperately looking for a way out. He must have been having sleepless nights.'

Bacher's views are borne out by a senior player who was close to Cronje. He, too, had seen a change in his captain; a man who had been cool and calm on and off the field during the mid-nineties had become moody and tense. 'It was easy,' says the player, 'for a top cricketer to get sucked into this web. There was easy money on offer simply for taking a phone call once a week and giving the caller basic information about the weather, the pitch, team selection and who was likely to bat first.'

There was another occurrence that further bears out Ali's theories about the change in Cronje. 'When in 1999 I heard that he had signed a contract with Glamorgan to coach there, I was livid. It had been done without my knowledge, behind the UCB's back, and I phoned the Glamorgan chief executive Mike Fatkin and gave him stick. When Jacques Kallis, for example, was approached to play for Middlesex in 1997, the county's representative phoned me to get our permission for him to play there for a season. With regard to Cronje, I put my foot down and refused to let him go. I couldn't understand how a player who was loved and respected in South Africa, who had a huge following, would want to go to Glamorgan to coach and possibly play. Now I believe I know why: he wanted to get away from the clutches of the bookmakers. He must have thought that this was his way out; go and play county cricket in England. He must have been going through sheer hell.'

HANSIE CRONJE'S DEATH in a plane crash on 1 June 2002 came as a terrible shock to Ali. When he heard through a UCB colleague, Trish Lewis, on that Saturday morning that the aircraft had crashed into a mountain outside George in the Southern Cape, he immediately phoned Frans Cronje. They maintained telephone contact throughout the morning as rescue workers were airlifted on to the mountain to search for survivors. There was none; the three occupants of the cargo plane, Cronje and his two pilot friends, were killed instantly. After confirmation of his death was received, Bacher issued the following statement to the media:

I was very close to Hansie Cronje throughout his cricket playing career. For much longer than that I enjoyed the friendship of his parents, Ewie and San-Marie, and their family. Hansie Cronje played a very influential role in South African cricket. Such was his popularity and influence in the game in this country that when he got caught up in a match fixing scandal that prematurely ended his cricket-playing career, it was deemed to be a national tragedy that touched the lives of everyone who knew him and followed him. The whole of South Africa seemed to be caught up in his plight. Yet Hansie's honesty at the King Commission of Inquiry facilitated a process for world cricket to address the problem and start stamping it out. I was very close to him from the time he emerged as a young cricketer and watched him grow into our senior national captain in which role he had an outstanding record. He was a natural born leader of men and his greatest attribute was his terrific ability to inspire and motivate his teammates. My heart goes out to his parents, his wife Bertha and the Cronje family.

Ali contacted the family home and spoke to Cronje's mother. He says she told him that perhaps it was a blessing that her son had died. He had suffered so much, had lost all his confidence, and would have had to bear the burden of the match fixing scandal for the rest of his life.

'That summed up the whole terrible tragedy for me; a mother suggesting that only in death could her son be freed from his burden.'

THE TELEVISED FUNERAL took place in Bloemfontein, in the tradition-steeped school hall of Cronje's alma mater, Grey College. In the days leading up to it, Ewie Cronje issued a media release that members of the UCB would not be welcome at the funeral. Strictly speaking, Bacher was no longer a member of the UCB because he had left his post on the national body more than 18 months before to take up his position as Executive Director of the ICC World Cup 2003. But, in this case, the term 'UCB' might have had broader connotations.

'I phoned Ewie and said, I feel for you; we've known each other for a long time. If you and the family don't want me to attend, you must tell me. And Ewie replied, "We want you to come." And I wanted to be there.'

On the day of the funeral, Bacher travelled by car with three companions from Johannesburg to Bloemfontein. During the journey, he received word from a security officer that somewhere ahead of him was another car transporting his friend and former colleague, Hoosain Ayob, to the funeral.

There was, however, another occupant in this car, and his name was Hamid 'Banjo' Cassim.

During the King Commission, Cassim was described as 'the biltong man' and a 'hanger-on' because he was often seen around the South African players; and, as a Johannesburg sweet shop owner, he had regularly supplied them with biltong and sweets. He was also the man who had introduced the bookmaker Sanjay Chawla to Hansie Cronje in a hotel room in Umhlanga Rocks, outside Durban, in January 2000. This was the same Sanjay who featured in the incriminating taped cellphone conversations with Cronje that were released by the Delhi police on the day that the crisis began. 'Banjo' Cassim himself had given evidence to the King Commission during which he appeared to suffer a series of memory lapses.

Ali called Ayob on his cellphone. 'Hoosain, would you say we have been good friends for many decades? Well, then, I am giving you some good advice as a friend. I want you and your passenger to turn around immediately and go back to Johannesburg.'

The world's media, photographers and TV cameras were gathered in Bloemfontein and Ali could imagine the pictures all over the front pages of the newspapers the next day, the image repeated over and over again on the television networks. He shuddered to think of the damage it would do. Hoosain took his advice and turned back.

As Bacher drove through the streets of Bloemfontein en route to Grey College, the newspaper posters on the lampposts screamed out at him: *BACHER, JY IS NIE WELKOM NIE!* (Bacher, you are not welcome!).

It was with a sense of foreboding that he drove through the gates of the old College and saw before him a surreal scene set in silence and witnessed through tense, tearful eyes. Hundreds of mute mourners were standing away to one side, the shiny hearse bearing stark testimony to the gravity of the occasion; and, probably doing their best to maintain a measure of decorum in spite of the frenetic nature of their work, an army of media people rushed at the car when it pulled up in front of the main buildings, as if the celebrity had finally arrived. As Bacher walked the gauntlet, with security personnel forcing open a path for him, a woman verbally abused him and had to be restrained.

It was a moving ceremony, attended by the majority of Cronje's former teammates. Peter Pollock delivered the eulogy and his son Shaun, fighting back the tears, spoke of his fun-loving friend and former captain.

At tea after the funeral, members of the Cronje family received Ali warmly. Hansie's mother San-Marie, his sister Hester and wife Bertha hugged him; others shook him by the hand.

ON THE WAY back to Johannesburg that evening Bacher received a phone call from the spokesman for the minister of sport to say that Minister Balfour was terribly upset because his presence, and that of other government representatives at the funeral, had not been mentioned in the long list of people who were thanked publicly for their attendance.

Even on this day of drained emotions and deep pain, when Bacher might at least have been afforded some solitude, there were matters of protocol, way outside his area of responsibility, that were demanding his attention. As always, he agreed to take up the matter, and he brought it to the attention of the Cronje family the following day.

Life was often like that for Ali Bacher . . .

Chapter 33

Inside the ICC

THE CROWNING GLORY for Ali Bacher was masterminding the first Cricket World Cup on the African continent; but first it is important to know how South Africa arrived at this point and about some of the politics of world cricket.

At the end of the 1992-93 season, Geoff Dakin bowed out of South African cricket administration after an 18-year involvement. His successor was Krish Mackerdhuj. In February 1993, shortly before he took over as president, Mackerdhuj went with Bacher to Lord's where he played a pivotal role during what Ali describes as a fractious 12-hour meeting of the International Cricket Council to decide the host countries of future World Cups.

'England were not happy with us because we went public about wanting to host the next tournament in 1996,' recalls Ali. 'We had pointed out that no fewer than three previous World Cups had been staged in England, and that Africa had never had one and deserved a chance. England's view was that they had been pencilled in to host the 1996 tournament.'

On top of this, India's Madhavrao Scindia put in a strong claim for India, Pakistan and Sri Lanka to co-host the 1996 World Cup.

One of Mackerdhuj's strengths was his diplomacy,[1] and Ali was impressed at the way the future UCB president played a key role in a meeting 'that was going nowhere' to effect a compromise. In terms of this,

---

[1] Krish Mackerdhuj was appointed South Africa's ambassador to Japan when he left cricket administration in 1998. He was succeeded by Raymond White.

with England's agreement, the subcontinent would get the 1996 World Cup, and England and South Africa would follow to host the 1999 and the 2003 tournaments.

'Krish's appreciation of the east-west sensitivities was well received and he also made sure that the agreed sequence was minuted which, as it turned out, may very well have saved the 2003 World Cup for South Africa.'

This was borne out when Pat Rousseau later became president of the West Indies Cricket Board and publicly expressed the viewpoint that West Indies should jump the queue to get the 2003 World Cup. In spite of the fact that West Indies was probably the most dominant team in world cricket from the time of the first World Cup in 1975, they had yet to host cricket's showpiece. The reason was simple: they did not have the capacity or infrastructure to do so. Rousseau claimed it was an unwritten agreement that they would get the tournament once these requirements were met, and now, he said, they were ready. His claim for the 2003 World Cup, however, was thwarted by the minute from the 1993 meeting that Mackerdhuj had insisted upon.

Ali liked Mackerdhuj. 'At the UCB, he was the right person at the right time. Before unity, he was the boss at SACB and he ran the show. When we united, he and SACB were quite smart by proposing that Geoff Dakin become president in the first year and he in the second. If that was their strategy, it was smart, because it would give Krish the inside track to continue as president once Geoff had had a year in office.'

This in fact transpired when Mackerdhuj stayed in office from 1992 to 1998; and Bacher's view is that he played a 'good ambassadorial role' for South Africa during these six years. He was, of course, a man highly regarded in the National Sports Congress where his black African colleagues valued his credentials and his democratic belief in collective leadership. He was a long-standing member of the ANC and his political thinking was crystallised when he attended the University College of Fort Hare; this being the alma mater of many members of the ANC leadership, including Nelson Mandela, and of many African leaders and scholars.

So, the 1996 World Cup went to the subcontinent where Jagmohan Dalmiya, secretary of the Board of Control for Cricket in India (BCCI), also chaired the three-nation organising committee. It was on the eve of the tournament that he tried to persuade Bacher to have the South African team switched from Pool B to Pool A – the two groups into which the competing teams were equally divided. Pool A included Sri Lanka, Australia and West Indies – and the Australians had cited security concerns for refusing to travel to Sri Lanka for their pool match. Dalmiya knew that the South Africans would be prepared to play in Sri Lanka – Bacher had said as much publicly – and he felt that if they went there, it would show up the Australians.

Bacher immediately said 'no' to this proposal; and not only did the Australians not play in Sri Lanka, but the West Indies also refused to go there. Both teams felt their security would be at risk in a country where terrorist bombings were rife.

There was further controversy when Dalmiya failed to invite the ICC president, Sir Clyde Walcott of the West Indies, on to the podium at the opening ceremony in Calcutta. This upset a lot of officials, including Bacher, and they met afterwards to discuss this obvious snub. It was agreed that Ali would raise the issue at the next ICC meeting of CEOs, and this he did. 'I made it very clear that we were not happy that the president had been snubbed in this way, and Dalmiya's response was, "I did it to protect him." What, protect Clyde? He was a legend of world cricket, an official who was highly respected by all member countries and I had never known him to raise his voice to anyone.'

Thereafter, the once warm relationship between Bacher and Dalmiya cooled by a few degrees.

Dalmiya's machinations in world cricket are noteworthy. Even before he became president of the BCCI, he ensured that he would be nominated as president of the ICC. This came immediately after the 1996 World Cup when three candidates – Dalmiya, Mackerdhuj and Australia's Malcolm Gray – were nominated to succeed Walcott. On the basis of a simple majority, Dalmiya would have won because he had the support of the smaller Associate Member countries of the ICC. What he did not have, however, was a majority support of the Test-playing nations, many of whom were nervous of this ambitious and dogmatic man heading up world cricket at a time when east-west relations were clearly strained. Amazingly, the rules of the ICC were unclear on the actual voting process but Dalmiya, who had enlisted a team of lawyers to assist him in his bid, insisted that a simple majority was the only requirement. Walcott, however, had the final say when he ruled that a two-thirds majority of the nine Test-playing nations was needed to elect the ICC president.

When Mackerdhuj withdrew from the ballot, Gray was confident that South Africa's vote would gain him the presidency. He needed six votes, and he was already assured of four from West Indies, England, New Zealand and Australia. He believed that South Africa, as an old traditional ally, would go with him and take Zimbabwe with them.

Dalmiya had the votes of Pakistan, Sri Lanka and India so, even if South Africa and Zimbabwe sided with him, he still would not have the required six votes. He simply could not win.

Ali recalls the tense meeting: 'The mood in world cricket at that time just wasn't right to have a winner. There were concerns about an east-west split in the game. So Krish had a brainwave, and South Africa abstained in the ballot. Zimbabwe followed suit.'

There was therefore no clear winner, and Walcott was asked to continue in office until 1997, at which time a new system of rotation would be applied for future ICC presidents. In terms of this, India would have the next president for a three-year term and would be followed by Australia.

The Australians were angry that the South Africans had not voted for Gray. Ali recalls: 'At a tea break during that meeting, I was involved in some short, sharp exchanges with their chairman Denis Rogers and their CEO Graham Halbish in the presence of (England's) Doug Insole. The Aussies were saying, "Ali, you've got a short memory", and by that they were referring to the fact that, during our two decades of isolation, Malcolm Gray was the first Australian Cricket Board chairman to examine our situation with some sympathy.'

Dalmiya, on the other hand, was obviously very grateful that South Africa had abstained. 'He later phoned me at the Westbury Hotel to thank us and say that this would give him some breathing space.'

In terms of the new system of rotating presidents, India would determine who the ICC president would be for the next three years. They chose Dalmiya. 'We all found this very puzzling,' says Ali. 'He was only the secretary of the BCCI, yet he was preferred above Inderjit Singh Bindra who was the BCCI president at the time.'

It was only after his three-year term as ICC president was complete that Dalmiya became president of the BCCI for the first time, heading a coup in 2001 to oust the incumbent A C Muttiah.

Of Dalmiya, Ali says: 'He was an excellent organiser. When we returned to world cricket in India in 1991, the matches were televised – but Indian cricket did not get a single cent from the national broadcaster. Nine years later, when I was in India, I was told by a senior official that the BCCI had $US200 million in the bank. It was all his doing; he made it happen. He turned Indian cricket into a multimillion dollar business.'

However, it was the perception of many who knew him, including Bacher, that Dalmiya was ambitious to the point of being power-mad. 'I have never known anyone who did not know the meaning of the word "no". It was a word he would never understand.'

Ali had always believed that Scindia, the distinguished Maharajah of Gwalior, had all the right attributes to make an outstanding ICC president. He was saddened in September 2001 when Scindia was killed in a light airplane crash while on his way to address a Congress Party meeting in Uttar Pradesh.

IN MID-2000 Ali Bacher told the UCB board that on 1 January 2001 he would have to move across to the World Cup 2003 position. 'If I leave it any later than that, I won't have enough time,' he told them. It had been decided that Gerald Majola would succeed him as CEO and Percy Sonn[2] had succeeded Raymond White as the UCB president.

For the first time, the UCB's two top positions were now in the hands of 'people of colour'.

Prior to the succession, Majola visited Bacher at his home to discuss his taking over as CEO of the UCB. 'I offered to be available for three months to lend a hand if he needed it but he said, no, it will have to be six months.'

So Bacher stayed in his UCB office where he concentrated full time on the World Cup project; but was also on hand should the new boss need him to resolve contractual issues that were still pending or any other UCB business that he had inherited and was not familiar with.

The simple fact of the matter was that Majola never called on him.

'I am told,' says Ali, 'that in the business world, when a CEO departs, there are two routes that can be followed. In the first of these, there is an agreement that for a period of three or six months he gets involved behind the scenes during a mentoring period to give the incumbent the benefit of his experience and know-how. In the second, the CEO packs his bags, walks out and is never seen again.

'I realised that Gerald, in fact, had chosen the latter option, which was his prerogative. Nothing would have given me greater pleasure than to help him behind the scenes for a period – I know I could have assisted him in the way I helped his late brother Khaya – but it was not to be.'

So, after three months, Ali packed his bags and moved to a new office a few kilometres from the Wanderers in a business and conference centre

---

[2] Advocate Percy Sonn formerly headed the elite Scorpions investigative unit of South Africa's prosecuting authority before being appointed an acting High Court judge in October 2002.

called Summer Place. This majestic suburban estate in Hyde Park was originally built as the palatial mansion of the enigmatic oil tycoon Mario Chiavelli and had since been acquired and developed into corporate office accommodation by the famous philanthropic Krok twins, Abe and Solly. Their family, like the Bachers, came from Rokiskis in Lithuania.

World Cup headquarters was housed in what was originally the main double-storey house and, because the main offices were converted bedrooms, the curiosities included en suite state-of-the-art bathrooms complete with gold-plated taps and imported Italian tiles. There were tennis courts and a vast swimming pool, at the centre of which was a huge Roman-style statue of a goddess-type figure of frightening proportions, but because of the immense workload that increased with each passing day, no one had the time or inclination to use them.

At Summer Place, Bacher assembled his organising committee. The first person he brought with him on secondment from the UCB was the commercial director Ian Smith, the man who he had personally head-hunted away from his executive position at SA Tennis eight years earlier. Smith would be his right-hand man. He liked him and trusted him, and admired his total commitment. 'Not once during the years we spent together did an external auditor ever question anything in the accounts. Ian was meticulous and, to his credit, was not averse to questioning me on items of expenditure.'

Bacher also hired from outside cricket a number of people in specialised fields for what he called his '50-50 club', an organising structure that reflected the black-white imperative. Some were appointed as managers, others as directors but, in keeping with his commitment to equity, he eventually designated them all as 'directors' in an organising committee that was stylised 'CWC 2003'.

Unquestionably, this was a huge project to which the budget bore testimony: a revenue stream of R732 million, a total expenditure projection of R513 million, and anticipated profit of R219 million.

In actual fact, the tournament realised a profit of R400.5 million, of which R131 million was spent on legacy projects in providing new facilities and equipment at the cricket stadiums. The remaining R269 million was distributed to the UCB, its provincial affiliates and the Zimbabwe Cricket Union who were effectively another 'provincial union' in terms of the original hosting agreement. There was also the good prospect that the profits would grow by an additional R50 million once certain contractual disputes were resolved between the ICC and its commercial partners.

The question was often asked what impact the World Cup would have on South Africa's economy. The Department of Sport funded a special survey by a specialist company which calculated that South African economic activity was in excess of R2 billion, and the impact in terms of net foreign spend into the country was R1 billion.

This was a World Cup that was unique in many ways. For example, for the first time since the inception of the Cricket World Cup in 1975 there would be three major role players: the ICC, who owned the property and its commercial rights, Rupert Murdoch's Global Cricket Corporation (GCC), who had bought the sponsorship and television rights as part of a seven-year package costing US$550 million, and the UCB through its CWC 2003 organising committee. It was the kind of arrangement that could easily give rise to damaging conflicts, yet the cooperation and teamwork in this tripartite alliance became the fulcrum for a successful outcome.

'At the start, the ICC was anxious,' says Ali, 'that we would run the event on our own, but I was told later that they were surprised by our level of cooperation. My relationship with Malcolm Speed (the ICC's CEO) was cemented and we had an excellent understanding.'

Bacher's respect for Speed had grown since the time of the Melbourne barrister's appointment as CEO of the Australian Cricket Board (ACB) in 1997. 'I remember the first ICC meeting we attended. He said, "I don't know" about seven times when questions were put to him, and I wondered where they had got this bloke! It was only later that I realised that he was a very astute administrator who was not prepared to commit himself until he knew exactly what was going on.'

Speed was appointed CEO of the world body in July 2001 and the mutual respect between him and Bacher became very apparent during the whole World Cup process. It would seem that Speed's admiration for Bacher had begun back in 1997, a year after Ali was appointed as chairman of the ICC's new development committee and at a time when 'globalisation' became a major priority in world cricket. Ali's intimate knowledge of development in South Africa made him the ideal man for the job – and his major achievement was the division of the world into five regions and the appointment of development officers in each of these. He continued chairing this important committee until mid-2000, at which time Speed wrote to him on behalf of the ACB to warmly congratulate him on a job well done.

The job now, in respect of the 2003 World Cup, was a huge one and the ICC's support was a comfort. As for the UCB, where again conflicts could have arisen, Sonn simply told Bacher, 'Make it happen!' and never once interfered. In spite of his lack of social graces at times, Sonn was an ally of whom Ali was fond. 'He was a forthright administrator who was not averse or afraid to take on fellow blacks on certain issues. Given his background and position, he was able to front up to people of colour.'

What Bacher had to front up to now was a project of immense proportions. Never before would so many cricket matches (54) be played by so many teams (14) for so much prize money (US$5million). At the 1999 World Cup in England, 12 teams played for a total of $1million. A total of 15 stadiums would be used, these had to be upgraded to meet the required ICC standards at a cost of R60 million, and matches would be played in three countries, including Zimbabwe and Kenya, in what would be a major logistical challenge. It was a World Cup of record-breaking proportions; and, in what would be his final journey to cricket's coalface, Ali pursued his goals and objectives with perhaps greater zeal than ever before. Wherever he went, he would tell people that 'this is much bigger than cricket'; and indeed it was. He was determined that South Africans in all walks of life should benefit, so one of the first things he did was to find out exactly what 'black economic empowerment' meant. He and some of his colleagues met for an hour with Cyril Ramaphosa, former ANC secretary general and head of the government-established Black Economic Commission, and came away enlightened, informed and enthusiastic. 'We discovered that empowerment was not about having a black chairman; it was about transferring skills down the line, uplifting people from the bottom up.'

Black empowerment became his watchword. It was championed whenever the CWC 2003 policy committee met under the chairmanship of Professor Jakes Gerwel, who was former president Nelson Mandela's director general, and whose composition reflected what Bacher described as an 'invigorating and dynamic mix' of people, including the country's top five cricket officials led by Sonn and other hand-picked leaders in their fields – the ubiquitous Professor Michael Katz, Professor Denver Hendricks of the Department of Sport and Recreation, top business chiefs Khaya Ngqula and Colin Hall and educationalist Coco Cachalia.

Having been given the benefit of Ramaphosa's wisdom on empowerment, Bacher now looked to the redoubtable Katz to enunciate the policy as it would apply to the World Cup. Indeed, empowerment was reflected in every aspect of CWC 2003 life. No company, no matter how big or important, could successfully tender for contracts unless it showed a significant transformation element in its operational structure or was prepared to enter into a joint venture with a black company. The awarding of contracts included the empowerment commitments of profit sharing, employment opportunities and skills transfer, and an independent auditor, Thulani Nzimakwe, was enlisted to oversee the process of the appointment of all the suppliers for the tournament. He and his company were also retained to monitor the ongoing implementation of the contractual terms by the suppliers, and also to review, at the end of the tournament, whether they had met their empowerment commitments.

In a detailed 30-page report after the conclusion of the tournament, he concluded that 'the CWC 2003 experience benefited black economic empowerment suppliers not only in financial terms, but also in terms of the experience in hosting truly international events. Comments from suppliers indicate a tremendous learning opportunity for all participants. For a significant number of suppliers this was a first opportunity to be involved in an event of this magnitude, both in terms of organisational logistics and international stature. As a country, South Africa can be proud of what was achieved both in terms of empowerment and organisational effectiveness. This experience stands South Africa in good stead for future major sporting events – particularly the 2010 FIFA World Cup bid.'

Black empowerment, then, was an outstanding success, and Bacher and his policy committee could take credit for it. The committee was later reconstituted as the CWC 2003 Board and at the head of it stood the quiet, reassuring figure of Gerwel, a soft-spoken academic with an immense wealth of expertise, skill and knowledge. 'No president that I served under chaired meetings as well as he did,' says Ali. 'He was passionate about cricket, he had enormous experience in chairing meetings and committees, he had political entrée at every level both in South Africa and abroad, and he never, ever lost his cool. If there were any serious political issues to deal with, his advice was always invaluable. We would always meet for an hour in my office before each board meeting. There were always major policy decisions to be taken, but his meetings never lasted more than two hours.'

If Bacher always saw eye to eye with Gerwel, the same could not be said about Ngconde Balfour. On at least two occasions, the rumbustious minister of sport slammed the phone down on him because he felt that Ali was effectively going over his head. 'He phoned me and said, "I'm warning you" and later, "this is your final warning!" . . . and I wondered if by that he meant he was going to send me to Robben Island!'

The major cause of his problem, it seems, was that the CWC 2003 chief was not following desired protocol.

'He wasn't happy with me because eventually I was having to go directly to various government departments without his knowledge. That's understandable, but the problem with government departments anywhere in the world is that the process can be slow; it can take up to two months to get an appointment. Also, government people are often overseas, they're in parliament and meetings, and I was running out of time. I had to take a direct approach.'

Bacher says he could understand Balfour's unhappiness, but time was of the essence. 'When I started the job, I had 25 months. If I had to do it again, I would insist on a minimum of three years.'

It was to everybody's relief that when play finally got under way in the World Cup, the relationship between the minister and the tournament director got back on an even keel. 'To give him credit,' says Ali, 'there were many occasions when he would contact me directly and offer me his support. He was no longer firing away at me but was endeavouring to be a calming influence – something that he has continued to do ever since the Cricket World Cup.'

After the World Cup was over, at a celebratory function in Cape Town, Balfour publicly thanked Bacher for the way he had handled government before and during the tournament. 'To my surprise, he then declared that there was only one South African suitable for the position of ICC president – and that was Ali Bacher. I phoned Percy Sonn the next day and alerted him to what the minister had said.'

The reason he did this was because Sonn had already expressed a big interest in the ICC position.

THE WORLD CUP, of course, was not without its controversy and disappointment – the South African team's failure to advance beyond the first round was a case in point – but chief among these, from a global perspective, was England's refusal to play in Zimbabwe. And the question remains to be answered: was it security or political priorities that persuaded them to pull out of their match in Harare?

Politics, as ICC president Malcolm Gray emphatically pointed out, was not cricket's game. He and his colleagues were simply not qualified to make decisions that were the remit of governments. What they could do, however, was establish that all security priorities had been met.

And, in the case of Zimbabwe, they did just that.

Bacher's major priority, in fact, was security around the event and the host cities; and to achieve this he and the government assembled the biggest security machine ever for a sports event in southern Africa, if not the entire continent. He knew that safety and security was paramount in a global event such as this and so he recruited a formidable Security Directorate with a CWC budget of R16.8 million.

For the first time, cricket grounds would be monitored by closed-circuit television, there would be metal detectors at all entrances, a 'moat' system of mesh net-covered frames would be erected around the perimeter of the playing fields, and the stadium security would be controlled from specially constructed Venue Operations Centres.

Bacher issued an unequivocal order to the Security Directorate that no unauthorised person should get on to the playing area at any ground at any time – and, remarkably, they achieved it.

Lord Paul Condon, director of the ICC's Anti-Corruption Unit, later accepted an invitation to join the Security Directorate in his stated desire to deliver a World Cup free of corruption – another goal the tournament ultimately achieved.

By mid-2002 the Security Directorate had completed a weighty major event security manual, a generic volume that was awarded to the ICC as the template for future major cricket tournaments. It also became a much sought after document in other world sports bodies.

The World Cup was declared a 'major event' by the South African government and, flowing from this, close cooperation with senior officers in state law enforcement agencies was established to ensure compliance with the special requirements. Central to this was Director Ben van Deventer, a member of the Security Directorate and a senior South African Police Service (SAPS) official responsible for the national coordination of major event security. His job was to oversee major event security on a national basis and he was a key figure in the success of the World Summit on Sustainable Development that was held in Johannesburg in 2002.

For the World Cup, no fewer than 4 500 SAPS personnel were deployed with a budget of R72 million from the government.

Van Deventer reported to Deputy National Police Commissioner Andre Pruis whose forte was event security and who, among other things, was responsible for ensuring that presidential inauguration ceremonies and general elections were incident-free. His basic method was simple and effective: concentric rings of steel security were set up in a pattern of ever tightening circles around the country, the region, the city, the suburb or district, the event precinct, and finally the central figures of dignitaries, players and spectators.

This was a man who left nothing to chance, and those who worked under him adhered to the same rigid discipline. In the wake of 9/11, Andre Pruis and his people worked 24/7.

In August 2002, the England and Wales Cricket Board (ECB) signed a Participating Nations Agreement with the ICC. This committed them to send a full-strength team to fulfil all their World Cup fixtures, one of which was against Zimbabwe at the Harare Sports Club ground on 13 February 2003.

It was not as if the world did not know well in advance that England was due to play there; the match schedule had been out since late October 2001. Now, almost a year later, when politicians and pressure groups first started voicing concern, the ICC sent a delegation to Zimbabwe comprising representatives of those nations who were scheduled to play there – England, Australia, Sri Lanka, Namibia, India, Pakistan and Netherlands. The ICC insisted that the delegation would examine security, and not political, considerations. The consensus was that it was safe to play in Zimbabwe.

Bacher, however, had a contingency plan in place in which matches scheduled for Zimbabwe would be switched to South African venues – but only if, for security reasons, the situation there became untenable.

As 2002 became 2003, the media was awash with reports about the inadvisability of the English team going to Zimbabwe; and while British prime minister Tony Blair said he had no authority to stop them, he did make an appeal to the ECB to do so. Reports claimed that if England did not honour their fixture in Harare, it would cost them 10 million pounds in fines and compensation; and the British government made it known that it would not foot the bill.

On 14 January 2003, the ECB chief executive Tim Lamb announced at Lord's that England would honour its fixture, a decision that Ali welcomed as 'a commitment to the principles of international cricket'. He asserted that CWC 2003 understood and was sympathetic towards the widespread calls for political change in strife-torn Zimbabwe 'but cricket takes decisions for cricketing reasons and is not qualified to do the job of politicians'.

Ten days later, an ICC Executive Board delegation travelled to Zimbabwe and asserted that the matches there should go ahead. Three days later the England players – still in Australia where they had just completed a long tour – asked that their match in Harare be moved to South Africa. After their arrival in South Africa shortly thereafter, the players' call for a switch received support from the ECB.

Politicians and pressure groups were cashing in. They had had more than a year to voice their disapproval about playing cricket in Zimbabwe but they timed their frenzied campaign until the eleventh hour to use cricket as the latest weapon to target the totalitarian rule of Robert Mugabe.

Throughout all of this, and to their credit, the Australian Cricket Board made it clear that their team would honour their fixture in Bulawayo. A year previously, Australia had cancelled a scheduled tour of Zimbabwe for security reasons following Mugabe's controversial re-election as president. Australian prime minister John Howard was central to calls for that country's suspension from the Commonwealth, but in 2003 the ACB defied his call not to play there again. Howard claimed the players were being used as 'pawns in Mugabe's propaganda campaign' which, given the Zimbabwean tyrant's irredeemable public image, was an ill-considered statement.

The World Cup's 'Event Technical Committee', chaired by Speed and including Bacher, rejected England's request to move their match. In Cape Town, South African Constitutional Court Judge Albie Sachs heard an ECB appeal against this ruling and also rejected it.

With the World Cup about to begin, the media was dominated by news of the Zimbabwe stand-off. 'It was unfortunate,' says Ali, 'that this detracted from the build-up to international cricket's most important tournament – and the first one to come to the African continent.'

ANDRE PRUIS WAS originally a military man who had studied and lectured in military strategic science before becoming a policeman and moving rapidly through the ranks. The late Steve Tshwete, while in his position as minister of safety and security, once described him as 'a cop who knows how to handle criminals'.

As Deputy National Commissioner, he headed the SAPS operational services and was responsible for coordinating joint operations of various departments inside and outside the police force. He had studied the Zimbabwe Republic Police file on its plans to secure its World Cup matches and 'it was excellent'. He sent Director van Deventer there to check out the situation and confirm these views.

Pruis' direct intervention was, however, demanded after the ECB's Lamb received an anonymous letter. It claimed to come from something or someone called the Sons and Daughters of Zimbabwe and it threatened that if the England cricketers went to Harare they would return in coffins. Furthermore, it threatened the safety of the players' families in England and described a disused swimming pool outside Harare that was filled with sulphuric acid and into which it alleged Mugabe's henchmen deposited dissidents.

If the ECB needed a reason not to go to Zimbabwe, this was it.

Pruis swung into action with his intelligence agencies. 'There is no doubt that these threats could have unsettled the English players,' he says, 'but there was a lot about that letter that showed all the classic signs of unmitigated propaganda.'

For a start, it was posted in Britain, it contained certain assumptions and disinformation, and it carried a subliminal message of government atrocities i.e. the alleged acid bath.

Pruis met the England team in Cape Town where he took them through the analysis of the letter by his intelligence people and, in short, told them not to worry about it because there was no authenticity to this threat. In his view, there was no such entity as the Sons and Daughters of Zimbabwe in the form that the letter suggested.

What subsequently upset and unsettled the England team, however, was a response from the ZRP's 'Interpol office' advising that any such threat should be taken seriously.

The mention of 'Interpol' clearly set off alarm bells, but Pruis explains that all it was, was 'our (SAPS) member at the Interpol office in Harare talking to our Interpol office in Pretoria' and conveying a theory from a Zimbabwe police superintendent that the letter might have emanated from within the opposition MDC political party. The words 'the threat should be taken seriously' were misinterpreted by the ECB as a 'serious threat'.[3]

As Pruis pointed out in a letter to Speed: 'Although an organisation by the name of the Sons and Daughters of Zimbabwe is not known to them (ZRP), the threat was taken seriously until proved otherwise. This is the reason for the response to the Interpol office in Pretoria . . . and is common practice amongst law enforcement agencies.'

In order to verify this, Pruis personally telephoned Commissioner Fortune Zengeni, the ZRP's chief staff officer for operations, who in turn spoke to his director at the Interpol sub-regional bureau.

---

[3] Andre Pruis interview, November 2003.

Pruis's letter to Speed confirmed that, after further investigation, these officers had concluded that 'Sons and Daughters of Zimbabwe has no known membership or organisation structure. An organisation by this name has not previously drawn any attention in Zimbabwe, let alone being involved in acts of violence. Commissioner Zengeni described it as an organisation on paper, possibly one person, who was only responsible for a single act – the drafting of the letter. Therefore, they are of the opinion that this so-called organisation poses no threat to the English cricket team or any other cricket team for that matter.'

Pruis did not let the matter rest there. He enlisted the help of the crime intelligence division of the South African Secret Service; and he contacted the national crime intelligence service in Britain and asked them whether they had launched an investigation. The answer was 'no'.

'They referred me to the London Metropolitan Police who were apparently looking into the matter. I spoke to them and asked them all the questions like, for example, did they take DNA samples (on the letter). They hadn't.'

There is good reason to believe from well-informed sources – although Pruis himself is unable to confirm this – that a senior superintendent of the London Metropolitan Police actually wrote to the ECB to say that there was no reason to believe that an organisation known as the Sons and Daughters of Zimbabwe existed.

According to Pruis, the crime intelligence division of the South African Secret Service performed an exhaustive investigation into the Sons and Daughters of Zimbabwe. 'They mined every conceivable database, they cross-checked against every known organisation and they conclusively reported to me that this group did not exist.'

In his letter to Speed, he confirmed the findings of crime intelligence: 'The letter was sent by a person or persons with the sole purpose of disrupting CWC 2003, especially as far as the co-hosting of the event in Zimbabwe is concerned. This person/s has no capacity to carry out any threat. From a security point of view, it should be treated as propaganda and not as a direct threat. In view of the above, and from my evaluation of the ZRP's security plans applicable to matches to be played in Zimbabwe, I am of the view that there is no reason why matches should not be played in Zimbabwe.'

The letter was dated 11 February – the same day that the ECB announced that the England team would not play in Harare.

Three days later, the Event Technical Committee met for six hours to consider a submission from an ECB delegation that was reinforced by no fewer than three senior counsel. Speed's committee ruled that England could not have the game switched, that it was therefore cancelled, and that the Zimbabwe team would be awarded the match points.

Bacher was very disappointed that England had not honoured their match fixture. 'The ICC and South African Police Service went to great lengths to ensure the safety and security of players, officials and spectators. The players were assured that they would enjoy the same level of security reserved for President Thabo Mbeki when he undertook state visits. My conclusion was that the views on security expressed by the ECB were unfounded and based on very flimsy information. In these troubled times, Harare on the 13th of February 2003 was probably the safest place to be.'

Pruis says he was sorely embarrassed on one occasion during the entire saga. 'During a meeting with the ECB, I turned on a very dapper lawyer – I was told in advance that they would be bringing a QC with them – and told him, if I go to your country the first thing I see at Heathrow airport is the deployment of military tanks. We don't need that here. I can also assure you that our Task Force is as good as your SAS, and he then looked at me with surprise and said, *"Maar, Komisaris, ek is 'n Suid Afrikaner!"* (But, Commissioner, I am South African!). I thought he was an English QC, but he was actually a senior counsel from Cape Town!'

At the same meeting in Johannesburg, at which the ECB made a second unsuccessful application to have their match moved to South Africa, Pruis took centre stage. He arrived in his full dress uniform and, according to one observer, proceeded to make a long speech, detailing exactly, point by point, how his investigation had been carried out. He claimed that the Sons and Daughters of Zimbabwe was a 'mystical thing' and that, like religion, it was intangible. He would constantly describe it as 'a phantom organisation'.

Pruis grew very heated when the ECB legal team persisted in asking questions about the efficacy of his investigations. He did not approve of lawyers questioning his ability and Ali was highly amused when he chided one of them: 'Ag, man, you're just wasting my time. I've got bank robbers, hijackers and other criminals to catch.'

ENGLAND, OF COURSE, was not the only team not to honour a World Cup fixture. In a sub-plot to the Zimbabwe fiasco, the New Zealanders withdrew from their match against Kenya in Nairobi. There had been a bomb a month earlier in Mombasa, 400 kilometres away on the coast, and the players were understandably nervous because they had once been traumatised by a terrorist bombing in the vicinity of their Colombo hotel while on tour in Sri Lanka.

Pruis, again, was of the firm view that safety precautions in Nairobi were more than adequate. He himself went there on a two-day visit during which it was decided to mount, with cabinet approval, the first-ever joint safety and security operation with another African nation. 'I briefed the New Zealand team and told them that the operational model of concentric circles of security was the same as in South Africa – in fact this is a concept in which we lead the world and which the United Nations wants to adopt – and I told them that my cellphone was always open to them. We mounted Operation Tusker into which we threw 64 top SAPS personnel, our bomb disposal unit and our special task force. I told the New Zealanders that if at any stage I was uncertain about the situation I would have told them immediately.'

New Zealand's decision was not as unpopular as England's because there were no political considerations involved. But not playing in Nairobi, and therefore forfeiting the match points, cost them a likely place in the semifinals. As it turned out, it was the Kenyan team that advanced spectacularly to the last four – benefiting from the bonus points from the New Zealand cancellation and the shock victory they scored over the Sri Lankans in Nairobi. The Kenyans were a popular team who attracted local support after the South Africans had been unceremoniously bundled out of the tournament.

On the question of the demise of the home side – a terrible blow after they had started the tournament as second favourites to the champions Australia – Bacher concedes that he might have erred in basing the team in Cape Town at the outset. 'There was so much going on there and they were obliged to attend any number of official functions, with the Mayor and the Premier and several others, that they were constantly in the spotlight and couldn't focus or prepare properly for the all-important opening match against the West Indies. The West Indians, on the other hand, were based in Bloemfontein where they could get on quietly with their preparations.'

The problems began for the South Africans when the West Indies narrowly beat them in the tournament's opening game at Newlands, and their darkest moment came when, in a rain-marred match in Durban, they miscalculated badly under the Duckworth-Lewis system of revised targets and failed to qualify for the second round.

'People said they were unlucky against Sri Lanka, but I didn't see it that way. They had not played well enough from the start. Allan Donald, possibly our greatest ever fast bowler, was just not the same player and, as much as I know how badly he wanted to play in a final World Cup, I believe he played one tournament too many. There were clearly problems in the team and it was said that Shaun Pollock did not have the support of all his senior players. Whatever it was, it showed in their body language.'

As for the Kenyans, their advance to the semifinals bore testimony in part to Bacher's crusading work as chairman of the ICC's development committee, a role whose universal acknowledgement is referred to by Steve Waugh: 'I have always found Ali to be genuinely interested in the development of the game on a global stage. He has always maintained that cricket needs to expand – not only to prosper but simply to survive and that it has to encourage non-traditional cricket nations to become involved. It says much for the man's resilience that he orchestrated such a magnificent 2003 World Cup that featured a team of "minnow" status that actually made the semifinals – this in itself I am sure would have brought a smile to Ali Bacher's face.'

THE SO-CALLED 'Cola Wars' broke out during the 1996 World Cup in the subcontinent. Coca-Cola was a sponsor of the event but, in what was to become known as ambush marketing, hot-air balloons were launched at the cricket grounds bearing the branding of their rivals, Pepsi. In addition, during the course of that World Cup, several high-profile cricketers playing in the tournament appeared in television advertisements endorsing Pepsi.

Since then, however, Pepsi had become one of cricket's Global Partners – the top bracket of sponsors – by signing a seven-year deal with the Global Cricket Corporation. The poacher had turned gamekeeper; and it was incumbent on CWC 2003 to ensure that ambush marketing, which was becoming less of a joke than a major menace, was stamped out.

'I went to see Alec Erwin (minister of trade and industry) and explained that we had a contractual and moral obligation to the ICC for the GCC's partners and sponsors to be protected in South Africa.'

The upshot of the meeting was that the CWC lawyers, led by Clifford Green, began work with Erwin's department on draft legislation. This would become an important Amendment to the Merchandise Marks Act and was promulgated on 6 November 2002, the day on which the minister told parliament that the amendment was vital to protect South Africa's small but growing position in the world sports and entertainment industry. 'The motive is to place South Africa in a strong competitive position to host this kind of event in the future. If we want to hold these events, we need very large sponsorships. We have to take the protection of those rights into account.'

'We took a hard line here,' says Ali. 'We warned that anyone engaging in ambush marketing either before or during the tournament would face the full force of the law.'

The new law carried heavy fines and long-term jail sentences for guilty parties, and it gave the ICC and CWC 2003 unequalled opportunities to act against companies trying to piggy-back the event to gain unauthorised exposure. Strict adherence to ambush marketing precautions at the World Cup stadiums ensured that there were no major breaches – but it did prove an irritant to spectators who, by way of one example, were not allowed to bring beverages through the turnstiles and could purchase only Pepsi products in the grounds. According to the letter of the law, this also applied to the Coca-Cola corporate suites.

Perhaps understandably, many cricket fans did not understand the necessity for this kind of restriction – one vitriolic newspaper columnist termed it 'commercial fascism' – but there were good reasons for it in a multibillion dollar global sports industry that would collapse in the twenty-first century if its sponsors' rights were not given adequate protection.

The 2003 World Cup, in a sense, introduced a new culture in cricket grounds by placing heavy restrictions on what spectators could take through the turnstiles. This was to conform to the commercial priorities, as well as the kind of security that was deemed necessary in the wake of 9/11. Whereas cricket watching had previously been something of a free-for-all, it now became sanitised to the extent that some people could not understand. It sometimes became extremely difficult for Bacher and his team to explain these new arrangements to a sceptical public.

Another area of contention was the sale of tickets. These initially went on sale to the public in various packages through three different purchasing channels – at stadium ticket offices, on the Internet or by phone through a call centre. It was advertised that sales would begin at 9 am on 15 July 2002; and it was not difficult to understand in hindsight why complaints poured in from people who were unable to access the sales website or the call centre. In simple terms, at exactly 9 am on that 'Black Monday', something like 100 000 people from around the world either dialled the same number or entered the same domain name on their computers. At the stadiums, meanwhile, thousands of people were queuing for packages and, at the Wanderers in particular, hundreds were left empty handed when the 'sold out' sign went up. The problem here was that people in other cities were buying up Wanderers packages to ensure that they would have tickets for the World Cup Final. Johannesburg cricket fans felt they should have the first call on tickets at their home ground and there were angry scenes when the crisis became evident.

Ali was at the Wanderers all day in the forefront of efforts to placate what had become an angry mob. At one point, as invective was hurled at him, he turned to a colleague and remarked tensely, 'It's like the Gatting tour all over again.'

It was here that Bacher's remarkable ability to think on his feet in intense pressure situations was demonstrated by way of the unorthodox turnaround he effected. He asked all the ticketless fans to provide him with their names and contact details, and assured them he would do his best to offer them first option to buy tickets if and when these became available. He knew that the Wanderers tickets already allocated to sponsors and other stakeholders would not all be taken up, and that these would flow back into the system at a later stage. When, in fact, they did, he kept his word and wrote letters to several hundred people who had confronted, and, in some cases, abused him that tension-filled Monday. Many wrote back to express appreciation for the unexpected tickets he now offered them.

Bacher's unorthodoxy in tight corners was not new; and it was something that Clifford Green would often remark upon. As Ali's 'legal frontman', he was constantly on call, and in the forefront of virtually all of the problems and challenges and crises that Bacher faced. 'From the time of the Cronje scandal and throughout the World Cup I would get at least ten calls a day from him, starting from early in the morning. We were also involved in countless meetings on tricky contractual issues and I would regularly introduce him as my "senior counsel" which he rather enjoyed. In fact, "Advocate Bacher" showed himself very adept at dealing with legal issues and would often defuse difficult situations. In one instance I can recall, he actually pointed out to the lawyers that they had left out a fundamental clause in a contract, which caused a few red faces.'

Like a shrewd bowler who gains the respect of an umpire by not appealing for every decision, Bacher would often disarm the other party during a meeting by departing from Green's suggested game plan and saying, 'Clifford, these chaps make a very good point and I think we should go with it.' This had the effect of making the other party far more amenable to his viewpoint when tougher calls had to be made later.

For Green, Bacher's tour de force in outsmarting lawyers through unorthodox manoeuvrings came in 1997 when the cellphone giants MTN and Vodacom became involved in a watershed legal battle over who had the sponsorship rights to certain major South African sports. In the midst of a highly publicised court case, at which the very future of sport seemed to be at stake, Bacher invited the warring parties to meet on the Sunday at his office. With a phalanx of high-powered lawyers ranged implacably against each other, and after two hours of futile argument, he called for an adjournment and quietly suggested that the respective chief executive officers, MTN's Bob Chaphe and Vodacom's Alan Knott-Craig take a quiet stroll together in the Wanderers Club gardens. When they returned, they had agreed on a truce, the crisis was over; and MTN's subsequent involvement in cricket translated into a R144 million grant for development, targeted primarily at the disadvantaged communities, as well as R102 million joint sponsorship with Castle Lager to fund Test cricket.

It was this level of ingenuity that helped Bacher solve any number of vexing problems during the World Cup; but there were times when his creativity was not enough and hard-nosed pragmatism would have to kick in. The best example of this was the seating arrangements in the VIP areas at the stadiums. 'Many local cricket administrators and former players were angry with me. They all expected to be seated in these areas where they usually sat for bilateral events controlled by the UCB. What they failed to understand was that the ICC and not the UCB owned the Cricket World Cup, and their member countries, sponsors and broadcasters had to get preferential seating. In addition, I was obliged, and quite rightly so, to give preferential treatment to members of the Cabinet and Constitutional Court; and, for the Final, many Indian dignitaries who had flown to Johannesburg to support their team.

'While we had the honour of organising the event on behalf of the ICC, many of the UCB officials and their guests had to be at the back of the queue. I was very strong on this and because of it I took a lot of flak. The simple reality was that the VIP areas only have a certain capacity and it was therefore impossible to invite everyone from the normal UCB guest list. When South Africa hosts the soccer World Cup, they will experience the same problem.'

To be a successful tournament director of a major event requires the incumbent to quickly develop an impenetrable heat shield or a very thick skin. Bacher clearly did one or the other because flak catching went with the territory. The Opening Ceremony was a case in point . . .

420

Ali developed the idea for it when he attended the 2000 Sydney Olympics as an invited guest of Sam Ramsamy's National Olympic Committee. It was there that Ramsamy arranged for him to have dinner one night at 10.30 with Michael Knight, chief executive of the Sydney 2000 organising committee. 'I asked him why they had spent $50 million on the opening and closing ceremonies and he told me that research had proved that spectacular ones – and Sydney's was by common consent the best ever – equated to a major boost in international recognition and subsequent increase in tourism and investment for the country concerned. This had been proved at previous Olympic Games and most notably at Barcelona in 1992 where economic benefits in Spain were still being experienced into the next century. He also pointed out that their Opening Ceremony had been a source of great pride to the Australian people. From that moment, I wanted an opening ceremony that would achieve similar success for our country and reflect favourably on all South Africans.

'My big obstacle was that it was going to cost almost R33 million and the majority of South African cricket officials were vehemently opposed to it. They did not believe that cricket should be spending money of this kind on a non-cricket event, and I accepted their viewpoint.'

Bacher, however, would remind everyone that the World Cup was 'far bigger than just cricket' and ultimately was able to convince the UCB and the government that the opening ceremony would be of great benefit for South Africa. It would be televised live around the world to an audience of hundreds of millions of viewers, and 65 per cent of its budget would flow into black hands.

'It was one of my most difficult and time-consuming jobs raising the money. I couldn't go to other South African sponsors because the World Cup partners and sponsors were allowed exclusive branding in the stadiums and therefore I could not offer a local sponsor any benefit for associating with the opening ceremony.'

It was during this period, while he was canvassing support from government departments, that Bacher had his run-ins with the minister of sport. Because of the time constraints, he had no option other than to make direct and unilateral approaches to would-be benefactors. In this way, he and Professor Gerwel elicited support of R2 million each from the government of the Western Cape and the Department of Arts and Culture, and R10 million from SA Tourism. The UCB, which initially was prepared to part with R2 million, eventually agreed to up the figure to R10 million. The remainder came from central government who directed him to the

Lottery Board to apply for one of the many grants they are obliged to make. There was, of course, the inevitable outcry when the latter funding was revealed to the public, and suggestions that the money could have been put to better use were not unusual on the thorny issue of the national lottery's choice of beneficiaries. Without this backing, however, it would not have been possible to produce anything of the magnitude of what was experienced and acclaimed on the night of 8 February 2003 at Newlands in Cape Town.

Doug Jack, the world's leading stadium theatre choreographer and the American who held that position for the opening ceremonies of the Olympic Games at Barcelona, Atlanta, Sydney and Salt Lake City, told Ali that CWC 2003 had produced a ceremony of 'Olympian proportions'.

The idea for an Olympic-style opening ceremony was not the only one that Bacher developed on his visit to Sydney in 2000. He also encountered a superb Volunteers Programme in which 47 000 proud Australians put up their hands and offered to make a contribution to their country.

Out of this grew the idea to use CWC 2003 to initiate a culture of volunteerism in South Africa; and 8 000 people from all walks of life were selected from the thousands and thousands who eagerly offered their services for no reward other than to be part of an unforgettable experience. Half of them took part in the Opening Ceremony.

He recalls: 'Two the most touching experiences I had were at Port Elizabeth and Bloemfontein when I went to thank the volunteers after the last matches had been played at those venues. They expressed to me in such a heartfelt way what an unbelievable experience the World Cup had been for them and that they were extremely sad it had come to an end. It was very emotional, many of them were crying; and I was fighting back the tears myself.'

The third idea of note in Sydney came one evening when Ramsamy took him to watch one of South Africa's Olympic boxers in action. 'Before the fight, there was an announcement over the loudspeakers, "Please welcome Dawn Fraser!" and this great former world champion swimmer walked into the boxing hall to great applause.'

Out of this came another Bacher-inspired project in which 41 men and women who had attained the highest honours in their respective sporting codes were appointed as the African Sports Ambassadors to the Cricket World Cup. Only two of them were cricketers – Graeme Pollock, as South Africa's cricketer of the century, and Basil D'Oliveira, for obvious reasons; but there were, in addition, six legendary global cricket ambassadors in

Sir Garfield Sobers, Sir Everton Weekes, Sir Vivian Richards, Sir Richard Hadlee, Ian Botham and Sunil Gavaskar.

'By awarding ambassadorships to Africans from a variety of other sports, we were able to embrace all South Africa and inspire all South Africans to support the event.'

We cannot leave Sydney, however, without telling of Bacher's modus operandi there. Not your average sports fan is he, so many Olympic Games visitors would have been puzzled at the sight of this man, armed with a camera for the first time in his life, taking photographs of toilets, and information kiosks, ticketing booths, big TV screens and sponsors' branding boards. 'I was unbelievably impressed and inspired by the way those Games were organised and run – spotless toilets, for example – that I wanted to show my team how we should present our event to the thousands of overseas visitors that would come to South Africa for the Cricket World Cup.'

As for the tournament director, his 26 months at the helm were remarkable for the fact that, for most of the time, he seemed perfectly capable of juggling about 12 balls in the air at the same time. 'I felt the real pressure for the first time at the beginning of January of 2003 when we had a month to go to the start. I was waking up between 4 and 4.30 each morning and sometimes I had to force myself out of bed and start the day. I kept telling myself that I didn't want to reflect back in April, once it was all over, and ask myself why I didn't do this or that. That's why my staff will remember me saying to them at the time, "It's going well, keep it going, keep it going, chaps!" and to their credit they did.'

Ali would proudly say afterwards: 'We proved that a World Cup could be run on a cellphone. At one point before the tournament, there were so many emails landing on my desk and causing such confusion that I stopped them. I told the staff that if they had a problem they should walk into my office – the door was always open – or phone me. I ran it on a cellphone, and it's even been suggested that I could go to Harvard and do a paper on that!'

By all accounts the 2003 Cricket World Cup was a resounding success as a well-organised global cricket tournament. At the presentation ceremony at the Wanderers, after Australia had beaten India in the final, Malcolm Gray, the ICC president, declared: 'South Africa, you have delivered!'

Bacher received a resounding cheer when he appeared on the podium; it was a far cry from three years earlier when he was roundly booed at the same ground when South African cricket fans slipped into their state of denial over the allegations levelled against Hansie Cronje.

Chapter 34

What They Don't Teach You In Medical School

A LONDON NEWSPAPER said of the man:

> *He prided himself on his old-fashioned, low-tech business methods; his working tools consisted of yellow pads and index cards and he claimed never to use e-mail or the Internet. He once said, 'You have to look into people's eyes and be interested in them as human beings.'*

The newspaper[1] was extolling the virtues of Mark McCormack,[2] but it might easily have been describing Ali Bacher.

McCormack's famous book *What They Don't Teach You at Harvard Business School*[3] espoused a style of management that was based on simple logic and the personal skills gleaned from understanding what makes people tick. Ali never read the book but he too formulated a method that was built more on street knowledge than a formal business education. Given the success he achieved during more than three decades at the forefront of cricket administration, and culminating in what has been

---

[1] *Daily Telegraph* May 2003 obituary of Mark McCormack, founder of the International Management Group (IMG) and the man credited with inventing the multibillion dollar global sports industry.
[2] In the 1970s, Dr Ali Bacher, the hotel doctor on call, was summoned to the President Hotel in Johannesburg where a guest, Mark McCormack, was suffering from an acute middle-ear infection. They met on several occasions later in England where McCormack would call him 'the doctor who saved my life!'
[3] Published by Harper Collins 1984.

described as the best-run Cricket World Cup, it is worth delving into his management philosophy. Indeed, what follows may well come in useful to those who are in similar management positions or are aspiring to improve their management success.

In effect, they are rules that he lives by; and although some might seem perfectly obvious, they are important enough to be cast in stone.

- Total commitment and passion sets the foundation.
  'In all the positions I occupied in cricket, I understood from the start that I was in the communications business, the PR business and the marketing business; and I accepted this was a seven-day-a-week job. Anyone who is a CEO in sport has to be available seven days a week. You're there at the behest of the public, the media and the sports world – that's your job!'

- So, availability becomes fundamental, and with it the common courtesies.
  'It was very rare for me ever to turn off my phone on weekdays or weekends. Even when I went out jogging, I would have my cellphone with me. In the office, I took 90 per cent of the telephone calls directed to me from the general public. By doing this, you are able to allay any fears that may have arisen, create good PR for cricket, and judge the mood of the market.
  'You must also be available to the media; and not only that, when I felt I had some positive news about the game, I would personally phone members of the media and pass it on. I also learned the importance of getting the message exactly right when I gave recorded television interviews to promote the game. Especially for television news, I would often ask the interviewer to restart the interview, sometimes as many as three times, until I was completely satisfied that I was conveying the right message.
  'It is absolutely vital to return all calls. If someone takes the trouble of leaving a message, you must attend to it at the first opportunity, and within 24 hours at the latest. It is also so important to have friendly, helpful personnel manning incoming calls throughout the day. In any business, everything starts with the switchboard ladies.
  'I also made it a habit to reply to all correspondence I received. I learned the importance of this from Charles Fortune who gave me the basic template to acknowledge with thanks letters from antagonistic

425

letter writers. There were times when I would even phone these people – and they couldn't believe it! Difficult issues are often solved by talking personally to people.'

- On the question of internal communication, brevity is imperative.
  'My staff always knew that memos to me had to be no more than two pages long. Anything more I would not look at.'

- Workplace structures are also meaningless unless the right people occupy them.
  'I would never look at organograms; it's the right people who are in the positions that count. Also, if you pay peanuts, you end up with monkeys working for you. All the cricket treasurers I ever worked with would know that once a year I would come and do battle with them. By nature, treasurers are conservative people when it comes to spending money but for me it was always extremely important for my staff to know they were highly valued.'

- Good working relationships, and confidence in the boss, are crucial to success in business.
  'You must always be available to your staff. I had an open door policy and 80 per cent of the time I would immediately sit down with the person who came into my office.

  'I also learned during the World Cup about the importance of allowing people to grow within the organisation. Before that I wasn't very good at this, but I read Jack Welch's book[4] and I learned from it. At the World Cup offices, I saw the potential in two front-office receptionists, Zaida Peck and Rae Israel, and they both were eventually promoted to become PAs to two of our directors.

  'Also important is that you divert responsibility to people that you have confidence in.'

- Small gestures of appreciation are not to be underrated.
  'In motivating staff, it costs very little to send flowers for a birthday, offer a weekend holiday to a staff member who has excelled in

---

[4] *Jack Welch & the GE Way* by Robert Slater (McGraw-Hill 1999), a biography of the chief executive of General Electric.

commitment and effort, or give people a long weekend without docking their leave. It costs you very little, but it makes the difference.'

- Honesty is essential.
'Never lie – because you'll always be found out! I once tried to hush up a story about an altercation between Brian McMillan (former SA cricketer) and a spectator at the Wanderers. When a newspaper reporter, Guy Hawthorne of *The Star*, found out about it, he castigated me; and he was right.

   'Another of my rules is never to break your word to someone even if it later transpires that this is not to your organisation's advantage. Keep your word and accept the consequences. If you go back on your word, you destroy the credibility of yourself and your organisation.'

- Useful advice also emerges from his dealings with sponsors.
'Never take sponsors for granted. Look after them. Give them more than you promised. Without them, you have no sport. If there's an important decision to be conveyed, take a third party with you to cover yourself in the event of any later disagreement or confusion.'

- In the case of disputes or arguments, always settle out of court.
'My late father-in-law Tuxie Teeger was a successful lawyer. He told me that the only party who benefits if you go to court is the lawyer. In all my years in cricket administration, I spent only one day in court – during the MTN/Vodacom battle.'

- During times of pressure or stress, there are also basic rules.
'In moments of anger or bad temper, never record your feelings in writing. Go home and have a good night's sleep. The next morning you'll be relieved that you did not overreact. Also, it is vital to remain calm under pressure; even if you're feeling the pressure, do not show it. Initially, I wasn't very good at this but with experience my body would tell me when I was getting tense, and I would condition myself to remain calm.

   'The same goes when you're disappointed. I always remember what Eric Rowan taught me about not showing disappointment in defeat: "Smile, smile, I feel like crying".'

- Finally, being proactive is the name of the game.

427

'Things don't just happen – you've got to make them happen!'

IN ORDER TO map out his working days, Bacher kept an A4 executive diary in which he would meticulously list everything that needed to be done, however small or trivial. When he woke up in the early hours of each morning, it was straight to the diary that he went, therein to inscribe the ideas and fresh plans that had crystallised in his brain whilst he slept. He would then act on each item on his list in the order he had noted them down. He did not prioritise items, but dealt with them in descending order.

As the day wore on, he would tick off items he had successfully addressed and, at the end of the day before leaving his office, he would carry forward those items still undone on to the next day's page. Then the list would start all over again. He would write down everything with an economy of words and a smattering of shorthand; and his retentive brain would record all of this like the back-up memory of a computer. When six months later he needed to check back on the details of an accomplished task, he would go to the right page almost instinctively.

If this all sounds like an uncanny talent, it is simply the work of an orderly mind capable of acute focus and concentration, and of a tried and tested working philosophy. By subscribing to the 'do it now!' principle, he would prevent issues from hanging in the air and complicating his thinking. It was not difficult to see why he worked seven days a week because just one day's absence from the diary system would have created a backlog that would be difficult to rein in. 'No, we'll do it now!' was a response that his tired colleagues, at the end of a long day, would grow accustomed to hear. Not for him a protracted exchange of memos, or emails flowing back and forth; no, the key was to deal immediately with issues and then move on. When memos did land on his desk from a colleague, he would reply by returning the memo upon which he had stuck a page from his small yellow adhesive notepad containing a response in no more than 20 words.

It is extraordinary that a man who 'ran a World Cup on a cellphone' had no inclination to expand his technological boundaries. He did not know how to send a short text message (SMS) or an email; and although he understood the benefits of the Internet, he would not know how to use it. He has in fact never laid a hand on a computer of any description.

ALMOST THREE YEARS before the 2003 World Cup, the UCB executive accepted a recommendation from its remuneration committee – former judge Mervyn King (chairman), Joe Pamensky and Raymond White – that Bacher receive

428

a fixed percentage of the profits from the tournament by way of a perform-ance bonus to be paid in US dollars. When the media got word of this, Ali was emphatic that he was not party to, nor would he accept, this arrange-ment. He did not want the public to think that, in organising the biggest Cricket World Cup, he was being motivated by personal financial considerations.

His response to the media surprised King who said it was accepted international practice for tournament directors of global sports events to receive a bonus based on a percentage of profits. 'Ali should have referred the media enquiries to me so that I could explain where we were coming from, but he didn't and that was that.'

Later, however, in reassessing Bacher's salary package, the UCB discovered that he had not been 'properly looked after' throughout his many years with the national body. His pension plan was inadequate and, although now past the age of 60, there was no realistic prospect of a normal retirement. The UCB then resolved that he should be given an ex gratia payment of R5 million before tax once his contract expired in June 2003 which would effectively give him a retirement package in keeping with a managing director's position.

When this was presented to the final CWC 2003 Board meeting after the tournament, the UCB resolution was unanimously approved in recognition of his devotion to cricket over decades. The R5 million was considerably less than he would have been paid in US dollars in terms of the original percentage of profits proposal.

Bacher insisted that a media statement be released in keeping with his commitment to transparency. This was drawn up for dissemination by the UCB at an appropriate time but, to this day, the national body has yet to release it.

For the record, the statement read in part:

For the exemplary work unselfishly performed by Dr Bacher on behalf of cricket over decades, the Board has unanimously agreed to grant him an ex gratia payment of R5 million before tax. It is the Board's considered view that this is a wholly justifiable reward for his dedicated and tireless work. In the interests of the transparency for which Dr Bacher has always been so committed, the Board is delighted with his agreement to make this public. Dr Bacher's work in South African cricket is now effectively over. His contract with CWC 2003 expires on 30 June 2003. On behalf of all cricket stakeholders, the Board takes this opportunity to wish him health, happiness and success in his future endeavours.

In November 2003, the *Sunday Times* heard for the first time of the bonus payment and ran a front-page story under the headline *Bacher gets R5m for World Cup.*

This was not correct and did not reflect the facts as contained in the media statement that the UCB never issued and which, understandably, the *Sunday Times* was not aware of at the time of publication.

THERE WERE THOSE who believed that Ali Bacher would wither away once his work in cricket was finally done, but as soon as his contract with the UCB expired in June 2003, he struck out boldly in new directions.

It was during a holiday in the Seychelles with Shira, their daughter Ann, her husband Darryl and their children that his future appeared very clear and simple to him. He was out jogging one morning when he thought to himself, 'I'm 61, South Africa has been very good to me and my family . . . I want to make a contribution to my country, however small.'

Back home he began sounding out business associates and friends in government about where he could or should be placed. At the same time, he saw the necessity to acquaint himself with the HIV-AIDS pandemic. 'I needed to know more about this, both as a medical doctor who had stopped practising a long time ago, and as a concerned South African. I did not have the time or inclination before to give it much thought, because I suppose it didn't affect me or my family directly, and I thought, hey, that's wrong!'

Ali began reading medical books on the subject, visiting hospitals and townships and talking to people living with HIV-AIDS to get a feel of this complex problem and devastating syndrome. 'I was horrified to discover the extent of it; and the extensive damage it was doing to the fabric of society, to hundreds of thousands of young South Africans and their families.'

It was during this research, and in his endeavours to do something, however small, that he met Nathan Geffin of the HIV-AIDS Treatment Action Campaign. He in turn introduced Bacher to Professor Edwin Cameron, former Constitutional Court judge, renowned academic, AIDS activist, and Chairman of Council at the University of the Witwatersrand.

Talk inevitably turned to Ali's future and whether there was anything in particular he wanted to pursue. There were a few things in the pipeline, but nothing firm; there had been exploratory talks with a major financial institution and a suggestion that he might perform some role on behalf of his country, perhaps a diplomatic posting. There had certainly been some communication with the office of President Thabo Mbeki.

'I told Edwin I wanted to make a contribution in an environment where I would be happy and have job satisfaction. He said there was only one place for me, and that was Wits University.'

Within 24 hours a meeting was arranged with Mervyn King, who, among his myriad functions, is also chairman of the Wits Foundation's Board of Governors. He and the new vice-chancellor, Professor Loyiso Nongxa, made him an immediate offer for the position of executive director of the Foundation.

Bacher attended Professor Nongxa's inauguration the following week, and it was there, after hearing the vice-chancellor's impressive speech, that his mind was made up. 'There were two aspects of what he said that ultimately motivated me to join Wits. Firstly, his vision for transforming the institution whilst raising the academic, teaching and research standards; and secondly, he expressed the view that Wits was a national asset and an institution that belonged to all, irrespective of their race, gender, religion or sexual preference.'

In accepting the position on a four-year contract, Bacher said it made sense for him to return to his roots, to the university from which he and his three children, Ann, Lynn and David, had graduated. In addition, this was the university that in 2001 had conferred on him its highest honorary academic distinction, the degree of Doctor of Laws, *honoris causa*. So he would return to his alma mater in September 2003, almost 36 years after graduating there as a doctor, to head up a foundation that the previous year had raised R104 345 385 in pursuance of the self-sustainability that was necessary for Wits to retain its position as an internationally acclaimed institution of learning, teaching and research.

In the mean time, he remained determined to do something, however small, to help raise awareness of those affected by HIV-AIDS who were in dire need of support and assistance. Not surprisingly, he found himself lending his support to the Nelson Mandela Foundation which had by now taken up the cudgels in the fight against AIDS. The former president and Robben Island prisoner No 46664 invited Ali to join him in a 'global call to action' and a worldwide '46664' fund-raising campaign that would have as its centrepiece a major concert, featuring some of the world's best-known rock musicians, at Green Point Stadium in Cape Town. Ali's role was to assemble ten of South Africa's top sportsmen and women – just as he had done with the African Sports Ambassadors at the Cricket World Cup – to make special guest appearances on the stage of the globally televised concert in November 2003 and to lend their support to this worthy campaign.

DOES HE MISS being part of cricket? Amazingly, not. 'I am fortunate that I have always been able to adapt to new chapters in my life.' He is, however, concerned about the administration of the game in South Africa where, he says, there are too few officials with cricket know-how and a passion for the game. He is adamant that cricket is for all race groups, and is worried that one group may be replacing another to control South African cricket. 'Dominance of one race group over another can never be good for cricket; and we should now start moving to a position where the best people get the top jobs, be it at honorary administrative level or in full-time employment.

'I don't subscribe to the view that cricket must ultimately represent the demographics of the country, otherwise the minority Indian population, for example, could only expect to have one player in the national team; and that is wrong.'

In truth, there is so much of cricket in his blood that he can never say that he is ultimately through with the game. 'Cricket has always been my passion and if someone or some organisation thinks that there is a contribution I could make, either in South Africa or abroad, I would consider it. But I am content; the game has been very good to me, and I won't lobby to play any further role.'

As a student of the game, however, he mentions two aspects of international cricket where he believes there is room for improvement. In the first – and as a logical follow-up to his pivotal role in introducing the Third Umpire (or 'Television Umpire', as he prefers to call him) to the international game in 1992 – he would like to see the use of technology being expanded to assist the standing umpire in establishing exactly where the ball has pitched or made contact with the pad before making a lbw decision. 'A ball may pitch half an inch outside the leg stump, or make contact with the pad just outside the off stump when a shot has been played, and in both instances the laws of cricket say the batsman is not out. There is no way, however, that the naked eye can judge this. Today's television technology makes use of the radar mats running wicket-to-wicket and this would ensure that the correct decision is made in either of these two instances.'

The second area of improvement is described by an innovation he supports called *The Million Dollar Test*.[5] This is the brainchild of Richard

[5] ©Richard Evans 2003.

Evans, an English sportswriter whose speciality is tennis; and Ali has elicited support for it from the former Australian captain and doyen of cricket broadcasters Richie Benaud. He has also apprised the ICC's Malcolm Speed of the concept. In simple terms, Evans' proposal is that a five-day Test match for a million dollars in prize money should be played at the end of every 24-month period between the top two Test teams in the world based on a new ratings system. He makes the point that no sport can survive in the modern age if the public does not have a clear understanding of which teams are the best at any given moment and if a series of matches does not lead anywhere. 'At professional level there is no question that cricket will die if it cannot compete to some degree with the financial rewards offered by other sports.'

In order to arrive at the right finalists, he has adopted the computerised ranking list that is used in men's professional tennis on the ATP tour. This is based on a 52-week rotating cycle with points awarded for wins. The total points are then divided by an optimum number of tournaments played. Modified for cricket, this could be changed to a 104-week cycle with points awarded for wins and draws plus bonus points added for any team winning a series of not less than three Tests. Each nation would be obliged to play in no fewer than 12 Tests in a calendar year. There would be a cut-off date every second year, and the two teams with the highest points average would qualify for the final.

Ali strongly supports Evans' contention that although cricket has done well to adapt to the demands of the modern commercial sporting world, the five-day game needs a really eye-catching, headline-grabbing initiative that can confirm its status as one of the world's greatest sporting contests.

IN THE NATURE of the politics of South Africa, Bacher's devotion to the game of cricket per se was often overshadowed by the intrigues in the corridors of power. First and foremost, though, he is a cricketer with a deep knowledge and appreciation of the game. To catch him in this vein is an instructive experience, and no book on him would be complete without his selection of a South African XI of players he has seen, from the start of his first-class career in 1959 until the present day. His team is notable for its five world-class allrounders*.

*1 – Eddie Barlow, the captain: 'an outstanding allrounder whose positive, confident approach rubbed off on his teammates'.
2 – Barry Richards: 'the most complete batsman I ever encountered'.

*3 – Jacques Kallis: 'formidable, he will go down in history as one of South Africa's most successful Test and ODI cricketers'.

4 – Graeme Pollock: 'in the words of Sir Donald Bradman, the best left-handed batsman of all time'.

*5 – Clive Rice: 'another outstanding allrounder, a tough competitor with big match temperament'.

*6 – Mike Procter: 'among many fine allrounders, the best of them all'.

7 – Johnny Waite: 'South Africa's best wicketkeeper-batsman; no 'keeper I saw stood up to the wicket to medium pacers with such finesse and class'.

*8 – Shaun Pollock: 'no South African fast bowler has been more accurate; as a batsman he is an exquisite timer of the ball who should have batted higher for South Africa in Test matches'.

9 – Hugh Tayfield: 'the best spin bowler ever produced by South Africa'.

10 & 11 – Allan Donald and Neil Adcock: 'South Africa's best-ever fast bowlers'.

12th man – Jonty Rhodes and Colin Bland: 'South Africa's greatest out-fielders'.

On 23 February 2003, Bacher accompanied UCB president Percy Sonn to Pietermaritzburg to watch the World Cup match between India and Namibia. It was there that they spoke about the ICC presidency in 2005 when it will be South Africa's turn in the rotation system to provide the incumbent. The conversation went like this:

Sonn: There are three candidates, you know, Krish Mackerdhuj, you and me.
Bacher: Do you want the job?
Sonn: Yes.
Bacher: If you want it, and the (UCB) board wants you to hold that position, go for it, Percy, I'll simply back off.

Later in the year the UCB's General Council asked the provincial affiliates to nominate candidates for the post of ICC president for 2005. Two senior provincial unions approached Bacher. The one had unanimously agreed at a board meeting that he was their man, and officials from the other union visited him at his home to tell him they wanted to nominate him. 'I declined both offers because I had made a promise to Percy Sonn, and I was determined to keep my word to him.'

For the UK edition of this book, a special Foreword was commissioned from Geoffrey Boycott, the renowned former England and Yorkshire opening batsman. Production priorities changed, however, and it was decided to drop the Boycott foreword, which included the following observation:

> Ali Bacher would make a great leader of the International Cricket Council. To my mind, when South Africa's turn comes around to provide its President, there can be no better candidate. South Africa must make its own choice and I appreciate that it has a priority to develop people who were previously disadvantaged. Having said that, he will still be the best man for the job by far.

Epilogue

NOT EVERYONE WOULD have approved of the road that he travelled; but none could deny he went the extra mile.

A simple yet complex man, he was accused on the one hand of being autocratic and hailed on the other as a nation-builder. In defining his vision for cricket, he first had to seek a personal transformation; and when they came together with mighty purpose he pursued his goal with a single-mindedness that bordered on obsession. Almost overnight, he cast off the shackles of the past and embraced his country's new democracy with an ease that startled even his former adversaries.

Sworn enemies became his friends; and his disarming personality would pull disparate groups together with astonishing facility. He was old-fashioned in his ways yet eminently adept at moving with the times.

He could walk with kings, but never lost the common touch.

He travelled at a speed that left many behind, some by design, others from sheer exhaustion. He set his compass and kept on going inexorably, unbelievably driven; and the end of the journey would justify the means.

He came to cricket as an introverted, inarticulate man who did not project naturally from the public stage, yet he developed the confidence to deliver a powerful message. A man who was not easily thwarted, he grew stronger and more influential through more than four decades in the forefront of the game.

For a man to become powerful he must have something extra; and in Ali Bacher's case, he ensured he had knowledge. He always had a bit more than anyone else, and his excellent sources kept him a step ahead. The

436

drawback was that he could not always divulge everything to people who thought they were entitled to know.

A paradoxical man, he was on the one hand capable of changing the course of history, and on the other of putting off an important meeting because his diary entry decreed it was time to take his grandsons for their haircuts. They were lucky, too, that they had him as their devoted cricket coach. In a family questionnaire sent to them by their Australian cousins, one of the questions was whether any person had said or done something that was considered to be a life changing experience. Shane Weisz, aged five, responded thus, 'My Ati taught me how to hit the ball straight.'

A man of no material ambition, he devoted his life to his family, to cricket and his country with singular loyalty. In 1999 he was voted the 48th most influential South African of the twentieth century.[1]

He would regard idle chat as a sheer waste of time; and he listened to everything he considered absolutely necessary before his eyes would glaze over and you knew you had lost him. What is often described as absent-mindedness was nothing more than his ability to clear his mind of everything that had no bearing on the moment. There were times when Shira Bacher would be in bed watching television; and Ali would remember to tell her that they were running late for a banquet. 'At half past seven, I'd be relaxing in bed; at eight o'clock, I'd be seated next to him at the top table.'

He is never happier than when faced with a new challenge; and then his focus is unshakeable. Once, on a perfectly clear day, he was so engrossed with an important passenger in his car that he drove the 20-odd kilometres from the airport with the windscreen wipers on, because it did not matter.

The tumult and the shouting is demonstrably behind him; but he is constantly in search of new challenges. According to his family, his stress level rises the longer he relaxes; and he terms as 'almost an illness' his inability to wind down.

There is a little essay in the latest primary school annual that includes this revelation by seven-year-old Daniel Weisz: 'My grampar is Ali he

---

[1] A list of top South Africans drawn up by a publisher and historians was placed on the *News24* website for the public to make its nominations and finally vote in order the top 100 people who 'irreversibly changed our country and society'. Nelson Mandela was voted No 1. Essays on the 100 people were commissioned by the publishers Human & Rousseau and published in a book entitled *They Shaped Our History*.

yoostoo play cricket.'

Daniel should know that his grandpa used to play a good game of cricket; and he used to do a lot of other important things besides. Daniel can be justly proud of him, as can Jesse, Shane and Rachel, and little Jarren, born in November 2003. Ali's pride in his grandchildren is palpable. In them, and his whole devoted family, he has sought refuge from a hectic, often complicated life. There were many times when his children would fear for his safety, privately phoning his colleagues to ask them to dissuade him from exposing himself to dangerous situations. He, in turn, would shield them from the threats that were made against him, deflecting their anxieties through his boundless optimism.

His wife Shira, in particular, deserves a medal for her patience, understanding and good-natured acceptance during the long and trying years. To her, he was always simply her best friend.

The memorabilia in the Bacher household includes a rich photographic tapestry of a full and interesting life. After the 2003 World Cup, the woman who delivered the latest batch of framed pictures marvelled at the photographs of famous people covering the walls of his study.

'You've been very privileged, you know,' she remarked.

'No,' he replied. 'I have just been very fortunate.'

Selected Index

Abbasi, Arif 387
Abed, Sallie 'Lobo' 148
ACB 192,193,198,199,376,406,412
Ackerman, Hylton 132,134
Adams, Paul 323,325,327,330
Adcock, Neil 32,43,44,45,61,120,121,
    131,138,434
African National Congress: See ANC
Agnew, Rudolph 229
Ahmed, Qamar 382
Akhalwaya, Ameen 246
Akhalwaya, Ebrahim 148
Akhtar, Javed 379,386
Akram, Mohammad 326
Alam, Intikhab 382
Alderman, Terry 195
Alex All Sports Congress 244,245
Ali, Basit 383
Allen, David 116
Alston, Rex 41
Amarnath, Mohinder 368,369,370
Ambler-Smith, Aileen 235,236
Ambrose, Curtly 305
Amiss, Dennis 178
ANC 209,211,213,214,216,226,229,
    230,263,275,308,324
Anderson, John 390,391
Anti-Apartheid Movement 99,126,210
Anyaoku, Chief Emeka 267
Arlott, John 41,98
Armstrong, Gregory 187,188,190,191
Aron, Cecil 11,12,20
Arosa Sri Lanka XI 183
Ata-ur-Rehman 382
Atherton, Michael 321
Australian Cricket Board: See ACB
Australian tour to SA (1970) 100-114
Avnit, Harry 64,65

Ayob, Hoosain 202,204,205,328,397,
    398
Azharuddin, Mohammad 298,385

Bacher, Adam 325
Bacher, Ali: addresses annual Wisden
    dinner (1989) 211; announces
    retirement from cricket 136;
    appointed as one-man commission
    to investigate unity in cricket 242,
    243; appointed executive director of
    Wits University Foundation 131;
    appointed SACU Director of Cricket,
    later MD 200; appointed Springbok
    captain 100; appointed Transvaal
    captain 53-54; appointed Transvaal
    Director of Cricket (1981) 164,165;
    as Transvaal chairman of selectors
    150; as wicketkeeper 43-44; at King
    Edward VII School 23-24,27-28,30-
    34; at medical school 35-37,49; at
    Yeoville Boys' School 17-18;
    'Bacher's Match' 87-92; becomes MD
    of United Cricket Board 264;
    business career 153-157; captains
    Balfour Park 42; captains Transvaal
    Schools 24; childhood in Yeoville
    15-16; compared with Bradman 25-
    26,27,49-50; cricket career statistics
    138; Currie Cup debut 43; first-class
    debut 34; first club match 22; first
    Currie Cup century 45; first
    representative cricket match 18;
    goes into private medical practice
    127; graduates with medical degree
    97; has cardiac bypass surgery 158;
    honorary doctorate conferred 431;
    introduces 'third umpire' technology

298-299; maiden century for Balfour Park 27; maiden century for Transvaal B 43; marries Shira 71; nominated for SA's Marketing Man of the Year (1992) 292; obtains permit for NSC demonstration 224; plays Premier League for Balfour Park 29; plays rugby for Wits 47; plays for SA Schools 24,26,34; promoted to MD of TCC 168; relationship with Hansie Cronje 317-320,331; scores 3 successive Currie Cup hundreds 99; selected for South Africa 67; testimony to King Commission 357-369,374-375, 377-385; tours England with Springboks (1965) 71-85; wins Jack Cheetham Memorial Award 241;

Bacher, Ann: *See* Weisz, Ann

Bacher, David 230,265-266,431

Bacher, Freda 11

Bacher, Issy 19,20,23,24,46,53,325

Bacher, Koppel 7, 10, 11-12,14,19-20, 35,157,232

Bacher, Lynn: *See* Weisz, Lynn

Bacher, Mushe: *See* Kirsh, Mushe

Bacher, Rose (née Nochimovicz) 7,8, 11-12,14,19,20,23,56,280

Bacher, Sarah 10-11

Bacher, Saul 14

Bacher, Shira (née Teeger) 16,46,66-67, 96,127,135,144,155,162,226,310, 311,346,350,430

Bacher, Sorrel 20,23,24,186

Bacher, Yitzchak Alter 7

Bacher, Yudel 19,20,23,24

Bailey, Trevor 84

Baillie, Trevor 42

Baker, Beryl 266

Bakers Mini-Cricket 206,334

Balfour, Ngconde 207,214,216,217,218, 228,233,372,373,399,408,409

Balfour Park: cricket club 42; sports ground 21-22

Bannister, Jack 214,215,378

Baragwanath Hospital 97

Barlow, Eddie 34,74,75,76,77,79,81,82, 83,84,88, 89,91,92,95,101-105,106, 107,111, 112,113,119,120,121,129, 130,131, 132,133,134,140,149,170, 171,319,433

Barlow, John 157-158,164

Barnard, Lee 150

Barnes, Abdul Latief 'Tiffie' 148

Barrington, Ken 43,68,83

Barrow, Errol 131

Basson, Brian 380

Basson, Willie 219,238

Bath, Brian 57,64,118,127,132,137, 141,142,144,237

Bawa, Nazreen 337

Baxter, Les 93

BCCI 269,386,389,403

Beard, Donald 289

Becca, Tony 302

Beckwith, Henry 25

Bedser, Alec 18

Benaud, Richie 43,89,94

Benjamin, John 30,31,157,164

Bennett, Fred 114,199

Berman, Rodney 8

Bhamjee, Abdul 147,148,167

Biggs, Anthony 134

Bindar, Inderjit Singh 403

Bing, Fritz 238

Birrell, Adrian 204

Bishop, John 286

Blacking, John 36

Blair, John 343,344,345

Blair, Tony 411

Bland, Colin 60,70,75,76,77,78,80,82, 84,92,96,97,121,434

Blogg, Stanley 16

Board of Control for Cricket in India: *See* BCCI

Bojé, Nicky 361,362,363,366,374,375

Border, Allan 197

Botha, Pik 185

Botha, P W 175,176,201,202,211

Botham, Ian 118-119,423

Botten, Jackie 78,147
Boucher, Mark 375
Boycott, Geoff 178,180,434-435
Brache, Frank 238
Bradbury, Daphne 165,202
Bradman, Donald 20,25,29,38,50,92,
   115,116,118,163,288-289
Bray, Cathy 165
Brink, David 292,293
Broederbond 229
Brown, David 74,78,172
Brutus, Dennis 215
Bruyns, André 132
Bryden, Colin 177,178,363,367
Bryson, Rudi 345
Bucknor, Steve 298
Buller, Sid 76,77
Burki, Javed 380
Burnham, Forbes 130
Buse, Bertie 28,31
Butler, Harold 75

Cachalia, Coco 407
Cagwe, Ezra 211
Camacho, Steve 306
Cameron, Edwin 430,431
Cameron, Jock 38
Campbell, Annette 165
Carlstein, Denis 200
Carlstein, Peter 57,147
Carr, Ronnie 39,64
Cartwright, Tom 98
Cassim, Hamid 'Banjo' 398
Cawood, John 132
Cebekulu, Edward 165
Chappell, Ian 106,109,112,113
Charnas, Morris 42
Chawla, Sanjay 355,374,375,398
Cheetham, Jack 39-40,100,114,133,235
Chessler, Delano 168
Chotia, Solly 148,149
Clark, Brian 62
Clarke, Sylvester 182,186,187,191
Coetzee, Carl 110
Compton, Denis 74,75,79,83,94

Condon, Paul 376,391,392,410
Constantine, Learie 73
Conte, Miles 150
Cook, Jimmy 138,171,232
Cooke, Peter 180
Coward, Mike 110
Cowdrey, Colin 79,83,267,270,271,272,
   285
Cowdrey, Graham 297
Cowper, Bob 87,90,95,96
Coy, Arthur 69-70,95,109
Cozier, Tony 380
Craig, Ian 41,44
Craven, Danie 309
Cricket Unity talks 262-264
Cricket World Cup 2003: 400,405-423;
   ambush marketing 417-418; black
   empowerment emphasis 407-408;
   budget 405-406; event technical
   committee 412,414; independent
   auditor appointed 408; opening
   ceremony 420-421,422 ; policy
   committee/CWC 2003 Board 407,
   408; security 410-411,418; sports
   ambassadors 422-423; volunteerism
   422
Croft, Colin 186,187,191
Cronje, Ewie 238,317,357,397
Cronje, Frans 396
Cronje, Hansie 20,281,285,305,317-
   320,324,325,326,331,342,343,346,
   351,394,395,396,397,398; & King
   Commission into match-fixing 355-
   376, 384-385,389,393,423
Crookes, Derek 281
Crookes, Norman 55
Crote, Mavis 127
Cullinan, Daryll 111
Curnow, Jenny 165

Dakin, Geoff 34,168,170,174,175,182,
   183,184, 185,191,198,200,213,214,
   215,217, 221,222,225,238,239,240,
   241,242, 243,254,262,263,264,269,
   270-271, 272,273,278,284,285,286,

289,400, 401
Daling, Marinus 229,230,231
Dalmiya, Jagmohan 269,270,272,273,
   282,368,381,386,390,401,402,403
Davids, Fariek 281
Dawson, Alan 334
Day, Adrian 294
Day, Chris 202
Day, Noel 150
Dean, Owen 156
De Klerk F W 211,216,226,230,231,275
Demaine, Mike 298
Desai, Zarina 36
De Silva, Aravinda 321
De Vaal, Peter 134
Development Programme 204-208,238,
   329
Dickerson, John 384
Dindar, Farouk 36
D'Oliveira Affair 125-126
D'Oliveira, Basil 98,422
Donald, Allan 319,417,434
Dove, Peter 155
Draper, Gordon 110-111
Dubb, Asher 97
Duffus, Louis 39,74,75,84,88,101,104
Dumbrill, Richard 55,62,79,80
Du Plessis, Attie 229,231
Du Plessis, Barend 184
Du Plessis, D J 37
Du Preez, Jackie 130,131
During, Albie 32,144,149
During, Roy 223,224,278
Dyer, David 171
Dyer, Dennis 69,235

ECB 411,412,413,414,415
Edrich, John 79
Elgie, Kim 140
Emburey, John 178,210,214,218
Endean, Russell 39,40,41,73,147
England and Wales Cricket Board: See
   ECB
Erwin, Alec 323,417
Esterhuizen, Johan 226-227

Esterhuyse, Willie 230,231
Evans, Les 61-63,64
Evans, Richard 432-433

Fairon, Gavin 34,37,38
Fatkin, Mike 396
Faulkner, Aubrey 88
Featherstone, Norman 118
Fernando, Tyronne 272,273
Fitzgerald, Michael 358
Fitzmaurice, Jim 290-292
Fleming, Stephen 318
Fletcher, Duncan 319
Fortune, Charles 41,76,133,193,200,
   234-235,425
Fotheringham, Henry 137,169,171
Fowle, Barry 206,208
Francis, Bruce 192-198,320,340
Frangos, Nic 34
Freedom in Sport organisation 227,234
Freimond, Brian 245-246
Fry, C B 118
Frysh, Manfred 154-155
Fullerton, Ian 53,57

Gaekwad, Anshuman 387
Gamsy, Dennis 84,112
Gandhi, Indira 130
Garda, Morris 149,150
Garner, Joel 300,306
Gatai, Fresti 387
Gatting, Mike 166,216,218,225,226,
   234,274,304
Gauntlett, Jeremy 334,335-337,338-
   339,357-369,374,376,377,378-383,
   385,386
Gavaskar, Sunil 423
Geffin, Nathan 430
George, Mluleki 217,218,219,220,233,
   247,248-249,256,257,274,304,324,
   328
Gerwel, Jakes 407,408,421
Gibb, Paul 76
Gibbons, Chris 281,285
Gibbs, Herschelle 188,303,323,325,

327,330,342,359,361,362,363,366, 373,374,375

Gibbs, Lance 300

Glaser, Phillip 328,340

Gleason, June 183,348

Gleeson, Johnny 105,107,108,117

Gleneagles Agreement 150

Goddard, Trevor 44,54,69,70,71,73,75, 95,104,106,107,112,113,119,121,171

Goldberg, Denis 268

Goldman, Arthur 26

Gooch, Graham 178,179,180,181,184, 186,210

Gordon, Norman 19

Gower, David 297

Grace, W G 105

Graveney, David 214,216,218,234

Graveney, Tom 43

Gray, Malcolm 381,402,403,409,423

Green, Clifford 156,325,336,356,360, 362,366,371,374,386,389,390-391, 417,419,420

Green, Niesha 165

Greenidge, Gordon 300

Greig, Tony 192,198,199,290

Greve, Viv 64

Grieveson, Ronnie 25

Griffith, Charlie 98,300

Griffiths, Billy 98

Griffiths, Edward 223

Griffiths, Hugh 267,271,377,379,380, 389,390,391

Gupta, 'MK' 385

Habane, Edward 136

Hadlee, Richard 118-119,423

Hain, Peter 126

Halbish, Graham 403

Hall, Andrew 344

Hall, Colin 407

Hall, Wes 98,300,301

Halse, Clive 45,71

Hani, Chris 276

Hanley, Rupert 169

Hansen, Joe 42,80

Haque, Sayed Abdul ('Mr S A Haque') 147-148

Hartman, Rodney 178,243,370

Hawke, Neil 91

Hawthorn, Guy 427

Hayes, Greg 204

Haynes, Desmond 186,188,300

Haysman, Mike 198

Headley, George 300

Heilbron, Lou 206

Heine, Peter 39,41,68,120,121

Helfand, Norman 47

Hendricks, Denver 407

Henning, Brian 16

Henning, Graham 16

Henning, Mark 31,42,51,146,149,161, 162,177

Henwood, Pelham 138

Hersov, Basil 294

Higgs, Ken 74

Highlands Park Football Club 64,129

Hirshowitz, Joe 61

Hlatywayo, Mi 218

Hobbs, Jack 115,116

Hobbs, Robin 77

Hobson, Denys 149,150

Hodes, Peter 335

Hogg, Rodney 194

Holding, Michael 300

Hookes, David 194,197

Hooper, Carl 306

Howa, Hassan 144,145,146,148,177, 206,207

Howard, John 412

Hubble, Jim 91

Hudson, Andrew 282,298,366

Hughes, Kim 193,195,197,198,199,242

Hunte, Conrad 300,347-348

Hurd, Douglas 292,294

Hutton, Leonard 76,115

ICC: 149,174,179,186,212,213,265, 266,267,269,270,272,280,383,386,390, 391,394,400; Anti-Corruption Unit 376,391

443

Imran Khan 118-119,172,387,388
Ingleby-Mackenzie, Colin 350
Innes, Gerald 55,56,57
Insole, Doug 175,179,403
International Cavaliers 43
International Cricket Conference/
    Council: See ICC
Irvine, Helen 127
Irvine, Lee 26,63,64,103,106,113,120,
    121,127,129,134,139,144,147
Isaacs, Wilf 48,85,126,152
Israel, Rae 426
Iverson, Jack 107

Jack, Doug 422
Jamieson, John 346-347
Jansen, Bets 204
Jardine, Bill 217,221,222,225,232
Jefferies, John 204
Jefferies, Steve 170
Joffe, Terence 42
Johnson, Lulu 275-276
Johnson, Shaun 301-303
Jones, Jeff 74,80
Jordaan, Alan 238,264,286,287

Kallicharran, Alvin 172-173,179,181
Kallis, Jacques 113,375,396,434
Kanhai, Rohan 300
Kapil Dev 118-119
Kaplan, Zunky 61
Kaschula, Richie 118
Kasrils, Ronnie 16,279
Katz, Michael 163,168,203,231,232,
    233,239,297,407
Katzin, Kitt 166
Kaufman, Gerald 179
Kekana, Charles 211
Kentridge, Sydney 156
Kerby, Jack 42
Kerr, Willie 116
Khan, Majid 377,380,381,387,388
Kimmie, Saaidin 148
King Commission into match-fixing
    (2000) 355-385

King, Edwin 356-357
King, Mervyn 163,203,375,428,429,431
Kinsley, Robin 158
Kirsh, Issie 153,222
Kirsh, Mushe (née Bacher) 20,153
Kirsh, Natie 153
Kirsten, Gary 111
Kirsten, Peter 170,189,305
Klette, 'Jumbo' 150
Klusener, Lance 188,309
Knapp, Bernie 197
Knight, Michael 421
Knott, Alan 178
Knox, Sheena 165
Knuttel, Hans 127
Koenig, Sven 344,345
Koornhof, Piet 144-146,151
Koseff, Stephen 8
Kourie, Alan 171-172
Krok, Abraham 8,405
Krok, Solomon 8,405
Kuiper, Adrian 304

Lamb, Allan 170,177,182
Lamb, Tim 411,412
Lance, Tiger 39,52,58,73,74,89,94,95,
    100,103,107,109,113,119,139,237
Lange, Frank 55
Lara, Brian 306,321
Larter, David 74,81
Latha, Osman 148
Latif, Rashid 326,383,387
Lawry, Bill 90,100,105,106,107,109,
    110,114
Lawson, Geoff 197
Lekota, Mosiuoa 'Terror' 221
Lele, Jaywant 386
Le Roux, Garth 149,170
Levenstein, Abe 30
Lewis, Eddie 129
Lewis, Isaac 9
Lewis, Tony 80,210,287
Lewis, Trish 396
Lindsay, Denis 70,71,77,78,82,84,92,
    93,96,100, 112,134,139

Litchfield, Eric 75
Lloyd, Clive 271,272,298,300,306,311

Mabena, Billy 295
Macaulay, Mike 53,79,147
Mackay-Coghill 57,59-64,68,70,88,90,
    101,103,116,117,121-122,129,132,
    133,134,137,140,143,144,149,161,
    162,163,165,167,168,187,200,203,
    236,341,342,394
Mackerdhuj, Krish 148,149,207,218,
    256,257,262,263,269,272,278,285,
    286,302,316,349,400,401,402,403,
    434
MacLeod, Don 238,240
MacMillan, Russell 349
Madugalle, Rajan 380
Mafole, Tebogo 302,303
Magiet, Rushdi 207,365
Majola, Eric 348
Majola, Gerald 325,328,344,345,404
Majola, Khaya 328,347,348,404
Major, John 271,280,293
Malamba, Rodney 211
Mali, Ray 334-336
Malik, Salim 326,382
Mallett, Ashley 107
Mamase, Max 248
Manack, Hussein 281
Mandela, Nelson 185,206,226,230,231,
    232,234,265,268,271,271,275,276,
    280, 302,306,310-316,323,324,326,
    381, 382,401
Mani, Ehsan 381
Manley, Michael 302
Mann, George 18,175,179
Marks, Sammy 9
Marshall, Malcolm 182,185,186,188,
    191,300
Masekela, Barbara 245,308
Masemola, Walter 295,296
Mashiloane, Solly 244
Mashishi, Moss 220,222,223,224,227,
    242,243
Mateza, Dumile 202

Mathe, Gift 211
Mathur, Amrit 282,284
May, Peter 41,175
May, Thoko 212
Mbebe, Mvuso 323
Mbeki, Govan 265,268
Mbeki, Thabo 209,213,229,230,231,
    232,249,254,261,265,266,276,324,
    431
Mboweni, Tito 277
McAdam, Sibley 127
McCauley, Ray 331,340-341,373
McCormack, Mark 290,424
McGlew, Jackie 27,32,43,44,54,55,80,
    104,111,117,121,139
McKenzie, Gavin 127
McKenzie, Graham 92,93,94,95,106,
    138
McKenzie, Kevin 127-128,129,138,140,
    141
McKenzie, Neil 127
McKinnon, Atholl 55,56,57,82,84,90,
    94,103
McLean, Roy 27,44,54,120,140
McMillan, Brian 427
'Mean Machine' 169,171-173,191
Melville, Alan 25,69
Mendelsohn, George 21
Menell, Clive 206
Menter, Alan 46,47
Meyer, Roelf 223
Mills, Tammy 31
Mitchell, Bruce 25,40
Modise, Joe 265
Mogodielo, Monica 212
Mokaba, Peter 276
Mokhatla, Masile 211
Monate, Akile 211
Morobe, Murphy 218
Morris, Richard 132
Moti, Razak 36
Mpofu, Dali 336,337
Msimang, Mendi 213
Mugabe, Robert 412
Munro, Wayne 247

Mushtaq, Saqlain 326
Muttiah, A C 386,389,403
Muzzell, Robbie 219,238,241,246-250,
   255,262,284,328,339,368,369
Mvumvu, Lawrence 202,203,204,205

Naidoo, Krish 217,218,219,220,221,
   222,225,227,228,231,232,233,234,
   239,264
Natalspruit Hospital 97
National Sports Congress: *See* NSC
Ndlovu, Judas 148
Nelson Mandela Foundation 431
Newman, Sid 47
Ngcuka, Bulelani 357
Nghona, Benson 36
Ngqula, Khaya 407
Nguni, Mzi 253
Nhlanhla, Joe 229
Nickel, Aaron 19,42
Nickel, Julius 18,19,22
Nkutha, Justice 204,211
Nkutha, Peace 204,211
Nkwana, Kapi 243,244,245,246,292,
   294
Noble, Clive 128
Nochimovicz, Louis 8,29
Nongxa, Loyiso 431
Nourse, Dudley 26,27,34,40,46,88,111,
   138
NSC 210,216,217,218,219,220,227,
   233,274,315,330,401
Ntini, Makhaya 318,319,321,322,323,
   325,327,330,332-339,341,357,366,
   389
Ntshekisa, Samson 148
Ntshinka, Harmony 204,211
Nurse, Seymour 300
Nzimakwe, Thulani 408

O'Dowd, Michael 245,294
Ogilvie-Thompson, Julian 294
Oldfield, Bert 120
O'Linn, Syd 53,56,147
Omar, Dullah 144

O'Neill, Norman 43,44
Opatha, Tony 181-183
Osrin, Ruby 30,165

Packer, Kerry 149-150,192,193,194,
   198,289,290,291,390
Pahad, Aziz 213,229,230,231,361,362,
   364,365,373
Pahad, Essop 265
Pakistan Cricket Board: *See* PCB
Palmer, Charles 175
Pamensky, Joe 143,146,149,162,163,
   168,169,174,177,179,180,182,185,
   187,190,191,192,193,198,199,200,
   203,206,214,216,428
Pan Africanist Congress 226
Parker, A C 104
Parore, Adam 318
Patel, Imtiaz 204,328,329,348-349
Patterson, P J 302
Paul, K K 355,356,374
PBL Marketing 192
PCB 389
Pearce, John
Peck, Zaida 426
Perkins, Arnold 16
Phillips, Harry 157,164,346
Phillips, Wayne 198
Pienaar, Francois 314
Pilgrim, Cecil S 267
Pillay, Ronnie 263
Pithey, Tony 69,70,71,75
Plimsoll, Jack 72,73
Pocock, Pat 74
Pollock, Graeme 27,34,70,75,76,79,81,
   82,83,84,93,95,96,99,102,103,106,
   111,115-116,120,121,133,134,138,
   139,140,149,150,169,171,181,422,434
Pollock, Peter 27,34,71,75,77,79,81,82,
   85,102,106,109,112,117,120,121,
   133,134,138,139,207,322,323,324,
   330,331,342,398
Pollock, Shaun 27,113,188,319,351,
   372,373,398,417,434
Popplewell, Oliver 390,391

446

Potgieter, Flip 254
Pressdee, Jim 80
Pretorius, Willem 229
Price, John 74
Procter, Mike 77,94,102,104,106,107,
    109,112,113,115,117-119,120,121,
    129,133,134,138,139,141,149,171,
    181,280,281,282,283,284,319-320,
    434
Proctor, Anton 28
Progressive Federal Party 227
Pruis, Andre 410,411,412,413,414,415,
    416

Quirk, Trevor 281

Raja, Rameez 387
Rajah, Goolam 351,360,362,363,364,
    365,366,373,374
Ramadhin, Sonny 300
Ramaphosa, Cyril 276,407
Ramsamy, Sam 210,215,218,220,231,
    232,257,278,421,422
'Rebel' tours: 184-191; Gatting Tour
    209-228,231; SAB English XI 181;
    West Indies 185-191
Redpath, Ian 106
Reeve, Anthony 293,294
Reid, John 40
Renneberg, Dave 93
Rhodes, Harold 76
Rhodes, Jonty 90,96,97,298,319,357,
    366,434
Rice, Clive 119,134,138,149,150,169,
    171,172,189,280,281,282,287,434
Richards, Barry 57,77,88,91,92,94,95,
    102,103,106,107,108,111,112,113,
    115-117,120,121,129,133,134,137,
    138,140,149, 181,433
Richards, David 199,269,381,386
Richards, Vivian 116,185,423
Ritchie, Gerald 53,344
Roberts, Andy 300
Robins, Derrick: team toured SA (1973)
    77,135-136,192

Rogers, Denis 361,403
Rokiskis, Lithuania 7,8,9,14
Rousseau, Pat 306,401
Rowan, Eric 39,40-41,54,69,73,94,134,
    143,144,427
Rowe, Lawrence 189,190,191,197
Rubidge, Abdullah 148
Rumsey, Fred 74,84
Rupert, Anton 194
Rushmere, Colin 182,183
Russell, Doug 382
Russell, Eric 83

SA Breweries 180,181
SACA 133,134,145,235
SACB 148,149,150,179,180,207,244,
    256,257
Sacboc 143,146,148
Sacco, Des 61
Sachs, Albie 412
SA Communist Party 226
Sacos 207,209,244
SA Council on Sport: See Sacos
SA Cricket Association: See SACA
SA Cricket Board: See SACB
SA Cricket Board of Control: See Sacboc
SA Cricket Union: See SACU
SACU 148,149,150,168,174,177,180,
    181,182,184,186,188,189,191,192,194,
    197,198,199,200,207,214,217,219,
    233,234,238,239,244,248,257
SA Executive Cricket Club 203
Samson, Andrew 120
Sanroc 215
Sasse, Gilda 165
Schmidt, Etienne 169
Scindia, Madhavrao 269,270,272,273,
    281,283,284,400,404
'Second Unity' 329,340
Seftel, Harry 37
Sexwale, Tokyo 224
Shafto, Michael 119,224,225
Shamroth, Leo 97
Shepherd, Don 74
Shilowa, Sam 373

447

Short, Arthur 134
Siebert, Kenny 65
Sime, Diane 165
Simpson, Bobby 87,90,93,95,96,100
Sisulu, Walter 224
Siwisa, Hintsa 251,255,256
Siwisa, Nolundi 255
Slabbert, Frederik Van Zyl 201,202,213, 248,254,376
Slonim, Lithuania 7
Slovo, Joe 266
Smith, Cammie 300
Smith, Chris 177
Smith, Graeme 20,111
Smith, Ian (former prime minister of Rhodesia) 130
Smith, Ian (UCB financial director) 296, 405
Smith, Mike 68,73,83
Smith, Robin 177
Snow, John 63,74,81
Sobers, Garfield 115,116,117,118,119, 129-131,191,279,300,347,423
Sohail, Aamir 387
Sonn, Percy 262,264,272,273,279,285, 316,325,343,344,345,361,363,364, 365,366,372,389,394,404,407,409, 434
South African Non-Racial Olympic Committee: See Sanroc
Sparks, Allister 230,327
Speed, Malcolm 361,365,406,412,413, 414,415
Sprague, Bridget 165
Stabreit, Immo 279
Stackpole, Keith 93,106
Statham, Brian 43,74,83
Stegman, Joe 294
Steyn, Gideon 329
Steyn, Godfrey 42
Steyn, Rory 314
Stofile, Makhenkesi 274
Stork, Ralph 22
Strauss, Conrad 60,296,297
Strydom, Pieter 361,374,375

Sunday cricket introduced 168
Sutherland, Stuart 296-297
Swanton, E W 280
Sweidan, Cecil 63-64
Swersky, Aimée 165
Symcox, Pat 325

Tambo, Oliver 209
Tayfield, Hugh 39,41,68,114,121,434
Taylor, Bob 77
Taylor, Lynton 289-290,291
Taylor, Mark 382
Taylor, Scotch 53
TCC 149,161,174,188
TCCB 179
TCU 136,143,145
Teeger, Debbie 72
Teeger, 'Nana' 43
Teeger, Shira: See Bacher, Shira
Teeger, Tuxie 30,41,43,53,144,168,232, 427
Telemachus, Roger 333
Tendulkar, Sachin 298
Terreblanche, Mof 229,230
Test and County Cricket Board: See TCCB
Thabethe, Vusi 245
Thatcher, Margaret 179
Thomas, Bernard 186
Thomson, Jeff 194,195
Thorne, Robin 42,204
Thornton, Julian 238,291,316,366
Tillim, Tony 55,56,91
Titmus, Fred 78,79,116
Tobias, Phillip 37
Townsend, David 345
Toyana, Geoffrey 344,345
Traicos, John 109
Transvaal Cricket Council: See TCC
Transvaal Cricket Federation 146
Transvaal Cricket Union: See TCU
Trimborn, Pat 55,113,134,137
Trueman, Fred 43
Tshoma, Kedi Sylvia 205,212
Tshwete, Pam 253,254,261,276

Tshwete, Steve 244,245,248,251-257, 261-277,293,294,301,304,305,317, 323,323,324,326,330,412
Tuckett, Lindsay 69
Turner, Arthur 236,343
Tyamzashe, Mthobi 217,218,219,220, 221,224,244,246-247,256,257,264, 274,304,305,324,328

UCB: 264,265,266,274,278,279,291, 292,311,312,322,324,325,327,333, 340-346,360,364,371,373,377,384, 428-429; 'Transformation Charter' 323, 329,330,348
UDF 201,205
Umkhonto we Sizwe 229
Underwood, Derek 79,80,178
United Cricket Board of South Africa: See UCB
United Democratic Front: See UDF
University of the Witwatersrand (Wits): 431; Medical School 35-37,97

Valentine, Alf 300
Van der Bijl, Vintcent 134,138
Van der Horst, Frank 207
Van der Linden, Wynand 150
Van der Merwe, Peter 71,72,73,74,75, 78,81,90,91,104,139,238,240,280, 281,287
Van Deventer, Ben 410,412
Van Wyk, Marinus 147
Varachia, Rashid 148,149,162,168,174
Variawa, Amien 148
Varnals, Derek 69,147
Versfeld, Berry 118
Verwoerd, Hendrik 149
Viljoen, Gerrit 223,234
Viljoen, Ken 38,39
Vlok, Adriaan 221
Vorster, B J 98,126-127,133,166

Wadekar, Ajit 298
Waite, John 32,,34,39,40,41,43,45,51, 52,54,118,121,143,147,148,149,434

Walcott, Clyde 270,300,383,390,402, 403
Walker, Peter 44-45,80
Wallace, Boon 149,174,235
Walsh, Courtney 305,306
Walter, Kenny 53,57,147
Walters, Doug 105,109,110
Wanderers Stadium 41,227
Waring, Frank 144
Warnapurna, Bandula 183
Warne, Shane 116,376,393
Warner, Jack 162,165
Watt, Michael 290,337-338,339
Waugh, Mark 376,382,393
Waugh, Steve 332,372,417
Weaver, Paul 225
Weekes, Everton 300,423
Weideman, Francois 204,238
Weiner, Paul 190,191
Weisz, Ann (née Bacher) 158,226,227, 234,314,385,430,431
Weisz, Darryl 227,430
Weisz, Kevin 234
Weisz, Lynn (née Bacher) 221,265-266, 305,431
Welch, Jack 426
Wellham, Dirk 198
Wessels, Kepler 177,193,194,196-197, 199,228,242,274,287,303,305,318, 331
Western Province Cricket Board: See WPCB
White, Raymond 26,143,149,187,238, 240, 241,242,306,312,315,322,325, 329,330,333,341-346,349,404,428
Whitington, RS 'Dick' 25,26,27,44,45
Wilkinson, Bronwyn 355,356,359,360, 362,365,366,371,372,373
Williams, Abe 275,276
Williams, Henry 359,374,375
Winslow, Paul 28-29
Witty, Andrew 294
Wood, Graeme 194,198
Woodin, Billy 146,235
Woodley, Ray 45,46

Wooldridge, Ian 225
Woolmer, Bob 178,318,319,320,324,
    331,367,368,370,371
Worrell, Frank 300,301
World Series Cricket: *See* WSC
WPCB 207,208
WSC 149-150,171,173,192

Yallop, Graham 193,194,199

Zengeni, Fortune 413,414
Zia, General 389
Zondeki, Monde 254,276
Zondeki, Namhla 254,276